IDENTITY AND CONTROL

IDENTITY
AND CONTROL

A STRUCTURAL THEORY
OF SOCIAL ACTION

Harrison C. White

PRINCETON UNIVERSITY PRESS

PRINCETON, NEW JERSEY

COPYRIGHT © 1992 BY PRINCETON UNIVERSITY PRESS

PUBLISHED BY PRINCETON UNIVERSITY PRESS, 41 WILLIAM STREET,

PRINCETON, NEW JERSEY 08540

IN THE UNITED KINGDOM: PRINCETON UNIVERSITY PRESS, OXFORD

ALL RIGHTS RESERVED

LIBRARY OF CONGRESS CATALOGING-IN-PUBLICATION DATA

WHITE, HARRISON C.

IDENTITY AND CONTROL : A STRUCTURAL THEORY OF SOCIAL ACTION /

HARRISON C. WHITE.

P.   CM.

INCLUDES BIBLIOGRAPHICAL REFERENCES AND INDEX.

ISBN 0-691-04304-3 (ALK. PAPER) — ISBN 0-691-00398-X

(PBK. : ALK. PAPER)

1. SOCIAL STRUCTURE.   2. SOCIAL INTERACTION.   3. SOCIAL

INSTITUTIONS.   4. SOCIAL NETWORKS.   5. SOCIAL CONTROL.   I. TITLE.

HM131.W443 1992 303.3'3—DC20 92-4072 CIP

THIS BOOK HAS BEEN COMPOSED IN PALATINO TYPEFACE

PRINCETON UNIVERSITY PRESS BOOKS ARE PRINTED ON ACID-FREE PAPER,

AND MEET THE GUIDELINES FOR PERMANENCE AND DURABILITY OF THE

COMMITTEE ON PRODUCTION GUIDELINES FOR BOOK LONGEVITY OF THE

COUNCIL ON LIBRARY RESOURCES

PRINTED IN THE UNITED STATES OF AMERICA

1   3   5   7   9   10   8   6   4   2

1   3   5   7   9   10   8   6   4   2

(PBK.)

For Lynn A. Cooper

TO WHOM I OWE INSIGHT AND TITLE,

AS WELL AS HEART

CONTENTS

LIST OF FIGURES

PREFACE

I BEGAN WRITING this preface on the morning of June 10, 1990. I was in Europe staying at a pension. This pension, called the Pauwhof, was waking up to its fiftieth birthday party. To environing Wassenaar, a Netherlands suburban idyll, the Pauwhof itself is a perfectly real social actor. I claim that its continuing construction out of network mechanisms, which cross-cut several distinct social worlds, is very much the same as your construction as you, and mine as me.

Like me and you, the Pauwhof is still seeking, which is to say creating, its self. As an identity, the Pauwhof keeps getting thrown together out of overlapping efforts of many at control, which thereby induce social spaces and times. The Pauwhof was willed into existence to . . . , well, that's just it, to do or to be what? There were some initial verbal formulae about hosting, about being *pension* for scholars and artists, about continuing the cultured hospitality of the owners' day. Then there emerged a production discipline. The hostess sits as head at the dining table, and also backstage she sits over the help. The help rotate just as does she, and as do we scholars in an ever-shifting crew. Production discipline and putative identity negotiate uneasily but endlessly.

Spun off out of past production discipline is a society, the Friends of the Pauwhof, whose charge is to create and re-create a charge and a correlate display. The society's emblem is the peacock, a bird which frequents elegant grounds thereabouts. For its birthday that Sunday, with rain expected along with hundreds of guests, the Pauwhof had a tent in the garden, just as guests and scholars had out umbrellas. Self-similarity is exhibited in such process that repeats across levels of organization and identity.

I have come to see social organization as arising from identity formation out of control efforts. I have come to see getting action as in tension with social organization. To develop and apply these conjectures I need to mine the resources of previous and current social science in a newly selective way. The great masters took everything as their scene and thus do not provide me with densely specific insights on which to build. Each of the theorists I consciously build upon is recent and quite specialized, and I exploit only one work of each as central. The works which served as early guides are by anthropologist S. F. Nadel (1957); economist T. Schelling (1960); political scientist V. O. Key (1945); psychologist R. Shepard (1962); social and behavioral scientists A. Rapoport (1961) and H. A. Simon (1950); sociologist S. Udy (1970); and modelers H. Landau (1965), P. F. Lazarsfeld (1957), and A. M. Spence (1974). Two other scripts provided core constructs but without explicit social theorizing: one by applied mathematician H. Landau (1950)—later developed by sociologist Chase (1980); the other by anthropologist E. Bott (1957). Both of them were later combined and developed by sociologist Mark Granovetter (1973; and see M. Schwartz 1966, 1967). The guidance from this particular set of works no doubt could also be achieved from quite different sets of specialized works by yet other theorists. In a similar vein, the sociology of science (Merton 1973) suggests that my synthesis here no doubt is, about now, being duplicated by other authors.

I aim, like Merton and others, for an epistemology of middling level, in between individualism and cultural wholism. But Peter Bearman and Ronald Breiger have reminded me of the kinship of these ideas to the micro-theorist Georg Simmel. And Granovetter pointed out to me that aspects of my results resemble formulae of the macro-theorist Talcott Parsons (1964). This latter kinship may descend both through Parsons's codification (1937) of yet earlier theorists and through the shaping by his ideas of such works as Nadel's and Udy's cited above. Parsons, Bales, and Shils (1953) is a key work here. Brownstein (1982) pulls together and critiques a number of Parson's writings, while Alexander (1983, 1988) provides a more favorable assessment. Conscious borrowings from other contemporaneous theorists are cited in the text. For one example, from Mann (1986, p. 1), see the Conjectures after chapter 7.

It was my experiences in applying mathematics to develop models for a diverse series of social phenomena which led me to search for a consistent and coherent framing in substantive theory. Mathematics comes in diverse subfields which did not map into what seemed to my intuition to be the major distinctions among social phenomena. To be more specific, my published applications deal with stochastic processes (White and Christie 1958; White 1962, 1970b, 1973, 1974, 1983); with networks (Lorrain and White 1970; White 1961, 1971); with combinatorics (Heil and White 1976; White 1963b, 1963c, 1970a, 1970c, 1970e, 1977; White, Boorman, and Breiger 1976); with semigroup representations (Boorman and White 1976; White 1963a, 1964, 1973, 1988b); and with comparative statics (Leifer and White 1988; White 1970d, 1981a, 1981b, 1988a). Inspection of the titles in Works Cited below will show that there is only a loose correlation between the substantive topics and the kinds of mathematics—for which latter see, in turn, Feller (1968); Berge (1962); Ryser (1963); Clifford and Preston (1961, 1967); Morse and Feshbach (1953).

Modeling social phenomena also came to seem as much akin to

engineering as to natural science. My background here was more limited, but my publications include five entries of this nature (Eccles and White 1985, 1986a, 1986b; White 1969, 1971), and I wrote many such reports as a consultant with Urban Systems Research and Engineering, in the early 1970s, with the Operations Research Office of the U.S. Army in 1955–1956, and with Raytheon Co. in 1953–1954.

The theoretical framing has to be abstract enough to permit results from different settings to inform one another. But yet the framing must somehow fit with interpretive routines at work in the phenomena, if the results are to have impact and validity. These are problems of reflexivity which suggest a turn toward humanist technique. Just a few publications of mine even touch on humanist topics: (Eccles and White 1988; White 1980, 1985, 1988b, 1991a, 1991d; White and Aubert 1959; White and White 1965) so that scanning of the literature in this direction was both more necessary and more problematic for me.

The great wealth of case studies came to be my prime impetus and resource, as will become evident in the text and as is reflected in the works cited. To weave phenomenology together better with theorizing, I have in each chapter introduced numerous concrete examples. Even the longer of these treatments can only hint at the richness of the underlying accounts cited. One set of key cases which could carry the entire book's argument are multidivisional-firm studies (e.g., Bower 1972; Chandler 1969; Vancil 1979; Eccles 1985), Roman form and process in the Augustan Principate (Badian 1958 versus Brunt 1988), aborigine tribes (Rose 1960; Spencer and Gillen 1903), convulsions of imperial China around the Taiping rebellion (P. Kuhn 1970), and Najemy's Florentine embodiment (1982) of commercial city-states, with, as centerpiece, studies of mobilization (Cuff 1973, Key 1945, and M. Schwartz 1976). These cases could be supplemented by study of a social movement such as the intertwined emergences of the Christian church and Rabbinic Judaism (von Campenhausen 1969; Flusser 1988; Gottwald 1979; Parkes 1960; Schoeps 1969; Segal 1986), by juridical study of the *Standestaat* of central Europe (R. Brady 1933; T. Brady 1985; Poggi 1978; and Barraclough 1946), by accounts of ethnic community (Furnivall 1948; Riggs 1964; B. F. Skinner 1957; and J. Windmuller 1969), and style fugues (Baxandall 1980, or Ennis 1991).

· · · · ·

By its own theory, both this book and myself are traces of interactions with others so that I should sketch some principle ones. Germination began long ago with two interests rooted in family. One was contingencies and how they chained together to override planned social life, as they did in my childhood of much moving. Perhaps science could override contingency! The other interest was kinship, out to mother's second-cousins-once-removed, and how much that resembled the Navy bureaucracy which embedded my father.

Years at M.I.T. under the tutelage of John C. Slater yielded technical tools from physics, a sense of theory for cooperative phenomena, and confidence. M.W.P. Strandberg suffered me in his (microwave spectroscopy) lab, as did W. Edwards Vacuum Ltd. in their industrial facility. I absorbed some notion of real mathematics from R. Salem and W. Hurewicz.

A call to social science came through the charismatic political scientist Karl Wolfgang Deutsch, then at M.I.T. A Ford Foundation Fellowship led to a second Ph.D., from Princeton University with Marion Levy, Wilbert Moore, Fred Stephan, Frank Notestein, and Stanley Udy, which confirmed me in sociology. Colleagues from consulting stints over the years have taught me much about surviving and modeling chance, effectiveness, and efficiency in social organization: Lee S. Christie, Anthony J. Blackburn, Bert Collins, Hermann Leonard, Warren Oksman, Richard Rosen, and Chris Winship. My thinking was also shaped by conversations with Ramon Alonso and with George VanDeventer, who each live for their ideas.

A year at the Center for Advanced Study in the Behavioral Sciences, one of the postwar national investments in the social sciences, gave me time and freedom for opening my eyes, especially to English social anthropology, and to the social context of art production in a seminar with Robert N. Wilson; later so did a sabbatical, taken up at St. Anthony's College, Oxford, during which I studied Roman history; and a Guggenheim grant, during which I worked through writings of Marx and Lenin. Business schools, at Carnegie Mellon and Harvard Universities, supplied settings for studying organizations and managers: I am especially grateful to Leland Bach and Richard Vancil, respectively, for help with this. My debts to libraries spread across many universities; the library of the University of Arizona, Tucson, was especially useful. Two months in 1990 in Wassenaar, at the Netherlands Institute for Advanced Study, and living at the Pauwhof, for which I am grateful to Siegwart Lindenberg, made feasible a final major rewrite.

My work and thoughts, which never left the two themes of contingency and context, have also been shaped over intervening years by colleagues and students in the sociology departments of the Universities of Chicago and Edinburgh, and in the departments of social relations and of sociology at Harvard University. Joel Levine and Morris Friedell, my first graduate students, have continued to share interests from our Chicago days in combining combinatorics and algebra (linear and modern) to develop notions of social space from process, rather than the reverse. Others who contributed to my thinking include Michael Adler, Serge Bogojavlensky, Richard Boyle, W. W. Cooper, Tom Ertman, Harold Guetzkow, David Krackhardt, John Lie, John MacDougall, Tim McGuire, Kazuo Seiyama, and R. Vargas.

I am grateful to the modern American university system (sketched in chapter 4) for making possible the huge stretches of time, and the stimulation from many young colleague-students, both of which are essential to research. Research also requires support of substantial equipment and research teams, which adds up to generous patronage. I am indebted for support received over many years from the National Science Foundation under Grants GS 2689 and 76–24394, as well as support under Grant Ser 76–17502 for the RIAS interdisciplinary mathematical-modeling workshop series at Harvard University, which I organized together with Stephen J. Gould and Richard Zeckhauser.

．　．　．　．　．

The theory presented here has had a long gestation. Michael Schwartz as head section man wrote up and circulated notes of my lectures in Soc. Rel. 10, a big introductory course which I helped teach in the 1960s at Harvard University. Ideas for the course interacted with my research in the 1960s on vacancy chains in big organizations, with which Schwartz helped in modeling and Ruth Adler helped in coding. As early as 1970, Granovetter and I sketched a possible joint book deriving from all that material, and he has patiently offered criticism and aid ever since.

In the early 1970s a whole crew of us worked on network phenomenology and modeling, including Ronald Breiger and Scott Boorman as leaders, Greg Heil as computer guru, François Lorrain and Steve Berkowitz as structuralist savants, the late Nicholas Mullins as institutionalist (1973), and with serious statistical computation from Joe Schwartz, mathematical computation from Paul Levitt, and a sense of reality from Paul Bernard and Nancy Howell. Our many unpublished working memos, plus dialogue at conferences we organized in 1970 (Camden, Maine) and 1973 (William James Hall), inform the present manuscript. In subsequent years, follow-up work was stimulated by informal rivalry with the Irvine group centered around Lin Freeman, Doug White, and Kim Romney, which initiated a journal, *Social Networks*, and by collaboration with the Toronto group centered around Barry Wellman, Bonny Erickson, and Steve Carrington, which for years ran a newsletter of concepts and computations for the International Society for Social Network Analysis.

In the late 1970s I developed interface models of markets, with help from Duane Champagne and Jeff Johnson. Starting in 1979, John Padgett and I ran a seminar at Harvard on large organizations in comparative-historical perspective, which generated notable contributions from Peter Bearman, Peter Evans, and Eric Leifer. This seminar led John to his own draft book and me to endless memos and syllabi. In 1980 Al Reiss was intrigued enough to encourage a revision of a general memo on interfaces, written for a Social Science Research Council symposium of his.

In 1980 also came my first systematic outline for "the book," circulated as notes for U.C.-Irvine students in a month-long graduate workshop there. Robert Eccles and I revised the White-Padgett organization seminar to emphasize control, in the context of a new joint doctoral program between the sociology department and the Business School at Harvard. Many working papers resulted; I remember papers from Jeff Bradach, Ken Dauber, Roger Gould, and Geoffrey Love which influenced the ideas now surfacing here. Soon after, Alessandro Pizzorno and I jointly offered a seminar on identity-formation which we used as occasion to trade and contrast our ideas, enriched by essays from Carlos Forment and field reports from Cal Morrill.

I thank the many who sat through diffuse and difficult presentations of some of this material by me during the years since the Irvine outline, as I continued struggling to meld disparate strands into a coherent theory. These include, as I remember, besides long-suffering graduate seminars, audiences at Boston University, Brown University, Caltech, U.C.-Irvine, UCLA, U.C.-Santa Barbara, University of Chicago, Cornell University, Dartmouth College, University of Edinburgh, European University Institute-Florence, University of Massachusetts-Amherst, M.I.T., SUNY-Buffalo, SUNY-Stony Brook, University of North Carolina, Northwestern University, University of Pennsylvania, University of Saarbrucken, Stanford University, University of Toronto, University of Utrecht, and Yale University, as well as Sunbelt Network Conferences in Tucson, Santa Barbara, and Tampa, and the usual sociology congresses and meetings.

．　．　．　．　．

The manuscript presented here itself has a checkered past. Again and again I stuffed and ordered years of bits and pieces into a draft of some part of "the book." Zeckhauser, as editor, helped shape the chapter (White 1985) which convinced me that I had finally grown a vision adequate for a coherent and comprehensive book. Then two years (1986, 1987) at the University of Arizona as head of the department of sociology exposed me to a broader range of substantive sociology to be included. There also Michael Hechter challenged me and Dauber, Carol Diem, and Gould to deal again with the perversities of rationality in social science. At the business school in Tucson, Shelby Stewman and I finally could talk vacancy chains up close, and Jim Lincoln, Calvin Morrill, Roberto Fernandez, and Doug Wholey debated with me sober uses for networks. My library notes for the book also accumulated at a record pace there.

Finally, as Director of the Center for the Social Sciences at Columbia University I found time and setting for writing a complete first draft in 1988. Most of all, I was aided and stimulated by a fellow structuralist, Ronald Burt, who also saw the challenge as regrounding social science. The unstinting support of Burt was vital, first as my department chair and then in creating settings of urgency in his own research and consulting shop, as well as in the Stamer Workshops. Fatimah Dornevil shares administrative responsibilities with me during my own stint currently as chair of the sociology department.

For their support as Steering Committee of the Center for the Social Sciences, I thank Burt, David Krantz, Helen Milner, and Richard Nelson. Debi Gilchrest, as Administrative Assistant, has kept the Center manageable, in collaboration with Miguel Guilarte, Robert Shapiro, and Van Rossem, who also helped me with software and hardware. The first full draft of the book was retyped into a word processor by Andrew Pollack.

Revisions of the manuscript were influenced by my experiences in activities of the Center. I remember especially the cognitive science/ decision-making workshops led at the Center by Lynn Cooper and Krantz; the elites workshop there with Harriet Zuckerman; a faculty group on conversation that included Douglas Chalmers, Carol Dweck, Priscilla Ferguson, Michael Hanagan, and Robert Krauss; and the seminar series organized by Charles Cameron on math modeling and by Richard Nelson on innovation. Author-meets-critic sessions with Charles Tilly in the chair were especially apposite. Helpful also was the dialogue at the first Shaker Inn theory conference, August 1991, which was sponsored jointly by the Center and by the ICS graduate sociology program of the universities of Groningen and Utrecht, the Netherlands.

Helpful in the last stages at Columbia have been discussions with Chris Canavan, Mark Clark, Andrew Cortell, Martin Gargiulo, Shin-Kap Han, Blanca Herredia, Sarah Mahler, Scott Martin, Peter Rosendorff, Ronan van Rossem, Kemal Shehadi, Ilan Talmud, and Clare

Ullman, all Interdisciplinary Fellows of the Center for the Social Sciences, and with other students including Bobbi Berenbaum, Wen-Rwei Hsu, Helen-Marie Lekas, Celia Lewis, Seth Rachlin, Marvin Reiss, Jae soon Rhee, Andrej Rus, Andras Szanto, Kuo-Hsien Su, and Yuki Yasuda.

The manuscript has also been shaped by suggestions, not recognized in the text, from Howard Becker, Douglas Chalmers, Robert Jervis, James Rule, Robert Shapiro, and Robin Williams, and from participants in the Russell Sage monthly seminar on economic sociology in 1990–1991, organized by Granovetter. The interactive structure of ideas in this book required unending rearrangements and revisions that would have been impossible or far more difficult without this embarrassingly large amount of stimulation and help over an extended period.

• • • • •

The hardest part has proved to be rewriting what I thought was already the book. Pungent commentary from Debra Friedman on the second draft in 1988 pointed out what could be important. It was Eccles who predicted, to my dismay and disbelief, that I would need three years of continued rewriting to achieve my purpose. Richard Lachmann and Tilly were generous in supplying suggestions for improvements in detailed memoranda on that draft. Granovetter's detailed critique of an early version of chapter 3 helped shape the present chapters 2, 4, and 5.

The third draft (December 1989), somewhat improved, benefited from incisive critiques by Kathleen Carley, Eccles, and Neil Fligstein. For other valuable comments on this draft I am indebted to Doug McAdam, and to Woody Powell and other participants in his Tucson seminar, as abstracted in notes by Friedman, and also to Lachmann, Leifer, Mark Mizruchi, and Van Rossem. Tilly understood, in some ways better than I, what the book in this draft was about and made many constructive suggestions, such as how to begin the first chapter! Padgett penetrated my murk to emphasize the centrality of molecular disciplines.

The next extensive revision was written in 1990 during two months at the Netherlands Institute for Advanced Study in Wassenaar (NIAS). There Lindenberg once again urged rational choice theory upon me. This revision incorporated improvements suggested by Burt's Columbia sociology faculty workshop, which included Ellen Auster, Henk Flap, Edward Mansfield, Mark Mizruchi, and Martina Morris as members.

Eccles and Tilly both were helpful early and then all the way through. I am especially indebted to Chuck Tilly for his endlessly patient and detailed commentaries, draft after draft, in which he also stood back to diagnose conceptual turbulence and skew. An insightful appraisal from Randall Collins for Princeton University Press motivated the last revisions, in which improvements in chapter 1 were guided by Bearman; in chapter 4 by Paul DiMaggio; and in all chapters by Leifer, who became the book's doctor, with the help of Holly Raider. For advice and help I am grateful to Jack Repcheck and Bill Laznovsky of Princeton University Press, and to Barbara Cohen for preparing the index.

For her continued interest and support I am indebted to Virginia White. The dedication acknowledges my main inspiration. She also helped to bring directness and clarity to this manuscript, especially to chapter 1.

IDENTITY AND CONTROL

ONE

INTRODUCTION TO IDENTITY
AND CONTROL

DESPITE the continuous flow of "new developments," the social sciences appear to be in the doldrums, suggesting that the foundations of these sciences are not yet right. Effective theory of social relations is hindered by assuming that social action comes only from individual biological creatures—humans—as a consequence of their nature and consciousness as persons. This mirage of the person as atom breeds an obverse mirage of a society as an entity.

The difficulty of the construct "individual as person" is shown by its being shunted aside from the center of activity in each social science separately. The construct although indispensable to current theory is opaque to research from that theory. Current economics proclaims the individual as foundation construct, but economics assiduously avoids any responsibility for understanding and predicting, pointing instead to psychology. Psychology as a scientific discipline disdains "the person." The active science today is rooted in cognitive aspects and emphasizes the "wet," the biological substrate of neural cell physiology, or else emphasizes perception and development and other correlates to the ecological environment. Deference to social psychology is low just because it gives some grudging attention to "person," and similarly with clinical psychology. A few bridges exist, such as those surveyed by Mischel (1990; see chapter 5 for development), but work of high scientific status tends to shun the "person" construct as polluting. This paradox, the shunning of a construct which is central in the axioms of current social science, suggests that social action is induced before actors, who derive from the action and need not be persons.

Entering an introductory class in any branch of social science can be intimidating. Professors lay out a world of uniformities—of rules, of seamless connection—and many treat change, disorder, or even improvisation as exceptional. Students, meanwhile, live in a world where disorder is around every corner and improvisation the only means of survival.

Everyday social surroundings also assert a normality at odds with students' improvisations and perceived chaos. News broadcasts do this as they imply an everyday life quite distinct from the contents of news stories. Students are correct when they perceive their social world both as improvisation in the midst of chaos, and as a set of smooth social stories shared with others. Social science should seek principles of social process which account for chaos and normality together.

Normality and happenstance are opposite sides of the same coin of social action. Students constantly strive for control, in efforts directed especially at each other, as part and parcel of the identity triggered by the chaos. Identity comes from moving to some sort of social footing, and the normality that students find is a veneer on these interacting efforts of identity and control. One theme of this book is that obfuscation is built into accounts of social organization.

Who "we" are is all bound up with what "control" is in social surroundings, and also depends upon our grounding in material production and the constraints from physical space. Much practical activity keeps on being done, and that translates into normality and habit at some level. But chaos and accident are the sources and bases for identities, and it is identities seeking control which give energy to practical activity in social context. So the questions become: How do identities intermesh to form social organization? When and by what means does it become possible to break through rigid blocking in social organization to get fresh action?

Much of this account will challenge existing theories, and in doing so will deny what we, of the present era, take for granted, namely the constructs of person and of society. Much of the text develops, as a second theme, how messy and refractory social organization is: there is no tidy atom and no embracing world, only complex striations, long strings reptating as in a polymer goo, or in a mineral before it hardens. The real riddle will be seeing how it is that anyone can effect action by intention in social context, and the book builds toward chapter 6, which identifies ways to overcome, sometimes, that blocking of action embodied in social organization.

Each of us already knows from experience how hard it is to push even the most local social organization in a given direction. For example, consider how students induct a newly arrived professor into the implicit standards of grading and cognitive framing in curriculum (e.g., that technical but not historical sophistication is encouraged) for their campus: they (as what I term a discipline) could not articulate, and mostly are unaware of, the complex of pressures they bring to bear. It is indeed effective control, but it does not rely on intention to get fresh action. Are there any reliable guides to getting action? But then again, if there are, would that not generate a paradox?

This book asserts and highlights self-similarity of social organization, as a first principle, according to which the same dynamic processes apply over and over again across different sizes and scopes. The importance of identity and control as primitives of the theory is manifest. The spread of a given identity plays off in control efforts against the spreads among other identities to enable some degree of balance and continuity to develop. The principle of self-similarity then suggests that dispersions are the key measures for all observed social formations. Dispersions are the sources of identities and control, which are the sources of social organization. Let this be a second principle: It is not averages which are crucial, but rather spreads across locale and degree of social connections. Particularly important is how events are spaced. These two master principles, dispersion and self-similarity, recur and complement each other throughout all chapters.

The next section develops identities, as distinguished from persons. Then a section on control follows. The last section of the chapter sketches the course of the book, in part through an annotated glossary.

Identities from Contingencies

A central claim of the theory is that identities are triggered by contingencies. Let us begin the analysis with a homely example. Consider the daily act of waking up:

Each morning's awakening requires the reproduction of a self that had been deconstructed in sleep. In this process of reproduction, pieces of the biophysical world are cobbled together with bits of social reality to produce the awake self in control. The argument is that this self is constructed and reconstructed out of prior, simpler identities. The deconstruction which yielded sleep had to be, at the same time, the provision of a protective order which affects both social and physical arrangements.[1]

Awake, there is much to be done; the need for order abounds. The physical and the social interpenetrate. A major juncture of the social with the biophysical environments is through work, whether the

---

[1] There is great variety in these protective orders, from Yanonomo fireside vigil to modern dormitory: see the survey in White and Aubert (1959).

material products be tools or food.[2] This juncture results in physical contingencies as well as activating social contentions. Contingencies and contentions produce identities.

Identity here does not mean the common-sense notion of self, nor does it mean presupposing consciousness and integration or presupposing personality.[3] Rather, identity is any source of action not explicable from biophysical regularities, and to which observers can attribute meaning. An employer, a community, a crowd, oneself, all may be identities. An identity is perceived by others as having an unproblematic continuity. Identities add through contentions to the contingencies[4] faced by other identities. Social organization comes as a by-product of the cumulation of these processes. When contending counteractions result in a dynamic equilibrium, we perceive social structure.

In life we continually have to restructure our understanding of what others are, and of what control is, even as we devise accountings for ourselves and for others who are in some relation to us. Furthermore, identities and their contentions come all wrapped in larger structures and processes that predate them. This book attempts to lay out some specifications of how identities develop into and result from social organization.

The Playground as an Illustration
of Interacting Identities

As an example both of how identities are formed and of how they help to create each other, consider groups of children on a playground. We can tease out some complexities from just this seemingly simple context. If the playground is observed over a long period,[5] certain clusters of children will emerge repeatedly. Choosing up sides for games partitions children into teams, each child going to a particular one. Any such crowd may repartition anew, or instead may dissolve into casual chasing or chattering. Or, a cluster of children may go about together when they are similar in their own and/or others' eyes. This recognition of similarity may be implicit, as when all the members are teenagers, or each child is a fan of singer X; or it may be explicit, as when the group are Hispanics, or teen-

---

[2] For elaboration see, for example, Udy (1970) and Howell (1979, 1988).

[3] See discussion on Mischel (1990) below and in chapter 5.

[4] It is important to point out that this usage is entirely unlike the technical usage introduced into psychology by B. F. Skinner (for an introduction to which see Skinner 1953).

[5] As has been done in a series of distinguished investigations in social science: e.g., Opie and Opie (1969).

agers. Initially these clusters mostly are unnamed, even unrecognized, as when they are "fatsos." They depend on the type and degree of activity going on. Such clusters can come to be perceived as and act as identities, if they reappear repeatedly or in a variety of other contexts.

Dynamic models can be based and tested on observation of spatial patterns in free play of young children.[6] Certainly what you observe at a given moment is only there because of some underlying orderliness of process. This orderliness partially comes from and is reflected in talk. One can listen to the same standard tales being offered across the playground in accounting for what this or that cluster does. The physical environment can play an important role in emerging identities:[7] how slides and swings are arrayed influences how children sort themselves into groups.

Much activity on the playground is casual. But there will be some appearance of orderliness, say in teams which make claims about specialization in relations and tasks. For example, even in kickball, such accounts of neatness only faintly reflect the real turbulence, energized by unending searches for self and control. When teams come to visit for tournaments, grown-ups often come along with the visitors, and this activates local adults to come out and spend time on the playground. These adults favor and slight various children, patronize them, according to how they themselves get caught up in the game. A much more elaborate social organization is created, or rather is shown to have been there in potential, and in the perceptions of some, all along.[8]

Likely as not, for a given child from this playground one identity first was triggered from playground contingencies, and others from mismatches between home and school. This may occur, for example, when a kind of food newly enjoyed at school with peers is rejected by parents when the child goes home. Or it may occur when the clothes that classmates insist upon, as their badge of belonging, are disdained at home and purchase resisted. Any identity comes out of diametrically competing energies, synthesizing many disparate bits, as when the child becomes the weird dresser in the family's eyes, or conversely, the nerd in classmates' eyes.[9] Having an identity re-

---

[6] Joel Cohen's thesis (cf. Cohen 1971) is a notable attempt. And see the observations of adult freely forming groups by James as modeled by Coleman (1964; cf. White 1962 for critique).

[7] But the correspondence may be more complex—perhaps geometric order compensates somehow for social disorder.

[8] This is Key's problem (1945) of interacting levels of context.

[9] This is a generalization of Garfinkel's problem (1967).

quires continually reproducing a consistent joint construction out of actions from distinct settings.

Persons and Identities

Persons, in the ordinary sense of the term,[10] are neither the first nor the only form in which identities appear. Much theory in social science stipulates persons, takes them as preexisting atoms.[11] In contrast, this book builds toward the conclusion that persons develop only under special social circumstances, which come late historically.

Persons should be derived from, rather than being presupposed in, basic principles of social action. One can usually impute ends from actions, but these "ends" often are, despite protestations, mere by-products of previous history as adapted to current circumstance. Actors, such as "Columbia sociology department" and you the reader, are social constructions in a practical and contemporaneous sense. Goals and preferences, being so changeable, are not causes, but rather they are spun after the fact as part of accounting for what has already happened.

Within sociology today, and other social sciences, there is a strong resurgence of an individualist mode of theorizing under the label "rational choice theory" (Bueno de Mesquita and Lalman 1992; Lindenberg, Coleman, and Nowak 1986; Lindenberg 1989a; Riker 1982). This theory takes identity for granted by ignoring the nesting of contexts and thereby tries to explain away control.[12] Rational choice builds upon a myth of the person as some preexisting entity.

The push toward rational-choice theory is itself sensible. Indeed it is rational, because it mimics the push in other sciences toward what

---

[10] It will take much of a chapter late in the book, chapter 5, to explain my own view of the etiology of person.

[11] These atoms perhaps can be equated to souls, the ideological invention of the Christian Church over long centuries. Means-ends schemes seem to be transpositions of the church's beautifully wrought theology of the soul; see further discussion in chapters 2, 5, and 7. Even among sociologists this methodological individualism is currently close to hegemonic, as Keyfitz and Keilman argue: "Of course, no one will argue that individual persons (the parts) do not exist. But it is certainly true that they behave differently depending on the context. Applying Capra's thesis to household demography might therefore imply that one should study the network of relations between individuals inside (and outside?) the household, in order to understand the behaviour of the individual—and many sociologists will wholeheartedly agree. Is our present preference for the individual as the object of analysis mainly due to the attention the individual receives in Western society?" (In Keilman et al. 1989, p. 277.) Just so.

[12] But see Hechter (1987) for an attempt at institutional explanation. Pizzorno (1990) reviews exactly this difficulty in Hobbes.

is called Mean Field Theory.[13] This is an approximate theory of long-range order through calculation of self-consistent fields. At first sight, of course, rational choice theory might instead seem to ape models of short-range order which concentrate on immediate environs. But no, the long-range order of a self-consistent field is essential to the calculations in a theory of rational choice. This is because the goals and ends in fact have to be read out of pattern, and only a larger pattern will sustain such attempts. Although any self-consistent field approach attempts to take great care of local context, it is at the cost of the subtle correlations that are central to actual process.

In contrast to rational choice theory, structuralism[14] disdains events, as when it explains the Civil War without Gettysburg, and the French Republic without the Eighteenth Brumaire. Structuralism thus takes control for granted and tries to explain away identity. Structuralism builds from the myth of society as some preexisting entity.

Abandon both the Talcott Parsons attempt to derive social order from values guiding individual persons, and the view common in economic theory of social order emerging from preexisting individuals' efforts to achieve their idiosyncratic wants and interests. Neither of these two approaches to social theory, themselves opposites, take persons seriously. As a result, neither can treat historical trends and cultural impacts with proper sensitivity. Neither rationalist nor structuralist approaches can give proper account of social action.

Control and Decoupling

Each identity continues discovering and reshaping itself in action. Identity is produced by contingency to which it responds as intervention in possible processes to come. The rush and jars of daily living are contingencies, as are ill health and contentions of other identities. Control is both anticipation of and response to eruptions in environing process. Seeking control is not some option of choice, it comes out of the way identities get triggered and keep going. An identity is as likely to target itself as another for a control effort.

Social processes and structure are traces from successions of control efforts. Yet control has most effect when it is fugitive, for it re-

[13] Also called the Mean Field Approximation, or Self Consistent Fields; see DeGennes (1979) and Ziman (1979), and, for an elegant and readable early account, see Van Vleck (1932). It is discussed further in chapter 5 as Scale-Invariance and chapter 7 as Self-Consistent Field.

[14] Whether in Parsons (1937), or Wallerstein (1974), or later forms.

quires disorder as material from which to attempt order. Control efforts are responses by identities to endless stochastic contingencies, to which others' control efforts should be added. Each control effort presupposes and works in terms of realities for other identities.

These social dynamics have peculiar features when compared with, say, chemical reactions. There is no single, unique, and isotropic space for context. The dynamics of control while they are playing out are also inducing and constructing their own spaces that accommodate possibilities of social action. These possibilities depend on perceptions that are only partly set by the biophysical environment.

Topologies of these social spaces are complex, and they vary over time and from one locale to another. Insights about a topology suggest leverages for control. The military drill is but one model of control, a model which subjects to caricature the preconditions and steps for control. In a drill persons are induced to move in parallel within a little group which is both literally and metaphorically cut off from other social relations for a time.

By contrast, one can seek control exactly from weaving a maze of uncoordinated and changing contexts around others. Consider a concrete example from a complicated setting. In an industrial firm, Bower studies control efforts moving up and down management levels, all high enough not to be constrained by production routines. Contentions are clustered around projects of capital investment, many being for the development of new products and processes:

> If one wishes to explain after the fact precisely why and when a project developed the way it did, situational elements are likely to be critical to the explanation. In the specifics, events tend to dominate patterns— which in passing is why history tends to be anecdotal. But, for the manager interested in influencing outcomes it is also clear that with one exception he should focus attention on the patterns. It is structural context that determined how the events of importance were perceived. Where the context seemed to be designed to serve strategic needs, events lost their disorienting impact. . . . Where traditional financial technique focuses attention on individual project plans separate from the businesses they are meant to serve, severe distortions in focus and timing can result. (Bower 1970, pp. 277, 279)

The internal arrangements of any particular firm are pressured by those of others. Let us locate the business within a second level. One avenue of pressure is the markets in which a firm seeks to find niches. The menu of actions thus reflects conforming to fashion among peers, but seeking control implies actions which are original at least in their timing. Bower avoids concepts that presuppose fixed systems and that stipulate management structures as being realistic and effective. His "context" is a residual term which calls for the kind of specification for social organization to be developed in this book.

Triage

This theory, if valid, should be reflected in at least some social practices. An obvious candidate is triage. An example of triage is admissions practices in hospital emergency rooms. When, to whom, and how an arriving claim thrusts itself upon attention calls for constantly monitoring the current congestion and activity across a structure of treatment locales which is itself changeable and negotiable. This monitoring requires acute attention to and assessments of arriving claims. Thus triage combines a context for control into an approach to control by indirection.

Triage binds the purely social in with biophysical contingencies.[15] It is a special pattern of attention to complementarities among arriving claims, and implies a dependency of the chooser upon a skeleton of other identities and their support structure. Triage also results in a pattern of responsibility. For example, assigning a gunshot victim to a nursing station treating bacterial infections is not responsible. This responsibility emerges as a pattern of evaluating claims not from the views of the claimants but rather from views of the interactions, and the interactions of interactions.

Triage can be highly formalized and elaborated, as in a system of appeal courts culminating in some court of final appeal. It can also take crude, unplanned forms. There are many terms for structures that may afford triage—board, committee, council, counselors—but the complete ambiguity in use of these terms corresponds to the difficulty in analyzing triage. There is more variety and ambiguity in terms than in the accompanying operational systems.[16]

Triage is a process highly dependent upon timings. Consider for example the implications of the seating strategies of airlines. Considered as an example of triage, they as a package show that intentional

---

[15] It is a special case of work, in Udy's (1970) formulation, and is thus subject to what he describes (1990) as the universal paradox of work organization.

[16] Current economic theory is all too likely to assume away the existence of options in triage: Contrast the assumption by economist Carlton (1979) in a prize-winning(!) essay on vertical integration—"Because a firm will always choose to use its own inputs first"—with the sociologist Eccles's report on triage in business (1985), based on observation in the field, in which he insists that managers as often shun as seek inside sourcing, depending on political context for control efforts.

forgetting is one prime component of the responsibility process in triage. Another component of triage which they suggest is arbitrary referral to some earlier history, jumping over a better present claim. Both forgetting and referral can be used in the triage process as part of the ongoing attempt to balance and optimize timings.

Triage supposes and allows for failure, as a component. Failure is an important social invention. Failure invokes the dramatic demise of an identity. In this sense, failure couples control to identity, whereas forgetting and referral are less dramatic erosions of identities.

Decoupling

Failures are not mere breakdowns of a physical component. A failure is the social recognition and construction of breakdowns which offers a fresh start. Failure thus permits and stipulates a sharp ending to what seemed locked-in by social pressure.

Every identity is engaged in control efforts. Even so, control slips away from each, and appears to go elsewhere. Control interactions come to seem determinate, as part of some order. Fresh control presupposes indeterminacies, with some breaking of connection between contingencies. These indeterminacies are the results and signs of decouplings, which are by-products of physical and social actions.

Triage generalizes decoupling, which is an aspect of process and extends across time and space. A queue for taxis at an airport decouples by abbreviating interactions among passengers and drivers to a focus in a single portal with queue. If there is a queue supervisor, the simple decoupling of fixed rule may become triage, with considerations of which parties might go in the same taxi, of emergency needs, etc.

A habit of saving from current income is an illustration of decoupling over time. In saving, conceded rights which are foregone now may be activated again, but at a time not stipulated. Saving, like other decoupling, depends on what goes on among many identities, in a larger pattern not perceivable by them. If the contrary were true, decoupling would not occur and there would be some sort of panic.

Decoupling provides lubrication which permits self-similarity of social organization across scopes and levels. Decoupling makes it possible for levels of social organization, such as cities and organizations and families, to mix and blur into an inhomogeneous gel.[17] Decoupling explains how it is that the same social formula can recur on different scales.

---

[17] For background on polymer gels see Appendix 2, part B.

The sources of decoupling always are attempts by identities to establish comparability: this derives from the second principle of the theory. These efforts have a paradoxical character, expounded in the next two chapters: comparability is established for perceivers (other identities) only through the most strenuous efforts at superiority. Attempts at dominance are exactly what set up the arena of contention within which comparability falls out as the unanticipated by-product.

One is surrounded by examples: professors vie for distinction and thereby become as peas in a pod to students in their classes; physicians strive as individuals—and also in much the same process as specialisms—for prestige only to exactly thereby become imbued by other identities as interchangeable. Burger King, MacDonald's, Wendy's and so on induce a new category of equivalence, the fast-food restaurant, exactly and only by striving to be better—which requires, and therefore induces as presupposition, being comparable.[18]

Stories

Stories are generated by control efforts which act as constraints upon identities. Signals ensue and cumulate. Sets of signals may get transposed from one situation to another, and eventually may become stories, fresh in application but familiar from before and elsewhere.

Processes which loosen constraints from control yield decoupling. Routine can be disrupted by contending projects of control, as these efforts generate stories. Decoupling induces a spread of alternative stories as menu. The conundrum is that these same stories play into control efforts elsewhere. Thus formation of identities itself is a form of decoupling.

Stories express perceptions of social process and structure, but stories also can and do conceal projects of control. Put chicanery to one side; concealment would still remain in social space. Failure requires accompanying stories. If all stories being told were valid, no story could ever be realized, even momentarily; there would be only some hypothetical tableau of stasis. Stories are numerous and can be mapped on actions in any number of ways so that they contribute to decoupling sufficient to permit some fresh action.

[18] There may emerge, as by-product, some one or more formulaic statements of the comparability. Here, for example, the formula may be expressed as a reshuffling of the time order among phases—say preparing, ordering, paying for, eating—which are standard in all restaurants. But the comparability emerges, first and painfully, as product of unceasing strivings for control by identities. In the present illustration, these can be seen, in agreement with the principle of self-similarity, not only as between concrete establishments but also at another level, such as among the franchises with whose names I began (cf. Bradach and Eccles 1989).

Identities emerge from action and counteraction, accompanied by stories which help create sufficient decoupling for fresh action; otherwise social organization would not persist long enough to be observed. An identity succeeds or not, and now rather than then, according to position from control struggles among identities. This position is subject to maneuver inasmuch as there is decoupling, even in extreme circumstances. Here is an example, from the autobiography by the former slave, Frederick Douglass:

> This (arbitrary) treatment was a part of the system, rather than a part of the man (Colonel Edward Lloyd, owner of 1000 slaves and many farms in Maryland in the 1820s). To have encouraged appeals of this kind would have occasioned much loss of time and would have left the overseer powerless to enforce obedience. Nevertheless, when a slave had nerve enough to go straight to his master with a well-founded complaint against an overseer, though he might be repelled and have even that of which he at the time complained be repeated, and though he might be beaten by his master, as well as by the overseer, for his temerity, the policy of complaining was, in the end, generally vindicated by the relaxed rigor of the overseer's treatment. (1952, p. 47) [19]

Scope and Terms of Social Organization

I focus as rigorously as I can upon the purely social. This is not to disdain the cultural.[20] This is also not to disdain, but rather to reemphasize the importance of geography and ecology and biology.[21] All social action regrows from those bases all the time. But their impacts are seen far better once the social is brought out by itself and into clear view—opening up its impacts, observed and potential, back with the biogeographical.

[19] Social organization, and the effects of decoupling within it, are by no means transparent, and indeed Douglass goes on to write: "For some cause or other, the slaves, no matter how often they were repulsed by their masters, were ever disposed to regard them with less abhorrence than the overseer. And yet these masters would often go beyond their overseers in wanton cruelty. . . . They could cripple or kill without fear of consequences."

[20] Distinguishing cultural as separate from social is a perilous undertaking. For the current state of debates on the matter consult the volume edited by Alexander and Seidman (1988); opposite sides are taken by Wuthnow (1987) and Swidler (1986).

[21] Haggett, Cliff, and Frey (1977) survey constructive modeling in geography. Levins is the genius of ecology, and some of his papers are readable (Levins 1966; Levins and MacArthur 1966; and see the adaptation to phenomena of human organizations in Hannan and Freeman 1977). Wilson's sociobiology (1979) is a massive synthesis of social with biophysical across all species.

Presentation

This book is not easy to read, because it aims for the largest possible range, and yet it does so in verbal formulation which cannot be completely shielded from ambiguity of terms, as will already be apparent. An ultimate goal is to formalize the verbal account given here, so that interconnections among the concepts become substantiated through specification within formal models subject to explicit test. But for now the scopes possible through models are so limited and so oddly scattered that I restrict discussion of them to footnotes, references, and an appendix.

The verbal formulation has several implications. The importance of case studies is one implication of the verbal formulation. Without systematic measures fitted by models to the principal terms, there is little help to be gained from existing statistical data series. And case studies also are apt vehicles for dealing with irregularity and happenstance, for dealing with them as an important causal pattern rather than merely a distraction. I argue further that case studies are the form taken by history in contemporaneous mode.

Yet another implication of verbal formulation is that I must work hard to establish a word for each principal construct, the relations among which are to serve as my axioms. Yet these terms often must be introduced in bunches, in succeeding chapters, which can be maddening to the reader. An additional problem is that all these terms, without exception, are also words in the English language, many with the numerous and subtle connotations captured by an unabridged dictionary.[22] A glossary section can help with these problems. Full definitions are not feasible, but at least all the terms are brought together, with some minimal explanation of how they fit together into an overall scheme. And it should be convenient to have this available for later reference. To site my usage among other usages, I adopt several conventions, just within the glossary.

Glossary as Overview

I *italicize* (in boldface) each principal term when it is first introduced, if there is possible confusion from ordinary usage. Each ensuing definition will be elaborated in a later chapter under that term in

---

[22] Any dictionary citation of mine is to *Webster's New Twentieth Century Dictionary, Unabridged*, 2d ed., William Collins Publishers, 1979. Even where there is good match with the dictionary, and but one principal connotation, however, the problems are not over, since ordinary language usage often serves to obfuscate ordinary social processes. Existing works on rhetorics and literatures can provide astute guidance as to such obfuscations.

a heading (of either a chapter or section of a chapter) which appears in the Contents. Special attention is given to the terms most at variance with ordinary usage, and there also is special discussion of variations from common usage in social science (when there is such).

For the reader's convenience, I also single out some secondary terms. At its first occurrence, any secondary term which is used in a sense special to this book is highlighted in bold face roman type. Some other terms common in social science, such as actor and action and especially the chameleon term "level," I use only as bracketing devices, or place-holders. These terms avoid commitment to a particular level: actor, for example, brackets identity and person and corporate actor, and so on.

Social organization, as distinguished from social structure, is the main object for theorizing.[23] The two primitives of the theory are *identities* and *control*, the former being triggered into efforts at the latter by **contingencies** which bridge physical with social. Identities are various, and include events. Once triggered, identities seek control and continue to seek it, first here and then there, while several other identities in contact with any given identity are doing the same. Social organization is both means and bar to control. The concrete physical and biological settings in which actions occur are crucial. It is thus the outcomes of contentions among identities which is what cumulates into social organization.

Social organization exhibits spatial grounding. Even sophisticated social action spins off from erratic and contingent aspects of biophysical realities: this is an aspect of a principle of *dispersion* as product of and basis for social formation. Social **comparability**, as both product of and basis for control, derives from this principle.

Human social orders derive ultimately from pecking orders in flocks of vertebrates, but respond to subtler irritants from their social and ecological environment. Pecking orders factor into three species of social molecules, three *disciplines*, which in the next chapter are labeled **interfaces, arenas**, and **councils**. Each is characterized by a **valuation ordering: quality, purity**, and **prestige**, respectively. Ef-

---

[23] In the words of Warriner, in Blau and Merton (1981), structure is "an observable social phenomenon involving the interrelation or arrangement of parts. It is in this sense that 'social structure' is often paired with 'social organization,' the two terms together referring to social actors in a regular interdependency created and maintained through interactor action. 'Structure' usually focuses attention upon the actors and their differential identities, while 'organization' emphasizes their functional or processual interconnections . . . the units, unlike units in physical structures, are not autonomous entities whose character is fixed by processes antecedent to and independent of the structural processes themselves . . . social 'space' is defined by what the units do in relation to each other."

forts at control continue between identities, and so social organization comes through cumulation and exploring which can be approximated in **catnets**.

A *tie* is a failed discipline. Ties are held together to constitute a *network* through the vehicle of *stories*, singly and in **story-sets**. Mutual patterning of ties of different types between blocks of actors can be interpreted according to *structural equivalence*. The interpretation, which proceeds from a self-consistent search, is called a **blockmodel**.

All larger social organization builds from *network-population*. The conventional definition of a population—as a bag of beans—is misleading, like the notion of a "society." To use such constructs is to mislead and hamstring the analysis. A network shapes and is its own population.

Institutions can result either from literal physical superposition of network-populations or by crossing them in other ways. Major institutions include **corporatism** and **clientelism**, each of which has many variants. An institution covers its concrete disarray with boundary claims of interrelations around **values** across a partition into distinct **corporate actors**. A different analytic approach, which erodes in concrete application, recognizes **positions** for actors, which cross between **role frames** in different network-populations.

Styles emerge in and structure environments characterized by wide varieties of social formations and stochastic processes, described in terms of **profiles**. Within such environments identities may be joined together into *persons*, and **careers** may result, as well as **professionalism** as a style.

The dynamics of social action come from and are expressed through layers of social formation that result from processes which recur at different levels and scopes: This is the first principle, *self-similarity*. By this first principle, examples of very different physical scope and social number can be used to illustrate the same construct, for example actor.

A diagram may help to fix this in memory. Figure 1–1 represents the principle constructs in a triangle, which then nests in a triangle for further level. (Figure 2-1 in the next chapter extrapolates and elaborates figure 1-1, as to disciplines.)

Social dynamics continue because they generate some flexibility for, while simultaneously constricting action through, accumulated social organization. This is the interaction between *decoupling* and *embedding*. Physical contingencies involved in decoupling and embedding are distinguished from social *ambage*, on the one hand, and from interpretive *ambiguity*, on the other. The basis is laid for a cal-

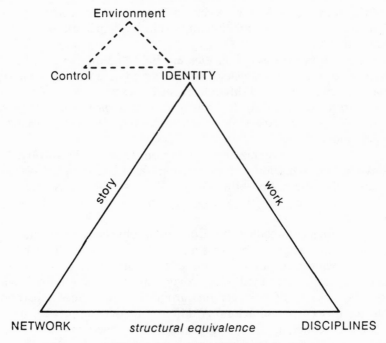

Fig. 1-1. Nested Social Triangles

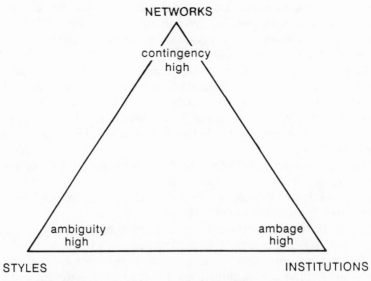

Fig. 1-2. Contingency trade-offs—Population Triangle

culus of trade-offs in uncertainty. Again a diagram may help fix this in memory. Figure 1-2 points toward a calculus for kinds of uncertainty in a triangle of populations.

The results of these dynamics include bridgings which reach both upward and downward. How a discipline embeds into its larger setting is summarized as three **embedding ratios**, called **differentiation, dependence**, and **involution**. How persons embed in careers invoke **story lines** as well as styles.

All the processes are accommodations—successively larger and more intricate—among efforts at control. Fresh action is blocked by the accommodations, which predominate over ecological opportunity. *Getting action* is difficult, given all the social involution.

There are many other secondary terms in the book not singled out above. The number of terms needing separate introduction can be reduced in particular applications. Identity and control, however, drive the whole enterprise.

Scale of Sizes

This book builds a scale for social organization. The resulting array of chapters is roughly cumulative as to evolution and as to scope in number as well as complexity. One thousand, and five, more or less, should be the two principal social numbers for the human species. A thousand, on the one hand, because that is the size of where it all begins, the size in number of individual creatures of a primitive tribe which is a more or less isolated aggregation able to subsist and to reproduce itself.[24]

On the other hand, five seems to be about the unit operating size. Five is the median number of comparable selves that work together effectively enough to keep reproducing the arrangement. The size of five cuts across all contexts and levels: nuclear family, men in a fishing party, producing firms making up a market, and so on.[25]

The absolute size of the constituent entities within a unit need not matter. The "accident-and-control" processes that generate identities recur again and again at very different scopes, with new levels of actor as by-products. The "friction-and-matching" processes that generate persons out of identities also recur at different scopes. Humans have techniques of naming and telling stories that help actors

[24] No one can now tell whether it is lemmas on minimal genetic variability or on ecological adaptability that make one thousand the key number, or whether instead it is the appearance of languages or kinship systems first at that cutoff size.
[25] This is also the effective number (seven, ± two) of discriminations by humans as argued by psychologist George Miller (in Miller 1967).

of different sizes deal with one another. And these techniques also apply within a person, apply that is to id, to superego, and to egos at the time scale of daily living, as well as at the time scale of professional ambition.

Support for this idea of bracketing size comes from across the social sciences. One source is the theorizing by sociologists such as Anderson (1974) and Tilly (1990) of the emergence of states from the fractious shambles of late medieval Europe. Another source is psychologists' recent theorizing about learned helplessness for persons (Seligman and Garber 1980), which is allied to sociological discussions of the self-fulfilling prophecy (Merton 1968; Rosenthal and Jacobson 1989). A third source is a historian of religion's tapestry of the emergence of Israel from turbulent ethnicities (Gottwald 1979).

Ecological siting in physical space is always present for social action, which continues to come into existence, and fade, in part as irritation from and spinoff into the erratic in biophysical space-time. Biophysical ecology shapes empire and tribe alike. Braudel (1972) makes this vivid in tracing agriculture and nomadism over centuries of urban and tribal polities around the Mediterranean. And Tilly (1964) traces this truth down through hamlets and micro-regions of Brittany in explicating who rose to support counterrevolution in the France of the 1790s.

Self-similarity in social action, across levels and size, reflects continuing impetus from the biophysical. Whether in work or demography or daily life, left untied to biophysical process, social organization tends to freeze up and to lose any possibility for change. A wide range of examples will be treated, from aboriginal tribe through medieval mosaics and on through contemporary social groups. But the focus is a middle range of size: markets, work groups, small cities, and the like. A thousand thousands is a million, so this focus in only a step or two permits tracing the tangles even of a big city or the internal economy of a Fortune 500 corporation.

Contributions to Social Science

Social science always has had weird problems, ones not shared by other science. Scientists of social phenomena are always amateurs, since those who make their living out of skilled understandings of the social condition are—almost everybody. The "molecules" of social science can confound practitioners of the science. By the rationale expressed in this book, practitioners of all sorts—including concrete-minded practitioners of daily living—must come to find the argument persuasive and also useful as a way to do other work. The argument can only be from within the social action in which we all exist. It is an argument about our continuing construction of realities sui generis, off to one side from other sciences. The task is akin to theory in engineering, as will become evident in the last two chapters, and is also related to theory of social engineering back through canon law (Berman 1983).

From natural sciences should come a desire to probe beneath common sense, which is chockablock with misleading notions. In social science the only sanity is to eschew sanity, common sanity. To be sane is by definition not to penetrate the common-sense that conceals the inner mechanics of social reality. This is the approach of the late Erving Goffman (1974), and Harold Garfinkel (1967), and many others in a tradition within social science tracing at least to Edmund Husserl. To be sane is to question, among the rhetorics of lay experts, only those rhetorics no longer in fashion: today we question theology but that was not true in the 1500s.

From the humanities should come some sense of the subtlety of interactions among ways of viewing—among your, my, and their ways, as well as among different realms such as historical, political, and magical. Literary criticism has much to say about stories and their grammars and voices. Ironically, humanists seem better aware than scientists of the paradoxical status of the person construct.

The phenomenological tradition should be developed and validated for larger and longer-lived and more elaborated social arrangements than those of the backstage of Goffman. Another prime target will be providing a bridge between social science and history. This will become evident both in the choice of examples and in the prominence of the case study as form.

This book outlines a theory of action in tension with social organization. It can be judged by the questions it raises, by how many specific new leads it suggests. These can be leads for research but also for action and insight. The first appendix offers lists of conjectures and questions to serve as examples. The last pages of text (pp. 312–16) reprise its grounding in identity and control.

TWO

DISCIPLINES

A MOLECULE is a spatio-temporal context which captures atoms from and using their own interactions. Each molecule continuously reproduces itself sited among whatever welter of outside influences obtain. The atoms are thereby embedded into a new level of action, the molecule, although still subject to polarization toward other molecules and atoms and thereby to some larger field of context.

Let social molecules be called disciplines: They are self-reproducing formations which sustain identities. Every identity is triggered by some contingency and strives for control over all the uncertainties that impact it. These uncertainties come to include other such identities and their searches for control. Social action and spaces are thus spun off from biophysical origins.

Disciplines are the most distinctive aspect of social organization. Social organization is a shambles[1] rather than a tidy crystal, but it is all the more important to be clear about any basic constituents for order, any social molecules. What persists, and thus is observed, builds from molecules within which urgent distinct searches for control have come into some accommodation. In such accommodation social spaces and times are being generated around, but recognizably distinct from, any observer's biophysical space-time.

Much of the fascination with theories of kinship systems (Needham 1962; White 1963, chapter 1) stems from the hints in Lewis Morgan (1877; cf. Trautman 1987) that a social space can emerge from

---

[1] A humanist, Barbara Herrnstein Smith, offers a similar assessment: "What I am suggesting here, rather, is that what all such terms and accounts (*homo economicus, homo ludens*, man as rational creature, cultural creature, biological creature, and so forth) offer to conceptualize is something that might just as well be thought of as our irreducible *scrappiness*. I wish to suggest with this term not only that the elements that interact to constitute our motives and behavior are incomplete and heterogeneous, like scraps of things, but also ('scrap' being a slang term for fight) that they are mutually conflicting or at least always potentially at odds. That is, the relations among what we call our 'actions,' 'knowledge,' 'beliefs,' 'goals,' and 'interests' consist of continuous interactions among various structures, mechanisms, traces, impulses, and tendencies that are not necessarily ('naturally' or otherwise) consistent, coordinated, or synchronized and are therefore always *more or less* inconsistent, out-of-phase, discordant, and conflictual" (Smith 1988, p. 148).

and persist in genealogies as molecules. Nadel generalized this (1957; and see White 1963). Parsons's means-ends chains (1937) are another entry, but they presuppose and depend upon choice as an unproblematic given. Economic theorists up through Chamberlin (1933; and see Marshall 1891) were serious about markets as constructions of and constituents in social order.

Gierke (1950) and Smith (1975), among others, generalized differently, generalized to corporate groups as the molecules. No one approach has continued and established itself as universal in social science. Much of social science has just given up on tangible disciplines with their required contextualizing, at least for research if not for teaching.[2]

But molecules are unavoidable. These are distinctive units of mutually constraining efforts at control, which survive contentions among identities that were triggered by happenstance. These identities survive with some uniformity and regularity only as they fall into self-reproducing configurations. Each such configuration is a discipline for social action which inducts as it embeds an identity into still further social organization.

This chapter proposes constructs together with measures for three distinct species of discipline. The internal aspects of molecule as discipline are distinguished from external siting as embedding ratios. The three species observed are interfaces, arenas, and councils, each of which comes in myriad variants.

Pecking Orders

Social molecule pushes person aside as being but a special case. Identity becomes the starting point. The question is what identity may look like, how to recognize it on the ground, especially in early times.

Social science today begins, without apology, from person. Most present social science theories can be seen as exegeses on Enlighten-

---

[2] There is a tendency to substitute for tangible discipline a computation of arbitrary measures abstracted from technicalities of statistical inference—as if they could supply structural and theoretical context to social mechanism (for elaboration of this critique see, e.g., Leamer 1978 for econometrics and White 1970 for social mobility).

Economic theory in particular has developed in recent times an apologetics for why "black boxes" are sufficient substitutes for explicit discipline: see the survey in Fusfeld (1980) of such tendencies as well as numerous commentaries by Wassily Leontief.

In this context, even an incomplete theory of disciplines such as this chapter seems justified.

ment myths. These in turn took their presuppositions from Christian theology. Thus, the Enlightenment was formed by, even as it fought against, theology of the soul, and the social sciences as its progeny remain enmeshed in the same presupposition. In order to combat homiletics one needs to start in the same pulpit. So let us start from The State of Nature created by Enlightenment *philosophes*, who preached the person as preestablished homunculus able to sign a Social Contract.

In our version of the State of Nature, material productions must start the scene. Unending interactions with the biophysical environment are the distinctive constraints on action for any species, and in particular on the generation of social space-time for the human species. The exigencies of material needs in a physical world underlie much of social organization.

Production, and especially material production as work, is the earliest occasion for social space-times emerging and tying in with physical space-time. Work is the human social construct which recognizes this most explicitly, but with or without such recognitions the pervasive constraints are there. Continuing material productions of all sorts are required in order that social action not cease, but social action itself also induces new productions that mix the social and material.

Stories and Valuation Out of Pecking Orders

Observation shows that a flock of hens, or of many other vertebrates, are mutually subjected in strict dominance order (Chase 1980, 1982, 1986; Richards 1974). Which hen eats or drinks what and when, whom to peck, even what physical space to move to, are subjected to the discipline of the pecking order. All the hens' interactions with the physical world are mediated by the pecking order. It is their social space, though one so primitive as barely to require separate recognition.

From this base we can improve on the Enlightenment myth for a State of Nature. Suppose, then, a pecking order among a baboonlike troop of humans.[3] The beginnings of identities would be triggered by the inexorable contingencies of life on this planet, and each would—from its construction rather than by pregiven intention as in Hobbes—seek control over its world, including control over other such emerging identities.

---

[3] There is a large literature on social relations among nonhuman primates; for recent overviews see Cheney, Seyfarth, and Smuts (1986) and Dunbar (1988).

Continuing struggles for control would, given the behavioral plasticity latent in human cognitive and manipulative capacities, break open the linear dominance ordering and generate wider social spaces. The dominance order would unravel and some sort of teams, such as hunting parties, would appear. These teams would reproduce as social disciplines that were awesome but not as ineluctable as the pecking order. Several species of social molecule might prove robust as disciplines within congeries of overlapping social formations.

Across social molecules, over time, some elaboration of signals and communication beyond animal level would build up. Gestures would come to be chained together in sequences of response that creatures would use repeatedly. This process leads to perception and then to mutual acknowledgment of just such sequence, call it story. Another story can emerge to counter any given one. And so on. The importance of linear ordering would continue after the unraveling of dominance, and would be perceived in the form of *valuations* through interlocking of stories, as seen most vividly in caste and pollution.[4]

There would be further elaboration of signaling. With stories, control struggles would take new forms and partners. More elaborate loops of interactions can get established. Some sort of language would eventuate as an aspect and by-product of pushings and shovings for control.

Such additional depth of signaling beyond that from pecking orders can serve to sustain distinct species of social molecule within larger social formations which become possible from such varied unit constituents. Each molecule comes to be perceived as an entity, and to constitute an independent source of social action. In being embedded within a broader social array it is also empowered as a distinct new social actor, an identity.

The "State of Nature"

Somehow, various sorts of material productions and other physical coordinations would stagger along, despite demise of strict dominance orderings, among groupings that survive. Other orderings would emerge to replace original pecking orders. The energies all would come out of struggles for control. And the energies had to have been channeled by stories which helped split up unitary orderings, stories which account for the specialized orderings that are their replacements. But many of the nascent orderings would break

---

[4] Themes which are picked up again in chapter 4.

down, leaving behind pair ties which then could trace into networks, as in the playground formations of chapter 1, further elaborating into clusters and multiple networks.

In short, social molecules would emerge and continue, largely oriented to work. Work and its contingencies remain a major coupler between the purely social and the biophysical. But work is not feasible, does not happen, except given considerable autonomy from social ordering. This autonomy would be achieved in a broader social context beyond work and discipline. There results a State of Nature fitter as basis for social analysis than Hobbes's disconsolate freebooters.

From Hobbes's own era we can cite exact examples of unraveling dominance hierarchies. Ferejohn reports from an overview of analyses of parliamentary elections in early Stuart England:

> Each locality had its own consensually recognized social hierarchy and only families near the top of that hierarchy were thought to have a legitimate expectation of a seat in the House of Commons . . . even within families with legitimate claims, the (socially valued or disvalued) attributes of the individual aspirants imposed further restrictions. . . . Thus, I argue that the interior understandings of early Stuart England had the effect of allowing costly contests to be avoided. . . . The interpretive reconstruction . . . requires that we see the local stakes of political disruption as vastly more significant to most people than distant and abstract goings-on. (1990, p. 25).

Ferejohn goes on to analyze how and why the disruptive innovation of contested elections came to disturb this basic ecology of dominance.[5]

---

[5] There are other paths to build theory from biosocial base toward human social organization. This first path through dominance orders, which plays off the Enlightenment philosophic tradition, leads to emphasis on work and control, and can be seen as deriving from ecological perspective. Another path is suggested by E. O. Wilson's sociobiology (1979). Within this path, thorough mathematical analysis of the genetic evolution of altruism and attendant social organization will be found in Boorman and Levitt (1980), who bring rigor to themes dating back to before Simpson (1952) and Wynne-Edwards (1985).

Perhaps the earliest path is traditional concern with human groups as behavioral contexts: for a recent example focused on deriving the size of human groups see De Vos (1991), who critiques and extends the game-theoretic, rational-choice approach exemplified by Axelrod (1984) and recently extended by Bendor and Swistak (1991). More informally, Elias ties emergence of hierarchies with emergence of organized sports as contests among elites.

Dominance Orderings and Comparability

A dominance ordering is the creation and adaptation of a flock or a pack in an ecology. Dominance orderings are by-products of proto-social situations which are driven by material productions and apportionment. In a newly social context, production can sustain itself only as some new social discipline establishes itself in place of a pecking order.

Inducing a dominance ordering is also establishing comparability. This is a necessary paradox. It is a paradox because comparability is equality, here being established through the strictest inequality. Dominance position is imputed regardless of the actual distribution on and the content of any underlying attributes in a flock (Landau 1950, 1965). Likewise, in even the most sophisticated intellectual or athletic circles, position is enjoined by social discipline with or without correlation to ostensible abilities. Achievements and their orderings are constructs of social disciplines. Mutual comparability is easiest established in terms of a strict linear ordering which overawes completely, even though individual positions may be arbitrary.[6]

Inducing any linear ordering whatever can establish comparability, as well as the reverse. In the course of a joint effort at material production, comparability may be achieved through inducing and participating in what appears to be antithetical to jointness, namely creation of a distinctive and memorable range of differences. In nonmaterial contexts, orderings can be established likewise. On grounds of perception characteristics which he establishes for human subjects, DeSoto (1961; DeSoto and Clinton 1968a, 1968b) has long argued for the overwhelming importances of the linear ordering, normative and manipulative as well as descriptive.

One can speculate that the hegemony of linearity in our speech, and in all our forms of language, may be as much a by-product as a cause of the dominance of linear ordering in perception.[7] One might even go so far as to say much the same about our insistence on, our fanaticism about, social time coming in strictly linear order—an insistence against all the realities of our phenomenological experiences and our historical sense.

[6] Tournaments (cf. the next chapter) achieve this by rigidly sorting entrants by skill level, then inducing winners and losers among them (Leifer 1991a,b).

[7] Irregularity and linearity in layout appear and disappear in one's perception according to strictness and leeway in pattern. This corresponds to an esthetic principle (Gombrich 1963; Thompson 1961), and it also can be seen in planned social arrangements (cf. Ascher and Ascher 1981 on the Inca).

One can analyze the pecking order into a fully interlocking array of pair relations, even though such relations remain merely implicit within an active dominance ordering. The dominance order can be transcribed as a mutual arrangement of pair ties together with a valuation, if one presupposes sufficient communication potential among biophysical entities involved, as they respond to stochastic triggerings. The path is there for valuation orderings to emerge.

Three Species from Valuation Orderings

Inducing some valuation ordering is also establishing comparability. Valuation levels replace direct pair comparisons. At the same time each valuation embeds a discipline within a larger context. In this context mutual accounts in a population can join issue with ecological production pressures as well as control projects from raw dominance orderings.

Control thrusts, which are erratic in incidence and unpredictable in direction, can settle down only in a limited variety of self-reproducing configurations. These are the three species of social molecules, the disciplines. They derive from pecking orders and like them each persists only because of powerful mutual reinforcings among its handful of participants.

Valuation Orderings

There are other ways besides dominance to effect linear orderings. New common footings, new sorts of comparabilities emerge from efforts to achieve material and social production, as circumstances become looser than for the simple pecking order. Once primitive dominance order unravels, there is enormous potential variety from attempts at control by identities, attempts that redouble contingencies and so mutually elicit one another.

On the one hand, control is attempted over specific occasions in social context. And on the other, control induces efforts to verify or regulate by comparison with some standard, if only implicit or relative or historical, which is to say to establish discipline by some linear order and thus some valuation. A discipline evolves together with an ordering. Each ordering goes with some sort of specialized valuation such that they induce each other. Each such valuation ordering replaces and supplements any original dominance ordering.

Unarticulated dominance metamorphoses into a valuation order in common perception. Dominance becomes merely an example. By contrast, in vertebrate flocks dominance was sui generis, because it was the only ordering conceivable, and thus there was no need for the generic term, valuation. Children also know this overriding dominance order from early on, from their experiences in achieving identity as an entity in a particular group of kids, or for that matter in a particular classroom.

Identities themselves are generated out of contingency and mismatch. Valuations are induced primarily for and by the impact of contingency over time, much of which is occasioned by exogenous events in physical space. Valuations can be seen as attempts to suppress knots (Crowell and Fox 1963) in social space-times, which represent eruptions or triggerings of identities. Valuations arbitrarily impose simple linear order.

Within a discipline, there is predictability in perceptions and actions by the identities caught up in that production, whatever the rhetoric in which it may be expressed. This implies feasibility of communication. After a survey of communication, bodily as well as linguistic, Argyle (1975) suggests two dimensions along which the communication can be interpreted: friendly-hostile and dominant-submissive.

Bales (1970) induced these same two dimensions from interaction data on years of observation of human discussion groups in laboratory situations. He was guided by theory consistent with Argyle's (e.g., Parsons, Bales, and Shils 1953). Bales also reports a third dimension, on instrumentalism, which appeared as a pair with friendly-hostile.

These three affective dimensions, induced from recent systematic observation of small human groups, can map into valuations for disciplines. This suggests three independent and distinctive valuations. If each tends to be preeminent in one species of discipline, three species are implied.

Valuations are the idiom in which social structure replaces irregular process, in the large as well as for the disciplines that directly replace pecking orders.[8] The three valuations are each induced from the juxtaposition computed as an ordering in that discipline. Call the valuation ordering induced in the first species **quality**, mapped from

---

[8] Valuations provide an idiom analogous to topology but in very simple format (Abbott 1981; Abell 1987; Coxon, Davies, and Jones 1986; De Soto 1961; De Soto and Albrecht 1968a, 1968b; Reiss 1961; and see Appendix 2).

instrumentalism; in the second species **purity**, from friendly-hostile; and in the third species **prestige**, from dominant-submissive.

There are three sorts of ravelings of control, corresponding to three sorts of ordered juxtapositions of entities which embed into an identity. There are also three abstract modes of triggering identities. In one mode an existing set of entities is triggered into an embedding whole. This mode embeds discrete entities all together into a discipline. A second mode is the converse, the splitting up of an identity into constituents, with differential rejections and retentions among identities. The third mode is when identities cross or intersect, that is, when constituents from several disciplines crosscut to also combine into other distinct disciplines, as developed in the next three chapters. (Ties are a special case of this third mode.)

Three Species

Control projects settle into precedence orders and their valuations, when they settle at all, through distinctive patterns of maneuvers to which correspond the separate species of discipline. Any discipline points toward a specific configuration of mutual control for analysis. This configuration is disciplined by a valuation ordering but can be examined in its own right.

The embodiment of **the first species, an interface** is the formation committed to continuing delivery of identity as tangible production, as in a hunting group in tribal context; this is production identified by its quality. In the embodiment of **the second species, the arena** the formation sifts itself apart and together into new identities characterized in purity valuation. And the embodiment for **the third species, the council**, is the formation of alliance and counteralliance in mobilization to retain existing formation in terms of prestige.

Consider some homely examples: meals as social processes. A cafeteria meal is an interface, effectively delivering foods into people. A sit-down urban dinner party among professional couples is an arena discipline. It is concerned with establishing some sort of identity of the evening. A church supper, by contrast, is a council, ordered by prestige valuation in an unending concern with balancing and disciplining conflicts as such.

The prototype situation inducing a discipline is recurrent team action for material production, from fishing party to assembly-line group. The interface is the reproducible discipline which is closest to this prototype, since it is interface between material production and social array. Disciplines occur also in contexts more purely social, divorced from work, whether these be the children's playground of the first chapter, or sports (Fine 1983), or an array of legislative committees (Padgett 1990), or bridge tournament.

"Interface" connotes passing through and transformation, as does the word "membrane." But interface is without the latter's implication of a sharply demarcated material body; instead, an interface is a mutually constraining array of contentions for control which yield as net resultant a directed flow, a committed flow. Interfaces are the most transparent of the three species. The matching of variances is the key so that the average or total sizes of flows being generated through this interface is divorced from the self-reproduction of the interface.[9]

The sift-and-exclude species, termed the "arena," is familiar in lawn sales and flea markets. It is stochastic in operation. It depends essentially on timing, the valuation aspect of which is speculation, that is to say, trading on averages.[10] Present-day discourse in economic theory obscures the distinction between this and the first species, that is, between markets as arenas and as production interfaces, which is remarkable since the two species are so different;[11] they differ in dynamic, and in valuation, as well as in concrete embodiment.

The council species, familiar in social mobilizations, are disciplines centered on a process of balancing contending but ever-shifting coalitions. Preexisting strings of dependency set up the endless process of mobilizing and remobilizing, as in an extended kin group with corporate rights whose allocations are balanced and rebalanced in a mutual discipline. The dynamics of contention keep this discipline going up and down in scale of mobilization.[12]

Now consider examples of the three species which are all from the same realm. A kinship example of a quality interface is a set of siblings working a farm or other task with eyes toward headship or ownership: to **commit** is shorthand for the dynamic of instrumentalism. Whereas for the council species, ordered around prestige valuation, a dynamic of **mobilize** such as an annual in-gathering of a kin-

[9] But there may be a fixed network of other such interfaces constituting an input-output system which serves to engender and constrain average flows. As we shall see in chapters 3, 4, and 5, larger context shapes constituents, as well as the reverse etiology of build-up to which the present chapter is devoted.

[10] The New York Stock Exchange and the Chicago Board of Commodity Exchanges are exemplars of large scope (cf. e.g., Abolafia 1984; Baker 1984, 1985), embodied on a much larger scale than individual human persons.

[11] In ways well established in their literature: see e.g., Newman (1965).

[12] In a production economy context, the mobilizer discipline is visible in procurement and supplier networks (Corey 1978; Porter 1976; B. Shapiro; Walker 1988). There too this discipline evidences the clientelist qualities developed in political contexts in chapter 4.

ship group works to reallocate turfs and settle disputes. For the purity arena a kinship example is a nuclear family with a valuation ordering that is intense yet opaque when seen from the outside: to **select** is shorthand for the dynamic.

The final lineup of species by process and valuation is

Discipline	Process	Valuation
Interface	Commit	Quality
Arena	Select	Purity
Council	Mobilize	Prestige.

The most succinct comparison of the three species is in terms of the equilibrating dynamic of matching: In the interface, variances are being matched. In the arena, averages are being matched. And in the council there are potentials being matched.

Embedding and Variations

Any discipline can be analyzed thus abstractly, but in actual functioning it is an awesome integral in which the components and their interactions are the taken-for-granted, the invisible, which ordinarily become visible to participants or others only in failed disciplines. And an identity induces designation from outside, perhaps by literal naming, which is the awesome integral of embedding.

Decoupling is a converse to embedding. Social action begins as triggerings of identities, each of which comes embedded out of a discipline of constituents but then is decoupled in seeking control. Specifically, the discipline for an identity couples its constituents while simultaneously offering them decoupling as some insulation from, and brokering to, the context. Embedding is mutual discipline sifting out of chaotic crisscrosses of attempts at control. Embeddings seed on now this happenstance and now that, but once started they call forth imitation and counterpart and survive as discipline by repetition.

Embeddings are a basic form of coupling. A name for a discipline establishes the commonness in action perceived among the entities making it up, which is one side of embedding; but a name also establishes commonness in relations to the setting of the discipline, and that is the other side of embedding. Measures which encompass this second side must be developed in order to go on and explore still larger social formations, but the measures must reflect the first side as well.

Work affects how control efforts generate identities, but work also affects how identities get embedded into context. Production itself comes embedded into some larger setting that keeps reproducing itself between the social and the physical. The discipline thus "lifts" production activity onto a further level marked by an emergent compound identity at the same time as it sites the activity in larger flows of production. Each identity becomes a joint formation that reconciles the social spaces with whatever is the ecological impetus. It is this dual process which motivates the term "embedding."

Index of Variation

Dominance ordering has devolved into three distinct valuation orderings. Pecking order is accordingly turned into three species of discipline. And there is more variation within a species of discipline than there is within pecking orders. Though disciplines of any one species vary greatly, one can attempt to index them all.

What is needed is an index space for variations in a discipline. At least three independent measures are required to index a given discipline. The goal is to find measures such that all species of discipline can be indexed adequately in a common space: the same three dimensions for each discipline.

Position in the index space must also report how a particular example of a discipline is embedded into larger social organization around it. Disciplines are perceived and characterized as concrete embodiments, but presuppose and generate a larger setting with which they interact and wherein they embed. Indexing this embedding can only be extremely summary, for the same analysis into disciplines is to be transposed between very different scopes.

Transposability is what makes the scheme of analysis worthwhile. Transposition of disciplines is first between different scales. A given discipline is transposed from say descent line to ethnic solidarity. A world of nursery schools—children, teachers, parents, inspectors, leagues—is to be disentangled in the same analytic scheme of social molecules as a world of investment banking or the interacting states of "the Arab nation."

Transposition is also from one realm of interpretation to another.[13] There is not a separate social science of economics or of politics, but rather only different parameters within systems using the same

---

[13] To what extent and how a set of viewpoints is integrated across realms into an observed system or theory will be developed in subsequent chapters.

models of disciplines. Differences in numbers, as of peers in a discipline, and in other input parameters are sufficient to generate widely divergent outputs from the same analytic model for a species of discipline.

Varieties of social forms may be agreed within a particular population as a linguistic convention and cultural frame without their having much reality on the ground. A great variety may be so reported, and it may differ arbitrarily from one population to another. By contrast, disciplines are to be universals which can be observed anywhere. Disciplines are not to be restricted to particular societies or by levels of technology, economy, polity, or the like. Only vertebrate fields of action are driven from this intermediate level, being called the molecular discipline, which can yield novel larger patternings.[14]

Aspects for Embedding

Transposability depends initially upon how the embedding of disciplines into broader population is modeled. Any identity embeds to a new level of social action through its discipline, but it continues being subject to ecological incident as well as to social unravelings. A social molecule combines setting with identity into a discipline which reproduces itself despite endless efforts to subvert it via projects of control that are not confined to the molecule.

A discipline survives only as it finds siting within its social population together with its biophysical work locale. A discipline ties to other disciplines as the various identities contend for control. There must be linkages for each discipline as it embeds in some larger formation touching on biophysical space.

Ties go between identities. A tie persists as it balances control struggles between a pair of existing disciplines. A tie is an abortive discipline, but a discipline compounds with all sorts of ties as it generates productions upstream or downstream. Elaborated social spaces are being generated, partly expressed in valuations within

[14] Ant societies (E. Wilson 1970) are coherent entities as wholes, wherein identification by pheromone communication is as stereotyped as are ant individuals. For insect populations, by contrast to vertebrate populations, individualist parsing from the bottom up can yield the same outcome as structuralist deduction down from rule frame and colony calendar. In physical science there are few analogues to the importance of a level of molecular discipline. For example, in astronomical analysis, planets may have identities in the sense of unique historical cumulations of past interactions and trajectories, but the "disciplines" for planets are mere passive niches in smoothly varying networks of other bodies. In biological science, there may be an analogy in colonial situations, of coral or even at the cell level where the nucleus of cells can be seen as a colonial assemblage of simpler cells.

identities, but partly expressed through ties and other embedding into population.

Analysis seeks abstraction of several aspects of any given linkage. Three embedding aspects are applicable to any discipline. They provide a neutral common base in which different species with their different valuations can be compared.

The first aspect, **involuteness**, which can also be called specialization, characterizes for a discipline the extent to which the given valuation ordering refers to and presupposes other orderings outside the given discipline. Involuteness reflects how the stringing together of identities in chains of ties, that eventually close back on their origins, impacts the valuation.

A second aspect is **dependence**, how the upstream valuation of each action or flow unit, in social and/or physical production, from a discipline correlates to its valuation downstream. This is the extent to which the particular contents of action within the discipline, in story or physical activity, interdigitates with the external.

A third aspect, how spread out the constituent identities become on the appropriate valuation, yields **differentiation**. Differentiation is a matter of visibility, recognizing distinctiveness by position in an ordering. Differentiation is the extent to which the ordering of entities by valuation inside the discipline correlates in its reception outside.

These three aspects of linkage will be used to characterize embedding of any discipline, for all variants of each of the three species.

Embedding Ratios and Index Space

Key for explicit models of disciplines are measures of the impacts which valuation orders have both within and outside a discipline, and the correlation between these impacts.[15] Reproduction of any discipline cannot be only an internal matter. It also depends upon external context, upon population.

Embedding is necessarily a joint or dual process between internal discipline and fitting to external context. An upstream and a downstream are induced for any discipline, and these go with change of level from embedding. The simplest way to capture this in measurement is through a ratio, of external face over internal disposition. A ratio scale (Stevens 1946; Krantz, et al. 1971) is generally appropriate

[15] Ronald Breiger suggested the embedding ratios and their importance. Extensive development of such models for interface disciplines appears in White (1981a,b, 1988b), Leifer and White (1988), and Leifer (1985).

for combining two independent impacts, here upstream and down-stream. The three aspects of linkage are thus to be measured as ratios. Call them **embedding ratios**, since each involves distinct levels as well as spread among like entities upstream and downstream. An embedding ratio is suitable to measure the impact from whatever valuation obtains. A diagram may help fix this in memory: see figure 2-1.

The important assumption is that the three ratio measures from the three aspects of linkage yield independent variables. Then the three embedding ratios structure an index space with ordinary Cartesian properties. The same index space will be used in subsequent sections to graph examples of all species of discipline. The three embedding ratios for disciplines correspond, of course, to the three aspects above, and are so identified. Each can be seen as relating to elementary constituents of social organization. Dependency deals with responsiveness along typical network ties. Differentiation reflects the third-party perception of the ordering. Involuteness deals with responsiveness across partitions. These embedding ratios each maps onto one sort of fixed valuation, but they also provide measures for variations able to sustain that given valuation ordering.

Discriminate a given species of discipline according to which embedding ratio is most critical. That embedding ratio is kept fixed at a distinctive level, which is sustained, or not, through the pressure

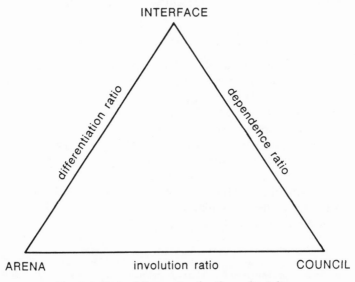

Fig. 2-1. Embedding ratios for three disciplines

from balancing off the other two ratios. Intensity is fixed on the principal embedding ratio, whereas the other two ratios differ across variants of that discipline. These other two embedding ratios thus shadow the other two valuations, which are subsidiary for that species.

No species of discipline can persist at all combinations of the three embedding ratios, which are aspects of positioning for its principal and shadow valuation orderings. In a given instance of any one species, social processes operate such that the ordering by that distinctive valuation is fixed along with that embedding ratio. Each species can be further outlined in terms of shadows from the other two dimensions. That is to say, the other two ratios and valuations, which are not being held fixed, are also measuring impacts.

Shepard Plane for a Species

Variations within the given species thus can be characterized by two ratios, one each for the two shadow species. Only certain combinations of these ratios will prove observable, for given larger social and physical context. In functionalist imagery, tendencies on the subsidiary valuations must balance each other in some way in order to sustain as stable dynamics a discipline of that species. Put it another way: Within a given species, two other competing embedding ratios or valuations, associated with the other two species, are compensating for each other to sustain the embedding.

A split is required between the representation of a given discipline as process—in the form of a mathematical model crafted separately for each of the three species—and the specification of constituents and context for any discipline. The specification takes the form of a plane. But it is a Shepard (1962) plane. This plane represents a topology chosen, as Shepard urged, because it suits the human eye and judgment rather than because it is explicitly called for by the mathematical solutions for that particular discipline.

To define a plane for a discipline requires two independently varying parameters. The essential concerns and context of its process must be identified by these parameters, and the ranges of variation laid out as a plane. Just these two may not be enough to identify the particular example to within a range of remaining variation deemed inessential, but any additional parameter provided should be on the same level of generality.

Let each of the two variates mapping a plane be a ratio, exactly one of the embedding ratios. Each single point in this plane will characterize a family of embedding contexts as matched with a family of profiles of participation. These particular combinations package into essentially the same outcome in the workings of the discipline: such is the claim which justifies use of an index space.

Heroic abstraction must be involved, if two parameters are to be sufficient to distinguish one variant of any species from another. Demographic trivia such as the exact number of actors must be left to one side, and idiosyncratic historical traces suppressed. There is also a confusing duality.[16]

Control and production are always the underlying sources of dynamic in any given discipline. For each species this supports a strict ordering which is engendered by identities' strivings for social-grounding, for control, in that context. Each strict ordering induces a valuation held fixed. The resulting three valuations can be assigned to permanent directions in a Shepard space of embedding ratios.

Interfaces

Interfaces are akin to dominance orderings in being driven by productions. Physical production and biophysical reality matter. Work is our adaptation to them. Much of life is work (Udy 1970), and work takes place in concrete ecologies. But much of work also involves coping with other identities and their control efforts, typically through interface disciplines.

Embedding into a new identity, which for the other two discipline species is a by-product, here in the commit interface is the focus. A set of actors can become comparable, become peers, through jostling to join in a production on comparable terms. They commit by joining together to pump downstream versions of a common product, which are subjected by them and downstream to invidious comparison. Children competing in hopscotch or reciting for a teacher, mathematicians in a test for a prize, manufacturers of recreational aircraft for the U.S. market, actors in a play—all can be examples.

"Quality" captures the connotations of the invidious transitive ordering induced in such interface disciplines. This valuation ordering cannot be sustained by the induction and routing of average flows.[17]

---

[16] Depending on which control struggles predominate as the discipline mechanism jells, the disaggregate side can be downstream, with the aggregate or embedded side upstream, or conversely (White 1988a, 1991c).

[17] Reference group theory long ago came to the view that it was dispersions in rewards among actors, not averages, that drove social action in small groups. In the classic formulation, from the Stouffer et al. (1948) study of World War II military, anticipation over time was equally important with dispersion. Recently, Tversky and Kahneman (Kahneman, Slovic, and Tversky 1982), among others (Lindenberg 1989a), have revived this notion.

Instead such valuations provide scaffoldings for dispersions in social formations that then prove able to reproduce themselves.

Asymmetry underlies all the variations of this commit interface. Asymmetry is built into the form. On one side individual flows are being induced amid jockeying for relative niche position; the other side is (possibly disparate) receivers appropriating the aggregate flow. The flow is always from the one, disaggregate side to the other. The social perceptions which discipline producers into order come from both sides, but behavioral cues to specific niches are on one side only.

Supervision and Identities

The "span of control" in modern bureaucracies is an unusually explicit formulation of the mechanism side of the commit interface, as distinct from the quality ordering. A superior is, aside from concrete abilities and achievements, also a place-holder, a symbolic representation of subordinates' embedding into a new joint identity. Their identity is as comparable peers with common, or rather parallel but differentiated, goals embedded within a common social production.

Embodiment like this of the interface in a tangible distinct actor, who represents the new embedded identity as indicated by the designation "supervisor," lays the ground for subsequent further embeddings. In these the supervisor can fold in together with others so as to become comparable peers embedded in yet another new identity, also a commit interface. Or the chain of embeddings can be initiated from above, in which case it can and usually does switch from one to another of the three species of discipline.

Pressures from contending efforts at control are so strong as to also support so-called inverted supervision. Here a set of peers interact with no common structuring beyond having a common flunky. This common underling may be a research assistant or a secretary. Or, at a different level, the underling of several personality components may be a sexual drive. In any case, the "underling" may increasingly come to cue actions of all and thereby achieve de facto apportionment and so supervision.

Interjections of manipulations, as attempts at control from within by assembling peers or receivers, find hard going within an interface. The equivalency in peer positions subjects insiders to very strong discipline by the comparable others. Effective oversight comes from those similarly located, and thus conversant with the information and perspective the subject is bringing. Supervisors symbolize authority but are substantively more important in linking to other levels of disciplines and context.

Interjections by outsiders also find the commit interface difficult to disrupt. The commit interface is robust to both external and internal control projects. Even the cumulation of authority through a supervisor is difficult.

Commit interfaces are directly concerned with identities. Since identities in action are refractions of what does not fit neatly into social organization of network and discipline, there normally is a multivalent correspondence, as in regards authority, between identity and any tangible actor. There is more than one correspondence between interface and identity, even fresh identity.

Commit interfaces appear to have a substantive identity which serves to distract from the sheer creation of a new actor identity. The competition is not about purity of some sort, for example, a kind of mathematics. Instead, the competition is about the importance of doing slightly better than your peers who in the larger context are so very similar to oneself; what is not necessarily signified is the strength of the new identity created by the competition. In the explicit supervisory structure a tale is induced of potential antipathy toward the supervisor which exactly conceals the fundamental effect of commitment through the interlocking externality of peers' impacts upon each one of them as the production of social action transpires.

There is a stripped variety of this commit species which is just the reflexive form of a human group putting on a performance for itself. One modern exemplar is the discussion group, and there has been a tradition of systematic measurement of interaction profiles (Bales 1970) across the group which permits quantitative analysis (Breiger and Ennis 1979). A village meeting in India (Mayer 1960), repartee in a barber shop, lunch table conversation—all illustrate relaxed social contexts in which the form is found.

Control Profile

Interfaces by their construction do not control for averages, cannot be programmed to yield prespecified flows. Instead, interfaces build their dynamics around the spread of contributions across the comparable set. The commitment characterizing an interface is best portrayed as a curvature or response across the variation in members' properties. Mutual attention of peers is directed toward jockeying for relative positions which yield each a distinctive niche.

It follows that the interface can become a control profile depending on skill in manipulation of social organization. Only variances and their ratios constrain the shape and positioning of the interface when it is operating autonomously. But rewards, severally and in aggregate, depend upon means so that there is latent a motivation to try to shift interface in concert. The shift can be accomplished only if the acceptable shapes of profile are retained so that they are envelopes for achieved control profiles. Participants can make systematic use of these facts: see Eccles and White (1986) for how Chief Executive Officers use these interfaces in achieving control over leading subordinates.

The interface comes in many other varieties, other institutional embodiments. "Star" systems, in entertainment and elsewhere, grow out of interfaces where imbedding induces perceptions of events which are greatly exaggerated from the view of actors producing them (Faulkner 1983). Even where the differentiation or dependence is limited, as among starlets in entertainment, there is the same pressure to generate events sufficient to embed them with a skew distribution of fame despite undetectable differences as judged within the interface. These star systems can be seen as closely analogous to the industrial markets.

The interface is a species with many more dresses than these few special types of competition or formal supervision, or the analogous pair of production market and Hollywood scene. Sitting around in a bull session or other conversation group is being in a commit interface. The institutional dress may be similar but the process shifted, or the reverse.

Actors ordinarily do not perceive and react to higher-order measures like variances; so this, like the other two mechanisms, must be realized through forms which are perceived and estimated directly in everyday terms. A model and its context must be specified in some detail to examine how this can occur.

Production Market as Example

Material production commonly comes in these interface disciplines.[18] Here the receivers are a distinct set and the context is not relaxed and social. The hunting or gathering groups described for tribal contexts (Firth 1935, 1978; Lee 1979; Udy 1959; Rose 1960) are early realizations which have analogues in sports teams (Leifer 1989) and in children's games (Fine 1979; Opie and Opie 1969). The basic mechanism does not require or presuppose distinct roles among the producers with explicit cues and assignments. Rather, a spread of perform-

---

[18] This example will be picked up in later chapters. As more scope and depth are introduced into the theory, production market in its larger contexts will provide a running example like the playground of chapter 1.

ances is induced by attention of producers to differential preferences by the other side, who can turn off their attention (or more tangible payments for production).

The same phenomenon of commitment, this same interface species can be seen on a much more massive scale in modern markets for manufactured products. The term "product," whether light aircraft or frozen pizzas (Leifer 1985), has no independent reality as a technical or engineering matter. Its reality is induced only through the commitment of producing firms into being peers in a differentiated set which organizes terms of trade around an induced order of quality among the producers. Note the analogue to the humble example of children competing in hopscotch or before their teacher.

The industrial production markets, from the previous century up through today, are exemplars of commit interfaces. It is an irony that current neoclassical economic theory has missed this basic fact (Leifer 1985; Leifer and White 1988; White 1981a, 1981b, 1988). Microeconomics (Mansfield 1975) has substituted a bizarre array of hypothetical "supply" and "demand" schedules to cover the mistake in basic phenomenology.

Take some production market as a particular institutional realization of the commit interface. Such a market is an ongoing social act which accomplishes the feat of reproducing itself to continue month after month just by their coherence as social acts (Leifer 1985; Leifer and White 1988). Nothing is passive about this. The producer firms, which usually are the actors in modern markets, are giant pumps expensively committed to spouting continuing flows of products more or less unchanged.

The set of pumps, the market as super-pump, is built up only in interaction with, and with confidence in, provision of an orderly and continuing social setting with buyers. The production market must induce, at the same time as it renders comparable, distinctive flows from a to-be-determined set of producers into the hands of an array of buyers becoming accustomed and committed here. This social process is what induces a definition of "product" from the common properties of this flow.

Underlying this mechanism is a matching of variances (see White, 1981a,b).[19] Producers differ in various combinations of abilities, say quickness and volume, and so are differentially attractive to receivers. The commit mechanism will not continue unless relative recog-

---

[19] Matching averages, as occurs in an exchange market, does not provide sufficient basis for sustaining a production market. This is contrary to the presumption of modern economic theory—but is just as the great economist Frank Knight long ago intuited (1921).

nition of producers can be matched to their spread on actual productivity. This matching must emerge and reproduce itself, which happens only when the producer set is arrayed in reward in the same order in which their productions are discriminated. Only if there is variance in abilities across producers, correlated with variance in their receptions, can the commit interface reproduce itself.

The interface here consists in the observable spread of terms of trade being achieved by various producers with their distinctive flows. At simplest, these terms are revenue for volume shipped (leaving aside the line of related product models which any given producer may supply). Gossip can supply to each producer an estimate of most of the terms achieved by peers.

For the market to reproduce itself, each producer must continue to see its pair, revenue and volume, as its optimal choice from the menu of observed terms of trade. Only this menu is known to be sustainable by the buyers, who themselves are comparison-shopping. Terms-of-trade can be a commonly observable shape which cues actors into niches by their own preferences which yet are agreeable across the interface.

The interface must be also accepted by the embedding side, which is the arbiter of the competition, the relative performances. The ironic implication is that production markets, whether at a micro level or the level of manufacturing firms, generate only the relative sizes of differentiated flows, not the aggregate size of flow. The aggregate size is a by-product of accident—so that aggregate "demand" so to speak is also an induced and arbitrary by-product.

Supply and demand are not operational concepts to the participants. Supply equals demand, after the fact each time, as a tautology. But it is the variation among producers in qualities, and the difficulties each confronts in production, that shape the interface which motivates and sets the terms of trade.

Shepard Plane for Production Markets

A Shepard plane for production markets as interface disciplines appears in figure 2-2; it comes from a specific family of mathematical models for production markets (White 1981b, and see White 1981a, 1988a, 1991b; Leifer 1985). As above, producing firms are the actors supplying streams of their differentiated products to the buyers who embed the flows into supplies to other markets and/or consumers.[20]

---

[20] The dual form introduced in note 16 has suppliers, say of skilled labor, as the problematic embedding with the ultimate buyers being represented by fixed schedule.

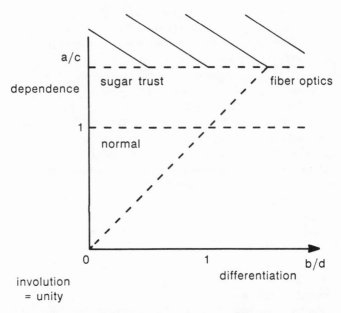

Fig. 2-2. Shepard plane for an interface: economic realization

This mechanism operates through the terms-of-trade schedule. The mathematical model identifies each shape of schedule which can sustain itself. A schedule can reproduce itself as firms confirm their distinctive choices of volume from the schedule and as buyers confirm their acceptances of the implicit quality judgments in the schedule (see also Leifer and White 1988).

Viable schedules yield comparability in aspects crucial to market members: for example, profits for firms and consumer surplus for buyers. Comparability can mean similar, that is, close together, or comparability can mean spread apart in fashion predictable from known measures of historical circumstance that can affect performance of the mechanism. The upper shaded region in figure 2-2 is packages of embedding and decoupling which cannot sustain a mechanism under any circumstances. At each package point in the lower right a trade schedule can be sustained but only under some historical starting points, and then it is vulnerable to manipulation by likely new entrants to the market.

The abscissa in figure 2-2 computes the ratio between, in the numerator spread (b) across different firms' products in buyers' valuations, and in the denominator spread (d) across the firms in their respective difficulties of producing as measured by costs. This is the realization of differentiation for the commit interface. The vertical, ordinate dimension computes a different sort of spread-ratio. The ordinate is a ratio of sensitivities across different volumes of operation. This is the realization of dependence for the commit interface. When the numerator, a, is small the embedding buyers are much more desirous of some initial small flow than of any subsequent increment in flow volume of a particular product. When the denominator, c, is large each producer runs into accelerating costs for larger volumes, and so on.

A great deal about the market is not included in the parameters forming the two ratios defining the Shepard plane of figure 2-2. The number of firms, as well as how they are spaced out in quality order, are not specified. Nor is the initial scale in volume and money at which terms of trade started sorting themselves out. The specific model of the mechanism incorporates these arbitrary descriptive features as baselines in the predictions of total outcomes, but they do not affect the structure of outcomes.

The operation of a production market may continue indefinitely and still be identified by a particular point on the Shepard plane, minor changes in descriptive features not moving it away. Social mechanisms are, however, unlikely to continue very long without impacts from above, that is, from the embedding situation. Embedding here is to a network of other markets and purchasers. Also, there are impacts from below, that is, within the mechanism itself, in which distinct actors may merge or come into the interface with new facilities or other change in attributes.

Qualitative interpretations of different regions in the plane are indicated in figure 2-2. To the upper right are embedding contexts where typically are found markets in exciting new products, such as color TV in the early sixties or fiber optics today. Toward the upper left are the sort of contexts in which trusts have emerged, such as the Havemeyer sugar trust of the early 1900s. Both of these upper regions presuppose "increasing returns to scale," which violate microeconomics textbook assumptions.[21]

In the lower left are more typical everyday markets. Only the immediate neighborhood in the Shepard plane is of much interest to participants in some of these commit interfaces, since there are massive inertias both in the distribution of context and of members' internal characteristics, which both underlie both ratios and make big changes difficult.

The logic of the commit discipline implies gradients in outcomes, that is, in dependent variables of interest to participants. For exam-

---

[21] But see, for example, Dehez and Dreze 1987.

ple, profit rates for all producers tend to go up together, the closer an interface is to the forty-five degree line, and to the point (1,1) in particular. And yet market shares tend under the same changes to become more equal and the market more vulnerable to chance unraveling.

That is enough for an illustration. One cannot expect other institutionalizations of commit interfaces to have the same shadings (the same pattern of instabilities) as in figure 2-2, much less the same dependent outcomes and trends in them. Only in a limited sense can a Shepard plane be seen as a state space in the usual scientific sense (e.g., Huang 1963). The plane is not a metric space in which some general actor moves. The two ratios are numbers, but they should be viewed more as library call numbers discriminating among scripts than as operational locations. Even where as in production markets participants are generating metrics and ratio scales for their own purposes, the parameters and their ratios and other variables are going to be crude approximations.

Three Dimensions: The Index Space

In a production market interface the valuing according to quality (which has devolved from dominance ordering) is taken for granted. And its embedding ratio, involuteness, stays fixed, whatever variations there are in context as measured on the other two dimensions by their embed ratios. The Shepard plane in figure 2-2 elaborates these two dimensions, the embedding ratios for differentiation and dependence, in which that production market discipline may vary. Figures 2-3 and 2-4 portray parallel planes for two different and extreme versions of the interface discipline. These planes are literally parallel so that among themselves they induce exactly the third dimension of measure, the embed ratio for involuteness, the ratio which this discipline species can be seen as fixing.

Figures 2-3 and 2-4 expand on the previous figure in order to suggest other institutional examples of commit interfaces at other values of the involuteness measure. These examples were suggested by and can be assessed from the published literature of social science case studies. A descriptive label of an institution/organization is entered in figure 2-3 or 2-4 near ratio values where examples of that variety of the commit interface seem common; footnotes in the figures supply background references which are the basis of these codings.

So any Shepard plane for commit interfaces can be visualized as one of a sheaf of parallel planes describing variations corresponding to different values on the involuteness ratio measure. Figure 2-3 por-

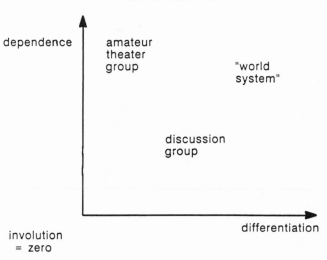

Fig. 2-3. Shepard plane for low involution (parallel to Fig. 2-2)

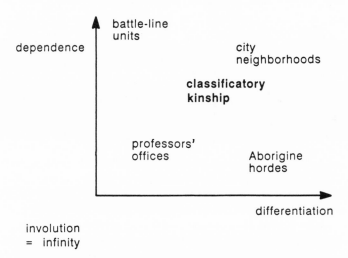

Fig. 2-4. Shepard plane for high involution (parallel to Figs. 2-2, 2-3)

trays ranges of self-reflexive mechanisms. One example is a discussion group being its own audience as well as cast of actors. The complementarity measure is zero for these self-reflexive commit interfaces.

Figure 2-4 portrays the analogous plane of variation for the commit mechanism at the other extreme on involuteness. This extreme is for localism, where the only criterion is a relative one: this here is a locality only by contrast to those other localities over there and there. The localism plane also can be seen as the special case of ecology, of physical space to which all the various valuation interfaces of social spaces reduce when social action evaporates. The usual story line is that all in a locality are the same—in tribes such as the Australian ones described by Spencer and Gillen (1903; cf. Durkheim 1915) all in a locality identify with the same potent totem. Locality is in fact always distinguished by live social process, with actual geographical dispersion only one of the occasions and excuses.[22]

For these three figures, the dimension perpendicular to the planes measures involuteness with respect to the quality valuation/ordering which defines the commit interface. The involuteness measure can be shown as coming out perpendicular to the plane of figure 2-2 (or 2-3 or 2-4), since it portrays the measure held fixed in that plane. But it is not restricted to the interface species. The three planes together outline a three-dimensional space (such as will be shown in figure 2-5). This same space then can be sliced up in other ways to represent other disciplines, as shown in the next sections.

Which is to say that the same three dimensions, for embedding ratios, give a measure space for each of the other two species too. The underlying valuation will be either purity or prestige rather than quality, with correspondingly different type of tie in transitive order, but that will not show up explicitly. The same space will be sliced by different planes depending on how each discipline works, what measure it tracks on.

Arenas

Comparabilities are the foundation in all species. The cohort in age as it moves into some age-graded mobilization is exemplary of how participants in social formations recruit themselves as available through preestablished comparabilities. These comparabilities are probed, in arena disciplines, so as to turn up and match complementarities. The talk tends to be about esteem, a purely social aspect, while the actual concerns in the productions being put together are with complementarities that may include the biophysical. The complementarities assessed can range from simple pair matching on over to a full team of specialties.

Let us return to the playing field of chapter 1. In choosing up sides the straggle of children are sorting out, from network context and

---

[22] See chapter 4 for further discussion under Boundaries.

proffered identities, the sorts of contributions and degrees of expertise which different kids can bring. The actual choosing of teams may be a commit-interface, a reification and symbolization of the new identity being created. But the choosing is based on a preceding select-mechanism of the arena discipline.

Selection and matching of diverse sorts are the activities of this discipline, which typically is episodic in time. In the playing-field case, formal teams may be only two in number, but the number of clusters in selections and matchings is various and shifting. Selecting is concerned with variously perceived real production tasks—throwing passes versus line play and the like—and corresponding degrees of social "fits." This transpires before the stylization of formal teams is achieved.

For many sorts of production to be induced, longer-lived and more complex teams must be matched. These selections also are often visualized as (and may in fact take place in) literal arenas, physical contexts given social identities from the matchings. The acquaintance dance, the production of Broadway musicals (Prince 1970),[23] and diagnosis and treatment of your current ailment, legal or medical, are some modern exemplars of the infinite variety of dress in which selection disciplines come, disciplines built out of exclusion for purity ordering.

The index space of embedding ratios is repeated in figure 2-5, analogous to figures 2-2, 2-3, and 2-4 taken together. Now the planes are defined by the dependence embedding ratio being fixed. For the commit-interface by contrast, dependence as embedding ratio was simply a shadow assessment. Exemplars developed below are recorded in appropriate locales in figure 2-5 without further comment.

Selection and Chance

Chance, the stochastic, is attracted to and tends to induce these select-arena disciplines. This is a socially problematic, chancy, and disorderly form. Most often we conceive it as an exchange market or a garage sale. It is an effective and predictable regulator of real network flows.

Arena disciplines are flexible for accommodating various and unexpected actors. The problematic for this species is identity formation for clusters. Selections into clusters of complementarities can be apt, and from an observer's viewpoint, effective social constructs in future production, yet they may come with inadequate induction of identities.

---

[23] See "Multiplex Network" in the next chapter, and figure 6–1, respectively.

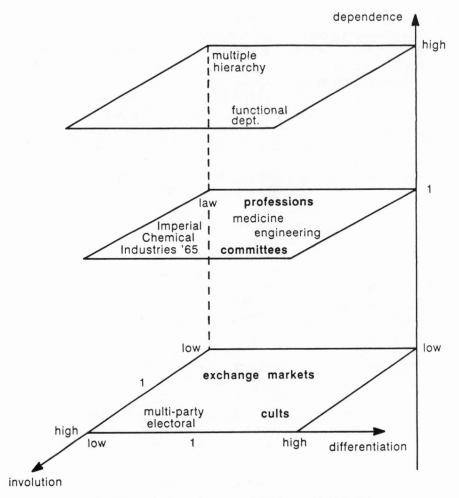

Fig. 2-5. Shepard planes for arena disciplines: the 3-D space

It is for this reason that fame, in various shadings and spreads, so often is articulated in matchings and selections. Fame can be purely social and arbitrary. Fame can supply a sort of universal currency of identity, a flexible spread of identities among the straggle that are matching into clusters. Fame is a way to make purity ordering tangible.

Selection-arena disciplines are robust with respect to eruptions of control projects, whether from within or from without. The robustness comes from the multicentered structure, combined with the fluid and stochastic nature of flows into and among clusters. Size distributions of freely forming social groupings in arenas have proved robust (James 1953; Coleman 1964; White 1962) and, on a larger scale, this is evidence of robustness across attempts at manipulation.

Arena Markets

A selection-arena brings together actors who can be disparate and inhomogeneous into a setting which is socially constructed to emphasize formal interchangeability so that actors are viewed as comparable, and concerned with exchanging this for that. Your earliest conscious experience of this discipline may have been choosing-up sides for a game amidst a bunch of kids on a playground. Pure-exchange markets (Newman 1965) are a mediated version of choosing-up.

The actors are there to make matchings, which can be of the most variegated sorts and which can appear as flows and/or stocks, or services, or intangibles. Exchange markets on all scales are obvious possibilities to fit this arena discipline. Consider a lawn sale, or for that matter a village market: From an operational social viewpoint what is being created are successive teams of actors who can "produce" what they both want by acting together. Money, while it eases barter, also obscures the underlying social form.

Within the interface discipline, by contrast, production was relatively unproblematic for individual actors. Inducing orderly reception and interpretation via a clear precedence order among producers is the focus in production markets. The arena discipline is an obverse in which the social production, the exclusion and recombining, can be accomplished only (and in diverse ways) from joint activity; so matching together into pairs, or more various teams, is induced. Mating is the homeliest example.

The production market modeled previously by interface discipline is entirely different from the arena discipline, which concerns matching and selecting. "Supply matching demand" is a syllogism for the arena, rather than a tautology as for the production market. There are fundamental differences in structure. This is true whether the discipline is on the scale of firms as actors or rather has Goffman personae as makers of the fleeting transactions of face-to-face life.

In the commit-interface, producers eye only each other, as reflected in terms of trade achieved, with the buyers being a confusion: The interface operates as a one-way mirror (White 1982). In the select-arena, in contrast, you are either in the arena, or it is opaque to you. You are equally "in" whether a seller or a buyer or both, and sellers are no more active than buyers in establishing proposed terms of trade. Select and exclude are obverse and complementary operations here.

There also is a basic difference in time construction. The production market presupposed and requires unremitting attention to the flows and to the interface by the producers; whereas an arena market can come in discontinuous and self-contained sessions. All those present in an arena are equivalent, rather than "marked" by side and fixed in niche by quality. Yet attendance at an arena may be fickle.

Money price to us is the natural idiom for matchings and selections. This is so much the case that we expend great efforts to impute and realize a monetary format even when remote from the immediate context. A more general way to view the ambiance is as degrees of purity. Purity, the designation of the underlying valuation ordering, is the apt idiom.

Arenas as Purifiers

The negotiated social logic which disciplines this select-arena species of mechanism holds fixed a purity valuation. "Exclude" could be used interchangeably with "select" in describing the mechanism of this species, in a designation using obverses. Selection may be a sort of purifying, and this discipline then be called a purifier.

Purifying occurs off to one side, out of the mainstream. Just how and why particular selections are carried out are not visible from outside. The purification is on the one hand an entirely public occasion, the general purpose of which is known and indeed disseminated. On the other hand, the arena of the selections and matchings is opaque from outside. That is, the rules and standards which take force within the arena are not fixed; they evolve and change within the disparate set of actors which the purifier exists to make comparable.

Membership in purifiers can vary from the most temporary and casual to the most permanent and rigid. There is a tendency to concentric shells of membership. The inner shells are the most pure, have the most weight in evolving changing standards of matching. Purity is created by achieving matchings which become defined as pure.

A village caste council in India (Mayer 1960) is a select-arena which explicitly emphasizes purity ordering. It is a purifier, whose business is the endless small matchings and adjustments of ceremonial requirements to ongoing productive requirements. From this example, as from examples of exchange markets, it is clear that arenas occur as one among many other arenas in a population of such.

The caste example is one where particular purifiers refer to and imply particular others, so that they imply a larger institutional structure. This fact of social pattern goes hand in hand with a fact of culture. The caste example is extreme in the explicitness of concern with purity, to the extent that there is an ideology tied to a religious institution to undergird it. This reminds us that disciplines of all species are analytical devices which presuppose as they also imply aspects of larger context. Disciplines do not come solo—anymore than do "persons." And in the caste situation, developed further in chapter 4, the insides of the disciplines may be strongly impacted thereby.

The arena discipline is an analytic category. There can be and are examples with but a single actor. Consider for example the office of Chief Executive Officer (CEO), which has evolved in business over a fifty-year period in this century (Chandler 1963; Fligstein 1988; Vancil 1979). Like all real evolutions it was blindfold. At first it seemed but an innocent alternative to "President"; it seemed at most an example of title inflation, where both CEO and President could bask in apex glow. Perhaps it also served to ease retirement transition; "President" itself was an uneasy concept. President was a temporary managerial servitor, in an environment of "owners" unlimited in term, and too many tried to assimilate to the time horizon of owner.[24]

Analytically, the CEO indeed is a select-arena discipline. The CEO is not the hands-on manager and decider of operations, but exactly the fixer, the healer—and thereby the controller, given appropriate networks of committees and offices below.[25] Which is to say that the CEO is a purifier. And over the past decade (Vancil and Green 1984) the CEO has come to be more and more commonly designated as a small committee of interchangeables who are to function in what we have described as the purifier way, as the select-arena discipline.

At another extreme, consider committees with which you are familiar in your own practical life. They too are purifiers, in a broad range of situations. The committee enables placements to be made in much less constrained ways; that is, committees may serve to pull, out of the main flows, streams of problems and opportunities and bring them to one side where matchings can be made (cf. March and Olsen 1976). Because the functioning, although not the provenance, of a committee can be private, existing memberships and networks can be temporarily suspended in devising rationales for matchings

---

[24] It eventually became clear that this mere change in terms went hand in hand with a shift to a very different, larger physiology of control, to the multidivisional form from the scalar functional one: see discussion in chapter 6.

[25] In chapter 6 this shift to CEO is also shown to be exactly a shift to use of arena disciplines in a new lattice of control.

and selections. The formal equality within committees, which neutralizes age and status and tribal distinctions and the like, is important to the flexibility.

Common also as purifiers are arenas **defined** as uncommon, centered on an inner core of purification specialists. A gathering of elders may function as a purifier in dealing with ill health, matching complaints to treatments. A gathering similarly may mediate conflicts, seen as a purification with wisdom. A gathering may similarly be consulted and give advice concerning sin and matching sin with apt contrition. In otherwise very different societies and institutional systems, purifier arenas of any of these kinds can be given explicit formal standing.

In this era, such "uncommon" purifier arenas often are known as professional settings (see Abbott 1981, 1988). Doctors heal, judges judge, priests offer sacraments, each in formalized settings fitting arena discipline. A joint, opaque arena of matchings underlies the formal setting, but the potential interventions from many and varying actors are not obvious. In each there is a logic of purity akin to that in the caste situation, keyed to an "inner," because more permanent, body of allowed practitioners. There is little tangible connection between the body of doctrine kept up to sustain purity definitions, on the one hand, and the tangible matchings of victim to remedy, or of actor to another actor or to material parcel: thus the setting can be understood as a discipline rather than some mere offshoot of overall arcane cultural prescriptions.

Councils

This discipline is the closest to the purely social. The concern in this species is to mobilize, as much in a gathering-and-foraging party as in a formal council with purely political concerns. Engrossing some, and sharing out much, of what is around, both social and material, are projects here which presuppose material production. The social processes are urgent ones, though the overall identity being induced and embedded by this discipline aims at time-rooted claims, and an appearance of immutability.

The arena discipline is an inverse, of sorts, to the mobilizer discipline. Actors are not embodiments of the rooted interests of factions, as in a mobilizer. Selection within the arena has actors functioning off to one side in obscured cliques of matchers, and there is mystification by systematic doctrine in the purifier format (e.g., committee or profession) of the arena. In the mobilizer-council, and only there, does each direct participant have attendant dependent chains.

Index Space

Differentiation is the given preoccupation in the council. Any mechanism emerging around mobilize discipline fixes the embedding ratio corresponding to prestige valuation, the ratio with respect to differentiation. When this embedding ratio is unity, there is an equality between the impacts perceived from standing within the prestige ordering for that discipline, on the one hand, and on the other the strivings for achievable differentiation being put forth by various actors within it.

The variations can be mapped in planes analogously to those in earlier figures. Figure 2-6 portrays a set of parallel planes in the three-dimensional ratio-measurement space built up originally for the interface species in figures 2-2, 2-3, and 2-4. The new set of planes are orthogonal to, but analogues of, those shown in these three figures. And the same is true vis-à-vis figure 2-5 for the arena discipline. The same space is to index all species of discipline.

In figure 2-6, on the middle plane, holding differentiation ratio fixed at unity, other illustrative examples of the council species are named. These are examples which have the advantage of being well known and studied from the historical literature. (They have the disadvantage of being confounded with explicit ideology and large underlying populations, and fuller interpretation has to await later chapters.)

Characteristic of embedding ratio for differentiation being unity, as shown in all these examples, are long-standing and stable dependency chains. Within the plane high dependence ratios correspond to longer strings of dependence. And representation—and also factionalization, another expression—tends to be imperialistic across all domains of practical activity. Thus the council discipline concerns mobilization.

Mobilizing

Mobilization cannot exist as an actual social process except in a set of foils and counterfoils. Mobilization means wrestling about ostensibly fixed and abstract claims. Mobilization also means inducting other actors via commitments that are unrelated to claims. Rather, these commitments focus on successive scopes of alliance and opposition from concrete commitments.

Correlation is the key, and it reflects what is being regulated, what is being held fixed in this species of discipline. To mobilize is to induce similarity, in actual social enactment, even though the story told be a unique claim. This is so because, objectively, mobilization

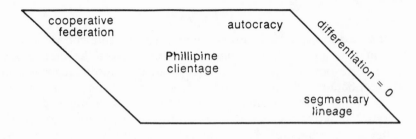

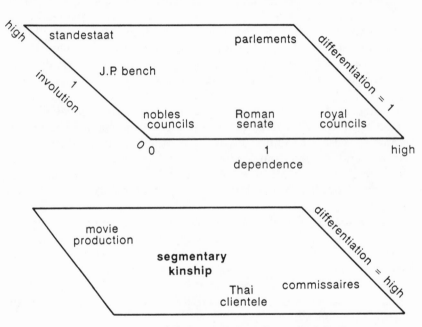

Fig. 2-6. Shepard planes for council disciplines: the 3-D space

always is a reciprocating process of inducing like claims and commitments in responses to other actors' (which claims and commitments need not be verbalized). Thus it is that differentiation is the ratio being held fixed across various instances of a kind of mobilization. One can best equate mobilizations according to whether they have the same differentiation among claimants—as seen embedded, from above, assessed in units of differentiation among comparables as seen in their own level.

Perhaps the best place to see the workings of this mobilizer-council discipline is in what was presumably its earliest embodiment, the lineage:

Our starting point is not the organized corporate group or the fabric of continuity and stability in the social structure (Part one, cf. Fortes 1945) but the individual . . . the standard forms and processes of person-to-person relationships . . . the gradation of rights and duties in jural and ritual relations in which lineage segments emerge as corporate units . . . every person belongs to a hierarchy of lineage segments lying between the maximal and minimal limits of his maximal lineage . . . relevant to his conduct in different degrees and according to variations in the social situation . . . even when only a segment of a lineage emerges in any corporate activity its status and functions are influenced by the total lineage field, including at the limit the field of clanship. . . . Conversely, a lineage always functions as a combination of segments, not as a collection of individuals of common descent. . . . Every lineage segment represents a dynamic equilibrium of mutually balancing segments. . . . It must be emphasized that these distinctions are not made by the natives. . . . The Tallensi have no term for the lineage . . . units of Tale social organization can only be defined by reference to the way in which they emerge in corporate action in relation to other like units. (Fortes 1949, pp. 10–11)

These lineage disciplines are not preset but rather are invoked as to membership and type of tie and occasion. The discipline in this species is from an ongoing, interconnected, and changing set of mobilizations. The identities being induced are about claims, and the content of social process activates chains of these.

The playground example of chapter 1 provides illustrations of mobilizer-council discipline. Children do not just appear at random, and where they appear is significant, where they appear among actors who may be mobilized for particular productions, here in play activities. Named street gangs give further color and recognition to what is a universal; namely, the interactive, the riposte nature of mobilization.

An effort at mobilization, for innocuous purpose as well as weighty one, is latent mobilization of what others might mobilize. Mobilization feeds upon itself, induces counteract and structure to any triggering action. This is as true among the Nuer (Evans-Pritchard 1940) or current business (Bower 1970) as on the playground or in government (Bearman 1989; Namier 1961; Opie and Opie 1969).

In figure 2-6 the middle plane is for a power mechanism that, so to speak, "counts coup." Here, an identity's standing within the council at the center of the mobilizer is achieved according to how many successes are being accumulated in paired encounters. The Roman Senate of Republican days (Syme 1939; Gruen 1974; Badian 1958,

1982) is an apt illustration of how this counting of coups worked out, persisting over centuries.[26]

Factions and Autocracy

Factions and their endless maneuverings around control of substantial outcomes can be seen as the substance of this mechanism. There is never a solution, a permanent alignment of factions, for that would contradict the central process. Mobilization and realignment goes on routinely in continuous adjustment. It is a context in which changes are embedded as routine. Membership enters and leaves particular dependencies, as well as the council structure itself, whatever the stories told.

Very much the same discipline appears across very different levels and different degrees of overall social-economic development. The Nuer tribe brilliantly analyzed by Evans-Pritchard (1940) can stand for the whole array of segmentary kinship systems—with their analogues in our boards of directors (Burt 1983; Levine 1972, 1989; Mintz and Schwartz 1985; Mizruchi 1982, 1984; Mizruchi and Schwartz 1986; Palmer 1984). There is endlessly breaking and recalling of old alliances and identifications, all as arbitrary circumstances change.

Council disciplines seem more stochastic in operation the more advanced is the overall economy and technology. Among the Nuer, exactly the same genealogical descent lines and groupings can continue indefinitely as the grammar in which power adaptations are made through fission and fusion—seen as moving further back up a descent line or further down. In more developed environments, there is a greater density of disciplines being worked up among a comparable number of actors. This greater density will have the effect, especially in the council form with its dependent strings, of shocks which unsettle particular alignments without changing the overall discipline.

In figure 2-6 "autocracy" is used to label council forms with the embed ratio for differentiation at minimum, and within that plane for high dependence. There are many particular council forms subsumed under that label. In autocracy the external or public differenti-

[26] The discussion here and later oversteps the bounds of a discipline proper, and will be taken up as uncertainty tradeoffs at the end of the next chapter. Clientelism is a term for dependency, especially in political institution, built around strings of connections such as are latent chains in mobilizations. The mobilizer discipline has indefinite boundaries so that it is natural to liken it to what are actually more intricate systems like the clientelism examined in chapter 4. Trust is more prominent and problematic in the larger system than in a mobilizer discipline, but the logic is similar.

ation of standing among all but the autocrat is squeezed to nil, however much effort is expended in jockeying for standing among this servile elite around the autocrat, be it Holmes's autocrat of the breakfast table, or Ottoman Sultan (Findley 1978). There is a contrast with the "counting coup" disciplines of the middle plane of figure 2-6.[27]

An important point is that, when differentiation ratio is held at zero, this council power mechanism also is central to the segmentary lineage systems exemplified by the Nuer. In Evans-Pritchard's words:

> The outstanding structural characteristic of Nuer political groups: . . . the distinction and individuality of a political group is in relation to groups of the same kind is a generalization that embraces all Nuer local communities, from the largest to the smallest. . . . The relation between tribes and between segments of a tribe which gives them political unity and distinction is one of opposition. (Fortes and Evans-Pritchard 1949, pp. 282–83)

In autocracy there also is substantial involution, as indicated by the placement in figure 2-6, but the same low differentiation-ratio mechanism can also work in a very homogeneous context such as for the Nuer with little scope for involution. The essential mechanism on this plane is the feud, which is endlessly particular to pairs and need not induce any recognizable status ordering.

The explicit demonstration of power is only occasional in the actual operation of this mobilizer discipline, in any of its variants. This power, which is potential and occasional, is also awesome when exhibited. It occurs when there is, temporarily, the fully joint action and perception by the constituent and competing strings of dependency whose representatives or embodiments constitute the council. It is overwhelming and unopposable when, occasionally, it occurs, not just because of the overwhelming preponderance of resources but because the perceived reality for all "involved" is starkly hegemonic.

Power, for example over engrossment and disbursement of social and physical material, is what mobilizing aims toward. Without mobilization there is no power, but without anticipation of power there

---

[27] This contrast seems to be illustrated by the distinction between French and German intellectual cliques as sketched by Lepenies (1988, p. 268): "The *ecclesia invisibilis* of the Georgeans (followers of the charismatic Stefan George) in fact had about it as much of the French *chapelle*, the demonstrative academic-cultural defensive alliance congregated around a patron, as it did of the informal, indirect and thus all the more influential coterie of an *invisible college*."

is no mobilization. Trust presupposes power; power is built out of trust in mobilizer disciplines.[28]

Catnets for Black Hole in Index Space

Molecules are analytical constructs. Exemplars of social molecules always come mixed with and colored by other such within larger social organization. It is the discipline aspect of molecule, perceptions of it as a source of action, as an identity, that tend to be tangible and discrete. As social action by given identities continues around a particular site it may, after first being captured in one variety of discipline, then shade into another variety. Or this action may change over into an exemplar of a different species.

For example, it would appear from a recent study (Eccles and Crane 1988, developed further in chapter 6) that American investment banks in New York used to be actors in a council discipline but then fitted into arena disciplines, as the network context changed and enlarged internationally, and as identities of the issuers of and investors in debt also changed. By contrast, American commercial banks have remained characterized by interface disciplines. On a smaller scale, the formal boundary role of purchasing agent within American industry has not just changed but oscillated between discipline species as distinguished here (see Corey 1970; Fligstein 1988; Pooler 1964).

And more limited, ad hoc processes can be seen within disciplines. Agency as process, for example, can be realized in different disciplinary species. One aspect of agency, supervision and "inverted supervision," was discussed above in terms of varieties of interface discipline. There the horizontal, peer aspect of agency was emphasized. When the vertical and cumulative aspect of agency is predominant, some variety of mobilizer discipline is likely to obtain. Compounded agency is, so to speak, just one arm of the mobilizer octopus cut off and treated as independent and free-standing.

Distributions in Index Space

Previous sections describe various tangible examples of disciplines which one expects to find in locales of the three-dimensional index space as indicated in figures 2-2 to 2-6. This search had to come in

---

[28] Compare Baldwin (1976) and Lasswell and Kaplan (1950) for accounts which are not referred to explicit social formations.

steps. First the species of discipline anticipated cuts down the space to a set of parallel planes, corresponding to the constraints imposed by that discipline. Then a particular plane was fixed by the embedding ratio corresponding to the valuation ordering being held fixed. Then changing locale within that plane, measured by the other two embedding ratios, went with changes in context imposed on or chosen by control efforts yielding that discipline.

Perceptions must underlie the three dimensions, since control attempts are being assayed as well as physical works done, but locating current and potential disciplines within the resulting index space is the analyst's choice. A wide range of descriptive material about discipline and its wider embedding has been drastically reduced into three numbers. This is the simplest index scheme which could be right. The three numbers that identify a location in the index space are embedding ratios for differentiation, for dependency, and for involuteness. Thus the index space is not isotropic since the three ratios are computed differently. Very simplified also is the underlying assumption; namely, that a linear ordering or valuation is central to the mechanism of each species of discipline.

A complete canvas of results is still distant. An initial spread of partial models of selected social organizations was the basis for proposing this set of three dimensions. These dimensions are conceived abstractly as embedding ratios, in order to index results for all varieties of all species of discipline. They require measurements of parameters which can only be specified within a complete model for a discipline, with upstream and downstream.

Measurement for a given discipline can only come from some definite empirical realization. A single point on a plane in the index space represents an array of concretely different exemplars of this discipline. The representation in index space lumps together from very diverse institutional contexts empirical cases that prove similar in fact. These exemplars, despite differences in number of participants and scope, all approximate to the same three embedding ratios. The argument is that the viability and stability of all examples in an array for a single point will be the same because the ratios reflect what is crucial in discipline and mechanism.

This representation in an index space also can suggest new settings in which to look for the same discipline species. A form of conjecture about a discipline is blank regions on a particular plane laying out its varieties. One cannot expect a given species to be adaptable to just any locale in the full index space. Examples were given above for the interface. Regions of a plane were noted (figure 2-4) where the given discipline could not sustain itself.

Some or all of those "impossible" situations for the interface discipline might turn out to fit viable examples of the other two species.
For example, there was a suggestion earlier that council disciplines
might be the only feasible option in a certain region. Actual calculations are formidable, since a complete discipline must be described
internally and in context for each point. And it is an unproven assumption that stability of form and other broad features depend only
upon values on the three ratio-measure dimensions.

Catnets as Residual

In some parts of the index space, representing whole skeins of situations for inducing disciplines, there may be no sustainable variety of
any species, at least so far as currently observed or modeled. This
seems to apply especially to the center of this index "space," around
where all three measure ratios are unity. Call this central region a
"black hole," inasmuch as any and all efforts at stable disciplines disappear without trace in such potential configurations.

Self-similarity of theory across levels is required in order to reflect
the complexities. Disciplines themselves can be nodes with social
ties, and at the same time participants within such a discipline can be
nodes as well. Thus a network of ties can appear connecting entities
embedded on different levels. It is only where a discipline is in action
and hegemonic that the context and contingency details, in the form
of ties and networks of ties, may fade from focus of attention.

Discipline mechanisms obviously are not the only social formations. There will still be social organization active in situations
which, if attempted as disciplines, would be indexed in the black
hole region. The black hole indexes the most febrile situations.

Identities emerge initially from rubbings together of mismatchings
engendered in aid of distinct control and/or production efforts in
given settings. So it is instructive to think of new identities as especially likely to be generated in contexts indexed around the black
hole. A newly forming interface (or other species) may embed a new
identity in cross-pressure from other existing disciplines. But, in the
turbulent contexts indexed around the black hole, sets of identities
may emerge in interaction. Uncertainty is likely to simultaneously be
high in all its guises, within situations such as this. And one would
expect agency to appear, as a stripped-down form of council or of
prestige discipline not constitutive of production.

When clear-cut disciplines do not emerge, in situations indexed
around the black hole, one can expect not only a profusion of identi-

ties of limited endurances but also much more prominence for aspects of social organization not captured in discipline representation. There are other representations as space and contingency, where identities cannot be grounded in terms of niches in disciplines. Ties and social networks may be all that is perceived. Attributes, of actors or of events, also become more prominent in the absence of place in articulated mechanism of discipline. Stereotypes, that is to say categorical attribution of character, appear among actors and events.

In earlier work (M. Schwartz 1966, 1967) the term **catnet** was coined to capture the involutions among network interconnections and personalization of attributes which, in present terms, seem most common in black hole contexts. Persons recognize indirect connections that are implied by the set of pair relations, assumed common knowledge, which can be represented as a network (in ways taken up in the next chapter). But these indirect connections are recognized only in part, and over a limited number of removes. These indirect connections are reacted to in concrete terms rather than as well-defined new types of relations. A "catnet" evolves from this and from the bunching of people by common attributes into categories.

The black hole in the index space for disciplines is at central location. The potential social context being invoked there teeters. It requires balancing at halfway point on each of the three types of linkage ratio, which means balanced between the internal and external sides of the potential embedding. Of course it is also the most complex context. The argument will build to an assertion in chapter 5 that persons, as distinguished from identities, only appear in such contexts, where, as the subsequent chapters show, more elaborate and cultured social organization is enabled through decoupling properties of persons, and of other like social actors.

The principal result of the evolution of a catnet is the definition, in the eyes of participants, of a new type of relation, equivalence within the perceived system. A catnet is less likely to be disrupted and shouldered aside by generation of a discipline in those contexts indexed by the black hole region. A simple example is the development of cliques in a network of friendship, developed in the next chapter.

Some terminology from the next chapter can be anticipated. As the density of ties among a subset of persons reaches some threshold value, the subset will come to regard itself as having an identity. Most of the pairs in the subset may not be connected actively at a given time by network relation, but because of the perception of an identity all relations will be regarded as present in a latent way. In other words, any member in a clique will feel free to "mobilize" the relation with another member in the clique.

A clique can continue to grow by the process of "folding-in" (e.g., Coleman 1957, 1961; Burt 1982). If one or more clique members have a friend in common in the network outside the clique, other clique members will tend to assimilate the additional person. When several types of network tie are superimposed in a population, cliques can form in each. Folding-in processes now work across the different types of relations and tend to yield cliques with common membership across several types of ties.

Given the catnet tendencies toward focusing and alignment of relations, it becomes easier and more common to perceive indirect relations with a wider segment of the population around. One reckons relations through clique memberships and the like, that is through the latent relationships, rather than tracing out some of the usually long chains of concrete ties that would be necessary to "reach" most other persons in the system. The network comes to be projected in perception into a net among the clusters or cliques, with persons in a clique treated as equivalent unless there is some short actual path to a given one.

Each person in the catnet system thereby secures a less fragile place in a social formation less definite but more ineluctable than any given discipline. When particular concrete ties are disrupted, there are clearly acknowledged sets of other persons with whom new ties of equivalent sort can be acknowledged and mobilized quickly. Yet at the same time the catnet system is more decoupled from random disturbance. Being surrounded by a wider range of reliable ties which are possible, a person can be less attentive to and concerned in every rumor and disturbance which passes along the concrete nets.

In still larger scopes around it, a catnet tends to become perceived in a broader view as an entity which itself grows links and evolves into membership in a still larger catnet system. That is one possibility, if the tense balancing indexed by the black hole characterizes the larger context also. We all have had the experience of leaving one early-life stage and moving on to another in which our previous highly refined and detailed perception of network and category among the young peers we leave is quickly distilled into a lumped representation of the whole stage as an entity, a catnet. Such is the genesis, and also the index space locale, of the more complex social organization which we seek to discriminate. And disciplines themselves can get caught up in catnets.

THREE

NETWORK AND STORIES

PROJECTS OF CONTROL underlie creation of ties, as both Schelling (1960, 1978) and Garfinkel (1967) insist. Such projects come from and can engender disciplines of any of the three species—interface, arena, and council. But many projects reproduce only in pair encounters because of both physical and social exigencies. The control struggle in such a pair has settled into a standoff, but the struggle in such a pair may activate both valuations and other pairs.

Identities come to perceive the likelihood of impacts from indirect relations to other identities in some string of ties and stories. The social result is called a network.[1] A mere set of disciplines and ties turns into a social network, seen as an envelope of ties formed from the flotsam of aborted disciplines. Pair balancing of control efforts become generalized through a set of common stories that the network-population makes possible. Networks, like their constituent ties, can be seen as the storied shadows from disciplines that did not come into being.

Until now, network constructs have lain undigested, increasingly indispensable for phenomenological insight (Granovetter 1985; Wellman and Berkowitz 1988), but inert theoretically. Theorizing social networks requires grounding ties in social molecules and then analyzing them in terms of dynamics of control, while recognizing influences from larger contexts.

Networks are phenomenological realities as well as measurement constructs. Stories describe the ties in networks. The contexts in which identities and their disciplines lie are shaped by further control attempts. It is the attempts that survive and concatenate which can be represented by ties in networks. These networks of disciplines will not persist just as they happen to be thrown up by sto-

---

[1] "Network" is retained as designation because of its familiarity, but it does have misleading overtones of nodes being monads and of ties as lines in physical space with Cartesian dimensionality. Terminology in social science applications remains loose and unstandardized, despite mathematical foundations in theory of graphs and binary relations (e.g., Berge 1962; Harary 1977; Ore 1965). Whether or not a binary relation is perceived as subsuming all the implied indirect paths (so-called transitive closure) it is known as a network.

chastic eruption, any more than will a particular discipline, with its projected identity, persist and reproduce itself independent of social context.

Consider an example. A new industry may (or may not) be emerging around the biotechnology being derived from molecular biology. This could be the triggering of an identity, a new industry as an identity embedded from one of the crisp discipline-mechanisms with clear boundaries imputed in the previous chapter. But there may be too many independent actors involved for such discipline to be likely. Also, there are many potential products being developed, each of which could separately key a specific market, though most would string together through their inputs and outputs.

What is clear is that there are social networks of ties spinning out among all the actors, networks sufficient to suggest a community evolving, an industry as economic community. These are ties of contention and of cooperation. Most important among them are contractual commitments between pairs or among sets of actors, commitments as to venture capital or joint development or marketing agencies and the like.[2] There will be many distinct perceptions, many stories about particular ties and interconnections of ties. Stories soothe identities' irreducible searches for control, which can be captured in stasis as sets of stories representing ties.

Abstraction of relations as ties in a network is a commonplace. Always this has been true in reckoning kinship. And today sociometry of acquaintanceship has penetrated general consciousness. Network is a verb, and we tell stories in network terms.

Ties and Stories

The triggering of one identity activates control searches by other identities with their own impetuses toward control of any and all exigencies, including each other's. An envelope from stochastic unpredictabilities of resulting struggles may fall short of becoming a discipline and in its stead become a tie. Ties among disciplines are themselves failed disciplines and, together with disciplines, constitute social space.

Ties as failed disciplines may in particular derive as residuals from complete linear orderings in disciplines that abort or break up, but ties become a distinct form, not mere degenerate cases of discipline. Ties reflect but also are implicated in activity for actors as well as for

---

[2] Four studies-in-progress are reported in Eccles and Nohria (1992).

observers. Every identity continually seeks control to maintain itself, and in that struggle breaks, as well as establishes, ties with other such identities. Ties are portrayals of connections,[3] but these are not once-and-for-all objective interconnections among fixed identities.

Control efforts by actors[4] presuppose and generate ties. Each tie encapsulates struggles for control, the ones which persist. Each of these ties is a metastable equilibrium of contending control attempts, and as such induces chronic reports. As such reports accumulate, with invocations of other ties, they fall into patterns perceived as stories. A tie becomes constituted with story, which defines a social time by its narrative of ties.[5] A social network is a network of meanings as Burns and Burns emphasized long ago (1973, pp. 16–18).

Everyday time spent with stories, building and hearing them in gossip or whatever, suggests that they are vital in social action.[6] And imbibing a formal story or film is so similar to imbibing "real life" that the authors and directors, like gossipers in ordinary life, must have found effective shorthands for expressing identities and control in social relationships. Other constructs may also underlie shorthand

[3] Description of a tie is, at minimum, two names in brackets to indicate juncture. A name makes an identity transferable at the same time as unique, so that a name is the primitive of "position," as developed in chapter 4.

[4] I keep to the term "identity" when what is at issue is original and unpredictable action by intention—and in particular and especially gaming. An identity may be short- or long-lived; neither it nor the bracket term, actor, is restricted to a person.

[5] And thus may bind actors into plots, as developed in chapter 5, p. 216. By "actor" I designate here the enactor of a social script: see previous note.

[6] If stories are kept distinct from ties, five major social constructs have shaped the theory thus far: control, identity, disciplines, valuations, and ties. One can speculate that from just these five constructs some sort of social network could be uncovered which would apply to other social species besides man, to wolves and monkeys, if not hens and insects (E. Wilson 1970, 1979). One finds pecking orders, ties, and certainly control struggles there (E. Wilson 1979; Wynne-Edwards 1985)—and by some definitions even consciousness. Disciplines build ties with ecology as well as with other disciplines.

One thus can speculate that it is stories which set human social action apart. Without stories, and thence networks emerging out of mere collections of ties, social action would have a monotone quality; there would not be all the "colors" that humans observe and use in social settings. The implication is that stories are the essential vehicles for elaborating networks so as to become base for further formations. A generic third party is required for the existence of any tie-as-story, just as the flock is third party for the compacted ties-into-valuation of the pecking order. The third party is the generic observer, without whose witness networks would not embed into further formations.

Cognitive science and linguistics will eventually be able to tell us what exactly the interrelations can be between the neural physiology of a species and its communication: consult volumes edited by Nadel, Cooper, Culicover, and Harnish (1989) and by Hechter and Nadel (1993).

effective for observers and actors, but the obvious feature is stories into which raw reports settle down. Ties emerge thereby.

Ties as Stories

Endemic efforts at control explain why there are not still other species of self-reproducing disciplines. These efforts are exactly outside any given discipline, fitting into ties and thence networks and other patterns by drawing on the outputs of uninterrupted disciplines. Understanding these efforts requires special attention to perception and thus to stories.

Put aside phenomenological observations and seek other indices of ties. Anything about which you tell a story is a tie. Instead of arguing, go listen to stories on the playground (Opie and Opie 1969), or go read stories (Burt 1978a).

A story in itself does not suppose or require identities as actors, nor does it require distinct actors. A story includes everything from the simplest line heard on the playground—"Ernie loves Sue, . . . true, . . . true"—through artful excuses and basic daily accounts and on through recondite nuggets of professional gossip.

Actors have no problem in recognizing other actors, other effective social identities. Likely they name any and all of these various bodies, somehow, if not with a proper name. And, without hesitation, stories are told.[7] A story is at root an authority, a transfer of identity, which explains its close correspondence to network tie.[8] Stories come from and become a medium for control efforts: that is the core.

Sets of Stories

Ties are stories so that stereotyped stories are constituents of a network. Networks and disciplines both are peculiar hybrids as constructs. On the one hand, actors themselves perceive some such constructs, fuzzily, and are accordingly shaped in their actions. Social spaces are built of multiple perceptions which interlock enough to sustain what we come to call a social formation as objective reality. But issues of identity impinge upon perceptions of relations and make these perceptions problematic.

An apparently simple pair-tie can be seen to be a considerable social accomplishment. A context and onlookers persist in recognizable

---

[7] Systematic data collection by social scientists would be much improved by more self-conscious application of this truism. Government clerks will use the truism, unless misled by discourse on methodology!

[8] This idea is attributed to Pizzorno (1990).

fashion, which means that some substantial interest obtains concerning the "simple tie." There also must be ambivalence and complexity built into a tie, since it is a dynamic structure of interaction in control attempts. It is this structure which is being summed up as "a tie," and interpreted in stories, both by its members and by onlookers.[9]

How is it that stories have become so universal? How is it that stories can communicate so effectively across diverse hearers and audiences, including social science?[10] Ceremony and ritual go from social spaces back to smooth the junctions with ecological space-time; they derive from discipline valuations. By contrast, stories and their rhetorics emerge within social networks from interacting control projects. Control is the driving energy of identities spinning out social networks and coping with ecology. Stories come from these energies to embody their spinning out; they give color to human social life, to shake it up.

A set of stories can go with or come from a tie in a social network. Conventions, sets of stories, emerge over time. This process goes on under our eyes again and again, as in the playground of the first chapter. Any such playground will have its neighborhood argot (Opie and Opie 1969). The occasion and arena are there for a primitive language to emerge as vehicle for contending accountings.

Stories go along with human action in identifying habits and habitues. It is conflicts and inconsistencies in which a child finds itself caught up that start generating identity. It is not repetitive family domestic life, and not playing with the same bunch, but rather clashing lines of descent, arguable residence rules, tainted ethnic assignments, and the like, it is these that cause, and work from, identities in adults and children. And both the tensions and their overcomings induce stories and require sets of stories.

Contentions for control, if they settle down, become told as stories. A tie can be seen as the whole set of stories defining the historical relation of that pair of identities. This is the multiplex tie, the overall tie folding in many aspects, the subject of the next two sections.

---

[9] We can conceive kinds of explanation that precede ties or are ties stripped to a minimum. Groups of animals have them. Such explanations are pragmatics of practical life, of productions. They involve communication, but at a simple level which need not rise above the pheromone level of say an ant society (E. Wilson 1970). Language is sometimes attributed to human action that should instead be seen as a simpler level of phenomenology (R. Brown 1965) accessible for other species too.

[10] Some social and economic theorists are working to adapt "preferences" and "goal maximization" to the realities of perception accommodated by stories. One rubric in this awakening is "framing" effects (e.g., Kreps 1988, chap. 14; Lindenberg 1989a,b).

Conversely, a story can be equated to a set of ties. The intersection of these relations amounts to that story. This set is the types of tie taken up in the subsequent two sections.

Tracings of Social Space

The spinning out of control struggles by identities, by which the stranglehold of pecking orders is broken, induces a larger social space. It is all too common for social theorists to treat space as unproblematic.[11] For example, in a recent collection of views on sociology of culture (Desan, Ferguson, and Griswold 1989) both Pierre Bourdieu and Alain Viala (cf. p. 292) accept physical space as the obvious arena of social action, just with the "forces" changed from their physical form. Field investigators in social science fortunately do better. Hackman's (1990) studies of interactions among three-person crews in airliner cockpits can serve as prototype for interrelating social with physical space in small scale.

Space and Network

Networks constitute social spaces among identities. The various sorts of ties which may devolve from and into networks lead to different framings, all of which help constitute social spaces. Without such networks there would not be enough elaboration of social spaces to warrant their separate recognition. Without networks, human social action, like vertebrate pecking orders, would need only be referred, as sets of discrete disciplines, to some geography and ecology in biophysical space. With networks, however, the phenomenology of social action becomes sufficiently developed to site persons and other complex constructions in social spaces, as in the biotechnology example.

Expressway networks are a bit like social networks, with interchanges analogous to disciplines, but highway nodes are not actors, and their ties are etched in the ground, rather than in the eyes of beholders. A polymer gel is more like social networks. These very long molecules reptate through messy, inhomogeneous environments which include other such chains and induce new ties (DeGennes 1979; Hearle 1982; and see below Appendix 2, part B). And polymer chains can be vulcanized into cross-chains, as in rubber.

[11] Except for some geographers (Haggett et al. 1977), but geography is out of fashion! Part B of Appendix 2 surveys models of space.

Geography plays some role. A big wedding, say, will roll up many hunks of social networks into the same hall and there may engender new ties and clusters. And yet pen pals may share only love of certain authors. Social networks need be controlled by ordinary physical space only episodically. Physical settings do give an easy start for visualizing social networks, as for the playground in chapter 1.

Always there are groundings of social networks in physical space, in various sorts of production. The important point is that network keeps approximately on a level in social space, on what B. Schwartz (1981; see also Moore 1988) would call the "horizontal."[12] Also there are groundings in physical time. Winship (1978) and Abbott (1983, 1984) have shown how to analyze use of time in social relations and their networks. Burt (1991) shows how even so obvious-seeming a category as age is best captured as an aspect of space generated by networks, and he goes on to draw practical conclusions, especially about cogent ways to group ages.

Social networks are spun off as by-products of signaling dynamics, which include stories and other verbal accountings. Counteractions may come to repeat and reinforce so as eventually to reproduce themselves as discipline mechanisms which spin out further reaches of social spaces. These processes build upon previous results, and in particular counteractions may cumulate so as to embed additional identities, which in turn can interlock further with one another, so that there seem to be levels.

Rapoport's Profiles

Draw a network of ties among the children on the playground of chapter 1. Represent each child by some point as node. The network is then a set of nodes with connecting lines each representing a tie between a pair of children. To define the tie, some cutoff is assumed on strength or persistence of relations in a dyad (Berkowitz 1982; Burt 1980, 1982).[13]

[12] The "vertical," by contrast, always requires cultural support, as does for example the style of chapter 5, which crosses levels.

[13] One can get obsessed with measurement problems and prospects. Eye movements can be as reliable as utterances (Duncan 1965) as indicators of ties. The possible cues are legion. One actor need not be abstracting from behaviors in the same way as another, or as an observer might abstract if called upon to articulate that social setting. Bjerstedt (1956) early uncovered surprising robustness across kinds of sociometric probes. A sociometric network is no more than an observer's coding or recording of a set of relations between pairs of people. Any network is less than a map known and attended to by all of the actors in the network. There may or may not be names that are known. A network is a matter of fuzzy sets (Zadeh et al. 1975).

Another helpful abstraction is to keep the nodes fixed in some social plane rather than having them rush around a literal planar transcription of the field. A final abstraction is to catch the pattern as ties in a matrix whose rows and columns for kids are in a social ordering which is not necessarily in line with location on the playing field.

Rapoport (1983) and associates (e.g., Foster et al. 1963) brought networks to life for modern social analysts with a brilliant innovation for tracing networks. Long since, sociograms, following Moreno, had been used to record small interpersonal configurations such as any teacher intuited in the classroom (Waller 1932). The question was how to extend the idea operationally to larger settings.

Rapoport proposed to measure large networks by frequency-profiles of traces through them. The idea of tracing a string of ties would be anachronistic in some early or tribal societies—though not in ancient Rome or Persia. The issue is just who are interconnected just how amidst the diversity of many distinct and often incomparable frames of kinship, work, and play; in particular, who are interconnected by that most sophisticated of notions, sheer acquaintanceship.

To bound a setting is to introduce the arbitrary. Like Coleman (1961) before them, Rapoport and associates used a (junior) high school, the simplest and most accessible exemplar microcosm of the modern polyglot social context. "Who knows whom," on one or another criterion,[14] is asked and answered within this school. The size of this school (approximately one thousand actors) turns out to be apt: big enough to exhibit nontrivial connectivity and yet small enough to be manageable.[15]

What are the significant parameters, what is the social "shape" of this network representation, this indigestible mass of claims and verifications of who knows whom? As observers, we do not, for example, care which Suzy is most popular, although we may be interested in how divergent individuals are in popularity. The single most interesting question to Rapoport, and predecessors, was how interconnected the school of youths was and how fragmented. This is a fundamental question about the interpenetration of disciplines with network spaces.

It is a question with limits. Social action always arises from accidents and speculations and gamings which become aspects of more

[14] In their choices, respondents prove not to pay much attention to the exact criteria stipulated—see previous note.

[15] As was mentioned in chapter 1, this also is the minimal size for relatively separable and independent populations in all sorts of contexts, from Australian aborigine on to modern village.

far-reaching and crisscrossing projects of control—even in surface ripples at neighborhood bars and acquaintance dances. Rapoport's traces are important tools of measurement, but they are misleading exactly in that they appear to abstract from and thus disdain details of framing and intensity (which we return to subsequently).

Rapoport exploited the combination of two ideas. First, conceive connectivity as how many people can be reached from some person, some representative location within it, and at what remove, at what number of steps through intervening acquaintances. Second, distinguish ties one from another according to the social relevance, presumably the perceived intensity of the relation.

Each idea requires many subsidiary notions to become operational. The conception must be of sampling from a statistical ensemble of possibilities. Try out a number of randomly selected actors, each as "the" center from which to trace out connections; useful parameters will derive from averaging the resulting traces. Trace out a given sequence as far as it may go. Realize that from some Sam at the "center" one may reach some given Suzy by any number of distinct chains, sometimes through completely distinct sets of intermediaries.

Rapoport presents simple curves reporting at j'th remove, for successive integer j's, the (averaged) percentage of the school that had been reached through any and all chains of ties, through whatever intermediaries, from the trial "center." The profiles of rising connectivity constructed in this way are reported in the diagrams of Rapoport and his associates. There are curves separately for different "orders" of acquaintanceship. Figure 3-1 is an example.

The second idea had been operationalized by having respondents list acquaintances in order of closeness or some such criterion. Rapoport then pretended as if the fifth choices, for example, really were a world of their own, identifying a certain intermediate "level" of intensity. Thus traces are given separately for successive intensity levels of ties.

The main message of the work is exactly in the neat nesting of successive intensity profiles: see figure 3-1. The monotonic rise in number connected is definitional, and the eventual height of the asymptotic proportion of the total school reached may be rather erratic as a measure, even after averaging. What is fascinating is that the indicator of intensity, which necessarily is crude and may not be valid, distinguishes whole trace profiles so neatly.

Ask yourself this simple question: in which of two directions should the trace profiles nest? Granovetter brought Rapoport's work to the attention of, and use by, the social sciences community by de-

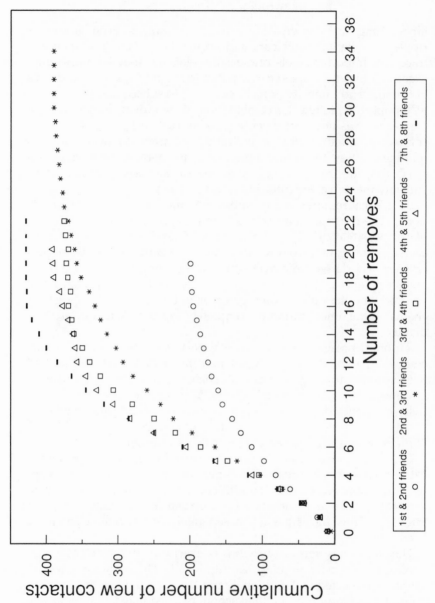

Fig. 3-1. Rapoport trace profiles

1st & 2nd friends	2nd & 3rd friends	3rd & 4th friends	4th & 5th friends	7th & 8th friends
○	*	□	△	-

Number of removes

Cumulative number of new contacts

monstrating that this was indeed *the* question. Moreover, Granovetter showed that it was most fruitful to simplify the question into weak ties versus strong ties; label this union of intense ties with weak ties Granovetter ties.

Tracing the Larger World

Granovetter derived out of Rapoport's results that ties and network were intertwined in a manner which was, at first sight, paradoxical (1973, 1982). Ties that were intrinsically weaker, more casual, yielded higher connectivity across the network: Weak ties are strong. That is, the way weak ties spread themselves around, they connect a larger fraction of a world together than do the same number of strong ties spread out in their way.

Strong ties, given precedence by the issuers, are weak in the broader context because they do not bind as large a fraction of a world into a corporate whole in connectivity. Granovetter elaborated all the nuances implied. Strong ties did fit into strong, if tiny, corporates so inward-turned as only to choose each of the few intimate others again and again without attention to the environment of persons.

To sum up: Close-knitness of a network is highly correlated with involuteness.

Access to jobs was shown to be dependent upon the implications of these Rapoport traces (Granovetter 1974), as no doubt could be shown for sexual access also. Not only are network perceptions shown to be intertwined with network realities, but also the accumulative impact of social structure is demonstrated. Granovetter captured so much attention because his results were not obvious; they could become plausible with thought but they were not accessible to uninformed intuition. They brought to fruition the theory of multiplex networks, where total relations within a pair are summed up in the one tie.

Rapoport's ideas were extrapolated to adult contexts. Milgram and others (cf. Kochen 1989) developed and applied chain-search techniques which permit specification and measurement of actual overlaps in acquaintances in current settings. Milgram understood how bizarre our world is: The Small World of acquaintanceships is the phenomenological world of Goffman and Simmel. Milgram had each randomly selected initiator aim to reach a named but unknown target through a chain of personally known contacts, each of whom in turn was to act as reinitiator, reporting by postcard to Milgram. They found overlap to a degree surprising only because of the apparent vague isotropy of modern social context.

The basic finding on chains was that an arbitrary pair could connect in about half a dozen steps, this within a hundred million persons.[16] The basic finding for phenomenology is that in our society ordinary people were acute sociologists who made sense of and carried out what to peasant societies[17] might seem a bizarre task.

It is not that acquaintanceship scope, the actual number of persons known to someone, necessarily differs by society. In all known times and contexts, from primitive tribes to empires, the scope of effective acquaintance, persons known in the relevant minimal sense, clusters around one thousand as median. Or, to focus on just the relations intense enough to persist indefinitely vis-à-vis ego, there seem to be around sixteen as a mode—in early societies all reckoned in a kinship frame, or in our own society dispersed over peer, kin, work, and neighborhood.

Siting Events

Identities and events are similar. Identities emerge out of turbulences in social process that do not appear accountable within any particular story. Events may be precursors to or consequences from identity formation, but they may substitute as a parallel to identities. Events are actors and so like identities are to be sited.[18]

A detailed case study of conflict over innovation supplies a striking analysis of the use of story sets amidst struggles for control, all of which centered on creation of an event, a discovery, as affirmation of values. This particular study is especially instructive because later we can interpret it to show the emergence of distinct types of tie and their subsequent spread as networks, all as a by-product of ongoing struggles between identities at several levels.

Originality and honesty are asserted ubiquitously in science. Susan Cozzens (1989) dissects a recent controversy over a multiple discovery in neural pharmacology. Five or so distinct research groups are struggling for some recognition as initiators, and many

[16] Dropouts from the searches terminated chains falsely, but the distribution of chain lengths can be corrected for the resulting biasing (White 1970a).

[17] E.g., the Tallensi (Fortes 1945).

[18] Consider their role in a political scientist's mapping of elite interactions into network portrayal: Axelrod's presentation of the Hitler-Chamberlain negotiations at Munich (Axelrod 1976). In an unself-conscious and practical way, Axelrod includes a number of events as nodes in the network on a par with human actors and organizations.

other groups and isolates are interested bystanders and contributors. Stories both of honesty and of originality are being negotiated in interaction with one another through various agencies in a complex social field.

Multiple networks—of collaboration, of training and sponsorship, of gossip, of friendship, and the like—are sources as well as products of rankings in Cozzens's case. These rankings are particular, as scientific pecking orders in specific subfields surrounding neural pharmacology. The rankings also are more general as status-layering, personal and institutional.

Mass-media news conferences were one sort of agency and arena used, but the focus was even then the consensus of fellow experts. Another agency was brokering and conciliating by other senior scientists. All meld into activations and adjustments of network and standing among the four different working groups being vied for recognition as codiscoverers.

Dual to all this is the semantic negotiation of concepts and perceptions. These negotiations are in struggles over whether there is an "it" to be discovered, and over bounds and shape for this "it"—the "opiate receptor." Scientific values do not operate as universal guides transposable as stories for this scene. The ordinary language terms of "priority" and "originality" dissolve in confusion amidst the bewildering struggles and claims. Participants manufacture, as convenient, new criteria of connection and information.

Siting in Social Times

Social structures often are made to seem the antipodes to, or at least unrelated to details and nuances of, sequencing in timing. This is in part because of the influence of structuralism (e.g., Lévi-Strauss 1969). Social times should instead be accounted as much part of structure as are network spaces. In the words of network theorist Granovetter:

> It is also important to avoid what might be called "temporal reductionism": treating relations and structures of relations as if they had no history that shapes the present situation. . . . *Structures* of relations also result from processes over time, and . . . without such an account, analysts slip into cultural or functionalist explanations, both of which usually make their appearance when historical dynamics have been neglected. (In Breiger 1990, chap. 2, p. 8)

Social times are woven together with meanings. Stories go with times as well as ties. According to the philosopher Ricoeur (1988), social time is reconciled with sidereal time exactly through the construct of narrative. Extend this to recognize that all sorts of social clocks are set and calibrated by stories, which are part of the fabric of social spaces.

Any theory of social action must deal with the recursion built into any reproduction, although the theory need not make recursion central as in the traditions surveyed by Hofstadter (1979). Skvoretz and Fararo (1980a) and Carley (1986) are sociological pioneers in this vein. It was opened by Newell and Simon (1972).

Self-reproduction of social formations can be taken for granted when engaged in induction from empirical reports. But self-reproduction can refer to a time scale of minutes as well as hours or seasons, indeed of seconds.[19] Social formations have no free ride, they are constantly being reconstructed out of the fluxes of endless social actions building and being built out of corporates and networks. This is equally true of person, community, and organization.

Networks themselves are always re-creating the social spaces of multiple perceptions. Social action creates and defines spaces for time just as it does for location, and with much the same fuzziness as patterns of network. These will not be common and robust enough to be observed unless they are compatible with timings which interlock. Processes, all the way from stringing ties to structural equivalence, are to be understood, by both observer and actor, only as to how they unfold together over time. Leifer (1990) looks at problems of timing in "simple" exchange reciprocity.[20]

Network as Population

Coupling can be traced in networks through strings of ties. But equally important is decoupling, which restarts social clocks and can buffer one chain of actions from another as well as freeing one actor from another's ties. There is some reality principle, in the sense of some restrictions for survival in physical space-time, but these are happenstance, now strict, now loose, as Udy (1970) has made clear.[21]

---

[19] Cf. Krauss and Bricker (1967) on effects upon conversation of delay in vocal transmission.

[20] The vexed issues of exchange and reciprocity (Blau 1964; Emerson 1962; Macneil 1978; Newman 1965) require analysis of embedding as well, which is a kind of dual to timing. Ideology can entrap us in the notion that specific local exchanges are the "realistic" version that should be modeled. Contexts of broader scope for exchanges, in the next chapters, should supply further antidote to this ideology.

[21] At the end of the chapter, a calculus among kinds of uncertainty is introduced which has decoupling and embedding as its vehicles.

Identities, of actors and events, come out of mismatches (chapter 1), and embed as disciplines. Disciplines spin ties which form networks or, when there are many balancing mismatches, give way to vaguer catnets (chapter 2). The resulting ensemble can be called network as population.[22]

A population has been a residual construct thus far. A population of identities who are seeking control is, through these struggles, coming to specify its own social space, rather than boundaries being imposed arbitrarily, as an observer is tempted to do. And within such population, disciplines become sited as summarized in the embedding ratios of chapter 2. Observable limits for a network depend on where one stands within it, and these limits also vary over time.

Action in a population spreads out in both physical and social space-times; so both affect the observable limits of population. Network entries are, as a set of pairs, what logicians and mathematicians call a binary relation. Ties do catenate together from one entity through an intermediary to a third entity as a mere fact of juxtaposition without prejudging some mutual knowledge. Tracing profiles registers this.

Much more subtle is network as population, as context for rather than mere juxtaposition of ties. Boundary of population is a theory, or rather a collection of theories rather than some singular outcome. One identity's boundary is another's neighborhood.

Multiplex Tie

A specification of tie as overall pair relation is called a multiplex tie. Rapoport and Granovetter dealt with ties as multiplex ties. Each multiplex tie sums up implications for ongoing processes that are perceived from some range of past incidents. Or, alternatively, each multiplex connection sums across some scope of specialized relations.

The relations being lumped as a multiplex tie imply sufficient familiarity with the other party to know to whom there is a further tie. For example, a friend's friend is a reality, gives orientation to action; yet the tie to a friend's friend need not itself be considered as a friend

---

[22] Until here, euphemisms—world, school, etc.—have been used for population, which is possibly the most deceptive term in the social sciences, just because it seems so obvious—"this set of people here." As if the reality of a social world in its boundaries (for which see the next chapter) can be mapped into a bag of beans! Demographers can be sophisticated about the time profile of population in its reproduction: on cohort versus generation see Ryder (1965). I avoid the term population in later chapters.

relation. Thus, a crude distance can be measured in steps away, given some calibration of intensity of relation required to code a tie. Some sense of distance and cumulation, of social space, is a by-product of, and motivation for, network thinking (Burt 1990). Connectivity is crucial (Freeman 1979) in any network, and it is the key construct for a multiplex network, in which much of value is obtained from even the crudest on-off coding for relations.

Corporates and Structural Equivalence

Connectivity is not the only basis for discriminating the social spaces of networks. These are spaces outside of, and which contextualize, disciplines. A corporate, at one extreme of network topology, exhibits full interconnection of all pairs, tangible membership as a group of comparable actors short of binding as a discipline. Such membership contrasts with that intimacy between a pair of identities which grows from subtle gaming interactions, and which can also be found in the larger settings of personages (chapter 5). Strategy and ambiguity mark the intimate, and they must be used to sustain action flows in delicate balance in order for identities to be maintained in such ties. By contrast, membership is, and is perceived as, a state which is exactly to be taken for granted.

Structural equivalence is a more general concept, which includes as a special case, but may be contrasted with, the cohesion of corporate interconnection (cf. Burt 1992). Membership presumes, as the norm, lack of questioning. "Character" is a suitable term for what membership is to reflect. As stories will be seen to characterize identity formation in general, so gossip in particular should cluster around character as a member. Members are to be deemed structurally equivalent to one another through attributes in common, relational or categorical. Comparability is achieved and presupposed as character of a group as corporate. Stability is to be guaranteed through ritual, as for clans (Durkheim 1915, chapters 2-1 and 2-3).

There may be no ties at all between structural equivalents, however. Two lonely kids alike alone on the fringes of a playground illustrate the pervasiveness of marginality in networks, what Romo (1991) analyzes as the "Omega Phenomenon." Also structurally equivalent are two "stars" who each reach out to gather the other kids into their respective orbits but have little to do with each other. Or structural equivalence can be abstracted from the particular others, so that two quarterbacks are equivalent even though there is no overlap between the kids in their orbits.

There are endemic intermixings of multiplex network with corporate groups. Baxandall (1980) is a recent example and Antal (1965) is a prototype of how accurately past corporate formations can be re-constructed, even in medieval European cities. Baxandall lays out the explicit guild-based physiology common to these cities. He goes further—he also goes into detail on the cognitive bases, and eco-nomic context, of the particular jurisdictional joustings among sepa-rate but interdependent structures of guilds. Baxandall builds from detailed studies of individual sculptors in their guild settings among a system of cities. Antal (1965) attempted the same for Renaissance Florence and Thrupp (1948) for all London guilds in a somewhat later time. Antal's study, like Baxandall's, is especially focused on art-work production, showing this cultural activity as very much en-meshed with all other aspects of the round of life.

High Schools, Bars, and Dances

For our own day, James Coleman (1961) reports with equal richness from a smaller and more specialized canvas, the American high school. Here it is initial networks, among youngsters feeding in from diverse elementary schools and family clusters, which are overtaken by corporate, but not much organized, forms of social space forma-tion. Coleman's is one of the few books which print actual graph dia-grams of networks, but the substantive theme of the book is the pre-occupations and machinations of actors situated in these networks to become assimilated to the "right" sorts of cliques. These are the "in" crowds on a social level, specializing variously around clothes, clubs, hangouts, sports, and so on.

Coleman's central vision is the importance of corporateness, of categorical identification at a more basic level of phenomenology. Adolescents above all are seeking a sense of belonging through emo-tionally grounded inclusion in the right sets. Coleman argues that school sports, especially in competitive leagues, are the single most important venue. Scholastic achievements have no broadly appeal-ing forms as representatives or even exemplars of school identifi-cation.

Abstraction in belonging is what high schools engender, it seems from Coleman's comparative study of eight near Chicago. Younger kids have corporate identifications too, but these are not only usually smaller, they are also specific and concrete. High school induces one to perceive and to structure one's actions toward corporates which simultaneously are real and abstract. This is not an easy learning task, so that one can expect intense emotions to be generated. Pri-vacy, away from the structures of larger contexts, is not as available for adolescents as for adults. Rituals come into being.

The dynamics supporting memberships in corporates are the main puzzle. Think of neighborhood bars and acquaintance dances as locales where corporates may be built across persons. Neither is or consists in disciplines. Both, like any processes in public space, intermix network and corporate aspects. Neither can be reduced to just groups or to just network graphs. But the differences between bars and dances are instructive for us.

"Neighborhood" can be vague and amorphous in delineating actors and their ties. A bar can be a significant influence in shaping perceptions that there exists a neighborhood and who and what pairs are in the neighborhood as a penumbra to the bar. But what determines an establishment's going down the road of locality? When is it a gay bar or an ice hockey hangout, or whatever—and when may several of these all roll into one consistent compendium?

A tie to another who is habituated to the bar is a major avenue of at least starting attendance there. You may have heard some other way that your kind of person hangs out there. To become a neighborhood bar is to grow a particular kind of corporateness. Networks are pressured. Over time, persons living near the bar are very much more likely than actors in a larger population to get caught up in a tie or identification with the bar. Just as real, others who do by chance come around do not have ties and identifications proffered but rather find some signs of exclusion and lack of welcome.

A neighborhood bar helps establish some corporate membership operating largely from networks, the literal geographical locale being an amorphous field of possibility that is consistent with endless alternatives (see Wellman 1988 for more extensive development). The corporateness is fuzzy, and in reality it is never inclusive of any complete local population. Wishful speculations and gaming calculations of social advantage underlie what we find; the supposed sociableness of drinking is less a truth than a stipulation conveniently shared among the speculations in the gamings.

An acquaintance dance or mixer is a converse to this stereotype of how neighborhood bars evolve. Arbitrarily defined corporates, say entering classes at certain colleges, were brought together.[23] This is just so as to generate still further ties and networks out of random seeding of dyads.

There is a duality. In the neighborhood bar, structural equivalence evolves from working networks toward corporate forms. In the acquaintance dance, corporates are worked about to generate ties, which modify networks and might lead to structural equivalence.

An acquaintance dance is a limiting case of explicit coordination

---

[23] This ceremonial form may be disappearing, its replacement not yet clear.

which implies more complex forms of organization, to be introduced in subsequent chapters. Spontaneous versions are common. Boys and girls use any occasion of corporate commonality as basis for exploring and forming couples. Men and women do so as well, usually in more complex contexts of organization, but there is always random rotation on a dance floor of opposite circles to switch dyads at the stopping of music.

Large acquaintance dances are but a first step in a proliferation of self-similar introduction settings nested within one another and across one another. Actors seek more restrictive corporates within the initial mass. More specialized mixers follow. There is a nesting of levels crossing simple partitions into groups. These embeddings go on in time as well as in organization. They go on among elites and in esoteric settings as well as everyday.

Networks also provide contexts for identities on other scales. Networks as well as disciplines grow around and with work and other material production, as the social emerges from the biophysical, as pecking orders turn into discipline mechanisms and open out into ties and stories. Markets are local disciplines which constantly produce and reproduce themselves. They must do so amid and drawing upon a bewildering profusion of networks and of larger formations. Unless input-output coupling for supplies to local sites becomes established, local disciplines will not reproduce. The settling in of production takes the social form of embedding.[24]

Story and Behavior

Stories cite behavior. Behavior guides stories. But behavior is actions on specific occasions involving essentially external and sometimes superficial relationships. Story goes beyond behavior to weave interpretation into relationships, which is what generates recognition of indirect ties, and thus of network as population.

The duality of story and relationship carries through on extended scale and higher level. V. O. Key (1945, p. 304) says, "Whether the

---

[24] In Florence and other Italian cities of the early Renaissance, production of cloth induced networks for "putting-out" aspects of producing a product, each of which aspects could itself become established as product of separate market (e.g., Lachmann and Peltersen 1988). There were similar developments into *verlager* and *kaufmann* systems (Kriedte, et al. 1981), in the hinterlands of medieval networks of German cities, as early entrepreneurs "put out" raw materials and/or tools to cottagers and then "marketed" the resulting production which they collected. And the process was elaborated further in subsequent periods and locales (e.g., Bythell 1978). Chapter 5 will develop further this account of networks in an economy.

existence of issues causes the formation of continuing groups of politicians or whether the existence of competing groups causes the issues to be raised is a moot point." Padgett takes a similar stance in a work on the Medici:

"Rationality" for us does not mean subjective expected utility theory; it means adaptive local action . . . leaders (as well as all others) carefully analyze their own particular situation, and intentionally scheme to improve it, in terms of the cognitive categories or continua laid down in the dominant culture. (Padgett and Ansell 1989, p. 4)

Their concept of adaptive local action is close to control operating in network of ties, and their categories and continua become here stories and valuations. The boundaries of adaptive local action are the boundaries of network.

Stories are vital to maintaining as well as generating social spaces for continuing actions. A recent study of a famous charity genre (Brilliant 1990) illustrates this: The initial purport of some Foundation disappears as a new and simple cure comes through medical innovation. The standard story-set about treated cures and untreated disasters from syndrome x no longer holds. The Foundation regroups by inventing a new story-set, again heart-rending. One story-set is substituted for another with no major changes necessary in the behavior and ties of the Foundation.

Types of Tie

The multiplex tie contributes, as a cause and mechanism of exchange, to allocation and to distribution more generally. For processes where undifferentiated connectivity is the issue, multiplex network is suitable: This is tie as coupler. But ties also go with decoupling, which fits with factoring into distinct types of tie.

Processes even of diffusion, much less of manipulations for control, cannot be treated properly by a network stripped-down to sheer connectivities. Ties and nodes alike are socially constructed and become embedded in social spaces while at the same time being constrained by ecological space. Much insight about connectivity was derived in pioneer network studies (e.g., Coleman, Katz, and Menzel 1966) and small-world studies (Travers and Milgram 1969; cf. Kochen 1989). Some of it derives from parallels to models for epidemics (Bailey 1957, 1982). But these studies themselves come to the conclusion that more depth in the phenomenology of ties is required, and simultaneously more depth of analysis about embeddings.

Leifer Ties

Control is sought in, and thereby it loosens, all formations. The smallest formation is the pair, which nonetheless defines subtle processes when both in the pair relation are actively contending for control. Leifer (1991) has developed a theory for such a tie of maximum intensity. He terms this a theory of local action, but as will become clear it can as well be termed robust action.

Robust action comes from unraveling of, but is a sophisticated replacement for, the dominance ordering which could override any particular tie within a discipline mechanism. Leifer's fundamental point is that unending gaming and speculation is a constituent of any tie significant to both its actors and to onlookers, which is to say an intense tie that is contributing to active processes and larger structures.

The initial example used in Leifer's work was tournament chess games. Tournaments are an unusually transparent structure and process for establishing and observing pairs as encounters, and then deriving identities from these pairs, for these tournaments are coordinated to yield public and reliable rankings of players across national populations. Yet Leifer ties are the subtle ties, constituted by skilled players locked in positional balance. Accounts heard about the ongoing relation between players in actual play are vague compared to the stories that accompany other instances of ties and disciplines.

It is exactly from this transparent example that it becomes evident that clear goals are antithetical to establishing identities. Robust action is just that which permits gaming and speculation to continue, which prevents anyone from seeing clearly an outcome that would end the tie. Ongoing relations lack the sharpness of a conceded game. The transparency of chess, tournament chess, as a social context makes apparent the cost of robust or local action. In good chess, the better the game the more likely a draw. Leifer goes on to show that players of tournament quality are, as persons, aware of and sustain ambiguity in their play.[25]

On the one hand, the long-established context of tournament chess has been worked out to minimize differences between players in a game. Thus only pairs thought likely to sustain a tie of robust action are encouraged. On the other hand, great care is taken about what population of pairs to form, what network of encounters to ar-

---

[25] Through careful dissection of samples of games and tournaments to support his interpretation of the extensive chess literature.

range. The arrangement is to ensure a clear spread of ranking and thus it increases the number and distinctness of identities.[26]

It seems a paradox. Robust social action, and identities as by-products, presuppose a veil over intermediate goals that may be driving play in a game. Furthermore, robust action is likely to negate the ostensible end goal, which is a victory, an assignment of asymmetry. The better established the identity of a player (that is, the higher his scores in the meticulously computed rankings of the chess world), the more his actions avoid events, which is to say striking losses or gains.

Events become important as medium in which already established actor-identities interact, fill out stories, and possibly lead to still further embeddings into identity. Leifer's ingenious dissection of chess playing among experts can be extended to a wide gamut of strategic interaction. Chess skill—and, by analogy, strategic social skill in general—consists exactly in keeping the state of interaction hard to assess through being pregnant with very many possible evolutions.

Skilled chess players come into existence by the blatant discrepancies in play with other players initially just chosen at random: in short, through events which later come to be reported as striking. Thereafter the skilled identity continues functioning by avoiding just the mismatches which gave rise to it; the identity is now embedded in a different level, almost a disjunct world where expertness is the agreed basis, to be demonstrated by avoidance of what can be seen by outsiders to be action.

Thus events and identities variously embed action in further levels of the creation of still further identities. The mismatches and multiplicities that generate identities are in turn themselves regenerated. As they are regenerated, stories adjust to changing ties.

Any such ties are stable only through being ambivalent and ambiguous at any particular instant and in any tangible action. A set of such ties can embed into a team, or into an identity, exactly because purposes and standings are unclear. Leifer both establishes and solves the paradox of such a tie, the conundrum of achieving comparability through attempted inequality.

Romantic love is another extreme case of Leifer tie. It is extreme, first, on intensity—but no more so than are competitive ties between chess masters. But here the conundrum is achieving inequality through the attempt at utter equality.

[26] This can be analyzed further in terms of the disciplines of chapter 2. Leifer has gone on (1992) to study long stretches of outcomes from professional sports team encounters, and uncovers a variety of larger institutions and styles: see also Mizruchi (1991).

The defining characteristic of romantic love is that it is not embedded in everyday networks; it comes "out of the blue," socially. Thus, romantic love need not concern sexual attractions, either hetero- or homosexual. Some bolt-from-the-blue relations have always been found, even in tribal contexts. Where we think of Jane Austen and ceremonial combat, Germanic tribes thought of blood brothers in physical combat.

Types of Tie

Stories come to frame choices, from among those innumerable distinctions and nuances which could be imposed upon relationships in hindsight or from the outside. This is a dialectic in which distinct hues, distinct types of tie can come to be recognized. For example, agency leads into a tie which has a single concern, even though it can be as all-embracing for a short period as is a multiplex total tie. Types of tie then become the alphabet of accountings, and evolve partly as a rhetoric of story-set.

A name for an identity makes it transferable at the same time as unique, so that a name is the primitive of "position."[27] Similarly, a label for a juncture, a "tie" type, is transferable. The colorings, the animuses of distinctive stories, that give content to types of ties are borrowed from discipline valuations.

A tie can be distinguished by intensity level. At one extreme is the multiplex tie of sociometry and casual gossip, the ties of everyday networks spun out in bar and acquaintance dance, and on playing field or in Rapoport's junior high. These are overall ties as commonly perceived, weak ties in Granovetter's terminology. The other extreme is the tie of maximum intensity. Such a tie embodies skilled sustaining of interchange and perception between identities, skill which perhaps helped to induce the identities.

Lump strong ties together with the weak ties of everyday networks into Granovetter ties. Granovetter ties, both weak and strong, are multiplex connections between identities.[28] Multiplex ties maintain themselves through narrative stories able to account for uncertainties both physical and social. But this gives only a black-and-white portrayal of the scene.

Types of ties also are incident between disciplines but are distinct from Granovetter ties. Types of tie occupy the middle range of inten-

[27] This is developed as a construct in chapter 4.

[28] It may prove to be the case that strong ties can only subsist between identities of the same species of discipline, whereas weak ties are like types of tie in having incidence possible between any pair of actors or disciplines.

sity in between the strong and weak extremes for Granovetter ties. Granovetter ties-of-the-extreme are less nuanced than ties of medium intensity.

All ties are defined by, and induce and respond to, stories. When control pressures between identities are either less or more than the pressures inside disciplines, stability over time can be anticipated for such networks. Then is when multiple networks by type of tie can't be recognized. Types of tie are factored from a set of stories. Any tie of intermediate intensity can be diffracted into one or more types of tie, where each type goes with a particular story from a standard set of stories, a menu.

A common menu of stories builds up over time across some array of identities, some population of disciplines brought into the same social space by Granovetter ties, weak and strong, which themselves are accompanied by narrative stories. Each story on such menu can come to be seen as a type of tie, at least for a particular period in that population. Some stories descend from the valuations for embedding identities as disciplines in the population.

Distinct types of tie form networks which are distinct not only to observers but to actors themselves. An identity can be very differently positioned in one and another such network. Two actors who are joined by one type of tie may have no connections in other types, or may have connections there to third parties which appear complementary to their joint tie.

Differentiation of ties is no passive, detached affair. Types of tie evolve as a by-product from endless trading-off among different control efforts across identities. Multiplex networks report how the various identities have spread their presences in the course of these struggles. As control struggles continue, the ties themselves, which report stymied states of struggle, are subject to splits into distinct types of tie. This factoring process can be illuminated by an extensive literature on observation of discussion groups, much of it distilled by Bales (1970).

New and additional control can be achieved by some actors when a network of multiplex ties becomes factored as by common agreement into distinct subnetworks of types of tie. One illustration is the trenchant analysis by Padgett and Ansell (1989) of the rise to supreme power of the Medici faction within the Florentine polity of the 1400s. Everyone can see that the Medici centralized control; what was less obvious is that they segregated ties to different dependents into different sorts of connections. This kept the dependents relatively separated and segregated, connected only via the Medici themselves and therefore not a good base for success in the chronic countercontrol attempts.

To recapitulate, identities become embedded into some narrative stories with respect to others in a network population during the course of continuing control struggles. Control struggles work upon strong and weak ties, and under pressure from identities' interactions with one another, narrative stories open out into sets of stereotyped stories across a population. A type of tie is a stereotype story, and its incidence on pairs of actors can be seen as a distinct network.[29] The control struggles open up a multiplex network into distinct networks for separate types of tie.

These types of tie, these stereotype stories, are social accountings, which are as much perception by third parties as by the "ends" or nodes of a tie itself. This third party may be an observer or analyst. Network now becomes an analytic construct as well as commonsense phenomenology.

Types of tie confound differences between relations with differences in their framing; that is, they confound distinctions in structural context for, with distinctions by asymmetries and strengths and qualities in, pair ties. Even so, types of tie have face validity and enable effective prediction of changes both in relations and their structure, as seen in the blockmodels of the next section. And theoretical interpretation of these blockmodels leads to rediscovery of "role frames."[30]

Blockmodels derive various possible implications for how multiple networks may imply aggregation of actors, and aggregation of types of tie simultaneously, into some articulated larger structure. Any such structure is one of an array of such structures latent in the context, dependent for activation upon impetuses of chance and control. Incidences of types of tie are not some extraneous analytic matter, they are part of the armaments of manipulation for control.

---

[29] This was formulated as the Axiom of Quality originally (cf. Lorrain and White 1971).

[30] As pointed out later, blockmodels derived in part from analyses of kinship systems, so that the rediscovery is hardly surprising, but it is nonetheless striking that sociometric data which is not referred in any way to role constructs turns them up through computation: see White, Boorman, and Breiger (1976). "Role frames" are idealized formulations of social relations which are rendered flexible through the use of story-sets. The construct of role frame will be defined and pursued further in chapter 4. Role theory is a general perspective in social science (Biddle 1986; Gross et al. 1958; Merton 1968; Nadel 1955), which as yet encompasses networks and embeddings only in latent fashion.

Specialization and Time Horizon

Specialization describes how the ecological is patched into the social in work (Udy 1970), and it then has a technical or engineering cast. Specialization also comes out of the emergence of disciplines. Types of tie can be explained and their number can be estimated in terms of specializations.

A recent definitive study of hunter-gatherer demographics (Howell 1979, 1988)[31] finds about sixteen relatives recognized by a particular ego. And every kind of relation, practical and emotional, is construed in kinship terms in this mode of human social life.[32] Thus sixteen is a good bet for the upper limit of distinct relations sustainable by human beings.

In modern society but at much smaller scope, Sampson,[33] in his meticulous and fine-grained study of a monastery's entering novitiate, differentiates eight types of tie, but he imposes them as a grammar of affections and they do not in fact all produce distinct configurations. This collapse to very few distinct types confirms extensive experience with sociometric testing on small populations: compare Bjerstedt (1956) on classrooms and Newcomb on fraternities; and on large populations see Burt (1985) and Fischer (1982).

Social times as well as social spaces are articulated by networks of ties. A strong tie, as seen from inside it, constitutes a continuing control struggle between two identities, and this struggle defines the phenomenological present, which in terms of biophysical space-time is a fuzzy set (Zadeh et al. 1975) rather than an instant. Other multiplex ties, Granovetter's weak ties, are seen more from the outside, by others or by observers. These weak ties can span and refer to years of biophysical time.

All the other, differentiated types of tie correspond to the whole intermediate range of times neither short nor long. Qualitative distinctions among ties hold for intermediate periods. One can confirm this by turning to how actors themselves distinguish types of tie, especially in complex and differentiated contexts. These contexts involve unbundling overall relations into the types of tie. One major example is the system uncovered by working out the connotations of

[31] Her estimate, for an African setting, confirms the most detailed data available in print for Australian aborigines (Rose 1960).

[32] To this end, marriage choice is constrained in terms of kinship, as are residence and foraging. Howell's findings are not inconsistent with the little deduced about early hominids by archaeological reconstructions.

[33] His thesis of 1968 has not, unfortunately, ever been published; see Boyd (1991) for definitive analysis.

the terms favoritism, nepotism, and venality. A variety of studies here (e.g., Kelsall 1955; Namier 1961; Mousnier 1971, 1984; Swart 1949) establish a time frame. Job placements commonly involve such unbundlings.[34]

Diffusion: An Example

Diffusion of information significant enough to trigger consequential actions observable across a population provides a basis for assessing evolution of types of tie in network patterns. Burt (1987, 1990) has built upon and summed up a tradition of study and modeling for diffusion of innovation. The tradition rests on a few definitive field studies. In particular, Coleman, Katz, and Mendel (1966) generated a reliable record of actual prescriptions of a new drug in a city by doctors whose network patterns they investigated: the strength of the study was its anchoring in specific events.

Innovations generate ambivalence. High standing can come from adoption, but so can scorn, depending on what comes to be accepted as the worth of the innovation. That worth in turn is no isolate technical truth but rather is negotiated by interaction of numbers of actors who adopt and are pleased, and it is also assessed with haughtier and more specialized verdicts likelier to shape cultural traces. To be crude, "early but not too early" seems an apt stance for those already of high standing, doctors as a group and within them the better-placed ones. The original study has much information and insight on corporate aspects of these issues.

There are ways to crudely allow for corporate effects, as Burt shows. But there is no data for discriminating networks by intensity of tie.[35] As often in social science, a good probe becomes unusable as the study of population examined moves from inexperienced and low status, like junior high school students, to loftier adult persons of affairs. But, on the other hand, for much the same reasons timing becomes more visible in actions, and these tend to be actions that are consequential.

Adoptions of the new drug among this town's physicians, controlling for corporate statuses and effects, generate a mosaic in time which Burt (1987) shows to be interleaved with the mosaic of structural equivalence in social space. Network ties are from a single crude measure of whom ego discusses professional medical matters

[34] But that depends on overall context. For example, under clientelistic spoils systems no differentiation of skills may be recognized and hence there is no unbundling of tie in awarding spoils.

[35] As from Rapoport traces of different order: see earlier in this chapter.

with among colleagues in the town. Social space is mushed into an artificial Cartesian representation, but on the basis of the quintessential social relation of structural equivalence.

Structural equivalence asserts how important it is that two actors see and relate to—especially on similar topics—rather much the same set of other actors, if there is to emerge, through a myriad of instant transactions, similarity in the views and acts of the given two. Close location in the Cartesian space conjured to the observer's eye boils down an average of a great deal of structural equivalence. Timing of major acts, such as first prescriptions of the new drug, should interlock with this array of locations in social space.

It does. A few clusters of doctors are so completely interconnected with each other in the cluster that stringing becomes cohesion and is indistinguishable from structural equivalence. And just here a particular tie of advice, between a particular pair within the cluster, does not stand out and predict closer timing. Such a cluster is so saturated with closeness that more elaborated cultural and hierarchical influences intervene in decision. Most physicians, as in any actual population of size, have little connection and thus not the raw material for much structural equivalence with most of the others.

A crucial intermediate set of doctor dyads are intermediate in that they are rather close in the Cartesian space—they share, and are structurally equivalent with respect to many neighbors in the space—yet by no means do they cohere into a cluster of near-complete connectivity. Timing is significantly correlated just in these circumstances. A reported tie of professional discussion activates similar adoption dates just when the physician pairs are acquaintances, so to speak. Time has different social meanings and results according to its interpenetration with locale and topology of social space.

"Boundary" is seen to be a problematic concept for social phenomena, in time or space. Boundaries are both matters of perception and of construction and thus subject to speculation and to gaming. The physicians are demarcated only fuzzily on their own account, as is the community in which they are operating. In fact it seems natural to think of several subpopulations of doctors, which overlap only partially and differ on locale, specialty, standing, and age.

Further layers of embedding and of control (e.g., of "certification" and of "residence") must be invoked and recognized to yield an edge for analysis, and there is little sign of that in this particular naturalistic observation of diffusion of prescription of a new drug. Networks and corporates were uncovered as explanatory pointers in field work and analysis among the physicians. In contrast, boundaries either were impositions of convenience to demarcate the field work, or pointed entirely outside the scenes accessible to this field work, like regulations on issuing and recording prescriptions.

The principal conclusion is that processes even of diffusion, much less of manipulations for control, cannot be described properly in a stripped-down network viewed as sheer physical connectivities. Ties and identities alike are socially constructed, not just imposed by observers. And multiple types of tie are generated, not just the overall multiplex tie. Thereby disciplines and identities come to be perceived as being embedded in more commodious social spaces while at the same time being constrained by ecological space.

Blockmodels of Structural Equivalence

Blockmodels parse distinct relational aspects among actors into feasible clusterings. This is the obverse to the focus on establishing continuity in character that obtained for the multiplex networks. Each focus has distinctive cultural accoutrements, and quite different procedures are appropriate for modeling and measuring the two.

A blockmodel[36] interprets multiple networks, one from each type of tie, in terms of a particular network-population. Blockmodels identify different possible stable balancings of control projects within that population, separated out from production pressures from the biophysical ecology. The outcomes are possible partitions of the original population, and each partition defines a set of possible identities called blocks, which are candidates to become disciplines if and as that partition emerges from control struggles.[37]

The Rapoport-Granovetter tracing of connectivity can be subsumed, in principle, in career analyses. And career analysis exhibits some similarity to blockmodels. Both are relativist, both are couched in terms of structural equivalence. Also both are concerned with specifying connectivity paths, the former in multiplex and the latter in multiple networks.

Career is another construct which can help analyze interactions among networks. But career does so at the cost of lumping together different aspects of relations within a given pair, as a multiplex tie.

---

[36] I use the term "blockmodel" generically to refer to several distinct lines of development which are surveyed most recently by Freeman, D. White, and Romney (1989). The one full-length treatment in print is Boyd (1991), to which I return in Appendix 2.

[37] And relations between blocks are candidates to outline a role frame: see note 30.

The contrast, in blockmodels, is to dissect ties into separate aspects and then treat each as a separate analytic network across the field of actors.

Dissection into Types of Tie

Summarize subtle, real-time interactions in a pair-tie, embracing all aspects of the dyad, as a dyad-as-process. To construct a blockmodel, one has first to pull apart these dyads-as-processes into a cross-sectional record. This is a record of which set of dyads share each of several qualities of relation that may be distinguished explicitly only by the analyst. A story set in the population both guides and reflects this dissection into a set of types of tie.

Discriminating among types of tie is a hallmark of expertness in the sociocultural milieu, but there are formal techniques for helping an observer sort out the discriminations (cf. Burt 1985, 1990). The problem is to sort out types in a particular concrete population. Techniques are needed that go beyond both tribal kinship lore and early sociometric studies. Some network of all-purpose multiplex ties of low intensity is what may be perceived by actors involved, as well as uncovered by research in a population. But upon further scrutiny the ties may be seen to devolve into special networks, each a network of ties with focus from a particular stereotype story.

From systematic case studies, such as Stenton and Searle made of the Normans, reported in the next chapter, one can argue for three universal ways in which types of tie get discriminated.[38] The first way discriminates a type of tie on the basis of the pattern of overlaps observed among disciplines and corporate groups. Especially in tribal contexts (e.g., Hart and Pilling 1960; Rose 1960), age and gender corporates spring into relief as intersections, such as "old men in councils."

Absolutist France is another unusually rich tapestry of enacted and self-conscious corporate forms, based on underlying disciplines, and offers an array of overlaps. Mousnier (1984) magisterially surveys the inclusions and exclusions among them which served to underline and define importances of various attributes. In our own day, classic field studies of communities (e.g., Hollingshead 1949; Gans 1962)

---

[38] This is aside from self-conscious cultural formulations such as Duby's (1980) three realms. Others also relate type of tie to the concept of "realm," on which I quote Tillich (1963, III, p. 16): "'Realm' is a metaphor like 'level' and dimension,' but it is not basically spatial (although it is this too); it is basically social. A realm is a section of reality in which a special dimension determines the character of every individual belonging to it, whether it is an atom or a man."

portray overlaps, exclusions, and nestings among less formal corpo-rates (especially class and neighborhood) as generating meanings and interpenetrations as a corporate calculus of lives and ties. The anthropologist Smith has attempted (1975) to raise an entire general theory of social action just on corporates and their interlocks.

The second universal basing for types of tie is asymmetry in rela-tion. Differentiation into distinct networks commonly grows out of tendencies toward persistent asymmetry in ties. Asymmetry gener-ates specialization of (symmetric) relation. In modern Thailand an unusually sharp example of the institutionalization of asymmetry in a tie seems to occur.[39] Agency seems to be at the root of asymmetry across even the most remote examples.

Indirect Ties

There is a third universal basis for separate types of tie emerging, besides overlaps and asymmetry. This is institutionalization of indi-rect ties. Participants and observers alike persuade themselves it is cogent to single out just such ties as a network of its own.

Kinship is the premier instance: for example, grandparents, cous-ins, uncles, in our Western parsing, or mother's brother's daughter, father's sister's daughter, or elder sibling's descendants, or mother's mother's brother's daughter's daughter and the like in various other kinship systems (White 1963). In Riggs's Thailand two clientship ties, if both to the same party, generate, by observable processes on the ground, a nexus of behavior between those indirectly connected that is sufficiently distinct to be recognized as such. Thus is encour-aged recognition in that society of other sets of parallel ties as a sepa-rable type.

It seems from the wide gamut of case studies available that the indirect tie will tend to be more homogeneous in intensity and in concrete attributes than the direct ties which occasion its phenom-enological construction. In the Norman case treated in chapter 4, magnates' conscious efforts to enhance recognition of indirect ties of fealty tended to generate a much more uniform quality of relation than the direct ties, despite the latter being much more uniform than in the preceding Anglo-Saxon regime. What makes the ambiance of Thai society so distinctive is not the patronage tie in itself, but rather the universality of recognition of indirect ties carried to the bounds of total population: it is the limiting case of network population as universe.

---

[39] Cf. Riggs (1966), but he has provoked rejoinders.

There is a countervailing process: Ties, once discriminated, may again be thrown back together into a common kind, with attendant acknowledgment of diverse and subtle multiplexities in particular exemplars. This can be part of embedding networks and corporates into still further levels. Again in the Norman example there are processes, mediated by money mechanisms, of *scutage* and *infangenetheof*, where indirect tie rights are made fungible, available in direct tie.

And just as indirect-tie formation tends to generate recognition of distinctiveness for other sorts of ties, at the same time the relevant scope of population is tending to be enlarged, which in itself would tend to weaken recognition of distinctness. The base kind of asymmetric tie may be changed so as to no longer generate indirect relations, as in the Norman development of the mere household knight; whereas symmetric ties universally seem to generate indirect ties that are recognized.

The combination of asymmetric and indirect modes for generating recognition of distinct types of tie yields a richer variety of patterns than indirect chaining of symmetric ties from overlaps. The latter tend toward a form of solidarity or mutual common reference. The former exhibit that also, as in the omnipresent formation of councils and courts among dependents at the same remove from a Norman lord, but they may further string into the mutually aversive chains of dependence which characterize clientelism (on which also see chapter 4).

Contrasts between symmetric and asymmetric in ties are developed and played out in the dissection by Padgett and Ansell of the rise and consolidation of the Medici. Their paper is unusual in the number of types of ties distilled from the historical accounts. There are nine, and then the analysis goes on (1989, p. 17) to argue aggregation into two families, one of strong types of tie—each one tending to inbreeding in the sense of Rapoport traces—and the other a family of weak types of tie which cluster the actors quite differently according to structural equivalence.

Each type of tie may be distinctive in formation of a species of discipline. There seems to be a loose correspondence between, on the one hand, these three universal ways or modes of induction for tie types, suggested by case studies, and, on the other hand, the three species of discipline from chapter 2. Asymmetric tie suggests the interface species, overlap tie the council species, and indirect tie suggests the arena species. It is instructive to match this abstract partition—based on overlap, symmetry, and catenation of ties seen quite apart from disciplines—with a substantive partition common in the literature (e.g., Laumann and Pappi 1976): business, honor, and professional, respectively. But it is a distortion of the social material to argue for the neat and tidy in either discriminations or mappings— except as imposed by the analyst for purposes of inferential computation.

A warning is called for, harking back to the earlier section on tracing. Even stripped-down networks are exceedingly complex mechanisms for any sort of process, diffusion, or manipulation. While the actors rely on intuition, context, and stereotypes, modeling is indispensable for the observer and analyst.

Blocks into Disciplines

Control efforts get reflected in the evolution of patterns across types of tie. This evolution can be modeled as the differing incidence of emerging compounds in types of tie on the population. Structural equivalence then suggests possible partitions of the original nodes. Each partition specifies a possible set of new disciplines that can become embedded.

A blockmodel is a conjecture as to partition into sets of nodes which may each take corporate form as disciplines under control pressures implied by the pattern of observed ties (see Burt 1978b). The pattern is assessed by examining the incidence for various compoundings of types of tie, for example clustering of friends' enemies ties may overlap enemy but not friend ties. The incidence for a given sort of tie is reported as a matrix in which nodes are sorted out the same for both row choosers and column receivers, and specifically according to the conjectured partition. The distinctive signal is the absences of ties of a given sort between particular pairs of conjectured corporates (White 1973).

A zeroblock appears as the absence of that sort of tie (either original type of tie or derived compound of types of tie) among its constituent actors. There is no necessary implication that a compound actor is cohesive, is bound together positively or is even aware of "itself." At some given time character as a discipline may not have been demonstrated despite structural equivalence as to interrelations with the other corporate actors across all the sorts of tie.

In practice these "zeroblocks," in the matrix reporting connections, are never pure. This is in part due to the unreliabilities in data, which are multiplied by the computational process for compounding ties. In part it is due to the fuzziness of social relationships.

This resembles the less abstract discussion of "catnets" in the previous chapter, which concretized the tangible process of social formation which obtains when more production-oriented forms are not feasible. Faulkner's (1983) brilliant account of evolution of movie-making teams in Hollywood appears to be an example. Here blockmodels can be used to describe the catnet process which stands in for production-defined disciplines in that context of balanced tensions.

Another example is portrayed in figure 3-2. In his participant-observer study of the staff of a psychiatric residential treatment center, Frank Romo predicted, from this blockmodel of network ties in the early months, who left as the staff disintegrated over a year.

Structural Equivalence

The blocks discriminate themselves as by-products of structural equivalence among the set of networks. Thus a blockmodel predicts how a set of disciplines may embed from a set of networks. This embedding is realized in a role structure, portrayed as interlocking mutual relations among blocks within the population. There is a parallel to a discipline as the embedding of an identity from a mechanism.

Structural equivalence is entirely relativist (for further discussion see D. White and Reitz 1983; Doreian 1987). It requires bootstrapping. That is, equivalence among a given compound actor is determined only with respect to other compound actors—but each of them in turn is defined only with respect to the presumed existence of the others including the initially given one. And this relativism is simultaneously dual with respect to the sorts of ties distinguished among the endless array of compounds as being distinct in implications for social action.

The effectiveness of blockmodels owes much to the native paradigms already developed (Boyd 1969, 1991; and see Appendix 2 below) in a number of cultures, tribal and other, for computing complex kinship corporatenesses as by-products of, and consistent with, particular kin relations and chains of relations. See Rose (1960) for exemplary data; such robustness and reliability in gathering data are essential to effective blockmodeling.

There are two distinct lines of technical development, in terms of graphs and of algebras. Wasserman and Faust (1991) offer a synoptic statistical perspective on both approaches to blockmodeling. Boyd (1991) provides the most complete mathematical exposition of both algebraic and graph approaches to blockmodels; and see Pattison (1989). Figure 3-3 reports the blockmodel which Boyd has subjected to the most intense scrutiny. It models the classic Sampson study of relations in a small, closed monastery, and correctly predicts the clusters of novitiates who abandoned the monastery in turn after a crisis from algebra and graphs of their relations.

RELATIONAL EQUIVALENCY & FORMAL HIERARCHY
STRATFIELD PSYCHIATRIC FACILITY -- TIME 1 DATA

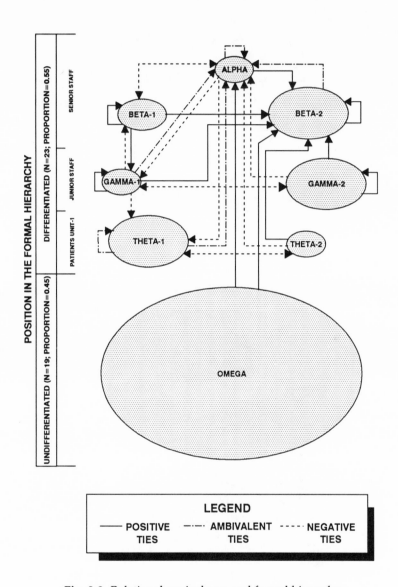

Fig. 3-2. Relational equivalency and formal hierarchy

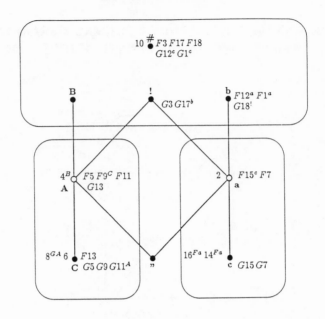

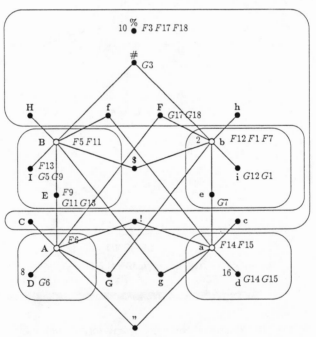

Fig. 3-3. Boyd's blockmodel of Sampson's Monastery

Breiger's model of semiperiphery systems is a substantive theory which utilizes both forms of blockmodeling. Using an algebraic equation discovered early, by Lorrain and Boorman, the so-called First Letter-Last Letter Law, Breiger (1979) interpreted leadership as a system. He interprets it in terms of core-periphery graphs.

In the first line of development, implied indirect ties are constructed in families of paths, each family compounding specified types of tie in fixed sequence. Blockmodels originally were generated as homomorphisms in an algebraic formulation (White 1973).[40] The models draw inferences as to likely inductions of structural equivalence, among actors and dually among ties. Partitions on the initial actors can be induced which suggest "blocks" of structurally equivalent actors. These blocks are candidates, on structural-pattern grounds, for acting as, and possibly becoming recognized as, compound actors, with respect to the dual aggregation into a few types of compound paths. The appropriate mathematical language is representation theory of semigroups of binary relations (Clifford and Preston 1961, 1967).

In this algebraic approach to blockmodels, one computes successively the myriad individual compound networks, that is, the pattern of incidence, for example, of friend's workmate from the incidence of friend and the incidence of workmate (Boorman and White 1976; Lorrain 1975). The principal conjecture concerns these patterns: Will one compound pattern be like another, or like one of the starting patterns? The basic axiom, the Axiom of Quality (Lorrain and White 1971), is that two compounds with the same incidence across all dyads of the population can be assimilated as equivalent in their implications about social actions.

Mathematically, this means that algebraic compounds of types of ties, different specified products of types, are equated if the resulting compound networks are the same. The rationale is that the endless cycling of messages and transfers and oppositions and the like, which are initiated and move according to impulses coded as separate primary ties, would not join exactly the same pattern of dyads to each other unless they had the same resultant form of impact, indirect and direct. The Axiom of Quality is an extreme form of structural equivalence which ties networks in with embedding, and which gets at a deep ambiguity—a tie is both part of the architecture of social

---

[40] Works in this vein, usually with computer implementations, include Bonacich (1980); Bonacich and McConaghy (1979); Boyd (1980); Boorman and White (1976); Breiger (1979); Breiger and Pattison (1978, 1986); Kim and Roush (1978); McConaghy (1981); Pattison and Bartlett (1982); and Mandel (1983). New developments include Pattison (1982, 1989); Winship and Mandel (1984)—on which see chapter 4 on positions; and Wu (1983). Some are surveyed in Bonacich (1989), and in Pattison (1988).

space and at the same time an action record having to do with quality and/or strength of tie.

The second line of development emphasized graph-theoretic reduction of the initial sets of ties (White and Breiger 1975; White, Boorman, and Breiger 1976). This was based on a concept of structural equivalence (Lorrain and White 1971) which was discovered independently by others (e.g., Burt 1976; Sailer 1978).[41]

In this second approach to blockmodels, the essential calculations derive conjectures as to which of the initial actors in the population of dyads can be clustered as structurally equivalent. A blockmodel is a partition into compound actors. The distinctive finding is where there are no incidences at all of a given tie or compound. Zeroblocks are where there is no example of that sort of tie between two blocks, that is, between two of the compound actors conjectured.

In fact, mapping into a partition of compound actors, blocks, is seen to be a dual process, in which at the same time sorts of compound ties are also being mapped into a partition, a dual partition which clusters together an array of sorts of compound or elementary ties into the same image tie. In algebraic terminology, there is a homomorphic mapping of networks into clusters such that certain equivalences hold among different compoundings. The latter can be called a cultural mapping of qualities of relations into a few clusters of relations.

Distinct types of ties are the base for generalization of identities within networks into further levels in social spaces. "Blockmodeling" of multiple networks is an attempt to capture this process. In so doing, blockmodels suppress physical productions, and instead interplay types of networks with story for disciplines.

Ambiguity versus Ambage

Each blockmodel sketches a possible partition into disciplines that results from pressures indicated in networks of ties. Contingencies have an impact on the outcome and are themselves affected by the

[41] It has been developed in a variety of ways in the social network literature (e.g., Everett 1985; Romo 1992. For overviews see Berkowitz 1982; Burt 1980; Freeman, D. White, and Romney 1989). Most applications (e.g., Breiger 1976, 1979, 1981a; Mitchell 1989; Padgett and Ansell 1989; Salzinger 1982; Snyder and Kick 1979) use this second approach, and most methodology investigations concern it (e.g., Arabie, Boorman, and Levitt 1978; Arabie and Carroll 1989; Breiger, Boorman, and Arabie 1975; Everett 1983; Heil 1983, 1989; Holland, Laskey, and Leinhardt 1983; J. Schwartz 1977; Wang and Wong 1987; Wasserman and Anderson 1987).

changes in network among disciplines. Stories emerge accordingly in sets to accommodate diverse outcomes. Chance effects thus proliferate and also assume interpretive guise and social form.

Discriminate between uncertainty in cultural and uncertainty in social contexts, a discrimination which is subtle and elusive. Analysis of uncertainty in cultural context comes first by itself. An apt term for cultural uncertainty is ambiguity. Then comes contrast with the social form, ambage, followed by a calculus of trade-offs influenced by ecological contingencies. As before, self-similarity is presupposed (for verification in later chapters) to allow a range of scope and level in examples.

Ambiguity in Council Disciplines

Discipline of the council species is highly ambiguous. There is little in the way of systematic doctrine, as already mentioned in chapter 2. It appears that connectivity is the essential to power; the key is being tied to the right faction through the right connection, whether in the Senate or in a family business. When normal reshufflings of faction are traced over time, however, it becomes clear that the essential aspect of structure involved is in fact structural equivalence. No factions and alliances ever stay the same. In the end what counts is the likelihood that your connections will be mobilized because of parallel hostilities and reflected interests with dominant sets of other factions. The combination of fission-fusion with stringing-dependency tends to generate aversive pillars as a by-product of structural equivalence.

The awesome yet ambiguous power of these disciplines goes with an openness and flexibility of agenda. Each council, miniscule and local as it might be in some broader survey, is sovereign in its own concerns. These concerns are limited in and by concrete fact, but they are not limited by any systematic doctrine or rationale.[42] In particular, there is little interpenetration of one council by another, in dependencies and wrangles.

In figure 2-6 the third plane is for maximum differentiation ratio (embedded over decoupled). Mountains out of molehills: the context insisting on imputing great differences in status between actors and strings, even though they are not much different on attributes as separately measured. The clientelism situations common at all levels in Thailand as described by Riggs (1966–1969) are examples. Riggs brings out that the strings are normally short, with dependency

---

[42] In Nadel's terms from chapter 4, role summation is common.

being very much personalized rather than leading to retinues—which seems to fit this plane in general. Thai clienteles are not specialized, as is indicated by their location on the plane for the power mechanism. Another example are the *commissaires* of Renaissance French Absolutism. These latter can be considered as councils making and carrying out wartime military requisitions (Hintze 1919; see Eccles and White 1989 and chapters 4 and 6 below). Dependence is higher, representing the much higher attention of *commissaires* to production.

Hollywood's production system is built around the council-mobilizer mechanism. This was analyzed and documented by Faulkner (1971, 1983), using a modern system of social structure measures derived from blockmodels, and compatible here. At first sight it might appear to be a marketplace, an arena-purifier. But it is the same specialists who come together again and again for packages to be formed, for productions. Major figures find minor ones, from same or other expertises, and bring them in tow into these packages. There is heavy inflation of tiny initial differences in standings.

Trust is required; power is constructed. The two presuppose each other. Mobilization spreads from some beginning link, which at the same time will trigger other, apparently distant links whose actors perceive mobilization toward their social locales. Some distribution, tangible or symbolic, is taking place as a result, but sharing is not built into mobilization automatically. Trust is presupposed and observably justified by some form of historicized tally. This tally must cumulate into a type of tie which is weighted by its history in a succession of chains of mobilization. There is an institutional inflation, as compared to other standards, such as arena ones. This is inflation in that the claims of different ties, if called all together at once, would bankrupt the situation more clearly even than would a run-down of confidence bankrupt a bank.

Now turn to a discipline displaying less ambiguity, but in trade-off with uncertainty in different form.

Ambiguity versus Slack in Disciplines with Purity Valuations

Chapter 2 introduced as the second species of discipline the arena, concerned with selection or matching. The importance of purity valuations in it was developed, and purifier is an alternate designation. Professions and committees both were cited as furnishing examples.

In all purifiers there is a decoupling of external status from internal standing. Within the purifier the practitioners, temporary or permanent, are operating in a collegial mode. There is no tendency toward inducing status discrimination within the purifier. Practitioners as such tend to have special standing when viewed from outside and this is associated with a tendency to impute differential status among practitioners—which need have no relation to any internal standings.

The opaqueness of a purifier permits it to seek matchings which can reduce social flexibility and unrootedness. At the same time it provides rationale for ambiguity being kept fixed, or even fixed up, as seen from outside. The very same committee members who may have just artfully patched up a social tie may, back "outside" the committee, not see that; or similarly not see how they have rigged a generally accepted cultural rule. The unusual degree of social confusion within the purifier is necessary to obfuscate the ambiguity which, according to the formal cultural rules, is being introduced by purifier action.

A purifier is a structure whose system of operation offers high slack. That is, there is not a tight constraint on timing, there is not a tight constraint on the amount of attention and other resources given to this or that situation brought forth. "Slack" is shorthand for uncertainty in social context. One further observes that not even the overall total consumption of attention and other resources is subject to much constraint. We have all noticed that committees tend to go on for unpredictable lengths of time, with unpredictable partition of attention by item. They are subject, even against formal rules, to being convened exceptionally.

High slack is a corollary of the purifier's being out of the main stream, available for unpredictable claims for social fixes. Open air markets are another major institutional embodiment of purifiers, here where the "hurt" to be fixed is a material one. The pure theory of exchange applies (Newman 1965). But this pure theory concerns only the formation of "prices" which are internal to the purifier operation. Left out is the huge slack built into the arbitrary times, occasions, and membership in the pure exchange arena—the swap meets and lawn sales of current times, the village fairs of Skinner's Asia (1964–1965), or early Europe and Africa (Smith 1975).

It may be because of high slack that one finds purifiers so often in whole sets—say lattices of committees for a larger environment. On a longer time-scale, careers are being negotiated more or less explicitly. High slack permits the subtle and endless probing and estimation which lead to invitations and acceptances, and possibly to careers. But this goes beyond particular disciplines to institutional systems.

Ambiguity versus Ambage

Confusion is to be treated as a lawful aspect of process, an aspect to be assessed. Refined distinctions are needed as tools. Assess phenomenological confusion in terms of trade-offs. Make these trade-offs be between specifically social slack and specifically cultural ambiguity.

"Slack" has too many extraneous overtones, of intentional carelessness and the like, to be effective as a term, a tool of discrimination. Instead contrast the term "ambage" with ambiguity. Ambage designates slack in the sense of uncertainty in purely social context. Ambiguity is as before to designate uncertainty in purely cultural context. From its origins the word "ambage" signifies winding or indirect and roundabout ways.[43]

Ambage can be operationalized in several ways.[44] A test of reliability of measuring ambage is needed. One test is correct prediction of the appearance of a tie of specified sort in some action context. This test applies separately for participant and for observer.

More difficult is the problem of transposing the measure to other levels. The nodes of a network, for example, may be identities or they may be corporate blocks such as derive from a structural equivalence analysis such as blockmodeling. And in the next chapter the theory moves on to embrace institutions and individual positions which cross network populations. Transposition of measure across such levels is essential to establishing self-similar theory that can hope to deal with the scrappy mess which is social organization.

The conventions actually used by actors, which may vary arbitrarily as gauged by the social mechanics going on, can be expected to be very resistant to change. These conventions are not mere matters of perception. Exactly because a convention, a set of stories, fits any situation very loosely, it is not subject to refutation by ongoing observation. Ambiguity can be measured as the spread in stories within such a convention.

Pressures for change of conventions will come as by-products of efforts at control. Control struggles that influence conventions in-

---

[43] In previous centuries, ambage also carried meanings of concealment and deceit, but, the Oxford English Dictionary (1933, vol. I) makes clear, that usage has become archaic. The established meaning is "circuitous, indirect or roundabout ways or proceedings, delaying. . . . "

[44] For example, Burt (1992, chaps. 1 and 2) introduces several relevant measures. These center around the construct of redundancy, which, being more abstract than structural equivalence and more concrete than role equivalence, is a good basis for measuring uncertainty in specifically social relations.

duce a further overlay of order, culture. And so the scramble of social organization wends on.

Ambage, on the other hand, concerns the concrete world of social ties, in networks of ties and corporates among nodes. Thus ambage is dual to ambiguity: fuzz in the concrete embodiment as opposed to fuzz in the rules of perception and interpretation. One can see there should be some sort of trade-off between ambage and ambiguity. Blockmodeling treats ambage reduction, measured through zero-blocks, and ambiguity increase from adjoining larger numbers of initial identities into corporate nodes of a partition. The particular blockmodel predicted is that with some intermediate level on both.

Consider how ties bundle and unbundle into types of tie. Uncertainty calculus reduces to a matrix whose focus is either for ambage or for ambiguity. Return to the example of venality versus corruption. The difference is whether those in the setting account for the unbundling and bundling by cultural rules or whether instead they do so by the patterning of social connections.

Consider an example of the trade-off at greater scope. Inviolable tradition, rigid in the way perhaps only found in church liturgy today (Thompson 1961), always goes with arbitrary, capricious decision in specific matters. The Ottoman bureaucracy was an extreme example of this theorem:

> The tendency toward a kind of bureaucratic formalism . . . and restriction of initiative appear at the top-most levels of the ruling class, just as among the clerks of the scribal bureaus . . . the routines of the office confirm that scribal functions tended to be conceived solely in terms of document-producing procedures. . . . The discretional use of power by those in highest positions had as a necessary concomitant the servility, in practical as well as formal jural senses of those who worked in their shadow. The decline of the empire surely compounded both this problem and the bureaucratic formalism. For the progressive loss of control by the central administration over the provinces created a discontinuity between the document-producing processes of the central offices and the world outside. (Findley 1980, pp. 90, 223–36)

American academics today often are bemused by the same phenomenon. In particular, this is when their standing committees on student certification rise to the challenge of "upholding standards." Powell's essay on hybrid network forms in bureaucracy (1987) can be seen as a study of the same trade-off.

Troeltsch's dissection of Christian church formations (in Gierke 1950) suggests how important the translation between ambage and ambiguity is in even the oldest social formations. Troeltsch is puzzled that it is the ecclesiastical church, fully rationalized in Thomism, which encourages heroic and extravagant deeds and sainthood, whereas sects, despite Gospel commitment to radical individualism, do not. Calculus of ambiguity and ambage suggests an explanation.

The ecclesiastical church greatly reduces ambiguity, but it attempts to do so for a differentiated set of roles and positions which yields an inevitable increase in ambage. This increase in ambage measures increased arbitrariness as seen in actual social patterns of relations. The resulting social tension can be eased by denying social fellowship, by instead insisting on an extreme pursuit of rules vis-à-vis the hypostasized residual actor, who is the summation of contextual uncertainty.

By contrast, the sect is Gierke's *genossenschaft* (1953). In the sect, fellowship is carried to a radical extreme in which ambage is minimal. But this is so only so long as all are in step, time after time, in beliefs. And then the ambiguity can be unlimited.

These arguments on the ambage/ambiguity trade-off resemble those of several current theorists of culture. For example, William Connolly says new

> unconscious contrivances of social control . . . (are) a political response to the disaffection many manifest from the roles assigned to them? . . . Foucault's texts seek to document the multiple ways in which modern attempts to liberate sexuality, madness and criminality from arbitrary and repressive controls entangle the self in a web of more insidious controls . . . they enclose the objects of treatment in a web of "insidious leniencies." . . . The conventionalization of social life renders it more susceptible to imperatives of authoritative coordination and those subject to that coordination more resistant to its claims. (1987, pp. viii, 91, 127)

The obvious quality of engagement does not vitiate the implied insight.

Turn to a contrast between two exemplars of social architecture, the English versus the Chinese countrysides in their interpenetration of class with lineage (Bearman 1989; Dibble 1965; Hsiao 1960). The contrast can be formulated in the respective trade-offs between ambage and ambiguity levels. In England daughters and younger sons do not generate or bind lineages; so socioeconomic status of particular families is clear while the abstract outlines of class is fuzzy. In China lineages are agglomerated into a huge clan with the same patronymic so that standing of particular families is buried in an overall repute, which however permits, and fits, sharply defined class and status in the abstract. The ratio of ambage over ambiguity is much higher for the English countryside. The differing trade-offs are the trace in that countryside of endemic struggles over control.

Other examples exhibit still greater transposability. Books and manuscripts are, in computer parlance, locked files for us as contrasted with our oral accounts. So our use of the written for formal reports means ambiguity is reduced, but thereby ambage is increased, which suggests that formal investigations and reports are ceremonial, with little impact on tangible social arrangement.

In Muslim tradition, by contrast, as in earlier Western epic poetry, locking is achieved by oral-code. So investigations conducted there in oral terms, without written reports, may lack the social bite of the public interrogations by committee of our day. Locking also is shown in a person's having an address, or in a larger actor, such as a tribe, having an address. Locking operates toward reducing ambiguity. Therefore locking must increase ambage.[45]

Ritual as Calculus

Mary Douglas (1970) sketches a symbolic approach in which aspects of human bodily functions stand for uncertain social contexts, which is to say for ambage in present terms. Douglas's work argues the possibility of a calculus for unbundling and bundling of action in the same metrics across both social and cultural patternings, for a calculus of trading ambage with ambiguity. Ritual becomes a solution to a problem which can be expressed in such calculus. Ritual becomes a basis for anthropology as a social science.

Douglas distinguishes two social contexts, groups and grids, which translate roughly into corporates and networks. Douglas takes her two contexts as total settings, seen from the inside, for correlations, rather than as boundaries, and so is the same approach as in blockmodels. Her first correlation translates into groups tending to exhibit high ambage, and low ambiguity, as gamings through agencies are played out in forming and reforming bundles of social connections. This group of Douglas is an ideal-type: her group is homogeneous, it is the *genossenschaft* of Gierke again, it is comradeship with its intense ambage that plays converse to minimized ambiguity in role and value—with physical uncertainty bracketed and held constant.

---

[45] Paul DiMaggio comments (personal communication, August 13, 1991): "Working social structures require a mix of bounded solidity and hazy obfuscation (so that the secret of the system is never so entirely revealed to the participants as to block all action)."

This ideal type is not restricted to small or simple settings. The classical polis is such. In the words of Gierke: "The state appeared simply as *the* human association. All social ties were entirely derived from it. . . . The individual had ultimately no autonomous purpose . . . (p. 87). No Roman corporation existed that had not first been recognized by Roman constitutional law as a political unit" (p. 117). The Roman state (Badian 1958, 1982; Mommsen 1885; Reid 1913; Salmon 1970; Stevenson 1939) achieved subtle and extensive policy through delegation of concrete tasks. As also in the Greek polis (Kitto 1958), the subtlety was in ambage and its yielding of policy by manipulation of gamings in social patternings. The polis, like the group of comrades, is insistently homogeneous in cultural terms so that there is little scope for ambiguity. Douglas's argument has only bodily symbolism at work, but it yields a rhetoric that can fit the facts.

The moral evaluative components of ritual should not be allowed to obscure their great importance in sheer representation and cognitive explanation. Ritual expresses a calculus solution as a rhetoric. Fortes argues this for the tribal Tallensi society:

> Even a very simple cultural heritage or social organization may be composed of a large number of strands and elements whose interrelations make up a very elaborate pattern . . . so complex is the overlapping of fields of clanship . . . that the whole system might be compared to a piece of chain mail . . . the basic rule of interclan linkage is that spatial proximity is translated into terms of putative genealogical connection. Ritual collaboration and common ritual allegiances [external *bxcar* cult, Namoo cult, earth shrines, etc.] are indices of common interests and mechanisms of solidarity. . . . The core is the sacrifice. Personal feelings are of secondary importance. . . . At the level of social and political relations between clans . . . the social interests are more complex and diffuse . . . an organizing mechanism of a different order comes into play, the mechanism of ritual. (Fortes 1945, pp. vii, x, 87, 98, 116)

The "chain" mail of corporates overlapping is laid out quite literally for members to learn. This is done by positioning and orderings at and among the unending succession of ritual gatherings, which also allow play for change, in a fashion reminiscent of Mayer's Indian villages with which the next chapter begins.

Douglas's "grid" is loose and porous as social form, but it is differentiated in role and rule, if one grants it enough continuity to warrant a treatment parallel to her groups. The logic of her argument suggests domestic circles, nuclear families in particular, as a paradigmatic example. Ambage—observed uncertainty of patterning in social ties—has little scope there, whereas there is high ambiguity in who is actually doing which role and following which rule. In the Chinese countryside of classical period, families were grouped into huge lineages which subsumed wide ranges of what we would call social class. By contrast, in the classical English countryside innumerable mechanisms decimated this nesting. The operation of ambage and ambiguity calculi thus can be shown to be entirely different, depending on whether levels are nested or rather crosscut.

Contingency and Decoupling

Ritual is specialized as a rhetoric in which a tight correlation of action in biophysical space-time is imposed; for example, as in church liturgy there is exact prescription of times and location. But except in such specialized contexts, contingency must also enter any equation in ambage and ambiguity. This is contingency from the physical world of work together with its social exigencies, from which the social spaces have been spun out initially. Ambage and ambiguity both exist only as a follow-on to contingency.

Any equation thus must sustain three very distinct variables, the equation must be in contingency as well as in ambiguity and ambage.[46] Ambage is especially associated with the connection between identities and network populations; ambiguity goes with aspects of connections of production disciplines with networks; and contingency, in a natural environment sense, is associated with how identities play off production discipline. These are not assertions about single disciplines or identities. These state tendencies that seem diagnostic in the social world of disorderly "gels and goos" as compounded by gaming.

Go back to enlarge upon earlier examples. One can suppose that there was less contingency in ecology—from devastation by banditry as well as weather—in England than there was in China. That difference will have shifted the balance between ambage and ambiguity. A similar shift can be argued regarding kin coding.

There also can be straight trade-off between physical and cultural. One example might be from Bynum's (1987) account of medieval women's stances toward food in religious context. But surely ambage in social pattern, as between genders, enters there too.

The subjects of these three measures are active processes, not natural flows. They are active processes among interactive identities.

---

[46] This deserves full mathematical development along lines akin to information theory: see e.g., Brillouin (1962).

"Gaming" is current idiom for interacting manipulations. Manipulations certainly trade on the concretely contingent as well as on social maneuvers and interpretive ambiguity. Manipulations often key on weather and shortages. Gaming finds ready, requires and resupplies ambage, ambiguity, and contingency, all three of which are its raw material, its medium, and product. So calculus of ambage, ambiguity, and contingency taken as a set is called for.

Decoupling is basic to networks. Coupling is more obvious to trace in strings of ties, but decoupling is equally important, decoupling which is the buffering of one chain of actions from another. Chance combines with network and story to yield patterns of decoupling and embedding. Decoupling is the phenomenological face of what the calculus among ambage and ambiguity and contingency asserts analytically. And from its introduction, in the first chapter, decoupling has been reserved for where contingency has a role. These material situations are where time and thence stochastic process has the greatest importance. Unfortunately, the greatest technical gaps in social science are in models for stochastic networks (for assessments see White 1973; Boorman and Levitt 1980), which are indispensable for capturing embedding and decoupling at the same time.[47]

"Equation" and "calculus" above are conventional shorthand for a much more complex interplay among "variables." These latter are assessments that may or may not prove to be measurable like temperatures. It is difficult enough to assess uncertainty in an objective or engineering sense, as Tukey (1977) will tell you. Shannon (for an appreciation and development, see Hofstadter 1979) pioneered measurement of symbolic uncertainty, here termed ambiguity, in information theory, but only in limited aspects. The overwhelming scope and subtlety of social uncertainty, of ambage, is a theme which can be discerned in Knight (1933), von Neumann and Morgenstern (1944), and Schelling (1960).

Tournaments and Liminality

Larger social contexts have been presupposed already both in examples and in analysis. Before turning to them explicitly in the next chapters, preliminary insight comes from viewing larger contexts in extreme forms. Tournament and Mardi Gras are two extremes that permit assessments of contingency, ambiguity, and ambage, cleared

[47] There are beginnings: on search in networks (Boorman 1975; Delaney 1989; Kleinrock 1964), on diffusion in networks (Boorman 1974; Burt 1989; Bailey 1957, 1982), on statistical mechanics of networks (Erdos and Spencer 1974), and on parallel distributed processing models: see Appendix 2.

of intricacies of historical specification. Both extremes evidence the dialectics of embedding and decoupling.

The tournament is a conscious enactment of a pecking order. It is a set of pairings among a population (Moon 1968; Erdos and Spencer 1974) in which within each pair one dominates the other. The pairings are to be strictly divorced from positions in other social networks and thus from institutional position.

The outcomes of pairings are to be arrayed to permit inference of a transitive ordering from the outcomes. A perfect, or near-perfect dominance ordering is one in which if one actor dominates a second who dominates some third, then the first also dominates the third in direct paired encounter. Call this a perfect tournament: it defines a transitive order. Examples from casual observation come to mind, such as among children on the playground of chapter 1; other examples are imposed by fiat, as in organized sports.

Define liminality, on the other hand, following Turner (1974), as an occasion, a Mardi Gras, for the suspension of all normal rules. This is a suspension conceded as legitimate by all. Liminality exemplifies decoupling and embedding in an extreme form that is the opposite of that for tournaments. Any and all network populations may but need not impact encounters.

Liminality is signaled by ceremonial boundaries; that is, there is a self-conscious embedding within an explicit culture, usually by rejection. At the same time the period of liminality serves to interrupt causal chains of agency and gaming. Usually this suspension holds only for some short, very specific period.

Liminality is a decoupler for agency even while it embeds in overall context. One can see this duality in Turner's Mexican fiesta, in student strikes, in pilgrimages (Christian 1980), in masses, in reunions, around a stage, at imperial apotheoses (Cannadine and Price 1987). Liminality copes with phenomenological confusion.

These two extremes, of tournament and liminality, are perfect converses. In the tournament the social standing of each actor is totally clear. This is a state of zero ambage, and there is, as a result, complete ambiguity as to the cultural basis of the social standings, as argued further below. In liminal formations, on the other hand, there is zero ambiguity, because there is an agreement on an extremely simple "new" culture of rules. Usually this is just an erasure of previous rules. At the same time, there is complete indefiniteness in social patterns of relation and thus extreme high ambage.

While liminal occasions mush together disparate and remote swirls of action, tournaments break apart larger contexts. Ambage is suppressed at the cost of erasing verifiable cultural content as criterion of dominance. By-products, such as hierarchies, may emerge in the larger context around the tournaments. Various tournaments, each with relatively arbitrary cultural bases, can be fitted together, in resultants of projects for control. Chickens do their flock's pecking order sincerely, but unlike humans they have no capacity to concatenate tournaments into ladders of mobility and hierarchies of control.

How real are these two extremes? In a profound series of analyses of the 1950s, Landau (1950, 1965) proved that the almost universal predominance of perfect linear orders of dominance among flocks in some species of social animals could not be accounted for by any plausible model of impacts from attributes of individuals upon outcomes of particular pair encounters. Landau rigorously proved that some form of heavy dependence upon existing overall social rankings was necessary.

Landau could not establish, just from abstract modeling, the kind of dependence that obtains. But recently a sociobiologist—that is, a comparative-species sociologist—Ivan Chase (1988), has presented evidence that for some species it is a cumulation of perceptions of gaming status. The principal species studied is chickens, who individually are stupid. Ambiguity does not figure, since there is no culture.

Among humans one never finds the near-perfect dominance order which emerges from naive encounters as among chickens. Instead a tournament may appear, but as a conspiracy, a joint conscious contrivance (Green and Stokey 1983; Rosen 1984). In this sense the culture around tournaments is clear-cut: the form is imposed from the larger setting. The result is that the ostensible basis, the cultural criterion of strength or brains, or what have you, that is used to account for ordering, is completely impossible to validate. Mandated dominance in social relation implies arbitrary placements on cultural criterion: Landau's work can be reinterpreted to that effect; and Leifer's work, developed earlier in this chapter, suggests some socio-psychological mechanisms. The Enlightenment myth approach in chapter 2 thus has been justified.

How does it happen that the human species, in our own time and sites, is so enamored of this social form analogous to that native to a vertebrate species characterized by stupidity? There can be no answer within the ostensible scope of the competing set of individuals. This set may be a squash ladder but it may equally well be a clutch of otherwise brilliant mathematicians jockeying for pecking order among themselves, possibly reflected in prizes. We must first examine the playing out of gamings for control, via decouplings and embeddings, and specify disciplines and how they may eventuate in hierarchies. Up several layers of embeddings and story formation, it should be possible to predict when and why this stupid form is reproduced and earns establishment.

Utopias are the imagined, long-term versions of liminality, compromised to various degrees for plausibility. The dictatorial utopias, the *1984*s and *Walden II*s, are as much liminal as the happily communal ones. It is not clear that liminal formations are observed in any other species. Mathematical modeling by stochastic process and encounter matrix should be feasible along lines analogous to Landau's, but there is no set of empirical findings to give bite to the analysis, in which symmetric ties would replace the asymmetric dominance ties.

What is clear is that liminality is common if not universal in known human societies.[48] It appears to be an episodic formation.[49] Why the contrast with dominance hierarchies? Liminality appears endogenous, in that no external pressure or trigger seems needed. Yet liminality is episodic, presumably from endogenous pressures of decay. Dominance tournaments often are extremely stable, in structure and even in exact mapping of member to rank, yet except in stupid species, where there are dominance hierarchies as a coupling between biophysical and social, tournaments are ceremonial contrivances not engendered in the routine operation of a social formation.

Liminality and tournaments both emphasize discontinuity. Time in social life has a picaresque quality overall, which I reflect in ambiguity and ambage measures, but moment by moment it is remorselessly Markovian (Feller 1968; White 1973). Memory, whether as vengeance or forethought, interrupts the Markovian quality only occasionally, with most of the generation of the picaresque coming, for each actor, from interruptions through gamings by others.

Liminality produces the illusion of an enlarged present in which Markovian chains are broken. Tournaments impose an enlarged present by fiat. Tournaments mock preceding continuities of interdependent action. Complete linear orders of precedence, complete sets of pair dominances without ambage, are antithetical to experiences of time, sequence, and interdependence.

---

[48] See Turner's cross-cultural survey (1969).

[49] However, sleep, it can be argued (Aubert 1965; White and Aubert 1959), is a liminal social state.

FOUR

INSTITUTIONS

INSTITUTIONS are, like disciplines, forced up from counteractions among efforts at control, but now on a larger scale. Institutions are robust articulations of network populations, articulations which draw primarily on structural equivalence. Institutions invoke story-sets across disparate discipline species.[1]

By definition, each institution is transposable from one of its concrete examples to another. Academic science will provide one example and caste another of the same institution. There is no reason, however, to think that institutions appear, as disciplines do, in only a few species that can be specified in advance.

Each identity has its own field of ties, which differ from any other identity's, in what kind goes to which others. There is a tension here. A clear differentiation is imposed upon, and enacted by, membership in a discipline of whatever species. Situational exigencies, however, determine in which particular network-population, and thus in which disciplines, actions occur. Institutions emerge when disciplines from distinct network-populations crisscross according to stories of regular patterns.

Network populations interpenetrate through migration and conquest and other processes, from which control struggles emerge on the new scale. These struggles may balance into robust social organization able to reproduce itself, for which new measures are required. One can compute within a network population, for example by blockmodeling, the recursive processes—the long loops of perceptions, control efforts, and causation—which, along with contingency, bedevil analysis of a network population for its own members as well as for other observers. Then, as network populations overlap and interpenetrate, complexity increases still further. For example, children, who their parents are and who they become socially, can be accurately construed only through deciphering interactions of distinct network populations as they settle down together.

---

[1] There are several other connotations for the term "institution" in social science usage: the broad architecture of functional areas (e.g., education, the arts, health, business as institutions); a special kind of organization infused by values (Selznick 1952, 1955); any social routine of behavior, such as a handshake; and so on. These alternatives are not hostile to my usage, as will become apparent.

When any larger social formation begins to emerge, control efforts proliferate and tend to obscure perception. Institution as a larger pattern can simplify perception and analysis of the details, and it in fact can be a realization of some special functional dialect common to its members, as well as visible to observers. But hazy discriminations are involved that necessarily are as much historical as analytic. The haziness of institutions is primarily historical. Any example of an institution is some deposit of accretive and evolutionary processes, together with intentional components, whose pattern, in self-reproducing itself, maintains some historical particularity.

This chapter and the next turn to social organization which is of larger scope than tournament and of longer duration than Mardi Gras. This is organization which is not at an extreme of ambage or ambiguity and which thus is less simple to describe and theorize than Mardi Gras or tournament. Computations of decoupling are required in the calculus for trade-offs among ambage, ambiguity, and contingency. As attention shifts to larger scale, analysis requires more explicit attention to decoupling—just as we become more attentive to decoupling when, in ordinary life, we move from conversation, with its instinctive decouplings, to arranging agendas with their strategic decouplings. Only pervasive decoupling can permit formations that encompass many disciplines and networks and much history.

It is impossible to derive from first principles some robust interlocking pattern to be an institution, just as it is beyond current powers of analysis to identify, much less to test for, all the institutions able to reproduce themselves across populations.[2] For the elaborately articulated architectures which are expounded in various social rhetorics,[3] one finds only scrappy concrete realizations. This chapter presents a few specific transcriptions of institutional order shown to hold across very different contexts and scales. Corporatism and clientelism are added to feudalism, caste, and science.

---

[2] Also beyond current powers of analysis is the simpler problem, in natural science, of deriving the observed few forms of crystalline order (Seitz 1940; Ma 1973) within the homogeneous and isotropic space which we owe to gravity and electromagnetism. This is not to even mention the problems of understanding the chief forms of gels and rubbers, problems more closely analogous to that of social forms (DeGennes 1979).

[3] Like many before me, I spent years on a vain quest for a portfolio of architectures. Padgett (1982) has reported some of his results on large social architectures from the joint seminar we ran for several years; my own partial results are in this and the next chapters.

Village Caste and University Science

Institutions precede and influence, as well as build from, constituents of discipline and network. In an institution, stories must continue to accompany local enclaves at the scale of disciplines and yet be configured so as to transpose across network populations. Caste as evolved across villages on the Indian plain does all this, and its structure as an institution will be brought out by showing how to transpose it to the patterning of science across American universities.

In both guises the institution is long-lived and of great scope. In the first of these guises, caste, change either in structure or production is generally thought to be precluded, whereas in the other dress the institution is generally thought to encourage change in production. The specific referent for caste here is the institution observed among central Indian villages and mapped out in networks of behavior and perception by Mayer (1960). The second illustration of the same institution, from an utterly different discourse, is academic science as a social formation in the United States, of which Cozzens's case in chapter 3 is a particular drama.

Castes across Villages

Accounts of Indian caste in general (Dumont 1986), emphasize the value placed on ritual purity and the strict demarcation of bounds for corporateness. A curious topology underlies and justifies both emphases, within the ongoing networks of kinship across villages. This topology very much depends on how networks weave together a corporate structure of purity. The topology can be tagged as a metonymy, specifically a synedoche: "the smaller contains the larger." This topology is then transposed to modern academic science.

Meticulous study of a concrete system is required to support description of an institution. Mayer's account (1960) of a field of villages in central India is used here. Purity is operationalized with extreme explicitness in villages. There is a ranked series of substances whose passing from one to another grouping permits precise imputation of purity, of sociocultural standing.

The groups ranked are local and constitute a partition of all family units within a given village into specific caste groupings. Rankings of each caste can be imputed from observed transactions, especially those on public occasions as in religious feasts and weddings. Party food, cooked in butter, comes at one extreme, then ordinary food, then raw food, and on through smoking pipes, drinking water, and on down through garbage and feces.[4] A generally agreed linear order of village castes is supported thereby.

The village is the site of primary economic activity, that is, farming and artisanry. Caste matters do not tie directly to most of this ecological activity. Nor do struggles over ownership, over improvement and change in property, which largely lie outside the scope of the village.

Through marriage, kinship cuts across villages. The unit of intimacy is the subset within a village caste who have married into a like subset of an analogous caste in another village, or rather the many such intermarrying sets across a number of villages in the region. Call this the subcaste, a network construction hopping across the region. It is a "sub"-caste because within any particular village the persons in the given affinal network are but a subset of the several clusters of blood relatives which make up the whole caste in that village.

Figure 4-1 lays out the institution as networks across a field of villages containing caste disciplines, whose subunits are the nodes of the networks.

Paradoxically, the subcaste is larger than the caste. The reality is that inheritance and marriage, the engines of major change, lie within the subcaste and outside the village. There is both village exogamy and caste endogamy. The corporate reality of a subcaste interlinked through affinal ties across a whole region, this intimate corporateness is broader than the only caste unit which is actually embodied, that of the village. Indeed the subcaste may be comparable to the whole village in size.

Only the subcaste has explicit organization, a council and like agency for regulating caste affairs. Wealth flows along subcaste lines, through marriage and inheritance, as do innovations, material and other. There are only the thinnest threads of purity calibration that can be spun out by the Brahman "priests," themselves scattered as local caste units in villages.

Some mobility can take place without disturbing perceptions of purity value. It is the mobility not of individual persons but of whole subcastes moving to new villages. They can do so because there are more distinct castes in the region than can ever be found together on the ground of a particular village. The Brahman argues primarily in terms of the four broad *varnas* of their scriptures; so a subcaste new to the village can appear and argue for a location in purity rank

---

[4] Explicit network modeling of such caste interaction data can be found in Marriott (1959, 1968).

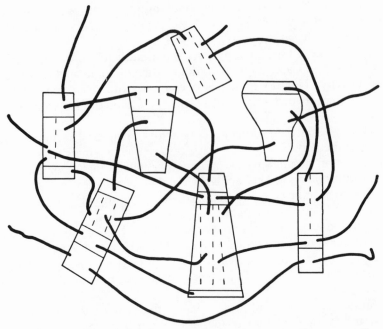

Fig. 4-1. Village caste and university science. Heavy lines represent flows of recruits among subcastes/research-specialties; dotted lines mark subcastes within graded castes/departments in a village/university. Only seven villages and selected flows are shown.

within that village in the only way that matters, getting the appropriate exchanges going.

Looking at Mayer's photos of separate caste groups hunkered down in separate locales at feasts, one can almost supply the story-sets used to account for and tidy up the value ranking by purity. Not amenable to photograph, but equally central, are the sprawling networks of kinship bonding across other villages that sustain and reproduce the system. A separate set of value facets is embedded in these ties among subcaste segments. The caste illustration is a vivid one which is easy to recognize in transposed dress in other institutional contexts.

The Institution

A general value—call it purity—is here operationalized in the strongest kind of social ordering, a ranking close to the full linear ordering of the mathematician. But this purity is confined operationally to a small locality, usually a geographic one defined by mundane activities. Purity thus is operationalized only for small populations separately, since linear order can be enforced only through transitivities in chains of behavior that cannot be monitored for larger ones. Despite its size, this institution is closest in form to the kernels of social action themselves, to the social disciplines of work teams and the like which come embedded in social networks.

It is the corporate membership, which intuition tells us should play the role of locality, that in fact sprawls out across localities without, however, interfering with behaviors whose patterns are sufficient to enforce purity. Other value facets, such as intimacy and wealth, accompany these corporate memberships akin to subcaste. What persists and reproduces itself as a robust social formation is the peculiar balancing with social patterns of interpenetrations across values.

Any examples of this first institution will tend to be pluralist in value terms, affording parallel sets of story and interpretation specific to locality. Such values have localized facets, which are used for *ex post* accountings. For a century, purity in caste, like analogous valuations in other climes, had hypnotized observers into treating the social formations of caste on a macro scale as automatic by-products of the values writ large.

With a new generation of anthropologists who were alerted to networks as analytic and phenomenological bases of social topography, values came to be seen as by-products from social pattern rather than as exogenous cause. And it became clear that particular values from the known package were tied together and mapped very differently in the corporate sprawl of networks from the locality layering.

Sociologists of science have been bringing this same new perspective of networks, and their results can be mapped into the same institution as village caste. On some matters one can argue for common predictions. All realizations of this institution exhibit social formations which are peculiarly resistant to attempts at external control. This follows from rumination on the illustrations, as well as from the institution's character considered in the abstract—a balanced and stable yet decentralized skeleton.

Caste is argued (Ghurye 1986; Hocart 1950) to be the resilient formation which has survived repeated waves of external invaders. Defensive or blocking action in the larger sense is the genesis of caste as social organization. The inner circles of recondite validation for caste center on Brahmin priests, who make no claim to economic or political predominance. Successive waves of external marauders common in these Indian regions are offered no obvious social foci through which to control and exploit, as opposed to plunder, the population.

The structuring of academic research science can be argued to be a parallel reaction against the emerging dominance of American universities by autocrat presidents in the early 1900s. It is not particular values as abstract symbols that accomplish this, it is an institution which embeds value facets operationally into a certain sort of balanced formation that is hard to unwind bit by bit.

American Academic Science

Academic science in the form of university departments is every bit as resistant to innovation as caste systems. When a genuine innovation comes along in academic science, there seem to be two likely fates: Either it is expelled to industrial application, as Charles Townes's laser seems to have been, or it is encapsulated within departments and spun out into what is, in social organization, a new network. The latter seems to have been the fate in the 1950s of the new biophysics of Delbrück and the Committee on Mathematical Biophysics and of Watson and Crick's molecular biology, and it also is occurring now with the new physics of matter, to mention only three which were unquestionably major innovations. Thus the social organization of a science as an institution is reflected in how existing theories combine with or reject any new theory entertained in that science.

There proves to be a close parallel of caste to the organization of American academic science. For village read university, and for village caste-group read department in a university. Purity becomes prestige, itself a stand-in for degree of ultimate truth. Subcaste translates into specialty, which is at the heart of science as research, as generator of originality. With this translation, the statements above on Mayer's village caste system can be carried over into the social setup of American academic science.[5]

A pecking order for scientific disciplines is operationalized only among departments within the particular university, physics or mathematics often being on top with sociology near the bottom.[6] Degree of scientific purity may be attributed to this order. Ritual pervades this scene, whereas action and excitement and intimacy grow along research networks spreading outside the given university.

[5] It may be that the dissection below carries through as well to the humanities, with whose organization I am less familiar. Better analogues to the humanities, as well as to professional schools and the like, may be the ethnic enclaves that crosscut villages and castes in a region like Mayer's.

[6] This pecking order varies a little between universities. The study of sociology, for example, is more prestigious at the University of Arizona or the University of North Carolina than in Ivy League schools.

Sprawling networks of collaboration and intimacy in actual research reach across the nation on specific subjects. Specialties are concretized in them. For specialty as subcaste read invisible college (Crane 1972).

Seen from outside within its university, a given department has meaning and indeed coherence. The meaning comes within and expresses a hierarchy of purity and accomplishment, which can vary from one university to another. The hierarchy is enforced by deference behaviors in committee meetings and luncheon interchanges. It is also enforced and expressed in larger and more solemn ceremonials, at which symbolic capital can be exchanged like any other.[7] Contents of interchanges can be typed analogously to the discriminations from high to low in the material exchanges among castes within a village, and there is a parallel range of meeting contexts within a village.

Seen from its inside, a university department of science, analogous to a village caste, is a shambles of unrelated specialties. Different collections of specialities will make up that discipline's departments in various universities. And universities differ in their exact menus of departments. All this is parallel to the caste/village/subcaste formation. A specialty spreading across scores of departments is typically much larger than a given university department—just as a given subcaste spreading into scores of villages has more members than are in that caste in a given village (see figure 4-1).[8]

Each specialty is the prime world of motivation for its working scientists. And when recruitment of new (faculty) members to the given department comes up, it is recruitment largely along invisible-college networks of specialties active in that department and competing with each other. Just so do marriages and children get formed through networks within a subcaste quite separate from the other subcastes which together in the eyes of that village make up the weavers (or the blacksmiths or whatever) as a single caste entity. Two specialties may be more closely linked to departmental counterparts in different universities, which is one more reason why they tend to operate separately and independently within their own de-

[7] Consider for example the annual Feast of Grades meetings held by Arts and Sciences faculties, at which higher honors for graduating students are negotiated and solemnized. One might speculate that in the university, as in the village, these local ceremonials absorb energies and distract attention from flows of main action and resources through corporative networks.

[8] Even the numbers are quite comparable, for sizes of units, subunits, and spread of networks.

partment. Again there is a parallel to Mayer's descriptions for sub-castes.

Familiarity of the reader with our academic setting can supply detail and conviction, though excellent case studies of science like Cozzens's cited earlier can help. For overviews to supplement case studies and personal experiences see, for example, Merton (1973), and Mullins (1973). For longitudinal perspective on values, showing how careers play out in science, see Cole (1979) and Zuckerman (1979), and Menard (1971).

Effectiveness and Efficiency Applications

As a preliminary to full topological measurement, the institution should be coded in terms of discipline species. This coding by hypothesis should be the same for science or other exemplar as it is for caste.

Operation of caste distinctions within a given village is that of arenas oriented by purity as value. By definition, the medium which codes exchange (here as *pacca* and *kacca* foods and so on) is stylized. Concrete contents of exchanges, amounts, and so on, are arbitrary, subject to negotiation in arena discipline. On the other hand, kinship organization is in the council species, adapted to mobilizing.

What is missing is the interface species, which is the discipline distinctive for effective material production. This is not to say that material production, here farming, is not key to the whole life of Indian villages. Farming does go on, in parallel exactly to the third aspect of the institution, the locality aspect which defines villages and is marginal to the institution. Thus production is divorced from the main social institution.

The Indian caste system may prove to be, upon close agronomic investigation, an unusually efficient one for farming. Our intuition on efficiency may be better for the academic science embodiment. Here too there is total divorce between social form and the actual accomplishment of the material task, which now is instruction of students. Teaching in the American university system[9] is efficient exactly because it is divorced from the main concerns of the professors and their social institution, which revolves around science research.

The important point for production efficiency—as we have learned from Udy's (1970) analysis—is that there be low correlation to social organization. The normal outcome of social organization is blocking action and thus inefficient production. Hence to establish a segrega-

[9] Most of the professors in which are scientists.

tion of social from productive organization is a major achievement in the Frederick Winslow Taylor sense. What it takes is an architecture in which values and processes from diverse species of discipline balance off. In this institution, the balancing mechanism is summed up by "smaller is larger"; that is, subcaste is bigger than caste.[10]

The other face of the coin is that the caste institution may prove ineffective in its principal social concerns of shepherding wealth within familial lines and purity within caste. Similarly, the claim must be that the current American science system is less effective than earlier European ones in the essentially social yet recondite task of establishing scientific realities. The European professoriate was principally concerned with and oriented around teaching, which it thereby was inefficient in, while behind its own back, so to speak, it was famously effective in its sideline or hobby of research. Discoveries were made, experiments run, all with precious little help from that earlier institution.

Control Applications

The Norman regime, whose multiple networks are dissected at chapter's end, may be a third exemplar of this caste-science institution, along with various other regimes which have been called feudal (Coulborn 1956), but data sources are poor. In feudal situations it could be that the network aspect, here vassal ties especially, could structure the local cells, with the strata ranked on purity, here noble rank, being spread widely.

Feudal cases suggest looking at control properties instead of production. There is no analogue to the Udy theorem as guide. And this caste-science institution has sufficiently complex structure that its processes may change drastically with apparently minor shifts in parameter, say the average number of caste ranks in a village, and its variability. A calculus becomes important.[11]

The numbers of subcastes within village caste groups, and the number of the latter within a village, seem about the same as the

[10] To go beyond such ad hoc and qualitative assessment, an ambage-vs.-ambiguity calculus is required. Unlike in the tournament/liminality extremes described at the end of the previous chapter, there is extensive substructure. In particular, trade-offs are among three interpenetrating formations so that qualitative assessment is difficult and unreliable. Contingency levels vary among these three, as well as within each, and it seems to me that it is these variations which will account for the different functioning of the caste and the science exemplars in ambage/ambiguity trade-offs. The sorts of computations required are of complexity like those in Jasso's (1991; and see 1990) application of relative justice theory to medieval monastic contexts.

[11] See previous note.

corresponding numbers for American science, as mentioned previously. What seems entirely different is in the average overlap between locales—villages and universities, respectively—in which ranked local groups (castes and departments) are present. This difference seems to correlate to a difference in control properties.

Different universities have far higher overlap in their menu of departments than do villages in their menus of castes. American universities have higher levels of central control, one guesses, than do Indian villages. This suggests a conjecture of exactly academic relevance.

During the continuing retrenchment in the American university system, there will be what in business is called downsizing. One likely component will be elimination of whole departments. There are two possibilities: First, university presidents clamber on the same bandwagon, as business CEOs do (Chandler 1969; Fligstein 1985), and choose the same academic disciplines to eliminate. Second, presidents react to or analyze primarily local context and history to choose sacrificial goats. The conjecture is that if the local adaptation predominates presidential control in universities will weaken. The reasoning is that diverse local choice will move the academic parameters closer to the caste parameters and thus to lower central control.[12]

Boundaries

As we have just seen, it is possible to pick out large and complicated patterns which seem to transpose across diverse settings. But to support institution as a general construct illustrated by such a pattern, analyses which are more general and systematic are needed. This section offers a number of perspectives on this task, all keyed around understanding boundaries.

Pervasive decoupling must underlie any institution, and so calculus of trade-offs among ambage, ambiguity, and contingency should be prominent. Related to this task, inhomogeneity of networks remains a challenge to measurement and perception despite attempts

[12] Such a conjecture made without benefit of a calculus is at risk because there is no way to allow for interaction with other possible changes. Exogenous (federal and business) financial support of science research may decline more or less than the number of professors. The different contingency flows implied could override the impact of changes in overlap across universities in departments. Such override could come through a change in the number of specialties within a department (subcastes within village caste). Once again it becomes clear that a calculus applied to reliable measurement is a necessary guide even to qualitative conclusions on sheer direction.

to sidestep it (Wellman 1981; Howell 1969), but it may be a necessary aspect of institution.[13] Boundary of institution must accommodate inhomogeneity of network.

Boundary as Theory

Social phenomena are least predictable and most interesting at boundaries. The world has long noted these truths, and boundaries are a basic concept of any folk. Ambage, ambiguity, and contingency, and their trade-offs are calculus of boundaries for analysts. The boundaries of institutions are constructs that result from, rather than being causes of, interpenetration between network populations.

To recognize a boundary is not an innocent activity. In natural science theories, boundary has proved to be a crucial and productive concept.[14] Experimental manipulation can impose boundary. Boundaries in social action are not given facts and they are not manipulable. Boundaries are, instead, subtle and complex products of action.[15] Boundaries are theories which can cause facts in the practice both of social science and of ordinary life.

Social organization is like some impacted, mineralized goo, some amazing swirl of local nuclei and long strands of order among disorder. In possible boundaries it is rich indeed, and this richness is resource for control projects. Some agreement on boundaries is sign for emergence of institution as balancing of diverse control projects.

The field for speculation is endless and their employments in control attempts are diverse. Stories are a form of agreement limiting the field. Communicable speculations by actors about recurrent acts by others, that is stories, have been shown to be part of the observable patternings which guide not only projects of control but also scientific observation. This aspect of the patternings taken as a whole can be analyzed as culture.[16]

Human cultures, each consisting in some discourses in story-sets and their values, concentrate on what nuclei of order can be found. Thus they set a tone of exposition which presupposes more orderliness than is really there. The main business of human discourse is to put an orderly face on the underlying messes. Human powers of per-

---

[13] And see the section "Catnets" at the end of chapter 2.

[14] Much of theoretical physics is structured as boundary-value problems (see for example Morse and Feshbach 1953). In biological studies, boundary as concept has not proved as useful, as discussed in the preface.

[15] Only persistent argument from John Padgett brought me to this realization.

[16] See chapter 7.

ception are limited, and it is not surprising that some agreed descriptions of boundaries are used for orientation to and within social spaces. The business of social organization is ultimately to make boundaries, which native theories attempt to portray.

Boundaries have to be constructed, negotiated, and maintained. Boundaries are not a free good, handily available to participant or observer. There are projects of control and disciplines of production which underlie and shape any putative "boundary." One boundary gets recognized from, and as a frequency distribution of, sets of social actions. Another boundary is constructed out of stories to dampen impacts of network.

The concept of boundary when just borrowed from physical settings induces one to take for granted just what is most central to explain. There are no analogues in social forms to such boundaries. Boundaries are contingent and tangible accomplishments, not exogenous orders of events.[17]

Social space is plural, not singular, nor is social space stable. Thus in social phenomenology "space" itself is problematic—a contingent, changing, and egocentric accomplishment. Control projects depend upon intersubjective decouplings and embeddings, among changing spaces, subjective and objective. Participants can each choose differently how to draw bounds to actors, but only among their own common frames as handiworks.

What remains to be disentangled is how important are stories and explanations in sharpening some edge of boundary in social action. Stories can be woven together into ideologies which compete with boundaries, as in this account:

> The social transformations which occurred in England during the 16th and 17th centuries culminated in the formation and articulation of abstract ideologies as guides to action, which, when carried out, transformed the world in their image. Common to these ideologies was a sustained attack on particularism, for example, the Puritan emphasis on the "godly community" over ties of kinship and locality, and the common-law emphasis on principled "right" rather than the exercise of particular "rights." As Weber has made clear, the distinctive feature of the West was the tenacious hold which these universalistic rhetorics held on the pattern and organization of social life. (Bearman 1989)

Understanding boundary effects requires a theory of the formation of culture. A beginning can be found in studies of artistic style

---

[17] Indeed, I think this holds true for physical and biological analysis too, but that discussion would lead afield.

treated in explicit relation to economic and political boundaries. One example is Baxandall's analysis (1980) of the evolution of limewood sculpture in the context of a system of competing and interacting late-medieval German city-states. It is at the same time necessarily a study of localities, how they are constructed as meaningful actors, as signifiers.

Localities

In coming to grips with some social actions, a first step is to fix on locales for actors both with each other and in regular space. Intuition teaches us that physical space provides metaphors for social relations, which themselves influence perceptions of space. Baxandall (1975) made this vivid through his comparison of Renaissance painting conventions in Italian cities with their emerging commercial routines. He shows how relations shape and are shaped by the newly crisp conventions of placement in artworks. Social theorists themselves have noted that the vertical as an earthly dimension is a potent metaphor in social stratification (see e.g., B. Schwartz 1981).

All social action sites in physical space-time. We live among irregular mixings between biophysical space-times and social action. This social action can be modeled as generating its own bubbles of space-time that are somehow adjoined to the biophysical. Such bubbles cannot be personal, one to each individual identity, because they come in populations and nest in levels. It is not easy to tease out what is the more purely social aspect of space-times, where to construe action out of control efforts by identities.

Every identity is giving some account for itself, which leads to sets of stories. Different sets of identities may generate and perceive different spaces, and all depend upon and influence an ecological level, like any other phenomena on earth. Locality as a construct implies some approximation to a partition of physical space in order to gain self-consistency in the social accounting of localities.

Locality has over ages been the basis of government (Whitney 1970). Locality seems important in economic realms across diverse periods as well. The meaning of cities as wholes can be entirely different depending on the kind of localism: "Basra grew from nothing to more than 200,000 inhabitants in 30 years in the 7th century. The merchant class of the great Islamic cities, of Cairo, Baghdad or Cordoba, was not indigenous as was the upper level of Western cities . . . the lack of localism in the Islamic lands deprived the cities of commercial aggressiveness" (*Cambridge Economic History II: Trade and Industry in the Middle Ages*, 2d edition, p. 405).

Locality is where social space must somehow be patched together with physical space or geography. Localities are—contrary to common sense—complex and confusing accomplishments of human social structure (cf. Durkheim 1915; Reid 1913; Rose 1960; Zeigler 1973). Social science theory has shied away from locality, except for specialized work by some geographers (Haggett, Cliff, and Frey 1977). To meld social with geographic concepts is very hard, as Koopmans emphasized (1957) within economic theory, and as Alonso demonstrated (1964). In the words of L. J. Sharpe (1979, p. 18): "Indications of a spatial variation of power has been treated almost as if all politics could exist on the head of a pin . . . scientific rationalism has a tendency toward uniformity and centralization."

Blockmodels and localities are two contrasting simplifications of social formations resulting from control struggles. Blockmodels ignore production. Blockmodeling is in purely social space. Sets of ties will be concatenated to suggest meshings with sets of stories. Localities, on the other hand, determine types of networks in terms of productions, weaving together sets of stories for the latter.

Locality is not a separate topic, but an outcome to be predicted and then carried through successive examples. Locality is a dependent variable, one requiring complex articulations within the theory. Localities are intersections between physical space and social networks, which also are embeddings. The main difficulty is modeling the uneasy mix between physical and social spaces required by locality as a construct.

This mix confounds interpretation in two general ways.

Stories and Localities

First, analogues to physical space confound the proper differentiation of levels within social spaces. Sorting out levels is a difficult puzzle, bound up with stories. Only a few classic studies are clear on such levels in interaction with the localities; for example, Sayles and Strauss (1967) on the local trade union.

Localities come into recognition from inducing ritual about physical space in terms of social spaces. This confounds theorists. A recent essay by an urban planner expresses the issues well, using the term "center" for locality:

> Let us define a *generalized center* as a marked place in space or time. . . .
> Surrounding a center is a structure or pattern that "supports" it and points to it. Centers imply inhomogeneity . . . and in the inhomogene-

ity there is either fall-off toward the boundary, or the periphery arises from (has its source in) the center . . . centers are often accidents that become facts: chance fluctuations . . . residents claim there is a down-town . . . the historian discovers a primitive act, . . . an act of founding . . . a center exists only because it is developed around. . . . Critics need authors and styles to organize the works of art they study, . . . one is looking for marked points in space, or in time, or in a collection from which and around which all complexity evolves . . . we can create differentiates of quality, through advertising and art, that make a place locationally justified just because it possesses those created differenti-ates. (Krieger 1987, pp. 1251–57)

Locality raises difficult subtleties of valuation, as well as of mean-ing. Locality embeds new levels. Localities build out of story-sets constrained around value.

Localities are constructed out of social networks and physical pro-ductions by the suppression of stories about actors. Not all stories correspond to the network etiology of social space. Some stories seem wedded to creating artificial localities, that is, to categorical at-tributions to sets of actors.[18] Such an account is, however, against the grain of the actual processes. The earliest story-form, the epic, was closer to real network etiology (cf. e.g., Scholes and Kellogg 1966).

The confounding of theorists by locality appears in the use made of ostensibly obvious geography to solve difficulties with social inte-gration. Nadel (1957) is trenchant in arguing the need to model within theory—in his case role theory—how the practical person of everyday puts together the disparate social worlds in which s/he has to live. From a philosophical view (cf. Kolb 1986), the only universal claims we can make are local performances, and it is a tempting sol-ipsism to claim these as the interpenetrations of social worlds. Local-ity, whether in space or time, is used as a folk-surrogate for role inte-gration.

Halévy (1974) gives a classic account of an attempted opposite structuring, of reliance upon local notables to guide and legitimate a whole system, the nascent Third Republic of France. This was a sys-tem in extreme shock, following collapse of the Second Empire in the Franco-Prussian war. Given complete authority, local notables in the aftermath of turbulence were utterly unable to cope. They needed to supply coherent story accounts to a larger population, which is ex-actly antithetical to their being local notables.

---

[18] Much survey research upon attitudes reports on as it builds up this.

Structuralist versus Atomic

There is a second general way in which the mixing of geography with social spaces as locality confounds theory. This second way is the conundrum of structuralist versus atomic hypotheses. The structuralist conjecture stakes out an extreme position, the antipodes to individualism, namely that all action is shaped mainly by the overall.

On the one hand, it is hard to deny that overall context or structure directly constrains and shapes action. This is true even more in social action than in physical systems, since there is a whole additional refraction of totality through perception and its embeddings in culture, a refraction into multiple spaces. Concrete examples jog this sense:

> Italian history is essentially local history, especially since centralizing forces are conservative and anachronistic (the Holy Roman Empire). . . . Heterogeneity was the essence of the Italian scene; the development of so many centers of contrasting types—trading towns and industrial towns, bankers' towns and agrarian backwaters—cannot be reduced to a single scheme. Each type made some contribution to the complexion of the whole. . . . It is hardly possible to write a local history without at least some working hypothesis as to its relationship with a wider world, so much does the assessment of local manifestations depend on the way in which the general and normal development is envisaged. . . . Those parts of Italy which were effectively linked to the empire of Charlemagne through innumerable local variations follow a single pattern, while those parts which remained outside—the South, the islands, and Venice—follow a course which is radically different. . . . By a gradual decline, the German Emperors in Italy passed from being effective though intermittent rulers to become the leaders of a faction until, in the end, they were merely the tools of factions. (Hyde 1966, pp. 8–9)

On the other hand, it is individual identities which generate the unpredictability at the core of history. And locality is not unrelated to identity: This also was in the Hyde account, though only implicitly.

The conundrum of structuralist versus atomic hypotheses mixes together boundary with locality issues. This can be shown vividly in a context of religious institution:

> Augustine's theology . . . conceives of an (priestly) order almost exclusively with reference to the individual who exercises it. . . . Such a view would have been impossible to hold but for the virtual breakdown of the old, jealously corporate notion of the local Church and its local

ministry during the two preceding generations. Augustine's theory is in itself a proof that by circa A.D. 400 that idea was extinct as a living force. (Dix 1946, p. 286)

And in a still earlier period:

Earliest Christianity began as a renewal movement within Judaism brought into being through Jesus . . . after A.D. 70 Pharisaism gained the upper hand in Judaism, and the Christians were excommunicated. . . . Wandering charismatics were the decisive spiritual authorities in the local communities, and local communities were the indispensable social and material basis for the wandering charismatics. Both owed their legitimation and existence to their relationship to the transcendental bearer of revelation. It was the homeless wandering charismatics who handed on what was later to take independent form as Christianity . . . the local groups of sympathizers remained within the framework of Judaism . . . entangled in the old situation. . . . Wandering prophets and teachers were still the decisive authorities at the time of the Didache (in the first half of the second century). . . . Their superiors were still the "apostles," who were allowed to stay no more than three days in one place. All these wandering charismatics had a higher reputation than local ministers. (Theissen 1978, p. 7)

Localities are spatial analogues to groupings of events in time. Sheer locale in physical space becomes locality only after considerable interpretive work with production arrays and networks. Anthropological studies have made this clear (e.g., Firth 1957; Fortes 1945; Hart and Pilling 1960; Rose 1960; Spencer and Gillen 1903; Warner 1937). Localities render concretely boundaries which are a form of theory, a profile.

Language and Thresholds

Language presupposes interaction among distinct network populations; so language is a by-product of boundaries. Like institution, language only appears when there are multiple populations. Kinship is the conscious-theory facet of the emergence of languages, which are not disjunct secret codes among isolate tribes but rather are broadly continuous idioms across sweeps of interrelated peoples (Bradfield 1973). Let us elaborate.

Network populations build from disciplines, which presuppose a set of valuations that mediate their embeddings. Identities make use of valuations to maneuver—but of course they can do so effectively only as other actors at least know what they are signaling, and thus only as they share a set of valuations. And this implies at least a language of practice, a parole, across some more-or-less definite population.

Stories are joint creations which evolve slowly and so only among social groupings that are self-reproducing. But stories are too flexible and numerous to be generated in a small setting. We cannot conceive of stories purely local, tied just to one network or discipline. Other levels of stories, with language as the limiting larger scope, are always implicit in any that we observe.

Language is coordinate to processes which lead to stories and to types of tie being discerned and factored out as separate patterns. Only the human species elaborates ties in stories. Social accountings ground social networks in a somehow-ordered heap of stories, only some of whose constituents map into physical space. The generation and spread of these accountings presuppose social contexts able to support language as structuring.

Language thus presupposes not just a population but interacting populations. Language is integration of distinct functional dialects (Culler 1975, pp. 57–59). Such integration comes only from control struggles across wide fronts of interaction with like other population. No language was ever known whose speakers were not keenly aware of distinct other languages, known to be languages. In short, language comes in only with metalanguage.

Language builds with multifaceted identities, and with multiple populations, and their reproductions as social formation, be it tribe or institution. Combinatorics suggests the underlying impetus for language. Combinatorial counts of possible social patterns are astronomical. Over enough time language is induced.

Make the same argument in more concrete terms. Control struggles proliferate out into, and generate, multiple settings. Stories in language are accompaniments induced as the scope of interaction grows beyond some threshold. The evidence seems clear that this magic number is around one thousand. According to the records of anthropology, at that size social formations can reproduce across a range of activities, and correlatively a language can establish itself. This is the size of the smallest self-subsisting tribe and also of the smallest language group observed.[19]

In a literally isolate tribe, the number of kin and production and

---

[19] I can leave to one side issues of physiological and neurological capacities for language. Identity in the guise of human consciousness may be triggered only across the interactions of distinct network settings sustained by such a population.

social ceremonial formations might be low enough, and their intercalation simple enough, to be described as just one population. There would be separate overlapping networks, but not necessarily further embeddings. And perhaps language might not have emerged fully; rhetorics might have been adumbrated.[20]

But any image of a neatly separate population with its own language is misleading. All known tribal languages appear in a nested roll of parallel, similar, and variational language. Each is in some use across a geographic region; each draws on neighbors as resources. There is not a need and occasion and goad for language until some such scope as one thousand actors is reached, interconnected across different settings, but usually the chain of mutually comprehensible languages goes further. In such setting each network becomes the site of struggles for control which cannot be settled neatly because they spill over into other settings, other populations.

Events

Corporate actors shape and are shaped by events. But events themselves may become actors. Eric Foner argues, on a macro scale, the need in us as observers, but implicitly also of the actors in the era of his studies, for a great deal of framing by distinctive events to build social reality, and a social calendar:

> The Civil War had by the end of the 1970s been relegated to the wings . . . (this was) more than a reflection of the overall crisis of academic history in the 1970s. . . . Traditional emphasis on institution and events, politics and ideas was superseded by a host of "social" concerns . . . (new) groups looked to history for a "useable past." . . . As historians intruded into the intimate lives of past generations of Americans, public events and institutions receded into the background. No alternative theory of politics emerged. . . . The Civil War is unintelligible if divided into the various subcategories of contemporary historical inquiry. . . . Problems appeared and disappeared, events simply happened, with no sense of systematic relations or underlying causes. (1980, p. 3)

Translate Foner's eloquent plaint into one for reconstitution of identity, construed at a higher level and of greater scope as corporate

[20] But not beyond some threshold: the Icelandic sagas developed, despite remarkable isolation, into an exceptionally powerful skein of stories (Scholes and Kellogg 1966, chap. 2).

actor. Confederacy and Union in his account are events as identities of large scope.

As Foner consciously makes clear, historians are social technicians who, *ex post*, impose a macro story on hunks of social space-in-time which, as seen by a Martian, would be mere picaresque jumble. Journalists are the current events analogue, joining historians in discounting ambiguity (Gans 1979; Schudson 1989). Administrators, when general managers, are the line-operation version, with the much more difficult task of suppression *ex ante* (Vancil 1979).[21] And the philosopher Ricoeur argues (1988) that narrative constitutes social time and thus that narrative is the bridge between sidereal and phenomenological time, so that he has stories as actors in some sense.

Values

From molecular discipline an institution draws upon valuation and generalizes it into value as articulation among stories. Values are important common elements across sets of stories. In a functioning institution, as also in disciplines, values are hegemonic, which means so predominant that other assessments do not come to mind.

Stories vary, but framing by value is taken for granted. It is this hegemonic quality that can afford the discipline or institution independent standing as an entity, as an actor on its own. For example, *The Right Stuff*, which is both title and theme of Tom Wolfe's novel (1980), exactly captures the inarticulate hegemony of a valuation, there prestige (which is closest to pecking order), and there within the group of test pilots. Previous exemplars have been large scale, but institution is an analytic construct applicable at various scales.

Stories and Values

The endless stories being invoked and applied in control projects confound attempts to understand and analyze what is going on. The stories obscure how in fact larger formations are being constituted out of disciplines. But the stories reassert values. Social organization is the deposit of previous interventions in social organization. This is the genesis of values. A value is reestablished as the intersection of story-sets from merger between network populations and over time.

---

[21] See section "General Management" in chapter 6.

An institution in reproducing itself around a value may flesh out into still other network populations. This is the genesis of corporatism, the most common form of institution. The modal institution is corporatist because corporatism explicitly organizes on stories around values. For example, the *standestaat* which preceded modern states across Europe for centuries drew resiliency from its expressive focus in value commitments, notably varieties of honor for aristocrats and holiness for clergy (Duby 1980; Poggi 1978).

Values embody the aspect of discipline orderings that can be common across a broader setting. The settings vary in boundary and in the contextual impacts they exert. Values trace back through discipline valuations to presumed ultimate dominance ordering. Repetitive levels in larger social formations thus may supply the grammars for stories, their stereotypes, and underlying meanings.

The meanings of values are to be inferred as much from the social architecture as vice versa. Analysts can predict movements within institutions by tracing contingencies in the story-sets and disciplines. Analysts seek a balance, which need not be reflected in any one of the stories current in a system about itself.

Values may reflect and explain away more than they cause. Change in values derives from fault lines in social patterns shown up by turmoil. An illustration comes from a recent case study of a social movement. Civil rights values, seen to include purity and effectiveness, were woven into the social fabric of movement organization. In McAdam's words (1988, 237): "Activism depends on more than idealism. . . . There must also exist formal organizations or informal social networks that structure and sustain collective action. The volunteers were not appreciably more committed to Freedom Summer than the no-shows"—among the college students initially recruited; so that it was position in mobilization networks that tipped who actually came, rather than intensity of individual beliefs in civil rights values.

Now look from the inside, from individual users' active perspectives. Valuations help each actor in a discipline orient in and deal with contingent interactions and environment, which are what give room to attempts at manipulation, and in particular to agency. Accountings of social actions as institution presuppose values common across social networks. Values fuel the unending conflicts for control among distinct actors, individual or composite, that are what generate the values in the course of reaching some equilibrium despite duplicity and contention. The resulting story-sets serve both to express and to conceal the conflicts and the orientations in that context.

Story-Set and Values

Story becomes story-set around a value. These quondam disciplines' story-sets are sources of stories as ties in the networks. The singular valuation order which interprets a discipline branches, upon its devolution, into values which no longer map tightly to a structure of discipline.

As identities provide accounts for and of themselves they jointly generate the device of values out of valuations from disciplines. Values are important common elements across sets of stories, so that values are couplers of stories. Stories end up as a set from which are picked parsimonious accounts which invoke a value but are consistent with control projects being pushed.

Story sets evolve and reproduce in a matrix of contending control projects. Whatever comes to pass, and thus whatever can be conceived, must be describable after the fact in terms of the story-set, the convention in which a value is expressed. But this means that there are multiple descriptions available as plausible description of the course of any value in a situation.

Goals are a device that bridges contradictions, goals stereotyped in terms of values. Values derive ultimately from the valuation orderings in molecular disciplines. Values are a peculiar hybrid between socially programmed reproduction of institution, on the one hand, and idiosyncratic actions by identities on the other.

There is the peculiar picture of identities sharing stories, no one of which corresponds to actual corporatist habitats any one of them is in, but which, together, form a sufficient base for constructing accountings that can be shared. Sets of stories intertwine structuralist with individualist viewpoints; they do so as decouplers. Values mediate.

Theories of Values

Earlier theoretical perspectives were typically focused on values abstracted from their context in social organization. Talcott Parsons, in his efforts toward a general theory of social action, pushed for transposability and separability of values so that the ultimate ends of different means-ends chains could constitute an abstract system. Thus for Parsons ultimate ends can be cultural facets of coherent social action across a society.[22] By contrast, Erving Goffman (1955, 1963, 1967,

---

[22] "Culture is . . . transmissible from personality to personality by learning and from social system to social system by diffusion. This is because culture is constituted

1971, 1974) denied this transposability in his push for local phenomenological truth: namely, a "backstage" where reality and valuation of even the simplest social acts must be negotiated afresh, endlessly.[23] He seeks to induce style as well as value out of everyday minutiae of social organization.[24] This reminds us that scientific discourse is subject, like any other discourse, to Ricoeur's (1988) contextual variability.

Parsons followed tradition as he sought to strip values out of forms of social organization. Eisenstadt (1981) returns to the principal source, Weber: "*Wirtschaftsethik* is, in a sense, a "code," a general "formal orientation," a "deeper structure," which programs or regulates the actual concrete social organization" (p. 172). In the present work the reverse direction is traveled instead, from concrete organization to whatever values there be. Others, such as DiMaggio (1987), Habermas (1975), March and Olsen (1976, 1989), and Merton (1968), also push for explanation of value only in interaction with tangible organization.

---

by 'ways of orienting and acting,' these ways being 'embodied in' meaningful symbols . . . which are the postulated controlling entities . . . unlike need-dispositions and role-expectations, (symbols) are not internal to the systems whose orientation they control . . . they have external 'objective' embodiments" (Parsons and Shils 1951, chap. 3, part II).

What had made Parsons's first book (1937) so stunning was its supersession of Pareto's synthesis of an abstract logico-experimental model of society with a biological/sentimental model. Pareto had relegated economics to a subordinate role, as unable to shed light on the general ends, the values, which drove and determined the whole means-ends schema of economics. Parsons argued, against Pareto's retreat to instinctual biology of the emotions, for a direct sociological interlocking of general ends into a web of values that was exactly *The Structure of Social Action*. Parsons's was a bold vision for linking society to individual by observable cultural fiat.

Parsons in his later work developed a positive theory of social system as self-similar system. He specified nested sets of functional structures as universals. This was the AGIL scheme: Adaptation/Goal attainment/Integration/Latent pattern maintenance.

Mark Granovetter suggests there should be a mapping into my discipline species. A possible mapping to the three species of disciplines is G to interface, I to council, and L to arena. The correspondent to Parsons's Adaptation is of another kind: it is the adaptation of social organization, taken as a whole, to the biophysical ecology. One can argue for a more general correspondence of AGIL to my principal constructs: G to production, I to network population, and L to identity.

However, there appear to be no analogues in Parsons to mechanisms of decoupling, apart from his "generalized media of exchange."

[23] For an overview of the recent phenomenological position, which situates Goffman with Sachs and Garfinkel, see Rawls (1989). For appreciation and critique of Goffman see Burns (1991).

[24] Even though Goffman seems concerned only with the evanescent, a principle of self-similarity suggests there should be similar stylistic regularities in large and ponderous institutions.

Either way, a value is made recognizable across different locales and periods by symbols and their use in social action. In the words of Michael Schudson:

> Culture is not a set of ideas imposed but a set of ideas and symbols available for use. Individuals select the meanings they need for particular purposes and occasion from the limited but nonetheless varied cultural menus a given society provides. In this view, culture is a resource for social use more than a structure to limit social action. It serves a variety of purposes because symbols are "polysemic" and can be variously interpreted; because communication is inherently ambiguous. (Schudson 1989, p. 155; and cf. Swidler 1986)

At any given time, any concrete actor always has available a number of alternative stories. Distinct frames of explanation (Simon 1945; Leach 1949) hold across several disciplines. But contradictions inhere in utilization of stories.

The first device that covers contradiction is exactly the use in common of sets of stories. The values used as foundation in many means-ends schemas of analysis (notably in Parsons 1937) were themselves derived by taking the intersections of story-sets in turn deriving from valuations across different disciplines. A value thus can be induced from intersecting interpretations across a set of stories. And specific values, as goals, are one of the common building blocks for creating and interrelating disparate stories into story lines and shared sets.

The second device to ease contradictions in social accountings is weaving a new value to enlarge story lines and sets of stories and their reaches. Either way, values conceal in the very process of affirming the contradictions. It is silly to regard each as being more cause than by-product of the generation of identities. But values may themselves in turn conform to some cultural logic, which calls for systematic development.

Packaging

Values operate in packages to form an institution. Lessons in white lies of tact and adaptability go along with lectures on honesty, and together they form a value set for living in institutional context. In one institution tact will predominate with honesty secondary, while another institution will have tact as shadow to honesty.[25]

---

[25] Until some proper calculus has been developed for analysis of narrative—perhaps along some such lines as Abell's (1987)—metaphor and intuition will have to

As an example, take values in science research in today's American academy. Originality (a variant of scope) is the preeminent value, with its complement and obverse in scientists' thinking and talk, the value of truth (a variant of purity) being shadow value; see the earlier discussion of Cozzens's (1989) case study in chapter 3.

From one institution to another, one may code different sets of values. But instead the same set may obtain, with the shift being in relative frequencies of use within the given set. The shift then occurs in how given values are mapped onto sorts of interaction, and in how actors sequence among the set in giving an accounting of action.[26]

No unique package, no single set of values is ordained. For example, priority and precision are another common pair of values, alongside truth and originality, through which to analyze stories of research within the discourse of a scientific specialty. At the level of "honesty" and "prudence," which is to say given the degree of abstraction in Parson's pattern variables (e.g., particularist, universalist: cf. Brownstein 1982), there is a whole package of values which can be operationally distinguished but yet which in subjects' appreciations may collapse into one. Distinctions within a set are correlated with concrete social context, so that the package in its concrete correlation is a moving target of analysis.

Take a concrete example from different discourse, Bob Dylan's adoption in 1965 of electric instruments, which then were adopted by many others. Within the preexisting (corporatist) institution of folkmusic, a general value—"genuine" hands-on music from and for the people—was no doubt violated by the shift of instrument; indeed there was a ruckus if not a schism. But among the active members of a world, operative values concern much more specific matters than such an abstraction. The change to electric instruments violated some but not others of the set of specific values, so that one could encompass the shift, cognitively, with rather small adjustments in the set.

---

serve. Linguistic theory of poetics (Culler 1975, pp. 197, 202, 227; Jakobson 1990, pp. 130–31) points toward some discriminations, as of metonymy from metaphor according to voice—discourse versus narrative—and theme, character, genre, and so on.

[26] Take a topical example. Senator Jesse Helms of North Carolina operates in a set of values which you hold too. A set of values comes with a scene, and the national political scene which you share with Helms as corporatist institution is huge, but it is also abstracted and limited to attitudes and accompanying ties as expressed in public media among entities and actions which themselves become defined as being public. It is the senator's priority, sequencing, and frequency in use, as well as his concrete mappings from values to social actors, that distinguish him from you on values.

The shift also at the same time would be impacting social relations, and in particular relations among performers, and between them and new sorts of technicians, all of which would be reflected in shifts in the specific values. Actors, like observers, are as much reading values out of accomplished actions as apprehending values for free-standing guides.

Corporatism

Corporatist institution builds from a soup of disciplines in which events and issues are generated in plenty, and in which arena disciplines are rare among the three species. Selections into corporates come early, as do routinized connections among them, so that continually forming teams of complementarities is not a thematic. Attention is directed to explicit corporate boundaries and positive identities, but equally distinctive are the suppression of many possible ties bridging distinct network populations. Many of the examples used will be historical from periods when the construct of corporatism was explicitly recognized, with an acumen from which we can benefit.

Work

Networks of disciplines do not build themselves from a concern with ecology. In shaping yet further structures of importance, it is control projects that continue to compete, and they only peripherally attend to effectiveness of physical productions. Each network as well as discipline depends crucially on the social context, which is supplied in large part by themselves as populations.

Work activities can induce each other and thereby temporarily outline a material population. But social life is about actors' importance within social settings; so work settings are not shaped primarily to effective joint operations on physical settings. As Udy (1970) early said explicitly, production in the ordinary sense of practical work is difficult to reconcile with the universal tendencies to elaboration and to embedding which come with the ongoing processes of social structuring. Udy worked out his argument from an extensive cross-cultural canvass of detailed forms of hunting, gathering, agriculture, and craft, as well as manufacturing and other contexts for work.

Succession is one major exemplification of this tension between work and the social. Performance in a work team can be seen as dependent on succession, day-by-day, to tasks of work. And the same issue recurs at larger scopes and periods. Solutions of social equations of balance are what deliver the successors and thereby impinge on technical equations of physical production.

Udy's theorem is that the longer and more fully developed the social context of production is, the less effective and efficient is the work process: hunting and gathering, he argues, dominates settled agriculture in efficiency, but not in social elaboration. Corporate institution deposited around work as a kernel, in a context of tribal and ethnic overlay.

Consensus in City-States

Corporatism asserts stories about itself as interrelated boundaries. The institution of corporatism is proclaimed as well as exemplified by guild systems of medieval and Renaissance cities. These systems and their cities are small and clearly demarcated so that all interconnections can be traced. The general picture is well known: Consult for example M. Howell (1988) on northern European and Hyde (1969) on Italian cities.

Studies of particular subsets of guilds for the arts have established contextual impacts, economic and political, associated with detailed changes in corporatist institution. Baxandall (1985) has done so for limewood sculptors across German cities and Antal (1965) has done so for all the art guilds of Renaissance Florence. Historical tracings of the overall governance of such cities, by contrast, can uncover variants of the institution as a whole.

Corporatism is defensive, and thus one might expect a corporatist institution to have some counterpart. This counterpart would have its own constituent corporates, it would be a counterpart corporatism shadowy in reality and ill-perceived by outsiders.[27]

Renaissance Florence is a city-state with highly articulate elites and extensive archives which have been studied intensively; so special transparency can be achieved there. Najemy (1982) has sifted a great array of detailed studies to draw a portrait of this polity, which he summarizes as a theory of consensus.

Consensus is not, paradoxically, the product, or even the goal of the collegial corporatist formation. On the contrary, Najemy makes clear that consensus is the urgent outer face of elite control which can only stay in shadows, given the brilliant light of consensus. Strings of dependency must abound in corporatism just because the

---

[27] The concept is familiar from Simon, Smithburg, and Thompson (1950) and has been developed further by DiMaggio and Powell (1983).

obscure, real struggle is over control of strings. Control by corporates is counter to the reality lying beneath consensus hegemony, which itself is manifested on the ground in strings of dependency, in some form of clientelism (for which see the next section).

The Frondé

The corporatist institution is not confined to cute little city-states. Nor, despite its story-sets, is it a pacific system. Consider a particular counter example.[28] When an irresistible social force meets an immovable social frame, paradoxes result. Such an encounter was *The Revolt of the Judges: The Parlement and the Frondé, 1643–52* (Moote 1971).

Earlier periods in France, as throughout Europe, had seen governments differentiate and evolve into largely corporatist forms (Major 1960), such as the *Standesstaat* of central Europe (Poggi 1970). A mosaic of collegial representations, a veritable tiling of the floor of state administration came into recognition. Always there were rights and privileges to be asserted for repeated recognition by a higher authority itself brought into being in part by urgent desires exactly for definitive recognition of turfs. These desires were expressed by not just one variety of discipline, not even a whole species for partition into interests and claims, but rather by an apparently endless spawning of still further subclaims and refinements and imitations (on Spain in addition cf. Carr 1966; and on Poland, cf. Anderson 1973).

Corporatism is the induction and defense of rightful meaning around right value. Corporatism is especially concerned with particular claims and rights about relations of agency. Corporatism is articulated by constellations of bodies which, in fact, produce the claims rather than the reverse. These are claims regarding three-party transactions, at minimum, which are being made to a supererogatory and embedding party.

The irresistible force of the Frondé period was the absolutist state of late medieval France, an unprecedented device of dual hierarchy and hieratic manipulation which was bypassing and smothering the *Standesstaat* (Lachmann 1989; Anderson 1973). The immovable body was the skein of legal corporations, the Parlements. This skein was triggered into stonewalling against royal invasion of their claims during a confusion of war and peripheral rural revolt.

The great paradox of the Frondé was the fact that a body of royal

[28] This early example is selected from among accounts of government corporatism because it identifies an explicit and tangible mechanism, whereas typical modern accounts (e.g., Schmitter; but see Lehmbruch and Schmitter 1982) primarily concern ideologies divorced from explicit social mechanism.

officials dedicated to the enforcement of law and the principle of royal absolutism—the story lines of parlements—could rebel against the king's administration. The singular article is inapt: even "the" *Parlement* of Paris was a complex of ten chambers which might only rarely meet together in plenary sessions. And this core complex itself was meaningful only because it was part of a formal network of other regional, local, and specialized parlements. This network combined law with registration and legislation, to express it in the modern idiom.

This Parlement lattice itself was resilient to being rooted out because it was contraposed to other lattices[29] which were more directly fiscal in operation. But these lattices were intent upon operationalizing meaning, each for its turfs and its members. This was the case with even a "sun god" king—who in their halls was invoked only to preside over their magisterial concordance of rights with rites.

The Frondé gained eventness, identity, just by the failure of Parlement to notice, as it were, to register absolutist decrees. Was registration a mere formality? No, registration was assignment of meaning by a pinnacle of a lattice of mutually recognized corporations whose own identities came from certifying meanings, which is to say from creating meanings. These corporations' historical (and etymological) origins always were to block action through asserting meaning.

These meanings were primarily and originally tangible. As meanings, they were socially operational, they were rights and immunities and the like. It was a late trick of the absolutist era, dressed up as a liberation and an enlightenment, to conceive and assert meanings so abstract as to have little social content.[30] There cannot be any self-evident corporate body to assert and define an abstract right.

> Absolutist arguments had no effect on the parlementarians, who simply countered with legal measures which forced the regent to make further concessions. . . . Any Royal legislation to enact their reforms (increase taxes in war crisis) then had to go through each court separately . . . (yielding) a many-sided scramble for redress of diverse grievances and a legal nightmare . . . at lower government levels petty bureaus had first to submit reforms to sovereign tribunals—provincial and national—and often lengthy appeals for and against from officials. There were provincial parliamentary Frondé's in the making, but the real re-

---

[29] Of *tresoriers* and *elus*.

[30] Just so did earlier Greek philosophy emerge in the age of tyrants, though it was the public relations of the occasional and momentary republican forms which impressed itself upon the later world as the character of the age.

volt of the judges in the provinces got under way only when the Parlement of Paris forced the regent to send legislation for the consideration of these local corporations. (Moote 1971, pp. 136, 140, 145, 150)

It was only special circumstances—a regency of notable ineptness, confused war mobilizations, and the like—that made corporatist institutions limpid to the observer and analyst. And also not every culture has the lucidity and consistency which the French show even when running amok. But the corporatist institutions whose bones are laid so clear here is no esoteric flower confined to France, or to the great, or to one era.

Pillarization

A colorful and instructive example of corporatist institution with dual hierarchy is *Verzuiling* in the Netherlands (Lijphart 1968; Bank 1981; Van Schendelen and Jackson 1987). In the Netherlands under public law there have operated not just cultural and educational systems separate by sectarian commitment, but also such organizations as chambers of commerce. In addition there have been separate *bedrijs vereningingen* for social insurance, and also *bedrijschappen* for self-regulation, which also are sometimes grouped into larger combinations, as for example Christian segregated from non-Confessional:

> In the mid-sixties this pillarised system of consociational politics essentially disappeared. Substantial political decision-making shifted from the level of pillar-elites to that of state officials and politicians . . . many pillarised welfare organizations had entered financial problems. . . . The state took over . . . accelerated the process of depillarisation. . . . The shift from inducements to compulsory regulation is related to the depillarisation of society. . . . New social groupings, including new or more modern-minded firms, ask for equal treatment, instead of closed-door clientelism and favouritism. (Van Schendellen and Jackson 1987, chap. 4)

The origins of pillarization, *Verzuiling*, show its focus on meaning woven into blocking action and energized along strings of concrete ties. The history is clear:

> *Verzuiling* is widely credited with "having brought stability to a society which is otherwise divided by contradictions and antagonisms. . . ." The "liberal" *zuil* should be regarded as an *omnium gatherum* which owes its existence to the presence of the others. The Protestants, or more precisely the strict Calvinists among them, the Catholics and the Socialists have in turn withdrawn from a society dominated by liberal

values. During the latter half of the nineteenth century they tried to entrench themselves within their own political and social organizations. . . . In the late 1860s Abraham Kuyper . . . a young minister (decided) Christianity stood in irreconcilable opposition to Liberalism . . . his well-known doctrine of the antithesis . . . he began setting up his own associations, his own political party, his own comprehensive system of education. The antithesis, originally directed against modernism, blossomed into a doctrine of plurality and diversity. His most ardent supporters were recruited from the artisans of pre-industrial Holland, the *kleine luyden*, the small men. . . . Kuyper in 1886 . . . forms his own church . . . *Gereformeerde Kerk* comprised seven per cent of the population . . . in 1880 the first priest to be elected to the Dutch Parliament . . . Schaepman, with his Protestant counterpart Kuyper was able to form a coalition government . . . ending the Liberal monopoly of power. (Bank, pp. 207–31)

Another expert, Windmuller (1970) emphasizes the subsequent labor explosions that became compressed into yet another, socialist pillar, leading to the full-blown pillarization system by the First World War. Such a plural society is held together by a grand coalition of the leaders of the significant segments, which can be seen as distinct subcultures around distinct meanings. These separations in fact greatly strengthen the tangible networks of favor and obligation which serve to freeze up the social formation. Such networks are energized exactly through strings of interconnections across the elites of different pillars, who, by their own public definitions, can have no meanings in common!

With this exoteric template in hand, one can recognize similar configurations around one. The system of faculties in a university may be like a *verzuiling*. Newer faculties, such as communications or even business, within universities are still negotiating what the pillars will be. Arts and sciences departments are not allowed to partition courses in such faculties. Unlike departments, the resulting clusters may not be able to interface with the outside, for recruiting and consulting. Disparate faculties within the university also are negotiating whether some professional institution or some frankly clientelistic style will be more apt than the usual corporatism, apt especially in the blocking action which is at the core of academic life.

Corporatism as Blocking Action

Recent popularizations of corporatism (e.g., cf. Lehmbruch and Schmitter 1982) have been misled. They have been deceived by the insistent rationalizations which are the very stuff of corporatism.

They have been duped into thinking of corporatism as something grand, esoteric, and different.

That is nonsense. Corporatism is a common everyday affair. Corporatism is an institution which exactly organizes around the assertion of specific meanings, rights, and immunities, for explicitly operationalized sets and nestings of actors. Corporatism is so at all scopes and in all contexts. The Old Testament is the bible of corporatism. The Ph.D. comprehensive exam is the text for corporatism. Corporatism is around you all the time, a stalwart of blocking action on every scale from boys' gangs to college departments and to bureaus within businesses. And of course we find it in the endless lattices of law courts and tribunals.

The elaboration of clothing into uniformities can define social ages and social classes and also local gangs. These elaborations are operationalized in the layouts of clothing floors in department stores. These displays are literal mappings of corporatism. Brains, energy, and loyalties are induced and applied in tangible fashion to the raw material of identity, story, and productions. All this is to the end of sustaining meaning by blocking action.

Listen to the reactions of a sojourner to Madrid witnessing the transition from what was hypostasized as a real corporatist regime (Franco era) into some other form:

> What is proclaimed, or even done, by the most organized and most conspicuous collective protagonists, the State in the first instance, is refracted, interfered with, perhaps even neutralized by the behavior of the other protagonists, over who, in fact, they have much less control than they would like to have, or that at times they think they have. Of all these collective protagonists, the State is also the one most given to overestimating the real effects of its own actions. It dictates rules, orders, projects, it announces objectives and wishes, all of which together it calls "economic policy," and it hopes that the real course of events will follow it to a significantly high degree. This of course only occurs exceptionally. . . . Economic policy becomes a mixture of government action and distressed cries from the political class, overwhelmed by circumstances and anxious to find some kind of psychological security in the trappings of decrees, laws or declarations. (Perez-Diaz 1984, pp. 1, 2)

Very similar quotes can be found for other esoteric locales, such as Riggs's accounts (1966) of Thai transitions cited earlier. But all this also can be transposed to the small scale of organizational life around yourself, as well as to the larger scale reflected in your newspaper's accounts of new administrations in business and in nation.

The underlying importance of an institution is its making comparable, and in so doing bringing together, otherwise disparate and unrelated clusters and network populations. Its story lines become so persuasive that onlookers come to mistake its intentions for tangible actuality.

Blocking action is omnipresent, as common in the economy as in government. Entrepreneurship was a striking characteristic of England when it was the prototype of industrialization; but so, even then, was blocking:

> The banking system that was constructed (by 1914) put the banks in a position where they acted as a block against the external forces that were necessary for industry's growth, and it has been the structure of the system rather than the attitudes and choices of bankers that has been at the root of the problem. . . . The banks have met industry's demand for credit all too comfortably, and, as a result, have developed a special relation with industry which has given them a blocking role . . . regulated their lending by a set of negative rules designed to minimize the damage that could be done if a loan failed. (Fine and Harris 1985, pp. 124, 130)

Another apt example is organization and management in the context of coal mining in Britain. As long as the industry was breaking new ground, all went well, but part of the evolution was addition of new aspects, professionalized and clientelistic, to what had been a corporatist form. When formal administration first took over from corporatist action, the so-called market or capitalist format yielded poor results for decades. Then the same was true under rationalization of mining by government. Corporatist institution remained, sufficient to block getting action but not free to exhibit its own low overhead.

Somewhat the same story seems to attend the electrical power industry, closely associated to coal in England. Krieger (1984) has analyzed the failure of a Weberian-bureaucracy scheme of impeccable rationality, the National Power Loading Agreement. "The failure of the NPLA was not a failure in the logic of planning production, but rather a failure located in the dialectic of control which attends centralized bureaucratic administration."[31]

---

[31] Granick (1972, 1975) found similar contrasts in his comparative studies of Western and of Eastern European managements, but the record is endless. In the USA after the Civil War: "By 1882 the (U.S.) navy had one officer for every four enlisted men. Vice Admiral Rowan retired in 1889 at age eighty" (Socolefsky and Spetter 1987, p. 95). President Benjamin Harrison did not block action here, he merely sat.

In social theory, conflict can be seen as a convenient dual face to solidarity, the two together offering both decoupling and integration. Conflict must be built into an institution to achieve some flexibility and some potential for the exercise of control.

Clientelism

Clientelism tends to be slighted, perhaps because of familiarity. It is by no means limited to small casts on small stages. Clientelism is a stratification system that centers on persons and their ties. It can be set off against professional style, including variants derived from the corporatist institution just described.

In its original Roman manifestation, clientelism had become adapted to structuring international relations across the complex field of cities, provinces, empires, kingdoms, and other flotsam of the early Mediterranean. Badian (1958) argues, "The year 146 B.C. sees the end of proper international relations and proper international law. . . . Henceforth all allies—free or federati—are *clients*, in the sense that their rights and obligations are in practice independent of law and treaties and are entirely defined and interpreted by Rome" (p. 105). This is Rome as concretized in particular senatorial families and senators as patrons. From the Roman case one can learn general regularities. For example, multiple "ownership" is what makes any patronage system "go," as when for instance in American academia, several older figures attribute the merits of any particular younger figure to their own—teaching, tutelage, favors, evaluations, whatever.

Nor is clientelism an all-or-none characterization of huge social formations. Suleiman (1987) describes the clientelistic ambiance in which persists the vestigial body of notaries in France. These notaries are neither public nor private; they persist amidst the contemporaneous French state and society, with origins in the times of the Frondé and earlier. Not even Crozier and his school (Crozier and Thoenig 1978) have argued that clientelism is the pervasive style in French social organization. Clientelism is however adaptable for intrusions. Suleiman says:

> Centralization concentrates jurisdiction . . . a private group need not disperse their efforts in accordance with jurisdictional dispersion as is the case in decentralized structures. . . . Clientelism is more dangerous in a centralized system, because the client need take over only one structure . . . agencies are created to protect sectors and groups . . . leads to a clientelistic relationship. (Suleiman 1987, p. 17)

There were examples of similar penetration of the emerging absolutist state centuries earlier. As Perry Anderson points out (1974, p. 49), grandee houses infiltrated the state apparatus with parasitic clientages of lesser nobles. Thus they formed rival patronage networks.

Some theorists are almost incensed by what they see as the inability of theorizing about clientelism to recover clean-cut institutions. Higgins says:

> In modern transactionalism these (common sense) descriptive categories are replaced by others of precisely the same [i.e., essentially descriptive] status: "action-sets," quasi-groups, "social networks," "factions," and of course patron-client and patron-broker-client relations. Social structure is again conceived as an aggregate of these relations. Its existence in both cases is only at a purely empirical level, and is given no theoretical determinacy. In consequence of the absence of any complex abstract conception of social structure which could account theoretically for unevenness and evenness within the totality. (In Clapham 1982, p. 116)

Here we see the analyst with the same obsession with imposing meaning that characterizes blocking action generally!

This last quotation also underlines a tension between the stringing aspect of clientelist dependency and the focus of blocking action upon meaning. The quotation suggests how the tension is exacerbated under clientelism. This is because clientelism does not make widespread use of style. In particular, clientelism does not ever generate issues, which are the event-analogues of style. In the soup of clientelism one will not find interfaces.

The dyad tie itself is what is carefully crafted in clientelism, even though the meanings built up around it invariably argue the cascading of loyalty along chains. Clientelism is a relation of exchange between unequals, which can be understood by itself without direct coupling to a next tie in a string of patronage: the coupling proves to have an obverse side; decouplings are and must be effected, decouplings from the past of relations and from ecology of concrete surroundings. A similar dialectic of decoupling recurs across all levels of scope and focus from localities on up. It is for this reason that clientelism as construct is so fluid as to bring endless complaints from analysts that it obscures distinctions.[32]

---

[32] I argue that another problem is confounding of institutions with styles in much existing theoretical analysis.

Blocking Action

Initial stages of forming clientelism are vulnerable because of the lack of explicit interlocking between dyads. Purcell describes post-Independence Mexico as having, locally, a stable clientelistic style; but

> the Díaz dictatorship had no organizational infrastructure . . . politics never became institutionalized. . . . The entire system depended on Díaz's ability to maintain personalistic linkages with the locally based landholding elites and their clienteles. . . . Two clientelistic systems are today operating in Mexico. The first is the chain of vertical, personalistic ties that originate in the Presidency. . . . The other patron-client ties characteristic of the locally-based networks are basically stable. . . . The clientelism that permeates the national political institutions, in contrast, is extremely unstable and fluid. (In Eisenstadt and Lemarchand 1982, p. 196)

There are large social formations which are argued to be entirely clientelist, at all scopes. Hausa city-states (M. Smith 1975) such as Kano, Katsina, Daura, Gobir, and Zauzau, which were contemporaneous with Medici Florence, had a repertoire of what can be called craft guilds and tensions with surrounding agricultural holdings which seem parallel to those of many of the contemporaneous Italian city-states. But he argues elsewhere that the

> basic bond was clientship. . . . Every free man regardless of his social or ethnic origin through the contract systems of *chapka* (allegiance) and *barantaka* found his place and his protection secured. . . . The ruler used this competition (for formal offices) to award title to lineages that lacked proper hereditary claims and thus reinforced monarchical power through the parallel system of client patronage. (In Griffith and Thomas 1981)

This is also reminiscent of the Absolutist French scene, but in Africa there does not appear to have been the lattice of corporatist jurisdictional bodies seen there, or the simpler lattice in Florence.

Thailand offers a special example: "Unlike the situation in many other societies where patronage is seen as something opposed to the structure of the system even if it does 'oil the wheels,' in Thailand it is analyzed as being an integral part of the system" (Kemp, in Claphan 1982, chapter 7). There is a highly complex society and yet one with an absence of corporate groups. Especially and above all, there is no sense for structural equivalence in Thai society:

> Any relationship is between unequals and the recognition of this fact is an integral and emphasized part of Thai culture . . . there are no kin-

ship groups in Thai society . . . a lack of role differentiation between political, economic and other types of activity. . . . Thailand can be seen as a changing population of entourages, the entourage joining unequal individuals in a highly personalized manner in a relation that lasts for only as long as it is mutually beneficial.

From all these examples of clientelism, it is clear that the dependent variable should be seen as immobility, as blocking action. Reports on all of them—Mexico, Hausa, Thai, and others—do insist on blockage. An equally common report is of a preoccupation with meanings, a preoccupation which is beyond any proportion to actual operation and accomplishment. Poggi argues both facets:

> By addressing all political energies and aspirations towards the pursuit of private advantage; by validating others' privileges in so far as one hopes to draw from them some petty favour toward oneself; by fragmenting and dispersing solidarities; . . . clientelism can *at best* conserve and reproduce the environment which generates it. Its "molecular" aspect, its ability to personalize, to make proximate and frequent the search for political protection and influence, is part of its deceptions, and as such it should be treated with diffidence or deprecated . . . it must be the task of political practice *to render* clientelism again vestigial and interstitial. (1983)

Another possible assessment is that clientelism may expand to permeate large social formations in a counterpoint of blockage exactly to periods of extreme and rapid getting of action. Such an alternation can be argued for the USSR, from the accounts in surveys like Brzezinski and Huntington (1964). It is implied in the treatment in chapter 6 of the current (1989) Gorbachev opening, which itself is an echo of Catherine the Great (Anderson 1987, p. 150), Peter, Ivan (Skrynnikov 1981), and so on.

Nesting

Without disciplines and issues, and with few identities, clientelist "gels" exhibit larger-scale ordering in ways other than those for corporatism or caste. There is a nesting of clientelism, a nesting into larger formation. But the nesting is derived from the context of other ties rather than from explicit three-and-more body chains of interconnection.

Consider, for example, the clientage ties of early Irish society, which have often been interpreted in mainly symbolic terms. Nerys Patterson shows how very practical and material these ties really were, and also how separatist. Yet she goes on to show how they were sustained and reproduced because of an intercalation of flows at different levels:

> The contract of free clientship was thus conditioned by and secondary to the relationship between lord and base-client. The terms of free clientship were sustainable by the free client only because he had reserves of cattle vested in base clients that he could draw on in a crisis. In the relationship between overlord and free client the overlord skimmed off some of the free client's profits that were generated by the base-clients' direct output, and their indirect contribution to the free client's productivity by permitting the latter to specialize in stock keeping. In return the lower-level lord received short-term injections of additional stock and was assured of the political support of other members of the cattle-lending class in maintaining control of base-clients. This class solidarity took the form of direct political alliance, and of the jural privileges accorded to members of the nobility by the jurists and genealogists. (N. Patterson 1980, p. 60)

Semi-Periphery in World System

World system theory can be construed to center on the distinctions and interconnections of semi-periphery with core and periphery (Wallerstein 1974, 1980). This theory can be seen as a claim that the present architecture of the world, taken in the large, is of clientage style.[33] The parallelism to Patterson's account is striking: an example of theory as self-similar.

Center on production and exchange, and let the physical space scale be maximal. The system of control is reduced somewhat arbitrarily to but three strata. The semi-periphery is where decoupling mechanisms become concentrated from cumulation over time of attempts at control in many institutions. Wallerstein construed semi-periphery at a macro level, as whole national economies which fit as brokers in between the two main positions that he conceives, exploitative center and exploited periphery nations. The awkward hyphenation of the term "semi-periphery" aptly suggests its awkward standing: as a structural locus which yet is defined by a process goal of decoupling, a goal which is exactly about subverting embedding. Wallerstein's account of a "world-system" reads easier, once the semi-periphery is understood in these relativist terms, rather than as some fixed and specifiable role or technical function, or as a halfway house.

Schwartzman (1989), in her account of Portugal, gives the most ex-

---

[33] One need only substitute economists as a modern equivalent to her early wandering jurists, and lawyers as a modern equivalent to her genealogists to get an analogy between her Ireland and our world.

plicit analysis extant of the mechanism of semi-periphery. Her formulation is that semi-periphery, as location within a system, must
imply "disarticulation" internally within the semi-periphery. In
short, semi-periphery is a position, as defined below, pp. 161–63.

What this semi-periphery does, viewed as a unit, is triage writ
large. This triaging is a complement to responsibility being taken
from above (see chapter 1), and more specifically it is the timing aspect. This and the structural aspect are in tension, and that is why
there must be the Schwartzman disarticulation.

Structural change in the world system is deflected and blocked by
the emergence and consolidation of this semi-periphery tier. A semi-
periphery unit permits and arranges just some changes in ordinary
flows. The presence of semi-periphery does allow for "policy initiatives," from below or periphery, as well as from above or core standing. Figure 4-2 lays out the brokerage pattern in flows, as developed
by Guillarte (1990) in an empirical study of semi-periphery in world
political context.

There are many other exemplars of the semi-periphery mechanism
which can be abstracted from Schwartzman's account. The key is
that the moves for decoupling, played against embeddings in the ongoing crossings of projects for control, that these moves tend to cluster in parallel locales. Consider for example Hsiao's account of a
nineteenth-century Chinese context (1960, p. 506): "Retired function-
aries, expectant officials, and degree-holding scholars far outnum-
bered officials in active government service . . . "; and it was these
figures, supernumeraries in a formal context, who were the actual
avenue of control, as gentry resident in a massive rural population.
It is in much the same way that, today in our economy, management
control subsists through the efforts of hundreds of thousands of officials with the MBA or other degree-analogues to the Chinese Imperial
examination ranks.

Tarrow's (1971) comparative account of French with Italian local
elites, as brokers vis-à-vis strong states, uncovers a semi-periphery.
His analysis is consistent with accounts by Ashford (1982) and by
Crozier and Thoenig (1976) of French as contrasted with English local
government; and it may fit the conundrums of Japan's local government as well (Funaba 1989; Steiner 1981). And in the economic
realm, the putting-out system, especially in its early *kaufmann* forms,
are exemplars of semi-periphery.[34]

---

[34] The semi-periphery is thus encountered at very diverse scopes and levels. For
blockmodel analyses of semi-periphery patterns in international trade, see Snyder
and Kick (1979), Breiger (1981a), Love (1982), and Van Rossem (1989). Missing is an
account of the dynamics that reproduce such a control process, at any scope. A recent
paper that moves in this direction is D. Smith and D. White (1992), which also gives

Influence Under Structural Equivalence

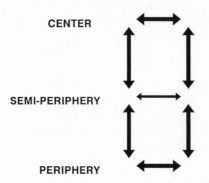

Influence under Cohesion

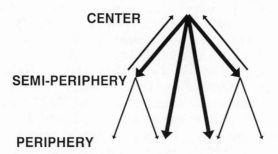

Fig. 4-2. Guillarte on role of semi-periphery

Norman Feudalism

Stenton developed the classic account of the first century of English feudalism, post-Conquest:

> The relationship between lord and man was as common in pre-Conquest England as anywhere in France. But in England this relationship was only one element in a social order based essentially on hereditary status, and in France it had become the basis of a new type of society organized specifically for war. No process of evolution could have bridged the gap. (Stenton 1932, p. 217)

It sounds like a switch from a more corporate to a more clientelist sort of institution.

---

a survey. Detailed analysis of examples, from diverse settings, is needed; Padgett's model under General Management in chapter 6 is suggestive.

The previous chapter on network analysis implicitly assumed an isolated population free of the complexities of interaction to which this chapter has turned. The Norman Conquest provides now a case unusually clear-cut in the interaction of network populations to form an institution. Much is known about story-sets, types of tie, roles, and the like.

Tribal contexts have been referenced earlier,[35] but tribes may be misleadingly simple exemplars. It is exactly because in tribes there are presumably fewer levels of embedding and decoupling—as well as fewer stories about, and intertwinings of, control projects—that we feel intuitively such direct access to anthropologists' accounts. No one in a tribe would or could write either this book, or the anthropologist's account. Likely it is that we over-conceptualize accounts of tribes. Any one set of concepts may be mappable into tribal reality, but perhaps that is so only because a tribe condenses what in more complex contexts we are forced to see as really distinct.

Instead we expound an example from early Europe. We draw general lessons on type of tie induced from such complex tapestries. Examining a case with written records will help open up distinctions among roles and position made only implicitly on the ground.

What populations are at issue? Whether one looks at aspects of economic exploitation, of Norman political insertion, or at interbreeding, no crisp answer is in view, and such answer could not be the same in the year 1086 as in 1066. Populations have clear boundaries only in special situations such as tribal invasion, where total extirpation of a population can be the outcome, failing the emergence of such an institution as slavery (McNeill 1983; O. Patterson 1982).

Turning to an account of the Norman Conquest suggests a return to the caste institution except that recent migration and immediate confrontation take the place of long-standing interaction among populations in continuing overlays, though the latter figures too in the emergence of settled feudal institution. The shock of the Conquest was both so large and so long-lived, that detailed stories are still known about patterns of interlock in relations down through individuals which proved to set the tone of how they evolved subsequently.

An esoteric set of social forms were brought across the Channel and implanted in the Anglo-Saxon society and they were to supplant its upper reaches almost entirely. There was no common language; it really was a foreign invasion, yet there was no massive migration into or killing and displacement of existing populations. Both sides

[35] E.g., see excerpts from Fortes on the Tallensi in the section of chapter 2 on the council discipline.

of the Channel had complex, large, encrusted social formations of known complex histories that were very different from what we are familiar with. It seems a fit setting for seeking wider applicability of network and value constructs in institutions.

Kinship Gangs

The Norman Conquest was sudden, though not unexpected, in 1066 (Searle 1988); for decades afterward William the Conqueror and his French barons were all too aware that Danes could pull the same turnover on them. The essential point is that one can hope to see the bare bones, the networks and disciplines in raw unmediated form, best during the turbulent period. The replacement of Anglo-Saxon by Norman was abrupt and by conscious intention. Searle (1988, pp. 238–39) is vivid on the consciously exploitative nature of Norman society and its takeover of England. Networks of kinship gangs were the Norman polity. The Norman invaders acted to set up an exploitation network akin to but more flexible than the one sketched below (p. 180) for a putting-out economy. In modern idiom, the Capone gang moved to add Detroit to Chicago as turf. Throughout history, kings often began their careers as gangsters.

Nonetheless, the conquest was limited in much the same way as is a merger-and-acquisition takeover of a big corporation by outside capital today. The point of takeover is to exploit even further the broad reaches of the existing structure with no more change than is necessary beyond throwing out the existing barons to bring in your own. As quickly as possible new stories, meanings, and identities are to be woven from speculations, gamings, and control crossings, but this is not very quick, given the scale and the shock; so for a while participants and observers are freer to perceive. And for a while there will be less of the actual embeddings into hierarchies of smoothly operating interfaces that are bound up with the stories and gamings.

Shift of Institution

The outlines of Anglo-Saxon society seem more firmly drawn . . . than those of the succeeding feudal order. The rigorous distinctions of personal status which run throughout Old English society essentially simplify its structure. (Stenton 1932, p. 5)

By contrast is:

The truth that the fabric of feudal history is composed of genealogical detail, that innumerable events which are unintelligible as related by contemporary writers presuppose an elaborate nexus of family alliances and rivalries (p. 3). The Norman settlers in England could not maintain the clear social distinctions with which they had once been familiar. They were a miscellaneous multitude (p. 27) . . . the fundamental distinction between Frenchmen and Englishmen overrode all the matters of detail in which the custom of one French province differed from that of another (p. 29) . . . the whole elaborate system of knight-service in England could be traced to the conditions which the Conqueror had imposed on his leading followers. (Stenton 1932, p. 3)

Much of the corporate outlines became blurred, as when the stratum of *thegns* evaporated (p. 116) within decades of the conquest even while many of the persons were adapting successfully. And it was not true that the parallel, but network-derived terms of the French, such as *vavassor*, were completely crisp, even just in Normandy proper. It was exactly that the conquerors could, and were vulnerable enough to, enforce much crisper definitions. And these were centered on military service, which in the technical conditions meant expert personal service under arms, and support sustained via grant of land actively farmed.

The tie was to be so well defined that it generated automatic indirect ties. That is, the king, and presumably magnates in their turn, asserted a claim to the allegiance of under-tenants overriding the claims of any intermediate lord (cf. pp. 11, 113). Conversely, although one man may well be subject to many lords, in *ligius*, the central feudal relation, he is bound directly to a particular one, of whom he holds his normal residence and whose contingent he must join if the host is called (p. 30). The term knight which eventually became the norm was itself Anglo-Saxon, showing that network ties in the new raw situation were being boldly redefined using all constituent material.

Interaction among corporate and string modes of perceiving and building social space emerged early in this rude conquest, and indeed each always, in any social context, shapes the other. Never did the conqueror or successors grant compact lordships, rather, lands even of the greatest barons were scattered widely, dispersed among the "fees" of other lords. At the same time that this inhibited forming new corporates of possible opposition, it also reinforced the long-standing corporate compound of the thegns whose lands were handed over as integral units.

As integral to dependency as the compounding of ties was the linking together as corporate of the men who worked the constituent farms of an estate. Peasant tenants with various forms of claims on the lands also had rights of consultation. Courts of a variety of forms were the most precisely defined instances of this conflation of corporate with networks forms, but justice was seen as so localized, both in the chains of infeudation and in the determination by local experts on local corporate custom, that it is anachronistic to draw a sharp line between court and council of advice (pp. 42, 67, 91).

Social standing, and authority derived from it, were not univocally set by location in the network of feudal dependencies, central though that was. "Many (lords or larger manors) held larger fees than the lesser among the king's barons held of him, and as a class they were men of the same social standing. And the word baron denoted a man's place in society without reference to the position which he happened to hold in the tenurial scale" (p. 98). The ideas of social standing melded network positions into corporate standings. "The reputation of a feudal lord in the world of his day, his influence in the king's court, and his standing in his own country largely turned on the number and quality of the enfeoffed knights who were bound to him by service" (p. 60).

Networks of ties become rigorously separated from corporate forms only in a very distinct line of development, that of **ministerials**. There were landless knights—roughnecks and layabouts in the terms of a later era—who proliferated in years of troubles and private wars. But there came to be built into this society officers, *dapifers* or *seneschals*, with definite duties of administration not related to war, not episodic, and not of right connected to courts and councils. Social standing, and corporate form, were largely erased for them. They are precursors to positions, which prefigure formal organizations which are prefigured by servile elites (see chapters 6 and 7).

Indeed, the Norman Conquest was a shift from more corporate to more clientelist institution.

Positions across Role Frames

Norman feudalism accounts itself in terms of roles and positions. These might seem the apt theoretical basis for accounting institutions in general. This section will show why this is not the case. In so doing, hints appear that some further sort of organization beyond the institution is necessary to generate individual persons, who usually are thought of as the actors in roles and positions.

The child is more than the playmate represented by a node in the playground network of chapter 1. Children also come from several elsewheres, from families, from schools, and likely also from neighborhood cliques. Each of these network populations in which a given child is found may contain few or none of its other playmates from that playground. To represent the child as a whole takes a bundle of such nodes-in-contexts from beyond any one physical locale and any one multiplex network. Maybe these bundles fit together as an institution, but maybe not—likely not for an American playground today. But perhaps there is no need to specify some larger environing social organization, such as institution; perhaps role theory, when enlarged to include positions, can serve as a theoretical matrix sufficient for all scopes. Nadel (1957) is convincing that this is worth exploration.

Each multiplex network taken separately can be analyzed, as in chapter 3, into multiple networks of types of tie and thence into a role frame. The first level of analysis is a blockmodel, which equates a set of children that shares the same types of tie to other such sets of children. The result is a partition of the children into a set of blocks. The role of children in one block with respect to other blocks is specified by the configurations of ties (direct and as paths). The role frame puts together these results.

A second level equates configuration of ties which are similar abstractly even though they do not connect the same sets of blocks.[36] This second level defines abstract roles that can have names and be transposed, as for example when one spots all the children on the playground who are playing the role of a halfback, or a socio-emotional leader, rather than, as at the first level, just the children at halfback in the particular scrimmage over here. A frame of fewer roles results, obviously, at this second level.

At either level, roles are interlocked together into a frame by construction. Hereafter, statements are written so as to hold at either level unless otherwise noted. The first level will be used below in putting role frame together with institution, and the second level will be used in putting role frame together with a new construct of style, introduced in the next section.

Positions

Social positions are presupposed by earlier role theory, but their provenance has been a continuing puzzle (Biddle 1986). So it is plausible to look for a set of positions within network data as a bridging

---

[36] This is Winship's (1974) generalization of structural equivalence. In other papers (White, Boorman, and Breiger 1976) roles were defined at the first level. The new procedure deals with structural equivalence abstractly, rather than confined within a given network population. It will come into its own, as elaborated just below.

structure among distinct role frames. And after all, until other role frames are activated there is no phenomenological basis for discriminating roles in a given frame. One will not be seen as a parent until one is also a workmate, scholar, or tribesman; you will not be seen as a playmate until you are also a schoolboy; and so on. This is true even though analysts can infer such roles from structural equivalence patterns on just one network.

In the playground example, the child will have some role in each of the frames.[37] Available in the frames will be braggart, bully, docile follower, and the like, sorted out by some familiar complementarities held in tension as a role frame. Separately, in the home there is some menu of roles vis-à-vis parents and siblings. Separately again, among groups there may be task leader, social leader, follower, and so on (Whyte 1943).

The social position of a particular child does not lie in any one such role of hers but rather in her being recognized at the same time in a role in each frame. Each position can be seen as a bracket specifying which role is selected in each frame and to which blocks in that network population. And the same position appears as an identity in each of several network populations.[38] The resulting position may have some tag associated with it, such as for the child teacher's pet, butt of ridicule, or big shot.

A particular position thus brings together a set of distinct identities, each supported by a discipline, from distinct network populations. They are brought together into a more-or-less integrated whole. This whole can be equated to the social personality: for a psychologist's perspective on this consult Mischel (1968). And also the present account seems compatible with the structuration perspective advanced by the sociologist Giddens (1979).

Seen as a whole, such a set of positions captures regularities in the intersection of distinct networks. This is a sophisticated structure, more so, even in this example for modern children, than in some involuted tribe. Relational data across and within a number of populations is required, such as for example Gross et al. (1958) collected in studies of school superintendency positions.

Accountings are sought by each identity for itself as well as vis-à-

---

[37] If only a residual role: see the discussion in chapter 3 of the Omega phenomenon of Romo (1991, 1992).

[38] The crucial step is to develop computational algorithms. It should be possible to adapt algorithms for finding roles (e.g., Pattison 1989; Winship and Mandel 1984; D. White and Reitz 1983). What level of divergence in detailed configuration to accept as still mapping together into a position: this is an issue of sociological theory, not of formal technique.

vis others. Choosing and telling a story becomes confusing. Identities in structurally equivalent positions across the set of networks are the first to share stories as types of tie. Identities share a set of mappings of stories onto the situation as they perceive it, structurally equivalent ones likely to share each mapping. Explicit interpretations result for roles in frames linked by position. They can also sustain some larger environing formation such as institution.

Positions and Institution

The chief point to be made is that not just any larger context will support reproduction of such a pattern of regularity—partial and nonuniform though it may be across the several network populations. The term "position" may be applicable for the location of an identity within an institution. The larger context may, but need not, be an institution. Conversely, an institution may, but need not, sustain a set of positions across role frames from all or some of its network populations. Some particular corporatism may be aptly described by positions across role frames, but not all corporatisms carry through so far as the individual level of detail on relations.

Among the youth of a traditional Elmtown (Hollingshead 1949), some institution may hold, with its corporate units being sets of kids well recognized by locale, class, age, and so on. But in Elmtown there may not be specification down to positions across roles for individual kids. Conversely, to describe the larger context across children seen on playgrounds in some suburb today as an institution, such description may claim a kind of order not there. And yet this suburban context may support a set of positions. That is, some combinations of distinct roles from different network frames may be recognized across the suburb as important or common, even though no embracing corporatism or other institution is found.

The context may be several institutions instead of one: From positions are enacted role relations both in this and in that distinct institution. For example, the guild merchant is also an official of Heidelberg city and also junior kinship-line head in rural contado, and so on. Or in our day the plate tectonics researcher is also professor of environment studies and reserve army colonel in Irvine, California.

It is this dual nature of positions, as intersections both from below and from above, that confounds much existing theory, for example game theory.[39]

---

[39] When most game theorists take on populations they disdain network topology to focus on subtleties of strategic interaction between persons as entities taken for

Nadel's Dead End

The anthropological theorist Nadel (1957), who also provides field reports (1946) well beyond tribal in scope, tried to model a whole social universe in terms of positions across roles in frames. He made reference only to a few very general positions; so the question of their being gathered into one or more institutions did not arise. The remaining question for him was what sort of diffuse structuring of the larger context might be observed and shown to be essential. He bypassed the whole idea of some sort of middle-range orders embracing network populations.

To elaborate into role frames carries a price, which is the necessity to somehow integrate location in one coherent role frame into the same position with locations in other role frames from different network populations who tell other sets of stories. How, Nadel might ask, can some individual make sense out of being father and professor and Celtics fan and taxpayer in different states? How can one make sense of a context of others each of whom has quite different combinations of, and different overlaps to others' combinations of, roles in frames, from a very large menu of role frames? How is such a common sense to be supported by the context?

These problems, as Nadel expounded with force and lucidity, become more severe when identities individually have more options as to role frames. Individuals do have some options in all save the most involute tribes. Nadel fell back on a generalization of institution (from the definition in this chapter) to a much looser usage (which is also standard in dictionaries): to avoid confusion, use the term institutional realm. Nadel distinguished political realm, economic realm, and so on. He then argued that certain generalized resources, such as money and power, were what correlated role frames, joined in a few abstract positions across institutional realms.

Nadel failed to produce a plausible system. It seems clear that no larger ordering which is deterministic either in cultural assertion or social arrangement could sustain and reproduce itself across so many

granted (Axelrod 1984; Bendor and Swistak 1991; M. Smith 1985). Boorman and Levitt (1980) take the opposite approach of folding strategic subtleties into robust response contingencies, in order to model how innovation can invade population by a network cascade process. Other game theorists (cf. survey by Riker 1982) turn toward very large but unstructured populations as in General Equilibrium Theory (Arrow and Hahn 1971; Scarf 1967, 1973).

See also Entourages in the next chapter; also, chapter 7 and Appendix 2.

and such large network populations as in the current world. Some sort of stochastic environment must be assumed and requires modeling. The next sections begin this, and in so doing will introduce the construct of style as suitable to capturing kinds of contextual orderings in a stochastic environment. Nadel's mistake was to take individual persons for granted as universals and build from them.

FIVE

STYLES AND PERSON

CONTINGENCIES may overwhelm any particular institution. But a more fluid social context can eventuate which proves able to reproduce itself, and which I will designate by its chief mechanism, styles. Such other context may to some degree support positions among role frames, just as it also supports institutions, or even some degree of integration of positions into institution. That is exactly the solution suggested by the playground example which has been carried along since the first chapter. One could even interpret this fluid context of styles as success by actors in imposing their own folk theory on their larger social reality, a theory necessarily shaped in terms of structural equivalences.

Such larger social context is necessarily stochastic, however. Social organization is heterogeneous, not tidy, at scales beyond the molecular, and even so it must survive stochastic flows of contingency. If it does survive, the larger context traces along strings of ties rather than across sets. Thus such larger context derives from and shapes the connectivity aspects of network more than its structural equivalences. And such larger context reflects and shapes the ordering more than the valuation aspects of molecular disciplines.

A style is a generalization of network, in that styles integrate behavior across disparate network populations, and they can do so whether or not there are institutions, or individual positions, that integrate role frames across these populations. For example, a profession consists in both an overall style, professionalism, and an institutional nexus of positions (see Abbott 1988). By the principle of self-similarity (chapter 1), styles can also characterize environments on much smaller scales, and below we shall begin with conversation as a stochastic context of styles.

Styles are discriminable as packages which combine signals with social pattern. A style appears only in a set with other styles, since theirs is an evolution by mutual discrimination. Styles order arrays of disciplines and networks, but style presupposes some continuing larger context, one which is sufficient also to support institutions. This larger context of styles defines and reproduces itself only on a stochastic basis, as in conversation. Even by its own stories, style, unlike institution, is not determinate.

These are vague assessments and must remain so until measurement has been deepened. It needs to go beyond that achieved so far, as in large-scale studies of mobility and stratification (Blau and Duncan 1967; Breiger 1981b, 1990; Hauser and Grusky 1988; Stewman 1988). Constructs are required which can discriminate such social organization as may underlie profiles and other stochastic regularities.

Institutions and styles both, unlike disciplines and networks, presuppose integrated skills at perception that are held only by human beings. Humans have capabilities for signaling, memory, and the like, beyond those already invoked above for all identities. Memory is a biological algorithm for decoupling actions over time, an algorithm from which language can emerge.

But these human skills need not come packaged as persons, in the sense current today. Such persons come into existence only in a complex stochastic environment. Human actors rally around valuations in constructing and interpreting institutions, but the irony is that persons only come into existence, as we shall argue here and again in chapter 7, through the exigencies of a stochastic environment built on quite other principles than the valuations to which persons, once formed, continue to orient.

Styles

Styles both couple and decouple actions among network-populations which overlap in physical space. Styles are set off by and thus appear in the midst of complex overlappings, of networks but also institutions and disciplines. In that sense they are analogous to identities. But styles are envelopes from innumerable attempts at control by identities, envelopes which thereafter limit and funnel control. The environment in which they appear is one of stochastic incident and process among actors.

Styles contrast with institution in how they respectively interrelate distinct network populations. A style is a rigid formula or prescription, whether explicit in a single story or in some other signaling idiom. In the stochastic environment, actions following a style are thereby ordered with respect to one another. But at the same time such actions are decoupled from the actions in other styles. The net result is that social ties can be maintained in a regular pattern; that is, ambage decreases.

The contrast with institution can be summed up in formulae about uncertainty. Styles make possible lower ambage in tangible social relations because they increase ambiguity: this increase comes despite rigidity within a particular style because its low correlation to other such styles permits a flexible match which supports continuation of a pattern of tangible relations. By contrast, an institution such as corporatism proclaims a coherent and integrated array of stories of regular rights and duties between cells within a partition of the actors. Ambiguity is lowered but at the cost of mismatch between the stories and changes in concrete relations, so that pattern continuance despite particular tangible changes is not supported and thus ambage is up.

Identities from the distinct networks figuring in a style are multiple projections from much the same physical creatures, but they are nonetheless distinct. Persons may get constructed out of these identities, as sketched in a later section, but as counterpoint to style, not as style. Persons are triggered by mismatches among styles. There is an irony. Styles can be sustained across much bigger scope in environment than can institutions; indeed typically actors across many institutions are subjected to the same style. Yet the actors in institutions are typically corporate and it is under the influence of styles that the individual person as we conceive it comes about.

Examples are needed. Start with an apparently simple and small-scale activity, conversation—which in fact occurs only in sophisticated contexts suitable for styles.

Conversations

Style presupposes decoupling among actors and events, as in conversation. The instantaneously interactive system by which we take turns in conversation rests on and presupposes decoupling as well as coupling. Only recently has this intricate dialectic been explicated systematically.[1]

Is a conversation a matter of style and form, akin to an art sketch? Or is it more an embodiment and building of a social tie, whether it grow out of council, tryst, or deal? Where does conversation come from, how can it be generated and sustained? Need a conversation coalesce around rhetorical figures—need it rely on metaphor and synedoche to tease the ambiguity of life?

The issue is how to conceive personal conversations. Must one bring an identity to a conversation, or does one grow identity during conversation, or can one share in the identity *of* a conversation? Is an audience in some sense crucial to conversation? Does conversation

---

[1] Consult, for example, Bilous and Kraus (1989); Duncan (1977); Kent and Shapiro (1978); H. Sachs in Rawls (1989); J. Wilson (1989).

permit, encourage, or insist on three-and-more-way involvements? How do dramatists and other authors "create" conversations? Did Erving Goffman believe in conversation, or did George Herbert Mead?

What is the demography: must a really good conversation be a descendant, have progeny, have affinal kin—or rather does it have an entourage? Can a conversation be episodic? Can it be among changing partners? Does it end or does it merely dissipate?

May conversation be but a Western specialty? Was it invented in Greece (Kitto 1958)? Was it revived in the Renaissance, or earlier in the troubadour period (Bloch 1977)? Is the Parisian salon still alive? How transmuted?

What is the analogue, if any, to conversation in music? Is shop-talk ever conversation? If among scholars, then also among natural scientists? Do teenagers converse? Do authors converse? Can a Barth or a Geertz be conversing in the act of observing? Is all conversation only questions?

Answering each of these questions requires some theory of control across populations in networks of identities. Within such theory, conversation is part of the dynamics, and it helps turn aside or postpone the usual social science formulations of persons as pregiven integrals, as stasis. In particular, personal conversation demonstrates the realities of decoupling at smallest scales of size and time.

Personal conversation has analogues at other scopes. Consider auction markets in many distinct species:

> The need to increase social distance in some auctions points up the fact that while communities are common to all auctions, there is considerable variation in the number of distinct communities to be found within a given auction as well as the way these various communities are interrelated. There can be a strong community of buyers, as in the New England Fish Exchange; a strong community of sellers, as in thoroughbred auctions; or a strong mixed community of buyers and sellers, as in wholesale automobile auctions. There may similarly be secondary communities such as the community of fish captains present in fish auctions; thoroughbred owners at horse auctions; and the loose, temporary community of casual buyers present at most art and antique auctions . . . there are buyers who attend auctions as purely self-interested individuals with a desire to buy certain goods for less than their assumed value. These buyers, in part because of their indifference to the communal dynamics of the auction, seldom get the items they want at their price and are usually disregarded by the regulars . . . their relevancy to the whole auction process remains minor because their low

bids do not hinder or interfere with the communal process of determining value and allocating goods. (C. Smith 1989, p. 75)

These observations can be paralleled for personal conversations considered in sets that partially overlap in time and attendance.

Styles and Meaning

Style generalizes the dominance orderings from within molecular disciplines, whereas by contrast institution generalizes the valuations from within molecular disciplines. Some institutions are themselves shaped from larger context by styles: they point outside themselves toward a well-developed larger social context which supports styles, as well as themselves influencing styles. But some institutions are not. Institutions get constructed through intentions, but are not necessarily intentional in the sense of conscious design by named actors.

Analytics of uncertainty and boundary are called for, application of the calculus of ambage with ambiguity and contingency. Style works through and takes form in stochastic variation, at the cost of increased ambiguity in meanings and stories, but with enhanced similarities in network clusterings. Institution, by contrast, is decoupled from stochastic contingency through its corporatism, its rigor of prescription in story, but at the cost of higher ambage in network pattern.

Stories are generated as explanations along with the embeddings and sets of them can come to constitute habits which define a style for an individual actor. A person, once formed, and a style can come to define identities for each other. The same duality obtains up through larger social formations. Styles can have still smaller, or yet more encompassing concrete referents, such as conversations and communities, respectively.

Style is most potent and yet most slippery to specify just at a middle range. Accountings of the cultural as well as the social can be played out together, from the tangible middle-range, played out as framings. Turn, for an example, to common-law systems. One might think that the reality of there being sets of stories available to rationalize whatever one chooses, once recognized, elides whatever force there is in just those framings. Not so:[2]

---

[2] The early provenance of common law is aptly summarized: "The introduction of written pleadings in the 16th century—soon followed by a requirement that the specific point at issue be unalterably set before trial. Once this happened, a court's opinion could be read with reference to definite fact situations, thereby making the scope

Llewellyn makes three points about "legal certainty" that stand out. First, the "operating technique" of judges and lawyers—a lawyer's craft and "feel"—is a powerful source of certainty in the law. Second, it is the fact situations of cases rather than legal rules that guide decisions, producing "the 'sense of justice' in the individual case." This pressure from the facts is what "makes different judges . . . despite their divergent analyses, generally . . . reach the same result" and thus act in predictable ways. Third, "legal rules provide certainty in the affairs of people whose interests are affected by the law if, in a lawsuit, they yield a result that accords with their real-life . . . evolving social norms." Fish writes, in his characteristically provocative way: "To be a judge or a basketball player is not to be able to consult the rules (or, alternatively, to disregard them) but to have become an extension of the 'know how' that gives the rules (if there happen to be any) the meanings they will immediately and obviously have." (Pp. xviii–xx)

Llewellyn's craft and operating technique, and also the know-how of his translator, Fish, are themselves embodiments of "style" for particular middle-range worlds. The sociologist Scheppele (1988) has developed further this theme of duality between example and rule at the middle-range of cases.

Styles with their packages of values and stories come in various scopes. A single person can embody a style, which then concerns component identities of the person with their stories and values as seen by given others as well as selves. At this level, conventional usage differentiates value facets central to the person, which are values proper or ends, from peripheral value-facets, called attitudes. Personality is style exhibiting consistency of ends within the person.

Formal Organization

Formal organization is an institution when seen as routine; it is a style when seen as a meaning system; and it is a hunting field when seen as opportunity. Formal organizations were patterned on early bureaucracies. Corruption and venality are built into bureaucracy, and early systems of venality coupled the beginnings of salary sys-

---

of a precedent ascertainable with greater precision than before. . . . It was not until the close of the eighteenth century that the now-orthodox theory of truly binding precedent began to be worked out and regulated by appellate review" (Llewellyn 1989, p. 6).

Here and earlier I resort in part to quotes of summary assessments by an editor (who is himself a law professor) and supervisor of translation of Llewellyn because of the notorious prolixity and elusiveness of Llewellyn's own prose.

tems with careers. The larger context and occasion for venality was a decentralized arrangement for raising capital; corruption was from a larger perspective just a more informal route to the same end.

These corrupt bureaucracies also at first served to decouple administration from networks of kinship among the nobles, those politically and socially privileged, but early became immersed in corporatist privileges, exclusions, and rights. Early bureaucracy was a new institution whose chief effect was to loosen earlier institutions, as is seen most clearly in this early format of explicit corruption. So at first bureaucracy cut through blocking action in a path of breathtaking decoupling, even noncomparability. But bureaucracy, like other institutions, soon settled into blocking actions even when it was set up to counter them, in particular to counter the corporatist institutions of the previous chapter.

Common adherence to a formal organization among any set of actors can engender careers as personal styles guided by it. In its insistence on boundary, formal organization becomes a native theory that argues for but goes beyond models of disciplines and other universals. Formal organization is a template which enables disparate realms, whether of governments or of nonprofits or business, to establish interpretive connection. For example, a business firm as a corporatist institution integrates a set of interpretive specialties, such as engineering, sales, and accounting, each a network population, but efforts at control are shaped, and deflected, by members' acceptance of a Table of Organization as style guiding them all.

So formal organization is a style, not an institution. Formal organization is a transposable set of directions about the interlocking of choice premises. Manipulations should not be conceived at just personal levels. Organizations are supposedly stable structures of rules, positions, and the like. Or in March and Simon's (1958) more sophisticated formulation, they are delegated sets of stable premises for deciding. As we all can see, but few of us learn, the only sure thing, in fact, is that forms, rules, and slots all change. Ambage and ambiguity trade off in a setting of uncertainty flows. Important manipulation comes to be (March and Olsen 1976) about the changes, and a cycle of changes becomes the steady if unrecognized state.

The formal organizations of our time are one side of an institution ordinarily related to work, perhaps only peripherally. Formal organizations also synthesize styles which can adapt and regulate meanings via a new type of tie. These are ties of authority which are explicitly public and which serve to bridge separate interpretive frames, which are being brought into some coherence quite aside from their connection to work.

One may argue that some formal organizations function as "inside-out markets." That is, they can be substituted, for the common image of markets as being sites where rigid social actors such as organizations can achieve accommodation and yet also sites that yield coherence of interpretation. An outfit with formal organization as its style can be the flexible negotiating ground to reconcile the rigidities of established markets. A publicly enacted organization is better able than most observed markets to supply ties by arbitrary fiat! So a single organization can provide bridges among incomparable strings of actors out in the social seas of urban life. The trade federation (Levy 1944) and the regulatory agency (Libecap 1978) both operate in that way. Each can be visualized as a common forum serving markets in much the way that exchange markets are visualized as serving to bridge and regulate firms.

Formal organization as a complete reality mixes hostility formats—such as authority trees which cumulate spans of control as interfaces—with corporatist binding through other disciplines, with this mix both overcoming and producing blockage of action. Today, formal organization is the commonest venue, into which older forms often are repackaged. But to say this is to say little, for the style, the stereotyped story line for organization, covers as much diversity as does the other common modern term, "market."

Evolution of Styles

Some orderliness of perception is presupposed and supplied in larger formations, and change between one kind and another is thereby made difficult. One example is the emergence of a system of dealers-and-critics around the French Impressionist painters of the last century, a system which eventually displaced an existing institution centered around the French Academy (White and White 1992). The new system became worldwide, and hegemonic in its ideology of the *avante garde* (for which consult Crane 1987). But the old, the Academic system in its day was hegemonic also. One could not continue to live in the same perceptual world through a change: in this case one had literally to see differently.

Members of the French painting world also had to come to regard the social organization of art production in an entirely different light. Interventions about symbols as about ideas can never be separated from social formations among specialized cultural producers themselves (Peterson 1976). The cultural producers' own use of "style" as a term captures both the made coherence and the claimed decoupling from social formations.

Changeover of social formation from a claimed definite institution to a fluid context of styles has to trace itself out in some phenomenology of trust. Trust is itself a term for a clustering of perceptions. An illustration within big business firms comes from Eccles's study (1985; and see Eccles and White 1988) of transfer pricing practices between divisions. He shows that the predominance, as rule in procurement, of "buy, or at worst make" over "make, or at worst buy," he shows that this predominance centers on considerations of fairness. In this era, division managers prefer to buy from other firms rather than from other internal divisions. The then current scene of managerial competitiveness within the firm was not such as to encourage trusting internal arrangements.

Another business illustration comes from the field study of auction markets cited earlier:

> This format [devised by the economist Vickrey], though mathematically well supported, is practically never used. The reason normally given is that it is too complex. Yet the more complex English knockout system flourishes. The true reason for its disuse might well be that the aim of this system is to maximize bids, whereas the purpose of the English knockout and other systems used in real auctions is to ensure fairness to all participants. (C. Smith 1989, p. 72)

A single manifestation of style, such as Vickrey's, cannot sustain itself separately. It is disrupted too soon by mismatch between stories and changing networks. An institution cannot be contradicted in that way; so isolated style may find a home within an institution.

Orderings and stories get winnowed into some style which holds across institutions as social spaces, in a loose stratification system. Stratification is stochastic system mediated by style. Stratification builds from pressures within and across institutions. These pressures can generate inequality in control among large as well as small actors.

Full treatment of concrete phenomena, for example the earlier case of recognition of the "opiate receptor" as innovation (in chapter 3) requires combining partial analyses. Experiences summarized in social networks and histories spread particular actors across diverse arrays of disciplines. Across positions within social organization, some social vision, some style, is locked in by the enormous pressures of joint action with others. Joint action will shape and generate perceptions into consistent patterns. Rationality, for example, may well become the style established within a locality.

A style does not come easy. Its history is all interwoven with some complex of social formations in an ecology, even for ostensibly purely cultural realms (Baxandall 1975, 1980; White and White 1965). A theologian puts it well:

> But dynamics is held in a polar interdependence with form. Self-creation of life is always creation of form . . . there is a moment of "chaos" between the old and the new form . . . the creation of a new social entity or a new artistic style. The chaotic element which appears here is already manifest in the creation myths . . . creation and chaos belong to each other . . . echoed in the symbolic descriptions of the divine life, of its abysmal depth, of its character as burning fire, of its suffering over and with the creatures, and of its destructive wrath. . . . Destruction can be described as the prevalence of elements of chaos over against the pole of form in the dynamics of life. . . . Disintegration takes place within a centered unity; destruction can occur only in the encounter of centered unity with centered unity. (Tillich 1963, p. 50)

Styles and Profile

In the control struggles which create and surround them, identities presuppose, and their disciplines contribute to, possibilities of order in larger contexts. Styles can be used to describe such a context, but not as a formation with definite stipulations such as in an institution. A style refers to context as if it were in the analogue of a gaseous or liquid state.[3] Stochastic models (Feller 1968) are one apt vehicle for the observer to use in modeling and understanding style, which emerges out of what is going on as disciplines get stacked, networked, cumulated, and aggregated. In chapter 3 these larger environments of social action have been characterized abstractly through a calculus of trade-offs in specialized uncertainties through decoupling.[4]

A discipline presupposes some orderliness of perceptions by each participant. Identities presuppose, in the control struggles which

---

[3] The distinction is like that drawn by the demographer Watkins (1990).

[4] It may be possible to characterize these environments with some construct modeled on temperature, which is the premier parameter that interlinks localities for condensed states of matter, and even gases. In bioecological phenomena, analogues to temperature—and even temperature itself—have proved themselves. And in engineering design, the Wiener feedback ideas of control theory exhibit some parallel to temperature. Interchanges among ambage, ambiguity, and contingency, through decoupling mechanisms, begin to hint at temperature, and stratification systems are a self-reproducing social organization under such exchange. But social formations emerge as insulation in between counteractions of identities seeking control, insulation that is too extreme to permit a temperature which pervades a whole system. Style does permeate across levels but, in contrast to temperature, allows for continuing inhomogeneities which result from blocking action.

create and surround them, and to which their disciplines contribute, networks and further possibilities of still larger contexts such as institutions. Obversely, pressures from larger context reach down to effect some orderliness of perception by a particular discipline. It is this dual orderliness that is reflected in the embedding ratios of chapter 2. The three species of discipline—the interface, the arena, and the council—are the configurations which proved robust to all these perception pressures, above and below, for varied contexts.

At one extreme, attitudes are the stuff of decoupling which yields fluidity sufficient for style. Attitudes are passive, however explicit their claim to goal and ordering, and attitude patterns change only in slow accretive fashion. Yet particular attitudes can gyrate to accommodate events to stories and comport with a style.

Decoupling at another extreme attends generational replacement. If generations came as discrete events, and so were absolutely separate and distinct cohorts, as among locusts (E. Wilson 1970), there would be less confusion in embedding and hence less scope and occasion for decoupling. Such creatures, no matter how "intelligent," would have little occasion, for example, to develop career systems.[5]

Styles are in part the residues of native analyses. No human observer of any social formations is truly outside the quandaries of style, since whatever scientific or other priestly garb is worn is itself constructed analogously. Styles come enmeshed in boundaries.

For example, topology and stochastic processes are two opposite scientific styles which analysts can use to try to make sense for each other of the messes of turbulent social polymer-gels, and they have ordinary analogues. Stochastic outcomes of social formations can be parsed also in terms of native styles. And surely there is a theater with stage for style. That is, one expects constraints on what concrete social arrangements, what profiles, disciplines, and networks, can house the story processes whose interpretive profile is termed a style. Some social calculus of uncertainty is needed once again.

A style tends to inculcate distinct sorts of perception which go with certain profiles of interaction among personal actors. The test of any calculus is predicting change. Changes in expression of particular values can be triggered by environment or by group and individual whim. But change in their structuring as a package, change in style, is difficult because style is coordinated to stratification system. A style has settled in only through continued reenactments. No change in style can take place without change in organization of networks and values together with profiles.

[5] Surely an apt topic for an Ursula LeGuin novel!

Fashion, in the everyday sense of a process of change in clothes, slang, and so on, is an existing version of a social calculus of style. Intersections of such calculi yield calendars and other computations that are common across identities. The conventional core of "fashion'" is cultural expertise:

> Levels of expression measured according to the norms of the day . . . but also . . . interactions between the framework established by formal conventions and the contents and themes it accepts or questions according to the period or current. . . . And it is obvious that stylistic choices are not only personal choices . . . but are also positions taken vis-à-vis society. Burlesque, for example. (Viala 1989, p. 262)[6]

Fashion is a melding of multiple styles into a profile. The meld pushes up ambiguity and thus goes with low ambage as actors in relations come toward the same behavior. Fashion is style purged of person. In fashion ambage is reduced as skirts rise and fall together, at the cost of heightened ambiguity about meaning.

Profiles

A revised construct of environment is needed. Boundary remains as problematic as it was for network, for the reasons given in the previous chapter. The revised construct still must serve both to frame action within itself and to summarize itself for action outside.[7]

Size profiles are one, simplest representation of order from stochastic process. These profiles do not include the before-and-after, and the ins and outs of actual system mechanisms. A profile reports a social formation in terms of mere distributions of constituents (Blau and Duncan 1964). A profile presupposes stable outcome along with stochastic process. Such a profile is useful in analysis only because

[6] Amidst an embarrassment of definitions, I can afford to give pride of place to sociological provenance.

[7] This environment, like a network population, exhibits complicated overlappings. Population ecology suggests instead a sharp partition, as of distinct biological species. Whole populations, each as defined by recurrent and patterned interaction, then may combine to constitute a super-population, within which each may be affected variously by biophysical ecology. One recent statement of population ecology is Hannan and Freeman (1989). In their approach, actors each may be an organization or other large formation of human persons, whose appearances and decays are to be modeled in terms of physical as well as social context. They apply the basic work of Levins (1966), for which E. O. Wilson (1979) supplies phenomenology. For approaches applying mathematical genetics to related social topics see Boorman and Levitt (1980) and Lewontin (1974).

decoupling establishes both flexibility and robustness, to degrees upon which Zipf (1949) insisted long ago.

First come some large-scale examples of economies. Then an elaboration of constructs is inserted, which leads into social stratification as the premier profile. The last example is of minimal scope: namely, a small group.

Tuck's Profile for an Economy

Profiles can be generalized from Zipf's raw size distributions, and correlated to human action patterns more concretely than he was able to do. Consider the analysis proposed by Tuck (1965, originally in 1954) to explain the distribution of earned incomes in a modern Western society. Tuck disarticulates the economy into a population of firms of varying sizes in number of jobs. Each job is held by an individual.

Tuck first asserts that a particular kind of interface can be seen as universal in modern business organization in its managerial aspects. This is the "span of control" in which a supervisor exerts authoritative direction over each of the "s" subordinates who are thereby put in structurally equivalent positions with respect to one another. These loaded terms—authority, supervision, equivalent, and subordinate—are justified to the extent that actors account identities in authority stories.

According to Tuck, to attain control beyond contending efforts by particular actors, which are contradictory locally, requires an actual cumulation of spans of control through networks. Tuck idealizes such networks as regular "trees." In each, from a top node there is a descent to "s" subordinates, and the same in turn from each subordinate node, level after level. Underlying Tuck's profile is the implications for cumulation of ranks and for multiplication of pay that come from embedding commit interfaces one within another over such a series, and for doing so across a whole population.

The identities in the nested spans of control for a particular firm's tree are sustained, Tuck argues, only if each span also marks a jump in salary.[8] By custom of the modern Western firm, the jump is a proportionate one. Tuck assumes the simplest form, not only homogeneous span of control but also a homogeneous multiplicative increase in pay with each successive level: Let "b" be the ratio for superior's salary over subordinate's salary.

---

[8] As confirmed by numerous studies of business practice (see Brown 1959; Granick 1972; Hedstrom 1988; Vancil 1979; Williamson 1970).

This is a simplified caricature of an authority tree. Given it, Tuck can first derive a prediction of the pay at the top level of a firm. Top executive pay is derived as being a power of the number of levels. In turn the number of levels of subordination can be shown equivalent to a logarithm of the number of managers in the firm. It follows that top executive pay grows only logarithmically with increase in the number of managers. The actual exponent is a ratio of logarithm of b over logarithm of s.

But the broader networks among identities, across the whole population of firms, can only reproduce themselves to the extent there are comparabilities among firms. Tuck argues that entry-level positions across different firms must have the same salary to guide the addition of successive cohorts into these continuing organizations. And he assumes the pay ratio is the same across all firms as well as across levels in a firm. All this is by a social logic of maintaining identities: It requires no references to marginal productivity and other such fairy tales (Simon 1957).

This simple picture, based purely on comparability across embedding interfaces, in present terminology, gives some fit to observed executive pay, and seems able to predict variations. It is straightforward to extend it as Tuck does to the distribution of pay across all employees of all firms. He shows distributions, but a summary profile or even coefficient will do. Any standard measure of inequality, such as the Gini coefficient, yields the same qualitative finding: One cannot obtain the extent of inequality commonly observed across whole populations with the orderly nested inequality from embedding commit interfaces upon one another.

Tuck seized upon this impossibility. A spread across different kinds of tree might be required, but even then it was hard to explain observed inequality profiles in the Britain of his time. One implication is clear: Observed inequality profiles, and thus perceptions and judgments of equity, are effected primarily outside of explicit schema of explanation.

Even inegalitarian schemas that have been agreed by some cultural process must not be dealing with basic aspects of the network contingencies which, from observer viewpoint, are in fact responsible for the inequalities. Social perception relates to the realities of control which underlie equity facades much as insect vision relates to human vision: the compound eye of insects cannot focus but rather is stuck with an array of partial and misleading perceptual reports that cannot be corrected within its own logic.

Tuck's most ambitious claim only then emerges. His profile has a sharp point, which he boldly extrapolates to the whole economy!

This claim comes from putting together the whole population of firms and seeing it as imbedded in a total social matrix which is observed to generate a social class structure, which Tuck translates into a cultural and normative claim to relative standing.

Tuck takes the claims to relative standing as a datum independent of the specific pay structure in business. That is, he asserts that actors have developed an independent (presumably complex and historically rooted) sense of where they should be standing in pay relative to others.

What does this massive mismatch lead to? It would be sheer accident if the profile of firms' salaries for an arbitrary collection of firms just happened to permit assortative filling of authority layers so that each person ended up in the relative position that suited the perceived stratification claims. Tuck argues that the missing match is achieved exactly by the creation (and dissolution) of firms themselves as compound actors! In particular, ambitious persons unable to obtain appropriate standing within existing large trees go out and start new trees, new firms.

Tuck's is a contribution to the demography of interfaces, and an exhibition of decoupling and coupling intertwined. His work prefigures needed theoretical modeling for more inclusive system. Tuck is employing a stochastic profile as envelope to report substantive structure.[9] The size distribution of firms and correlatively of pay are profiles impacted by roles and style. Such profiles are, after all, accommodations into institutions spanning a wide variety of specialized role structures. His idea is exactly that the persons in the system themselves are using in common a simple role-structure picture to guide actions. Thus Tuck's profile is for a style. He elides the specific structure of these economies of many markets.

Putting-Out as Economy

Such a complex system as Tuck presupposes must have developed out of local institutions of production in interaction with migration and trade over longer distances. What we recognize as "an econ-

---

[9] Many other examples could be cited. Padgett (1989) develops an analysis akin to Tuck's but derived from the mechanics of judicial systems within courts at a city level in the U.S. The stochastic profiles become ghost players in the social arena, ones which are hard to beat by changes in policy.

Stewman (1976) and Stewman and Konda (1983) in mobility studies at organization level work at the difficult margin between such envelope effects and explicit decoupling through vacancy chains (for which see White 1970).

Back at Tuck's scale, Sattinger (1980) walks the same tightrope, as do Ijira and Simon (1977). Zipf (1949), following the lead of Pareto (1966), is the fullest exposition.

omy" builds up slowly from earlier systems that concatenated agency and occasion. These were so-called putting-out systems, in which profiles of repetitive transactions were cumulated. Putting-out systems evolved from networks of traditional work groups.

Udy (1970) uncovered a general truth: Material production is limited mainly by the ubiquity of control projects concerned with their mutual standings rather than with production. Decoupling has been recognized before as an essential to output in production. First, within what we call firms, the engineer R. W. Shepard (1953) has done so, from the factory insides of manufacturing.[10] Decoupling is also recognizable within all varieties of markets and market systems. Objective social forms, such as the species detailed in chapter 2, are needed as components whose specific design eases decoupling in building input-output systems of markets.

Udy (1959) originally focused on societies where historical context is not generated explicitly (as distinct from implicit embedding in a past via culture), even though most of the field examples which he uses came from contemporary sources. Udy (1970) then shifted his account to current industrial societies, where he implicitly presupposes decouplings across many levels in order to discuss work groupings on the scale of the "early" societies.

Udy's main argument is that history has provided some accidental concatenation of various windows-of-opportunity sufficient to define the new system of industrial capitalism, all of a piece. This system henceforward is undefinable except as a unique and all-encompassing universal context. In this claim he anticipates Wallerstein's (1974, 1980) account from a macro-historical side.

Lawrence Stone (1965, chapter 6) supplies an account of work arrangements on the largest scale known during just the intermediate centuries that Udy skipped, in which the all-encompassing history which we take for granted was coming into existence (cf. also Anderson 1974; Braudel 1982). It was a context where, especially at the scope of noble estates considered by Stone, decoupling mechanisms were new and raw, more visible and transparent than either for prehistory, or for now as settled within history and rhetoricized (Myrdal 1931) by economics.

The decouplings necessarily are all mixed in with the criss-crossings of embeddings and reembeddings through which were appearing the new system for which Udy argues. "This intellectual and technological revolution—for it was no less—meant that by the beginning of the seventeenth century it was at last possible for the lord

[10] This was followed up by economists Fuss and McFadden (1978), but their formalist adaptation seems to miss his central phenomenology.

of many manors to keep a close check upon his agents and his agents upon the tenants" (Stone 1965, p. 311).

The apparent paradox was that to free production for effectiveness one introduced decouplings of one manor from another, one form of husbandry from another, even decoupling of one accounting language and format from another, in order to achieve some control and some choice in operation exactly because there was some separability and accountability. There are parallel accounts, such as Chrimes (1950) and Roseveares (1973), for the parallel and earlier seizure of control in production by the state in England. Each of these occurred via new forms of decoupling and devolution, so that the painful awkwardness of each step makes it easier to trace and to understand the resolution of the paradox. There is no slick layer of rhetoric from modern economic theory to obscure the reality.

The new forms of decoupling were made possible—and extensive deployment was made feasible even while alert actors fuzzily began to perceive the new forms—because new forms of embedding had been evolving. The putting-out system, actually later in Britain than on the Continent, enabled regular flows of product not embedded in and through the operation of manors (Bythell 1978; Kriedte et al. 1981; Lachmann 1987; Najemy 1982).

Markets come under a new light. Exchange markets exist even under the simplest contexts. They are couplers into a distinct species of discipline: arenas concerned with selection based on purity, in the terms of chapter 2. Systems of exchange markets spanning large distances come between Udy's main context and Stone's. Such a system is complex, it is both a means of embedding and coupling and a means of decoupling. Speculation appears as a possible commitment rather than an occasional aberration.

Speculation can decouple production from use and yet at the same time guide in structuring exchange networks: speculative activities sketch the routes actually followed by emerging putting-out systems. Control struggles will move to this level: exploitation is achieved there. Speculative gyrations are one possibility, an extreme form of decoupling. Rationality seems a side-show, since speculation is far more concerned with timings and interaction than with considerations of optimality and the other apparatus of formal rationality.

Berle and Means in their recognition of managerial capitalism (1933) are but an especially distinguished example of the recurrent lauding of rationality for production organization. Rationality is used to mean tight coupling, within the firm. It apparently is hard to come to terms with Udy's truth (1970) that decoupling is the main problematic for achieving production. The literatures on "decision-making" and the like are often just attempts to assert embedding rather than to uncover decouplings for achieving tangible ends like production. This is ironic since often it is those convinced of the merits of decoupling through markets who emphasize decision-making (e.g., Fama and Jensen 1983; Jensen and Meckling 1976).

The fruits of bureaucracy, level by level, bear no direct relation to its necessary internal disciplines, span by span. The formal rationality of administrative dogma is the analogue to the formal rationality of microeconomic theory: each is based on chimeras. In fact there must be some alternation in species of discipline for any successive embeddings in a hierarchy, as there is also for successive aggregations in a production sector.

The whole debate on "market versus hierarchy" (Lazarson 1988; Williamson 1975; Walker 1989) is a misspecification. Production markets and hierarchies are similar fields for mobilizing the same species of discipline, interfaces.[11] The real problematics are struggles for control, which are played out over both fields as combined terrain (Eccles and White 1985). Efficiency is secondary.

A conclusion is that production markets, if not interfaces in general, cannot themselves directly become individual actors embedded into a further interface. Aggregation must take some other form, which allows decoupling. Decoupling, together with some sort of balancing among species, requires a network of production markets in association with an input-output system.

Each production economy is the result of a slow historical evolution from a base system of markets in long-distance trade and exchange into networks of production for feeding the system. Today's systems of production markets evolved from putting-out systems in previous centuries (cf. Bythell 1978; Kriedte et al. 1981). On technological and transportation grounds, whole networks of such markets were needed to weave into input-output requirements of production.[12] Such networks avoid one another as they reach out to coax supply. Slow change on the surface does not contradict intense social

[11] Interfaces—as so-called spans of control—within some formal organization can be seen to be analogous to some sector of production markets, and thus different from exchange markets.

The importance of retaining "make or buy" decisions becomes manifest: A given production actor disciplined within a particular production market cannot rely on that interface to give protection in transactions with other disciplines; so each actor retains the ability to partially pull out of the input-output chains among disciplines. There is a dual form of decision, "sell or use," which faces downstream instead of upstream.

[12] Fligstein (1990, pp. 295–96) develops an alternative view emphasizing the immediate neighborhood of firms coming to a market. His trenchant conclusion fits well with my account: "The forms of social organization produced the market, not the reverse" (p. 300).

pressures of competitive style for and to sustain distinct position in the resulting system. The process began independently many times in Europe.

Putting-out systems are the form taken in production of goods by the same sort of projects of control that led to what was called venality and corruption in state administration contexts. Each may be seen as lowering efficiency; at the same time each can be seen as increasing exploitation. Many stories are possible and are used in these networks. There is no neutral ground in actual social organization which permits meaningful measures of efficiency which could differentiate it from exploitation. Exploitation itself can be seen in terms of interacting projects for control amid numerous passive social actors. These concepts are relative and social rather than absolute and technical.

It is a lemma that specialization always signals corporatist efforts at embedding to escape projects of control. Putting-out and venal systems are less specialized than bureaucracies became as they grew common, but that is not just a matter of architecture. They are processes which exemplify decoupling and introduce stylistic elaboration. Decoupling is an active process which cannot be frozen into a form but is always playing against existing embeddings.

Embeddings into flows and counterflows of product, at successive technical stages of treatment, could go abroad or elsewhere. Such flows were in tracks unrelated to explicit routines of discipline across the manorial (or city) economies. And the producers and intermediate agents could move not just from place to place but from one mode to another, between safe sinecure and evanescent putting-out network. Putting-out networks became profiles rather than institutions. Habits had been replaced by profiles.

Envelope from Profiles

Aggregation into populations is best seen as a continuing process, not a static matter of putting beans in bags. Tuck's model is too static and simple to suggest how an economy could have come about. An economy grows as some painful accretion of styles out of original institutions. The process can be contingencies which yield a profile of occurrences.

The process can be a by-product of counting and sheer accumulation without any embedding via discipline and tie. Network population need not be the only social construction of population. A prototype is the pattern of congestion in a city's road network. The term "envelope" captures that it is only the outer limits of the cumulation of contingencies that has impact. This is a new sort of embedding where there is no reforming of identity, but rather a factual accumulation which shapes or reflects a constraint on action which is comparable to embedding.

Tuck's model of pay structures described above predicts an envelope which in turn explained a lot about income inequality. For some road network, a simple analogue can be drawn. Queue lengths across the set of intersections is the size distribution. Green-light times, in number of cars passed, could be the control parameter, with the analogue to status distribution being profile of acceptable delays.

A population then defines itself by the aggregate produced from contingencies observed across networks linked one to another through common actors established through interaction among discipline, identity, and network, possibly as positions. The envelope which an observer can draw as the high-tide line of contingencies, is one operationalization of population. A city can be defined as the population within which interactions are observed to yield a stochastic pattern of congestion that reproduces itself (White 1973). Control over population definition, over boundaries, can be achieved by influencing the topology of the network of flows (Kleinrock 1963). Similarly, Tuck should examine actual mobility flows among and by firms to induce the actual population to which his profile applies.

The same principles apply at very different scales. Take the layout of aisles and wares in a supermarket (Kuehn 1958). By changing the positioning of products, paths of movement and perceptions of customers can be reclustered, so that a different set of (micro) populations emerges within the store. Perhaps yuppies segregate out as a population in their movements, from mothers of families and from retirees; whereas before it was drinkers, the poor, and the ordinary middle class. And, embedding this is a similar process of population formation by location and product alignment of supermarkets across a region of neighborhoods.

On a larger scale too, a product is an aspect of population clusters mutually induced among actors and products and subject to some control through the ecology. This is what market in the larger sense is, and perhaps someday economic theory can be brought back into connection with this network reality. A Leontief input-output matrix could be derived as the result of carrying this principle to national scope (Carter 1976). Burt (1990) carries the approach yet one step further by specification of sector boundaries from organizational principles (and see previous section on putting-out system).

Manipulability of population boundaries is not unlimited. For example, an accident (Calabresi 1970) is a natural population, a cluster of contingent happenings and context. An epidemic is a large-sized social accident (Bailey 1957, 1982). Some epidemics, for example malaria (Cohen and Lewontin, 1981), embed and are embedded in a number of levels corresponding to different organisms and stages involved.

The diffusion of the use of a medicine can be seen as a species of epidemic (see chapter 3). Here too the populations involved—in this case of professionals and of users as mediated through a third population of agents (Coleman, Katz, and Menzel 1966; Burt 1990)—are best defined reflexively, as the contingency envelope of the stochastic processes of influence and action spreads. Reanalysis (Burt 1988) of the classic initial study underlines the structural effects of topologies.

Envelopes can be specified in narrower focus as well, where differential involvement with different species of discipline may become apparent. A tie of influence and dominance from one actor to another may chain through several actors treated successively as intermediaries. Whatever factual connections, of the diffusion sort above, obtain as a result, joint perceptions of the concatenation of links into a chain can have major impact on continuing action. Such perception is likely only in mobilizer and commit disciplines: councils and interfaces. Reputation or fame, on the other hand, is a perceived result of clustering of ties to the same node, and envelopes of prestige and the like may be recognized as significant only in match and mobilize contexts: arenas and councils.

Envelopes of any scope can be important indicators of boundaries, as seen either by participants or observers, even when explicit perception of construction, as in chains, is not generated or is not possible. Collective protest activities (Tilly 1978) and panics (Granovetter and Soong 1983; Milgram 1977) have a phenomenological reality not dependent upon perceptions of cumulation of contingencies.

Return to the supermarket product-display example. It is an established rule of thumb that one-fifth of the products account for four-fifths of total sales. The rule is robust in that it holds whether one discusses "brands" within a so-called "product" or discusses distinct products, which supports the earlier contention that categories like "product X" are socially induced rather than neutral "technical" facts. This particular rule of thumb is widely, but by no means universally, known. The rule marks a significant decoupling in the merchandise system whether or not particular actors or disciplines explicitly compute in terms of it.

Stratification

Always formulating social organization in institutions has the unfortunate implication of not recognizing macro-regularities like social class. The issue is how to bring that in without losing correct analytic insights into the self-similarity of social structure and the arbitrariness of social process and boundary—and in particular without invoking myths of some reified "society" such as the nation of today. Stratification as system of styles in social phenomena provides a resolution. Stratification can be seen as a super-catnet (chapter 2) of profiles resulting from stochastic interactions in a soup of distinct institutions as well as networks and disciplines.

An earlier section confronted puzzles of scale in analyzing stratification. It turned to a modern economy for a bold study of how individuals and style can cumulate into social stratification. Another section laid out the evolution of putting-out system from earlier institutions in Europe, an account which drew on chapter 2 models of disciplines for markets and chapter 3 models of networks. Stratification now becomes an envelope of disciplines and yet also of institutions.

Stratification system builds following style but out of the same constituent disciplines and ties as an institution. Styles in stochastic environment can apply even when no institutions can be discerned. But the usual situation is stochastic environment which is a context for styles as well as institutions which may or may not themselves be crosscut by positions across roles. Continuing coexistence of network populations in a population envelope depends upon flexibility from their couplings through positions and/or institutions.

Styles cut across realms of meaning as well as levels of embedding. Styles are parses in meaning upon stochastic profiles that follow from actions. Styles can join together with institutions to make up systems. Styles normally draw upon values in several institutions and so cannot correlate to each. Institutions tend to be leached out through the play of styles from stratification system. Such system is to institution as catnets are to disciplines.

Choice being blocked by an institution is not some mere abstract notion; it impacts upon lives in the small and in the large. Opportunity and misery are but two sides of the same hard social die. Misery can be articulated only as it comes embedded into a social formation, only when it is an aspect of a position. Likewise, opportunity knocks only as a signal to one position concerning other positions. Both misery and opportunity are facets of blocking action, of which stratification is the chief expression.

Stratification may appear hard to explain without reference to some total world. Social classes and stratification seem to extend indefinitely far all around us, which might seem to argue against scale-invariance for theory. Yet at the same time classes and stratification are curiously elusive to detailed analysis. This elusiveness should be juxtaposed with the intensity of phenomenological experiences of invidious distinctions and blighted chances. It is not surprising that the best analyses (e.g., Svalastoga 1957; Hollingshead 1949) require tangible groundings in institution, tie, and locale as well as style and persons.

Stratification induces native theories of orderings and their boundaries. Sociology itself can be seen as an example (as the concluding chapter develops in some detail). It is fitting for a substantive denouement to a general work on sociology, as opposed to some other social science, to be stratification, to which I add getting action as its dual.

Whereas elites and control are elusive shadows of process and manipulation, and thereby are at the edge of social perception, by contrast social stratification is the manifest solidification into invidious formations of what initially, at micro level, are just the happenstances of opportunity supplied by momentary positioning. Control struggles among identities come to be constrained by the stasis of stratification. This stasis consists in size distributions thrown up from the specific and particular blocking patterns into which control interactions of identities settle down.

One bias obscures perceptions of stratification: only occasionally are the same story-sets which account action for lower strata made available in high culture, as for example Rabelais did centuries ago (Bakhtin 1968) and the War on Poverty did for a few years in street murals (Cockcroft, Weber, and Cockroft 1977). Ennis (1992) shows how tensions with an older generation motivated acceptance of rock 'n' roll music, which grafted black onto white popular music, at first across all social classes of preteens. And, conversely, high culture is made unavailable to lesser folk (DiMaggio 1992; Lynes 1958) by a host of devices.

Carley's Group

Consider the human group, and build toward a fresh analytic approach from the work of Carley (1984, 1986), who also supplies data as detailed as one only expects to be given in the biography of a personage. Its "smallness" is a deception uncovered by probing its profile of actions.

A human group (Homans 1950) is more than a set of individuals categorized and cross-categorized according to some attributes of value and story—location, heroes, age, roller skates, whatever. The human group, in Homan's sense, casts as its shadow and indeed is self-similar to an arena discipline.

Yet, like a personage, a human group does not have a singular identity, with its unique discipline. Nor need it be one articulated set of roles, such as task versus emotional leaders of the tradition of small-group experimental research (cf. Bales 1970). Nor yet need it be a concretization of one institution, although both these frames are shadowed in the results. A so-called "small group" is large enough to be a social world, rich enough to exhibit style as well as institution and network: the combinatorial complexity is immense.

One can attribute identity to any group which evinces a subjective consciousness, as well as attributing identity to a joint production as a discipline. In some theories, group replaces discipline. M. Smith (1975) is only one of the latest to erect a complete theory of society on the basis of corporate groups and their embeddings.[13] Perhaps "corporate" should be reserved to connote subjective jointness rather than being the catchall term that it has been in this manuscript. This subjective jointness cannot be modeled in fashion consistent with the internal mechanism of discipline except through the construct of decoupling.

"Household" is a familiar term with the connotation of a corporate group. Demographers have found its definition surprisingly—and increasingly—problematic. Consider the following remarks:

> For too long, demographers have hesitated . . . related to the relative paucity of methods of analysis and of modeling efforts focusing on primary group dynamics. . . . Nevertheless, the excuses remain unconvincing. What is perhaps the most puzzling is . . . that family and household . . . are the basic decision-making units regarding most phenomena studied in conventional individual-based demography: fertility, nuptiality, divorce, and migration. (Keilman, Kuijsten, and Vossen 1989, pp. 4–5)

We need to understand how a corporate group can come to share, and be aware of sharing, social characteristics and evolve to share a subjective sense of identity. How is such corporate nature established? The answer must be by endless stories talked by identities to each other, as part of their ongoing struggles with each other for control with respect to one another and concerning all sorts of matters.

---

[13] See, for example, Tellenbach (1946) and the discussion of Douglas's groups and grids in chapter 3.

Rather than arguing this from scratch we can rely in part on observation in the tradition of small discussion groups. But this observation needs to be intensified enormously in scale of time, with the aid of computer programming and simulation technique.

In particular, consider Carley's participant-observation study keyed to a simulation model in which she has developed an explicit and operationalized theory for how character develops for corporates, for groups (1984, 1986). She has grown it from a matrix of theories about artificial intelligence, which use "frames" and scripts and related formulations that evolved along with computer science.[14] Implicitly she has thereby assumed decoupling.

The group, in Carley's formulation, builds itself out of profiles from interactions. Carley assumes existing human identities as the beginning point and develops her model on that basis. In her words:

> Constructuralism is the theory that the social world and the personal cognitive world of the individual evolve reflexively, and are continuously constructed as individuals, as they move through the series of tasks that constitute their daily experience . . . not just one individual but all of the individuals' structures. . . . As the individual's knowledge base evolves it affects his position in the social unit. As knowledge is acquired individuals reposition themselves cognitively. . . . Since interaction leads to knowledge acquisition . . . this is a case of positive feedback . . . tacit consensus produces social knowledge . . . each piece of social background information is in itself a social tie . . . that social fact, that piece of social knowledge, in and of itself becomes a defining characteristic of that social structure. . . . It is a research decision as to what level of consensus produces "social knowledge." . . . The level of social validity chosen when constructing the social knowledge base leads to different predictions. (Carley 1986)

Then transcribe her analysis to actors at nonpersonal levels, in order to argue that character there too can be inferred by the same phenomenological principles of measurement.

March and Simon's (1955) formulation of organization theory revolutionized the field by basing authority and decision processes on "decision premises," on their distribution and control, as judged from the profile they generated. Carley's theory is a generalization of

---

[14] The formal mathematical structure of Carley's theory is not unusual. What is crucial is that the loops of calculation can be performed thousands instead of scores of times, which generates outcome structures that can be qualitatively different and much more interesting. To put it another way, steps which were too miniscule to motivate modeling before, being bypassed by more wholistic modeling attempts, are modeled very simply in Carley's scheme and then accumulated so as to generate veridical and surprising larger structure.

that early approach to handle corporates in general. Her computer programs go much beyond the early attempt at operationalization carried out by March, in collaboration with Cyert (1963).

Carley's work goes further in showing that explicit "decisions" are not where the real action is. The real crux is how "frames" or structurings of social knowledge (Schank and Abelson 1977) get formulated. This determines how a particular frame comes to be invoked for a particular occasion which may, in accordance, become defined as locale for a decision. Decision "premises" are not marbles which can be acquired and mixed arbitrarily by "authorities" and then thrown out upon the arena of decision. To calibrate her model, Carley carried out a highly detailed reconstruction of the evolution of a corporate living group at M.I.T. around the replacement of an official leader.[15]

Cohen's (1971) model is an earlier alternative to Carley's for analyzing style of a group. Cohen combines the tradition of Zipf (1949; and see Ijira and Simon 1977) with combinatorial insights (Erdow and Spencer 1974) to achieve the simplest models that can yield the profile shapes observed.

One can anticipate applications of such models in larger and different contexts, even some in the remote past. Breiger (1976) has dissected the underpinnings in multiple network structures for prestige—and associated stories—in a biomedical research specialty. One could see how group formation and consciousness here correlated to network positionings.

Entourages

An entourage centers on a noteworthy figure but expands to some depth, even extending into historical time.[16] The topic of entourages, like the schematic playground example carried through from the first chapter, illustrates a fundamental tension between individuality in the sources of action, on the one hand, and constraint from larger context on the other. The topic of entourage also illustrates three further themes of this book: that action precedes and generates actors; that control comes from identities; and that variabilities serve as causes.

---

[15] Carley's other initial explicit application (1984) was to the adoption of an innovation (homomorphic filter analysis) by electrical engineers. An analogous line of analysis, for the diffusion of a medical innovation in a city, was discussed in chapter 3.

[16] I borrow the term from Hull's study (1982) of the crowd around Kaiser Wilhelm I.

Entourages serve as a commentary on the preceding discussion of complex textures of social organization that is beyond institutions in scope, if not necessarily in scale. Entourages have many components, which may come as close sets or long strings, and among both individual figures and corporate actors. The purpose here is to show that crosscuttings among networks can be stable on a small scale.

Entourages will also serve as introduction to person in the next section. Historians have developed diverging tracks for dealing with persons, arguably because of the uncertain scientific status of person as concept. Summarize such debate as follows:

> Human beings are not ignored [by the *Annales* school], of course, since the study of history is by definition the pursuit of knowledge and understanding of men, but the focus shifts from individuals to their context. . . . Lucien Febvre wrote in his *Combats pour l'histoire*: "The historical individual . . . or more exactly the historical personage develops in and through the group. . . ." Fernand Braudel went considerably further . . . in terminating his massive *Mediterranean and the Mediterranean World in the Age of Philip II*, he argues that the great king's death had no effect upon the established trends of Spanish history. (Church 1976, p. 97)

This *Annales* position is doubly ironic. Studies of ordinary persons, even in such apparently detailed form as psychoanalysis, are not and cannot be undertaken with the resources needed to report the larger social context for their action. "Movers and shakers" of earlier eras can be reconstructed, however, indeed even better than current elites. It is more likely to be for past ages than for the current scene that "professional investigators," scholars and/or scientists, have enough clout and perspective to gain full access to elite life and the full context. But it is just such study which undermines the *Annales* conceit that fresh action of importance did not emanate from such as Spain's Philip II, Pippin, etc. Instead it becomes evident that the *Annales* approach is suited to the history of, but only of, corporatism, or more generally, institutions.[17] It will not function with this variant of style as profile, the entourage, say of Philip II.

Personages Making History

Take a biography of a very different historical personage, Rowen's (1978) of the great Dutchman, John DeWitt. It is the very turbulence of the Cromwell-Orange period, when the Netherlands emerged out

---

[17] The *Annales* approach is in some respects a throwback to an older form of history, the annals, which, rather than fitting the myth of history-as-a-general-form, suits

of an ambiguous fog of towns and polders, that triggered the identity of DeWitt.

He started out as a bright young man from a middling line of patricians in a city of medium importance. He learned to operate among contending place-seekers in the unrationalized mazes of pensionable offices which made up Holland and the lesser Provinces. He carried on extensive administrative routine in a turbulent time. All these fit together from separable contexts into what goes beyond an identity or person: into a distinctive personage, also labeled DeWitt:[18]

> The government led by DeWitt should not be seen, however, as an emanation of his personality. . . . DeWitt as councilor pensionary exercised his leadership not only by the undoubted power of his words and his skill in manipulation of the system, but also by the existence of . . . not a modern organized party, of course, no more than its competitor, the "[Prince of] Orange party," but a clique or a congeries of cliques . . . and it always remained a narrow party of the elite. (Rowan 1988, p. 98)

This personage was importantly an expression and creation of the larger convolution that was the United Provinces wound around Holland; it was not a mere person, no matter how able and multifaceted. Yet this personage was such an exceptional success at creating control—out of thin air as it seemed to his contemporaries, especially to smoldering royalty—that it is hard to deny unusual individuality to DeWitt as central person. Notably, DeWitt embodied a double genius: he contributed, as an equal among other great European mathematicians, a complete theory of conic sections.[19]

Nonetheless, across this exact century there is striking evidence for the claim to personage as being shaped primarily by social confluences. A generation before, for years very much the same personage had been dominant, centered around another extraordinary human person, Oldenbarnevelt (Rowen 1988, p. 37; cf. Tex 1975). The social confluences, the system then, were also congeries of cliques, in "a political current . . . that is usually called 'republican,' but more precisely was 'Staatsgezind' (literally, 'in favor of the States') and denied the sovereignty either of the 'people,' however defined, or of the House of Orange" (Rowen 1988, p. 37).

As if to confirm the similarity conjecture, even the human fates of the two central persons were identical: Both were assassinated by

---

well only to value-centered corporatism which, as observed on the ground, is a shambles of high ambage, by the argument made earlier.

[18] See Rowan (1978) e.g., p. 28 on the system and p. 252 on the identity.

[19] Perhaps DeWitt would today have contributed a mathematical theory of control covering issues such as those sketched in chapter 6 below, but perhaps not, since particularity may have been key to his method and his cognitions on control.

royal interests, Oldenbarnevelt under judicial guise and DeWitt by the agency of a street mob. The context had changed considerably in concrete terms, and they were different persons, but the personages were parallel.

Strategy and Intimacy

Such personages evolve as corporate actors, compounds of identities. Disorder that is apparently unneeded and unusual in the context is a clue to shifts in the personage. Strategy and intimacy are involved, which cross distinct social worlds and institutions. Intimacy seems to be a delicate by-product, confined to equals, of exactly the multiplicity from strategy that can permit simple beliefs among some array of third parties. Intimacy is of course a situation of lowered ambage, and the strategy invoked increases ambiguity.

A biographer of President Lyndon Johnson comments on his important base of power in Senate years as follows:

> The biggest, the most efficient, and most ruthlessly overworked and the most loyal personal staff in the history of the Senate. . . . Those who made up that staff found that working for Johnson subjected them to unpredictable expressions of feelings. One minute he would turn right around, give him an expensive gift, and say to him, "You know you are my right arm. . . ." Johnson justified his violent swings in feelings and conduct by the need to keep his staff continually off-guard in order to ensure that they would not relax their efforts. Everything— from staff meetings to rides in his car—was by invitation only, allowing Johnson to arbitrarily freeze out or bring in anyone at any time. Yet if one of his staff decided to leave, Johnson would become desperate, begging him to stay, attempting to bribe . . . to pressure . . . so the aide who thought of leaving remained, perhaps because he felt he had acquired the intimacy that Johnson had hitherto denied him. (Kearns 1976, pp. 78–79)

Kearns is looking from LBJ's side, and these strategic ties proved to have been asymmetric, in tune with the hierarchic structure of a Senate leader and his staff. An earlier account of Johnson (Evans and Novak 1966, pp. 410–12) comments on anomalies in his relation as new President with the press. There were sudden summonses and bizarre privileges here too, but the overwhelming tone is a consistent one of uninterrupted wooing. The outcome (which Evans and Novak are confused by) is exactly a failure to build intimacy, but not a failure on either side to establish identity.

Around the world from LBJ, "big men" in New Guinea mountain tribes appear to develop strategy and intimacy and achieve identity in a similar way, according to one account. Strathern guided his field work "by reference to Radcliffe-Brown's definition of alliance relationships . . . those which are characterized by an interplay of conjunction and disjunction, by antagonism and yet by mutual friendship and aid. Such relationships occur between persons who are outside the sphere of incorporation relative to each other." Ceremonial displays and ostentatious conveyance of gifts, called prestations in the literature, are held in scattered sites, with one or another increased according to the strategizing of big men. There are numerous preliminary negotiations of who is to supply what to which others, and what they, variously arrayed in tribal distance, deign to accept.

> But prestations themselves are always part of a further sequence . . . of alternating between a number of partners . . . I distinguished between the main flow of prestations between a number of partners . . . I distinguished between the main flow which is the moka chain proper, and auxiliary flows, which can be thought of as further "ropes of moka" attached to and feeding into the chain. (Strathern 1971, pp. 121–33)

Strathern emphasizes the strategizing and gaming from which moka emerges; for example "a deputation of engambo Minembia men came to big-man of Kawelka Kundmbo late in July 1964 and complained strongly that he had not yet given pig-moka to them; had he done so in time they could have passed his pigs on to the Kitepi to whom . . . ; such demands are part of the general effort of gamesmanship which is put into moka relations. . . . Each side knows fairly well how far to insist."

In addition to both assessing and representing political maneuvering among hierarchies amid tribal composites, Strathern's account also is a specification of one, albeit restricted cycle of actions that can be seen as economic; someday they may be woven by some native entrepreneurs into the beginnings of a putting-out economy. Any economy anywhere is built only from such tangible mechanisms brought into some resonance with work and its cumulation; consult Granovetter (1985), and earlier Polanyi, Arensberg, and Pearson (1957).

Strathern's account also shows how intimacy[20] is bound up with creations of identity as by-products of superficially erratic mixtures of actions.

> The large size of prestations is partly a result of the desire to show temporary superiority and dominance over them . . . in this context, moka

---

[20] There is a striking similarity to what Leifer calls local action among skilled players (see chapter 3).

gifts are a true functional alternative to warfare. . . . Indeed, if one group were overwhelmingly "defeated" in moka exchanges it could become politically dependent on the victor; hence recipient groups, in order to retain their independence, *must* reciprocate." And "Allies are also rivals, competing for prestige through the size of their reciprocal moka gifts.

Strathern sums up the "rope of moka":

> Donors' formally announced intention is often to compensate the recipients . . . to make them "feel good" again. But underneath the formal rubric a good deal of antagonism may show, especially when the social distance between donor and recipient groups is great. This point might lead us to suppose that the largest gifts, expressing the greatest antagonism, would be made to *major* enemies. But . . . between these there is insufficient trust for groups to risk very heavy investments in each other. . . . The upshot is that most effort is put into prestations to groups which are allies . . . but are also in some way politically and socially opposed.

Personages form from strategic ambiguity in maintaining intimacy in ties. This etiology can be illustrated as well in U.S. national government as in the highlands of New Guinea—or for that matter on any basketball court. This same process is at the root of the creation of stories that tell about identities as a core part of ordinary social life. There is a paradoxical combination of ambiguity and intimacy which must be there to weave together stories and establish the fascination from which personage can emerge. Resulting stories are likely to come in sets that accommodate each other.

Persons

Persons come into existence and are formed as overlaps among identities from distinct network-populations. Identities and positions do prefigure persons, but persons emerge only as the contexts become more sophisticated. Persons build in terms of styles across distinct populations. Conversation prefigures personal identity.

Return again to the playground of chapter 1. A network spreads through many nodes but it need not catch up all the nodes embedded in any given identity. A child as a person, itself a compound of identities, comes late in sequences of other disciplines of family and gang. Personhood never would have emerged in the child had it not also placed as a node in some other networks than the playground, in networks across some other populations as contexts. Conversely, a personal identity may touch on many networks but does not encompass all of any network. A personal identity presupposes distinct networks—not just in different locales but also with different tones. Consider, as illustration, games versus storytellings right on the playground.

Identities are the basis from which persons are constructed. Identities are triggered. They are contingent by-products from mismatch between embeddings of disciplines, on the one hand, through contingencies upon ecology and network histories on the other. Identities are as real—they function about the same in relation to environing social organization—however they fit as actors into the complex interlocking of gels and strands of social process and organization. But persons are special: for example, not all the sorts of actors considered can converse, despite all having identities.

Person should be a construct from the middle of the analysis, not a given boundary condition. Personhood has to be accounted for, which means specifying contexts where it may, where it will, and where it cannot enter. But in most present social science "person" is instead taken as the unquestioned atom. This is an unacknowledged borrowing and transcription of the soul construct from Christian theology.[21] Before general theory in social science can be attained, "persons" have to be assimilated as being but particular embodiments of a class of socially constructed actors, and that not the only class.

Persons come to be generated only out of large-scale frictions among distinct network-populations. It is through common style that persons link across network populations. Ordinarily, persons and styles coexist, but the charismatic is a person purged of style. While style tends to reduce ambage at the expense of ambiguity, personhood tends to reduce ambiguity—to sustain orderly interpretive frames—at the cost of increased ambage.

Etiology of Persons

The emergence of identities from irregularities is traced even amidst the smooth life of the isolated island of Tikopeia by Firth. These are natural irregularities from storm or fishing upset, but also social irregularity from health degradation or randomly triggered brawl. Firth, in his reports (1957) across two generations concerning this tribe, isolated on a Melanesian atoll, weaves an account in which one

---

[21] Christian theology worked out "soul" during centuries when a strikingly dual polity was emerging in its region, and this secular context helped shape and limit the construct. But the ultimate fixity of the soul, carried over to hobble social science, was a Pauline theological imperative.

sees persons emerging only dimly and partially in their own eyes. Persons become vivid and real only in consequences of and as by-product from bridging across to distinct populations, be they Firth's and our society, or Asian sailing-bark crews.

In the much more complex tribal spread across the hills of upper Burma, Leach (1954) painted a very similar picture of how persons emerged—and faded. They did so in sequentially invoking and ignoring two competing forms of social portrayal, *mayu* and *dama*, which appeared and then faded as a by-product of eddies of social action. Populations analytically distinct, though only partially segregated, were bridged by actors who maneuvered from one to the other according to political situation and thereby became persons.

Our access to other ages through what we call history is not usually sufficient to reconstruct social milieus and contexts in which then ordinary persons would have appeared. There are, however, exemplary studies which appear to support the conjecture about personhood; for examples, consult Tilly (1978, 1990) and his students on contentious assemblies, Bynum (1987) on medieval spiritual life, and M. Howell (1988) on medieval practical life. Usually there is not enough precision to establish or refute the conjecture that persons are by-products of interaction between populations.

But in our own day and cities, field work confirms these ideas. Personal identity can come from turbulences in early life which result from and carry over into several realms, of family, neighborhood, and the like. Willis (1977) gives a vivid characterization of this for working-class British teenagers. Many if not most of these youth participate for long periods in social scenes in which they never step outside routine role performances; so there personhood is never induced or invoked, despite inevitable chronic mismatches among alternate role performances and role complementarities.

All the earlier chapters on ties and disciplines and institutions may sound impersonal, and much too elaborate. But in fact our consciousnesses as persons result from and are caught up in style for these mazes. Each "I," in the common parlance, is a more-or-less rickety ensemble; it is firm and whole only temporarily as a facet of one particular constituent discipline energized in some situation and style. In a specific context we may recognize some particular self operating in one or another of the three species of discipline. But, overall, persons are aptly seen as walking wounded, who evolve out of stochastic processes of continuing bruisings and coalescences among networks and disciplines. Take an early example.

Luther comes from a period long known for its induction of person in the modern sense. The book *Young Man Luther* is unusual both in its impact, and in its authorship by a psychoanalyst (Erikson 1960). Historians have always re-created Luther, like other "world historical" figures, as a strain point at confluences of significant social tides. They do not agree on some preexisting uniqueness and strength of person but do join in a re-creation of the entourage. And specialists in theological history (Obermann 1970) are engaged in a revisionist debate as to the originality of Luther's ideas and of Luther's systematic formulation, as opposed to a revived perception of liveliness in late medieval nominalist theology preceding Luther. But they too will join in an "as-if" account of Luther's importance, minimally as an expression of incoming major cultural reformation.

Erik Erikson contributes a highly original view, of the importance of dynamics in young Luther's family constellation, which is fed into, rather than used to contradict, the historical and theological perspectives. Erikson's accomplishment illustrates one major theme: each social reality, of whatever scope, is caught up in and affected by other scopes. Erikson is convincing on Luther as being quite literally created as a person by cross-pressures of his immediate family life, as both interpreted and, simultaneously, concretely shaped by the late medieval theological and institutional context. The person as a pearl shaped in a family bivalve of turbulent flows: this could have been Erikson's subtitle.

Persons and Styles

The ordinary person is a late construct, by the standards of archaeological reconstruction of societies. As Nissen argues from the archaeological record of Mesopotamia, persons are like pottery in this respect. A lot of corporate actors evolve and reproduce as disciplines before there is pottery with its styles, and before persons are recognizable. Pottery provides not just an illustration of style, but what seems from an archaeological perspective to be the principal early vessel of style. Pottery came in relatively late, and it came in along with persons (Nissen 1988). Pottery combines the story aspects of style with physical substrate in transparent form. The correlation continues to this day (Dauber 1992).

Persons in seeking control cannot and do not attempt to deal severally with the enormous, the astronomical array of paths and influences upon them. Instead they come to deal with combinations as styles. Persons work with sets of perceptions both of their own and of others' situations, social and physical. Only some such sets prove able to reproduce themselves and thereby become objective constraints. Such sets are styles in that they exert constraints, like molecular disciplines but in more sophisticated context. Style goes with a patterning in physical space that survives turbulence and reproduces, and likewise for style in social spaces of ties or stories and of values or roles. Stories are generated as explanations along with the embeddings within habits that, all together, can define a style for an individual actor. A person and a style can define each other, and the same duality obtains up through larger social formations. Styles can have still smaller or much more encompassing concrete referents, such as conversations and communities, respectively.

Individual actors watch one another within disciplines and social networks and imbibe patterns in how to maneuver and how to account in stories and values for the maneuvers. Thereby individuals acquire a style, as they jointly reproduce profiles through their mutually patterned actions. A style may come as a distinct pattern of combining and embedding disciplines, as well as personal actors, into an overall network topology. Gearings for action, intentional and unintentional, rely on common styles as well as on profiles.

In Simmelian milieu of strangers on downtown streets, style is the only skim on the surface of chaotic social process. Styles are byproducts of turbulence in tangible structure and process, in institutions. Style and turbulence presuppose each other. They arise across many ranges of incident and network, and across the many levels mixed up in social organization. The social economy of different relations is not developed only or primarily at a level of individual dyads and actors.

Formations at higher scopes must be reaching down with contextual pressures as styles through any particular discipline to effect an orderliness of perception. And conversely from lower scopes, where, for example, conversations as prototypes become elaborated into further disciplines or styles of perception. The three species of discipline—the commit interface, the select arena, and the mobilize council—are those which have proved robust to all these perception pressures, above and below.

Selves and Multiplex Ties

"Real selves" cannot be disentangled from "intimate ties," as we see in modern social contexts, which have been so concerned to create "privacy." The modern concept of friendship is wholly aside from tit-for-tat, from favor for help. Silver (1989, esp. p. 274; 1990) provides convincing argument and evidence for this evolution of friendship: he fixes the beginning as the Scot Enlightenment. Equate Silver's tie of friendship with a multiplex tie, the kind of overall tie that we take for granted as the basis for civil and civic life.

This overall tie presupposes a lack of concern with the detailed balancing of obligations found in traditional formations. There is no tangible, concrete mechanism perceived as concerned with enforcement of obligation. This kind of multiplex tie itself comes to seem a recent, modern innovation.

A tribal or feudal society does not know the luxury of a single, overall tie not built into concrete economy of obligation. Such social formations rather make use of relations each part of which is lucidly factored out by audience and occasion—as kinship, as village, whatever. This multiplex tie is a late and sophisticate construct, on this interpretation of evolution.

Yet the modern multiplex tie need not be fraught with fearsome potency from balanced duress in gaming. Romantic love is merely representative of extreme examples, not of medians in multiplexity. Some extreme examples, notably feud, can also be found in traditional formations.

What this overall tie can bring about is the person. By this argument, the person is a late construct in perception. "Self" becomes the creation as well as the creator of person, with multiplex tie as the occasion for perception of a self. The tie of marriage is an example.

The key is a multiplex tie that requires and builds to disparate populations. Elizabeth Bott (1957) emphasized this. She showed how to predict differences in marital personalities from underlying divergences in partners' interlock in their concrete social relations. Marital person was read by Bott from immediate context of social networks, which changed from couple to couple in London. A "joint" form of marriage relation was distinguished by Bott from segregated roles of domestic wife and "pub" husband. Only the joint-form, requiring straddling different populations, yielded persons.

The world of romantic love, discussed below, is a precursor and correlate of the joint-form marriage. Romantic love is induced by the same modern contexts in which attitudes become reified. Love is an induction of person, but as only a metastable state. Romantic love is so important because development of this sort of subtle, ambiguous, gamed bond of some duration is a main path to unique personal identity in Goffmanesque social contexts. Here is where the esoteric game theory which economists misplace onto "rational decision" might yield empirical insight.[22] Stable identities as persons are difficult to build; they are achieved only in some social contexts; they are not pre-given analytic foci.

[22] It could be argued that the crippling of game theory is the worst effect of rational-

Community

Silver (1989, 1990) also argues that distinct identity as a person in the modern sense followed from rather than created a multiplex tie, the overall tie. Across levels of identities similar interpretation of multiplex tie should be possible. Persons are not the only constructions made out of identities. Identities are a much broader class than persons, or than facets of persons, or than any other entities that are embedded by any particular discipline.

For example, communities can be seen as built out of identities rather than persons, and as being only partial analogues of persons. Consider this analysis of the concept of community:

> We need to develop a conceptualization of community which allows us to penetrate beneath simple categories . . . to see a variable of social relations. . . . The relationship between community as a complex of social relationships and community as a complex of ideas and sentiments has been little explored (p. 107). . . . What is important about "sense of belonging" is . . . his modification of consideration of alternative courses of action on the basis of the communal relations to which he belongs. (Calhoun 1980, p. 110)

Then he continues, "The self-regulation of community is dependent on dense, multiplex bonds. . . . The crucial issue is the breakdown of the structure of hierarchical incorporation which knit local communities into the society as a whole" (p. 115). Recast Calhoun's point. Earlier forms of community had types of tie well defined and built into explicit disciplines, so that sense of community was not relevant. The development of multiplex tie from community to other actors is what induces and permits the appearance of community persona akin to the modern individual person, as signaler.

A large-scale exemplar of the signaling argument for identity is how "lost," "saved," and "liberated" communities are not successive stages, but rather alternative structural models:

> Many scholars believed that community ties were now few in number, weak, narrowly specialized, transitory, and fragmented. . . . These scholars feared that community had been "lost." . . . Others argued

---

choice theory (for which see chapter 7). At its introduction by von Neumann, game theory had the potential of refounding the theory of social action. Unfortunately, it devolved into the hands of economic theorists. Except in the work of Schelling, who eschews systematic theory or modeling, the results for many years were increasingly arid exercises. New developments may be afoot, but effective game theory has to concern the induction of identities and disciplines, of social organization.

that people gregariously form and retain communities in all social settings. . . . By the 1960s their "Community Saved" argument had had much the better of the debate empirically. . . . Both the "Lost" and the "Saved" arguments assume that a flourishing community can only be one that replicates the standard image of preindustrial communities: densely knit, tightly bounded, and mutually supportive villages. But such bucolic imagery not only disregards widespread preindustrial individualism, exploitation, cleavage, and mobility . . . but it also restricts the criteria. . . . Scholars who have avoided this mislabeling . . . argue that large-scale specialization and personal mobility have "Liberated" community—encouraging membership in multiple, interest-based communities predominantly composed of long-distance friendship ties . . . people are not so much antisocial or gregarious beings as they are *operators*. . . . Each model speaks to a different means of obtaining and retaining resources: direct use of formal organizations (Lost); membership in densely knit, all-encompassing, solidary groups (Saved); or selective use of specialized, diversified, sparsely knit social nets (Liberated) . . . all three models are likely to be reflected in current realities to some extent. (Wellman, Carrington, and Hall 1988, pp. 133–35)

These are alternatives for community identity, they constitute a story-set for it. This set of stories is in fact used both in common parlance and also simultaneously in professional jousts by scholarly analysts within their own world. The set of stories clusters around some value(s).

There is community as identity of personal sort at still larger scope and higher level. Identity acquires theophany, covenant, and law before gaining the most universal recognition, as for example Jehovah (Jahweh in Gottwald 1979, p. 94). All three of these aspects—pronouncement, reciprocal commitment, and rules—presuppose and can only be observed in social context. Social context is not opaque like the "insides" of persons, and so it is requisite for the three aspects even regarding a particular human person. All three aspects presuppose value. This is true even where the "actor" is least personal.

There is analogue to community at smaller scale. Ties are the detritus of discipline formations. Ties are fragments of what might have locked into disciplines, thus yielding identities enabled to generate social action. Within a discipline there are strong connections among the constituting entities, which may themselves be identities, so that other types of connection exist between identities. These connections are mutual pressures which come to fit together so as to support some transitive order, perhaps some personhood.

Modern Person from Love and Attitudes

The modern vision of social milieus is exemplified by Goffman's (1963, 1967, 1971) and Simmel's (1955) strangers. These are persons who are so little reinforced by siting in specific social structures as to have only shadowy existence, to be creatures mostly bracketed, to be abstract actors triggered into concreteness only through encounters. Turn back to romantic love.

This modern vision fits as well a province of romantic love, which at first sight seems so surely and purely a matter of one preexisting person intensely attuned to another. Perhaps. But in fact the two persons are meeting in the Small World. This Small World has been emerging since around the time a phenomenology of romantic love was spreading beyond troubadour circles (Bloch 1977).[23] It is just when persons are shadowy in their social sitings that intensely personal attractions are generated, as Swidler (1989) argued. But this modern vision also reminds us that an identity may have just one or two facets or personae (out of its corporate self) exposed to observation at a given time. These facets are cobbled together, by the identity, from different frames, perhaps spun together in stories.

Romances are outcomes of mutual searches among networks and groups which are keyed to occasions, to specific times marked by assemblages of persons as at acquaintance dances. Attention can only be given, in social as well as physical perception, to limited numbers of "contacts" at a time. Romantic acquaintanceship can only be pursued one "date" at a time. Romantic personages are a construct out of, a by-product of distinctive eddies and enclaves which emerge as by chance in a Small World in which "eligibility" itself, perceived active participation, is induced by the states of queues in what can be visualized as a system of stochastic social servers.

Romantic love is a colorful topic. The same truths can be argued about more everyday stuff of our life in Small World contexts. Attitudes are perhaps the most distinctive invention for modern contexts of social life. Substantial portions of time and cognitive attention are given to the adaptations and replenishment of hosts of notions on topics remarkably far removed from any tangible aspect of the actual living of the persons concerned.

Persons become unique in identities, yet must be validated as stereotypes. So today to some extent the person is the attitudes.

[23] There are no person-pheromones which signal one person as special to another; i.e., there is no doing ant societies (Wilson 1970) one better. A queueing system of stochastic servers (Kleinrock 1963; Riordan 1962) is a formal-modeling way to situate romantic love.

Each set of attitudes can distinguish an identity.[24] Each such set then can find it comfortable to recognize and define as persons other such combinations, variously alike, or compatible, or neither.

Modern democratic politics and its incessant stream of "news"—events made meaningful by episodic campaigns and elections—can be seen, in part, as contributing to the sustenance of personhood, to the creation of persons as distinctive combinations of attitudes which can be perceived as having meaningful continuity over time. Modern politics is a very inexpensive way to create the voters as civil persons, whatever the significance of the ostensible processes of decision and governance. Modern politics can be seen as a phenomenological by-product of the Small World. Milgram's (1977) unknown names as "targets" do not seem bizarre to us as civil beings in part because we have come to attend to and "know" remote names as politicians.

Politics is just an example. Sports is another, or rather each is a cascading modern family of examples. Persons are defined and define themselves most easily and inexpensively, within the Small World which also yields romantic love, by what particular families of attitudes they penetrate into, as much as by particular attitudes upon topics apparently portentous enough that every person should indulge in a "holding." Trivial Pursuit is a parlor game emblematic of an age.

Mischel's and Burt's Persons

The general point is not to distinguish between great personages and ordinary persons, nor between the latter and corporate personal actors. On the contrary, the point is that the ordinary person, so-called, is a late and sophisticated product from interplay of larger social formations, of populations. This is to stand on its head Durkheim's call on religion, as explicated in detail by Swanson (1960). Every person is a god, since a god is exactly any actor required and generated as intersection of multiple social worlds. Making persons atoms in a social science makes as much sense as asking gods for predictions.

Recent research in personality has led to similar conclusions and so have developments in psychodynamics (for an assessment by sociological theorist see Swanson 1988). The classic view, shared by both trait and psychodynamic approaches, was that the gist of the person was stable and broadly generalized dispositions which

---

[24] Combinatoric calculations show the number of possible combinations or sets to be astronomically larger than any human population: see Appendix 2.

yielded substantial differences between individuals within the same social situation. By the late 1960s extensive research had shattered these core assumptions. Yet the theories, the cognitive constructions, that persons have about themselves and others were found to have consistency and continuity and

> suggest a world in which personality consistencies seem greater than they are and in which the organization of behavior seems simpler than it is. . . . Actuarial methods of data combination are generally better than clinical-theoretical inferences. Base rates, direct self-reports, self-predictions, and especially indices of relevant past behavior typically provide the best as well as the cheapest predictions . . . and usually exceed those generated either clinically or statistically from complex inferences about underlying traits and states. (Mischel 1990, pp. 113–14)

According to Mischel the focus has become

> the idiographic nature of each person interacting with the specific contexts of his or her life. . . . Indeed, the tendency to focus on dispositions in causal explanations soon was seen as a symptom of a "fundamental attribution error" committed by laypersons in everyday life, as well as by the psychologists who study them. . . . Going beyond lip service about the importance of person-situation interaction to generate and test theory-based predictions of those interactions became and remains high on the agenda. (Mischel 1990, pp. 115–16)

Indeed so, but personality psychology remains grotesquely naive about the constituents of "everyday life." Mischel goes on to explicate a brilliant continuing series of experiments on cognitive process in social prediction which seem consistent with the approach in which persons become products through social organization.

Much the same conclusions about person are drawn from recent sociological investigations by Burt, where he approaches persons from the outside, in field studies of managers in competition for careers. Burt (1992a) writes a primer for effectiveness in social action which is at the same time a theory. He jumps directly into tangible empirical materials: in particular, mobility of individual managers in hierarchies (and, as an analogy, interconnections of various industrial markets within economic flows). The myth of the person—with specified goals and a drive to optimize—seems to be accepted. But it is from analysis of dependencies evidenced by relative movements and flows in networks that Burt induces his central construct: This is the structural hole of his title (which can be generalized to structural autonomy).

You are one of the black dots in the dark grey circle; but the dot isn't all of you. It is a piece. Specifically, it is a piece of you that is redundant with structurally similar pieces of other people. . . . The other black dots at the center of the network would be the other professors connected to the same clusters of students, colleagues and administrators. The distribution of holes in this network defines the structural autonomy you have. . . . Still another piece of you . . . involves another network. . . . As a physical entity, you are an amalgam of these structural pieces. . . . But structural autonomy exists for each piece of you defined by a network of others concerned with that piece. . . . At a higher level of aggregation, structural autonomy . . . with a functional division, . . . at a lower level . . . jobs could have been subdivided into project networks. (Burt 1992a, p. 144)

As Burt points out, the structural hole replaces the "weak tie" of Granovetter and Rapoport (see chapter 3), but I argue that this is exactly because the idea of weak tie relies on person as construct; whereas, Burt is forced into constructs much like identities seeking control, with persons as by-products only under some structural conditions. Furthermore, the nexus of ties, which Burt has shoulder aside person as chief actor, resembles the disciplines of chapter 2. In particular his generic third party resembles a council discipline.

The point is not that these theories are identical or the same as the present theory, but rather that, despite different stances toward the myth of individual persons, the substantive contents of the prime constructs arrived at are similar. All the theories must then depend on specifying what mixes of distinct larger context—institution versus style in my terms—can coexist, and how they may shape persons into existence.

Scale-Invariance

Both actors and events are socially negotiated, both are derivative from ongoing productions. Both can cumulate into new actors and events. Both also can partly shake free of context through decoupling mechanisms. It is this derivative nature of events and of actors that encourages the theory to be scale invariant, or what is called in natural science self-similar (see chapters 1 and 7).

Scale invariance has been queried; for example, in the study of Italian city-states. "The real state, the state felt all around one in the form of potent commissions or as a source of income (via speculation on the Monte), existed in the corporate and individual holder. . . . Nothing in the Florentine constitution emphasized the principle of indirect representation. . . . The contact with power was direct, immediate, sensory" (Martines 1966, pp. 391–92). But on the other end of scale, whether in interpreting international relations (Ashley 1980) or in perceptions within sports leagues (Leifer 1991b), the personalization of embedded actors such as states (Tilly 1975; Wolin 1987) is universal. The plausibility of this personalization is evidence for self-similarity across levels.

Control efforts are attempted every which way across levels resulting from embedding. The idea of levels comes with embedding, but social spaces are not tidy layerings, and actors on presumably different levels can relate directly through control projects. It is all the more important that the analysis be universal, or self-similar, so that the same terms and analyses apply at all scopes.[25]

It is not self-repetition at successive levels in a system that can be claimed. If it could, chapter 3 could have been the last chapter. Levels build up in social formations as by-products of interacting control struggles. "Actor" can become anything from a multinational giant firm to a Goffman creature of the brief encounter. It is for this reason that stories can operate as gears, as transcribers between actors and action on different levels.

Identity is a social fact which can be discerned and takes effect only with respect to ongoing social process, whether or not there is an internal subjective sense of identity on the part of human persons. Signaling is the key. Clans, firms, and Goffman fugitives also signal, and receive signals (for a broad perspective see J. Wilson 1989). It follows that identities are embodied in and take effect concerning some definite context and circles of process as perceived by and recognized among the actors involved. A given entity may be an actor with identity in one context or setting without having identity in other settings in which that actor's disparate entities might or might not cohere into any sort of personage or compound actor.

Persistence through crisis is where identity emerges. Mere announcement of a new business, or a sports team, or a farm, or a lineage, or a political patronage line, cannot effectuate an identity for a corporate actor. The new compound actor will not be taken seriously, considered to have the inertia and staying power of an identity, by others and by its own constituents, until after some nonlinear eddy of affairs, some crisis. Ian Watt (1957) traces the rise of the novel as exactly this sort of birth from irregularity: the principle car-

---

[25] For similar arguments on self-similarity, restricted to a macro scale, see Bergesen, Fernandez, and Sahoo (1987), and Caporaso (1989).

ries over from person to larger sort of identity, and thus the construct of corporate personage is justified.

Clinical psychologists are forced to cover this same ground and are aware of levels in formation of corporate character—and also of unique identity—even within a human being. Consider two different developments in clinical psychology. Stage theory deals with acquiring and evolving corporate characters; for example,

> when a mother responds to anxiety with the intention to relieve it, she brings the culture of embeddedness to the defense of a given evolutionary state (the state of equilibrium). . . . She directs herself to the individual . . . rather than to . . . the movement of evolution itself. She responds to the protection of made-meaning rather than to the experience of meaning-making. . . . Support is not alone an effective matter, but a matter of "knowing," a matter of shape, as well as intensity. (Kegan 1982, pp. 125, 260)

In contrast, group therapy (e.g., Napier and Whitaker 1978) deals with subtle and ambiguous ties as the generator and base of unique identity formation.

On the one hand, Kegan's book is adapting Kohlberg's stage theories (1981) of learning to a personality theory of four stages. Each stage should be seen as a theory of character, which is an essentially corporate matter of joint learning, necessarily concerned with rituals. On the other hand, theories descending from Freud's therapy approaches, such as Erikson's introduced in chapter 1, take as their focus the problematic, gaming, and strategic pair. Thus, ironically, group therapy follows one side of Freud to achieve insight into unique individual identity in a way not available to stage theories. The lines between personal and corporate often blur.

Suicide as Envelope

Identities can appear in person or as event, and either packaging is continually being reshaped by contentious accountings of the contexts of their unions. Surely the ties between identities are then Leifer ties (p. 85). And these comings together are in networks under impetuses of control efforts and pressures of production. Stories are the form taken by the accountings, stories as everyday framings.

To explore simultaneously persons and events, turn to suicides as a unique combination of person and event that is designed to erase identities and end story.[26] Suicide is a personal speculation about

---

[26] Stories apply as readily with other scopes, such as tribes, nations, age sets, clans,

context. Suicide can come when the set of stories available fails to account for how disciplines are woven together as this person. Suicide is the identity disembedding, perhaps without external stochastic trigger. Suicide is rare, for sets of stories have evolved over time to give maximal flexibility. Priests are never caught short in explaining, and other persons can imitate that skill.

Durkheim pioneered systematic study of suicide, and some of his arguments carry over here. Persons in common patterns of disciplines with others are less likely to be focuses of mismatches which generate identity, without which suicide will not be conceived. And such homogenized contexts are not going to generate the intensity of rules—that is, the prominence of story line only evoked by mismatch and inconsistency—to which Durkheim attributes an "altruistic" suicide (Bearman 1991).

Suicide is best seen as an event being generated as a means of filling in and making effective an identity, which always is the product of mismatches and is expressed in the idiom of stories. Durkheim would require that events of suicide must be construed in terms of the larger groups in which they are embedded. But on social analytic grounds, suicide then should not be rare because it is a technique by which stories among events and group actors are further developed so as to accommodate the contingencies and mismatches which are their origins.

When social formations are dissected into disciplines and networks, rather than into reified groups of actors, many of the anomalies in the theory of suicide derived from Durkheim are reduced. There will remain others, since suicide is also in part a phenomenon of a different theoretical venue, of organism as part of biophysical space and its ecology. It may make more sense for social research to look at more purely social analogues and antinomies, such as the creation and destruction of actors through manumission and enslavement (O. Patterson 1982).

The higher the skill stratum, the less clear-cut the events, as judged by identities participating in the disciplines producing the skilled action. But this stratum in turn is embedded in, indeed is materially dependent upon, a larger world of inexpert playing. Events now must be regenerated so as to sustain the interest of the larger world as umbilical cord. Not only wins and losses but also definite strategies and ploys are required. Rankings in particular tournaments as events become themselves assertions of identities rather

---

cities, markets (e.g., Cornell 1988; Deutsch 1953; Eisenstadt 1956; Fortes 1945; Waley 1969; White 1981b), and the suicide construct can apply there as well.

than identities inducted out of contradictions. Chess players generally avoid suicide.

Learned Helplessness

Learned helplessness (Seligman and Garber 1980) is the empirical accompaniment of consistency in role; for adults it is the analogue of the state of innocence for children. If you are in a wholly consistent social position, if you and your compatriots have roles that actually do dovetail, you have no basis for and no irritant of capacities for dealing with the unexpected. You are helpless outside the confines of your tied roles. You are not a person.

The issue is slippery. If one has a role does one gain or lose control thereby? It is slippery because "having a role" can be just a story. If the story is one of a set among which you can change easily, one may be able to gain control. If the story is a fixed one, you lose control, whether or not the story is, on the surface, an attractive one.

The puzzle is mixed up with the standing of goals and the like. If one gains action by having and following goals, then having a definite role should contribute to gaining control.[27] But on the contrary, control, according to the present argument, comes only out of fluidity of role, because then one does *not* have goals imposed upon oneself by the social process.

Learned helplessness has an unpleasant ring to it, on its own; yet it is engendered by what is quite literally the utopian situation. Utopias all share the trait of roles fitting together. Negative utopias may seem unpleasant but they are as bland as utopias in removing the basis for identity.

Regular life, by its own account, is a utopia. Regular life seems to supply you at any time with an accounting, a story of what is going on and where you fit. If this were the whole story, there would be no triggering by happenstance and you would not be in existence as an entity outside of prediction. You would not have an identity; you would not need it—any more than you would need an identity in a utopia.

Regular life is shot full of contradictions. They are less obtrusive to us than they are to children. They may be invisible. Everyday life has trained us to and supplied us with neat packages of stories, as argued in chapter 3. At any given time we have learned to apply just some of the set, and suppress memories of the switchbacks and

[27] Bailey and Morrill (1989) so argue: their example is the emergence of the "skinhead" role on the streets of contemporary Britain.

changes which we use and embroider to get along. Much of social science has been an auxiliary to this provision of packages of stories sufficient to account for most anything we find—but only by suitable *ex post* selection of one rather than another story.

Learned helplessness can recur in an abstract sense at some higher level of social formation. Not just persons but other social actors can be subjected to it. It need not be naive; it may be part of efforts of control, and of getting action. The psychologists' concept of learned helplessness should be elaborated and generalized by other social sciences.

Careers

Persons come into existence not singly but all together, as by-product of and set within an envelope of network-populations. Yet, there are varied ways in which any given person may emerge and develop, ways worth studying. A person comes as a hybrid of ties with disciplines, a hybrid held together with stories. Any person is an uneasy balancing of disjunct identities which were triggered independently. A "person" is a continuing balancing act among distinct identities, often very disparate, so that some unilinear track of interpretation is not feasible. The term "career" is misleading if it implies a unique track. Career will be developed as a construct applicable to other than personal actors, also.

Development and Stories

Begin with the precursor to plots, the use of stories to frame the disciplines of chapter 2 and the ties of chapter 3. Stories do not cause social action, nor need they guide it. Rather, they account for it in much the way a CPA keeps track of the financial activities of a firm. Stories come as sets. Each story-set can account for a wide array of possible events, after the fact, in some range of social and ecological settings, to sustain a discipline or a tie. Pressures to sharing a discipline can themselves come as stories, in sets. Stories as told are always about particular ties. Meanings are not separable from structure, any more than social action is. The other basic constituent of storying, besides language and social spread, is time spread. Events strung together are a story. This is story as realized in time, just as ties realize story in social space.

There is nothing weird about being weird, in fact it's perfectly normal. Our accustomed stories are just too tame to singly match reality, even of the everyday. Each "normal" story defining some "normal" path is itself a one-dimensional abstract of any real life segment. It takes a whole set of stories to incorporate a segment of real life. It would take an abnormal, a weird story to, by itself, describe a normal patch of an identity's existence. So in a sense we're all weird; it is the stories that are "normal."

Sets of stories are eminently practical tools, rather than mere decoration. They are tools analogous to gears in mechanical machinery. That is, stories are ways to bridge between different scales. For example, by personifying a giant state or bureaucracy an actor is enabled to conceive and maintain ties to such. Differences in scale make it all the more inevitable that stories come in a set able to accommodate to a given value whatever happens.

Dramas are another matter, being stories which interlock and imply a discipline and embedding. It is appropriate to distinguish these dramas as a contrasting sort of rhetoric, call it vertical.[28] A longer story is harder to match to actual happenings. That match is important to the identities involved. But actual happenings are nearly unpredictable—even now despite all our vaunted social science we could not predict next week's social climate in some second grade classroom!

Story Lines

Given multiple stories available for *ex post* explanation, feedback is not tight from actual ravelings of networks among disciplines. Accountings are accepted whether or not the series of events would seem explicable to an observer. This is possible only because story lines organize the perceptions. Any particular story by itself would quickly get so far out of step with the ongoing situation as to be unusable.

A calculus requires more specification of intervening mechanisms for decoupling than was developed at the end of chapter 3. Indexing of one role by other coincident roles is what yields position. In this city, say, a citizen may be a member of an assembly, the head of a family, and a soldier. There citizen is a resident of a locality who participates in an economy. Decoupling is presupposed and must be enacted to make possible this identification of several identities as one position with several roles in distinct network populations. Story lines build out of such constrained stories. The times are social times,

---

[28] For other social science usage of horizontal/vertical imagery see, for example, Moore (1988) and Schwartz (1981).

which are constructed out of application of story lines. Hence these times are multiple and not necessarily consistent (cf. general equilibrium models in Winship 1978).

Social time interweaves *ex ante* and *ex post* in ways that may not be available to many or any of the conscious persons or other personal actors always being regenerated in ongoing social patterns. Social time consists as much in switchbacks and other nonlinearities as in any linear sequence. Story lines accommodate these irregularities of social time (cf. Ricoeur 1988). Social time is as much a by-product as a shaper of social pattern, just as social space is. So social times are by-products of story lines. But physical realities of work also contribute to shape time and to shape population.

An institution can emerge with story lines. A story line of stories is analogous to a path of ties, is in a way an expansion of the path in words of that language. Each position generates at least one recurring path in a story line as part of its continuing reproduction across distinct identities. Sets of stories become partitioned into story lines able to accommodate whatever occurs with that position, in the reality of a stochastic, fluid context.

Story lines must serve a number of contending identities. There must be some correspondence between stories and the facts in physical space, and also facts as may be seen by an observer in social space. But stories are best thought of as members of a convention, which depend on each other as much as on any other facts.

Story lines survive in a matrix of contending control projects. Story lines end up as a set from which is picked a parsimonious account that is consistent with control projects being pushed. Whatever comes to pass, and thus whatever can be conceived, must be describable after the fact in terms of the story lines and the conventions. But this means that there are multiple descriptions available as plausible descriptions.

Stories are paths both to the frames for and to the by-products of multiple levels of control. Each by-product is itself a resultant trace from interspersed movements of decoupling playing off embeddings. Story lines are devices accounting this confusion, before and after the fact; they do so as decouplers. They intertwine structuralist with individualist viewpoints; they do so as decouplers.

Story lines constrain accounting of process, constrain sifting into events as well as arrangements. Ambiguity is then the slippage between one example and another of articulation into a given story line. Then there can be further slippage between articulations by different story-sets, both invoked as elements in a larger codification, a framing.

Story lines appear to be similar to Collins's (1988) concept of ritual interaction chains. So too does Goffman's frame (1974) concept. The story lines approach also seems analogous to that taken on a much broader scale, for whole institutional systems, by Berman (1983): He has realities being dealt with in terms of parallel discourses of statute law, natural law, common law, local customary law, merchant law, Roman law, equity, and so on.

Story lines are rational expectations, in the modern phrase (Muth 1959; Hechter 1987), but only in a limited sense. Identities come from mismatches in contingencies and so perceive and try to control turbulence. An identity must have multiple possibilities from a story line available so as to be able, *ex post*, to give accounts of whatever in fact is happening concretely. The constituent stories from a story line must be shared.

Story lines are explanation spread over time. A story line comes at least as a pair; its members form what mathematicians call a basis set. Each story line is a kind of orthonormal basis (Birkhoff and MacLane 1953) in terms of which to account for whatever observable comes along.[29] This is an accounting which does not itself lead to further shake-up of the events and actors already generated out of preceding mismatches. The pair or more in a story line in some context cover all possible outcomes, they express the logic of the narrative (Scholes and Kellogg 1966).

Stories thus take form in social organization as distinctive sets over time, packages of accounts that provide the multiple story lines which are needed by a population of identities to situate themselves within the contradictory situations which gave rise to the identities. The identities include events as well as actors. Identities are shaped mutually so as to fit into sets of story lines.[30] A person can be seen as a set of story lines.

Positions and Plots

Location of a particular identity requires tracing how that identity came to embed in and be interlocked there. Position then is elaborated into a historical statement. Position of an identity is its posture with respect to several disciplines and networks and across levels.

[29] Price systems are in our day the best known exemplars of such sets of story lines: to develop this claim however will take another book.

[30] Story lines as well as sets of stories should be correlated more explicitly with blockmodel applications. A new line of development is Abell (1987); another is Cicourel (1980); a third is Skvoretz, Fararo, and Axten (1980); and see Breiger (1990).

Position correlates with story line, but requires several because of the reality of fluid, stochastic context.

To see persons, or organizations, chatting back and forth in everyday life is to see one primitive sort of plotting in operation. This is the framing of picaresque stories about the concrete particulars of happenstance in a population, such that all actors stay within a stereotyped format. This is also a stereotyped content, which would be for us today, variously, with sports, or children, or floppy discs as actors in the skits.

A plot decouples events in one role frame from events in other frames. Dually, events serve to decouple plots. The material for plots are story lines. The plot deals in stock characters and scenes so that it can be transposed from one story line to another. The combination of stock elements into a plot gives it an inner side which can furnish accoutrements for melding identities into a further level as career.

It is when certain occasions always trigger one from some given set of story lines, that one speaks of a plot. Plot is built from a given set of story lines. Plot accommodates positions, and yet plot can be transposed across a larger fluid context.

For example, all viewers know conventions in cowboy movies. The conventions work by relying on stereotyped positions for actors, call them positions or niches: greedy rancher, corrupt sheriff, heroic knight-errant, beleaguered family, and the like. And in a production market, complementary stories are used about niches for price leaders and the like which also constitute a convention (see the earlier sections, and White 1981b). Stories can be understood by identities not themselves active in the convention and also are consumed by them.

Careers in General

Careers, on micro and macro scales, generate envelopes in the perceptions of those involved. Careers also are product of contingencies that can be described by envelopes of contingencies. These can and do embed persons across induced network populations, and do so through social interactions not heavily mediated by perception. Envelopes are large-scale alternatives to disciplines in constraining joint action. These are whole venues rather than disciplines such as interfaces. So these envelopes provide a basis for styles, in particular career as style.

An actor succeeds or not, and now rather than then, according to position, to specify which requires a more general concept of social spaces. Such a space is only in part a matter of concrete ecological context, nor is it enough to add a social network. In major part, embeddings and their stories fix position in a full social matrix. The whole of religion and magic wrap around this (Durkheim 1915; Niebuhr 1959; Tillich 1963). So do modern descendants of religion: embedding is part of the realization side of the wishes encapsulated as justice (Zajac 1985).

Embedding thereby gives a lead on the vexed issues of exchange and its natures (Blau 1964; Emerson 1962; Macneil 1978; Newman 1965). Institutions are contexts for exchanges of broader scope across different network populations. With mutual disciplines substituting for spontaneities, institutions ward off the ideological notion that specific local exchanges are *the* realistic version which should be modeled scientifically, as in theories of rational choice (cf. chapters 1 and 7). Institutions come in a stochastic environment too fluid to sustain rational choice, but fluid enough to induce it.

Institutions can become embedded in a larger stochastic context of styles that proves sufficient to induce and sustain individual persons in the modern sense. Exchanges are also among personages, as in the kula rings of the section on entourages. A whole new layer of interpretation can be superposed—as is done in some microeconomic theory—upon an economy actually grown out of a putting-out system but which needs, in the present, sufficient social "software" for continuing running.

Career is a general concept applicable beyond persons, and beyond positions for persons. Terms in which actors perceive their social organization, and particular embodiments of those terms, also have careers. For example, the vacancies intervening between incumbencies can themselves be construed as entities having careers: for development of this theme see White (1970b) and Stewman and Konda (1983).

Budget construction is also about the shaping of identities for social organizations which are themselves treated as actors. Budget construction is about the shaping of an interacting set of identities: Identities for leader disciplines require the promulgation of goals, that is, require kernels of interpretation from which successive strings of particular targets can be spun off in story lines.

Stedry (1960) models the budgetary process in just such terms of aspiration level. Existing networks of contingencies and interrelations are hard to reshape to goals. These networks are reproduced among the actions of yet other disciplines which are closer to tangible production sequences, and which in a context of accounting take the form of projected budgets. Seams must be welded somehow across these independent shapings of identities as budget lines from above and from below.[31]

The disciplines indexed as in figures 2-2 to 2-6 each also presupposes some sort of time embedding, some memory. But there is neither the loose-jointedness of career, nor the decoupling of career and anticareer as played out together. Within arena discipline, complementarity of specialty being held constant presupposes long-term memory. Within council discipline, the endless shifting balancings of coalitions exhibit short-term memory; the string architecture of kinship underneath this mobilizing discipline codes in long-term memory.[32] And commit interfaces generate embedded identities which are material to careers. But none of the disciplines are loose enough in construction to support or require such loose coupling as in careers.

Not just disciplines and budgets in place of persons, but also the ties that analysts use to code connections into networks can have story lines. A long time frame for a tie is partly unavoidable given its phenomenology. Even the most intimate connection is only enacted occasionally, so that a tie must always in part be a memory, negotiated among parties in control struggles in that neighborhood.

The time frame for network ties is also the focus of much struggle for control, for discipline, and for standing. Field studies (Jacques 1956) have demonstrated systematic variation in the length of time before ties have to be reenacted. There is very high correlation from this length to official status and to leverage for actual control. Discretion over spacing of reports, and thus autonomy, are a main focus of larger structures of control.

The time-course of an agency-form can become reified, but it also can be enacted so variously that it is recognized once more as broken apart, as having a career. Take an example: the evolution of administrative formations through the medieval period of the English monarchy (Chrimes 1950). The Wardrobe, the Exchequer, the Chamber, the Council, all began as interfaces, in present terminology, con-

---

[31] Associativity (for which see also notes 32 and 36) in this welding process must be surprising. It matters very much whether the initial integration of disparate lines of interpretation is done first between B and O and then between the pair and L, or on the contrary the first reconciliation into a joint social form is done between L and B and only then is an overall reconciliation attempted; all this without changing that the sequential order is L, then B, then O!

[32] This guarantees the nonassociativity of mobilizing; Boyd (1991, pp. 8–9) gives a lucid prose discussion of associativity in network relations, and see also notes 31 and 36.

cerned with running a household on a royal scale, with feudal technology.[33] What the detailed historical record shows is the subsequent evolution, slow and painful, of these royal interfaces into what we recognize as today's instruments of administration with general and abstract fields of activity.

The point is a double one: First, the form of a discipline itself—one of the species of chapter 2—can split and evolve. Thus, that species throws up exemplars of new embeddings for specializations, new locations as summarized in figures 2-2, 2-3, and 2-4. Second, a particular discipline will be defined, for its constituent actors and for others, partly through its particular career. This career can lie within a single point in these figures, a point which can cover the succession of network locales in which it is embedded.

Contingency Chains and Careers

Objective, measurable traces of connections among disparate social spaces are needed, across both networks and populations. Such traces are best sought in changes and motion, for it is too easy to project some elaborate architecture into any static, cross-sectional view. The obvious focus is contingencies, and the traces sought can be called contingency chains, of which careers and vacancy chains (White 1970) are prime examples.

A vacancy in a job decouples, and it can move in a chain of decoupling among jobs at a given time (White 1970). In addition, jobs fit into careers, whose manifest content is coupling over time and among identities hypothesized to evolve. But careers also exemplify decoupling. Career is meaningless if preordained; so where careers are perceived, flexibilities of decoupling exist as well.

Careers like queues become the occasion and context for control efforts, as persons emerge and try for style. Story lines, told around identities, are where stability, permanence, and coherence can be found because they are sought there. They may be propounded and also enforced upon careers in the building of networks and of disciplines for production.

A career links disciplines which may be mediated into yet another identity, and a career acquires uniqueness only in that way. Career as construct implies activism and some search for agency. Career is not merely a neutral measurement construct.

Think of tenures at given jobs as a sort of tie between job and per-

---

[33] No doubt each also had come as the later career of a yet more primitive interface in smaller households.

son. Careers are made of tenures and so go beyond social space and site networks in social time. Careers and blockmodels provide contrasting approaches to uncovering compoundings, that is, the equivalences and subtle interactions which must underlie identities as disciplines. Through blockmodels we can conjecture, from reports treated as a cross-section in time, about the enormous pressures toward equivalence that must come from the endless cycling of transaction and signal along paths in networks. Career concepts and constructions pick up more on contingencies and build upon overall subtleties, in particular dyads.

Careers may be touted as objective reports of realities and realistic choices, but there must be much of both speculation and hindsight. Rationality may be attempted in the career, as part of a broader search for control, but the very meaning of rationality depends on structure across levels embracing many careers. Careers are actors time-extended in terms of contingencies; careers are perceived as such and embedded by others into larger systems.

Career and Anticareer

Anticareer goes along with career. An obverse of embedding is decoupling. When business consultant Jacques is showing the increase in unsupervised, unaccounted time span that comes with higher control in business firms,[34] he is also showing a change in boundaries of career. At one end, the clerk under close programming of time is enacting career on a micro-scale within daily activity. However, that same clerk may have no career horizon at all in the perspective of longer intervals with which we started. One can contrast micro-time career with macro-time anticareer.

Upper managers show the opposite rhythm to clerks' rhythm. Life is picaresque on a daily, hourly scale as their binding in disciplines and identities calls forth erratic fire-fighting following upon perceived contingencies.[35] But at the same time, these managers are always pressed to be endlessly shaping their possible changes in position over the longer intervals into structured sequences, into careers. Managers have careers on a macro-scale of time but anticareers on a micro-scale.

Careers and anticareers alike relate alternative identities to network contexts, to changing contingencies. They both presuppose and induce joint perceptions, which are of some complexity and

[34] That is, with high standing as confirmed by observed autonomy.

[35] This has been modeled formally by Radner (1975a,b), who demonstrates desirable efficiency properties for this fire-fighting mode.

which can only in part ever be realized in actual patterns. Spilerman (1977) offers systematic exposition of the stochastic envelope of such patterns. A career embeds identities from different chunks of time. So a career is partially analogous to a discipline, as well as careers constituting networks over time. But also careers, and in general anticipated memories, induce multiple possible identities in their story lines. Without it one imagines systems which could not contain beings whom we would recognize as people. Persons have unique identities thrust upon them as the beached litter of ongoing social processes and embeddings.[36]

Projecting Reality

Meaning construction is vivid to actors in connection with their whole careers, not just initial selection. But their perceptions, colored by the agreed set of stories, may not correspond to ascertainable facts. This is not a mere convention of our era and locale.

In the tenth century A.D. transition from T'ang to Sung dynasties in China there was an important innovation in tangible social mechanism of middle-range order (Whitney 1970). It well illustrates the unusual importance for social ordering of time embeddings in all their multiplicity. Careers were implemented in three functional sectors (civilian, financial, military) into which administrative activities were seen as divided. No doubt there was a long period of merely factual

---

[36] There is a further basic aspect of time cumulation in social process. It goes beyond the Markov property and its negation. It is yet another way to put, in more general terms, the career versus anticareer confrontation. One tends to assume associativity in any formal rendering of processes. That is, only time-order counts—to know that the sequence of three events is L, then B, then O is to know the important aspect of ordering.

But when the events occur in a process across a network of changing identities of actors spread among interfaces, the sequence aspect may be minor. In projects of control and joint production, efforts at shaping joint identity continue with great energy before, during, and after the "present." Bindings into one or another interface, embedding, story line, and envelope are the turf of contest.

Nonassociativity in the mathematical sense (Kurosh 1965; Birkhoff and Maclane 1953) may result. That is, if B and O are wrestled together into a joint form which imposes its reality, the outcome of the sequence with L may be entirely different from the flows and other outcomes when it was L and B which were first bracketed together into a merged form. See notes 31 and 32.

The letters L, B, O suggest one family of examples, the recent wave of leveraged buyouts on Wall Street (see Eccles and Crane 1988). The most familiar field of examples around us are in accounting, the shaping of budgets, and the "control" of expenditure. Zero-based budgets, policy budgets working down from goal figures to concrete program expenditures, provide ready illustrations (Padgett 1981).

sequences of distinct local positions held by particular persons; "careers" then came into existence as certain shifts became anticipated and consciously enacted. The significance of a later-held position is different according to whether it is merely a fact or is also a fulfillment of an anticipation: this is precisely the significance of career.

It does not follow that careers must interlock through networks or through levels of embedding. The formal positions in a sequence can, but need not, be identified within some cumulation of disciplines; for example, embeddings of commit interfaces into an authority tree. Positions also can be defined by localities and other ad hoc designations. Careers can come about simply on a basis of concrete population.

Careers can be more than stereotyped particular sequences, or choice between sets of subsequent stereotyped sequences. When the subsequent position cannot be predicted adequately just from knowledge of present position,[37] careers have a more formative influence. They contribute in this way more to the embedding of levels into one another over time. The corresponding tracks of positions which are reported therefore are more varied.

"A good career," or vita in modern academic parlance, is more than just the quality of the particular job, it is the balance and diversity of the track as perceived contemporaneously. Non-Markovian careers give scope for control projects. These can be both by incumbents and by others interested in playing a hand.

Since careers are as much perceptions as they are accomplished tracks, their scope of influence can be the greater. In the Sung period it seems that triple the number of persons actually in any position regarded themselves, and were regarded, as eligible for and therefore participating in the system of careers. We can see the same phenomenon around us today in common use; this is the basis for our credentialling industries, schools of business, law, and medicine, as well as faculties of liberal arts for awarding degrees. Careers tie to the style of professionalism.

Professionalism and Regimes

Connotations of professionalism include obsession with appearance, form, and meaning. Professionalism is a style and as such presupposes a larger context which is fluid. But professionalism further presupposes a corporate institution or some other tangible social

---

[37] Careers are non-Markovian as probabilistic sequences (Feller 1968).

grounding. Professionalism is especially concerned with the nesting of meanings, with, so to speak, the mobilization of meaning substituted for mobilizers that are more tangible socially; but professionals do eat. Start with the general, and then in the further subsections turn to tangible social groundings (cf. Sarfatti-Larson 1977).

Abbott's System of Professions

The system of professions, to use Abbott's term (1988), induces a distinctive style primarily as the outcome of control struggles in a context of increasing specialization in role structure in a given population. One indication is the extent to which professions, as recognized in the contemporary USA, form a single lattice or tree of cultural domination and subordination.[38]

Jurisdiction is the obsession of professions, as part of a focus of concern upon meaning. It is not a mere jostling for agreed partition, as in the guild fights of corporatism. It is rather a struggle to shape as well as allot a structured order of legitimate interpretations.[39] Professionalism always orients to and thus generates a succession of depths of interpretation, as the texture of jurisdiction, a texture reflected in social organization as well as in ideas (Abbott 1988). The style is willing, but the social flesh is disorderly and unmalleable; so there is never in fact any tidy social structure of nesting and depth.

Mobilization is the antipodes of jurisdiction. Mobilizer disciplines there will always be in any actual social formation, but since the impetus of professionalism contradicts it, the incidence is lower. Events are a form of identity compatible with jurisdiction, and they can fit with professionalism.

The term "professionalism" has modern connotations, but the professional style has historical depth; however clientelism and corporatism are much older and more widespread. Before monotheism, social formations especially imbued with religious interests exhibited the nested jurisdictional tendencies of professionalism. Priests, shamans, and the like tended toward professionalist distinctions, in contradistinction from magicians and the like who fit variously into

---

[38] The Brzezinski and Huntington survey argues that professionalism is the style of Soviet Communist leadership. Professionalism could be the style of a whole stratum, rather than just the accoutrements of specialists. Simirenko (1982) went further, and argued this extreme view in his title *The Professionalization of Soviet Society*. Whether for a society or for middle-range formations, professionalism is a style that inhibits innovation.

[39] In the strict mathematical sense, this ordering is a partial order; cf. Birkhoff and MacLane (1953).

guild institutions or into corporatism (cf. Stark and Bainbridge 1986). Monotheist religions, after coming to be used to permeate social formations, also can spin off sufficient distinctions of sacerdotal standing to undergird professionalism as style. Tellenbach (1946) spells out this process among Roman Catholic clergy and other orders during the Gregorian revolution (and see Berman 1970, chapter 2).

The elaboration of canon law was one aspect of this professionalization of Catholics into complex partial-orders of sacerdotal standing and expertise; the elaboration was parallel to spelling out theologies of different depths. Control projects are intertwined with professional as a style. Deference is extended to experts in ever deeper layers in the centripetal process of ideation within professionalism (Abbott 1981). But the deeper layers are also but reserves to strengthen efforts of control on those in outermost circles. The Reformation was a reaction to this professionalization of the church (Oberman 1981).

Control efforts induce counters as well as parallels and refinements. The priestly hands always find themselves being sheathed in secular gloves, though with professional style far along the secular sheathing itself perforce has to find professional garb. Perhaps many secular legal systems emerge in part out of some such confrontations. And in turn lawyers build a field which is of professionalist style, with differentiated and concentric layers of interpreters. The sheathing process then reemerges: a striking illustration is the commercialization of American law as argued by Horwitz (1977).

Defensive power is much a concern of modern professions, within a social formation of organizations (Johnson 1967; Sarfatti-Larsen 1977). A not unexpected counterpoint to professional style is a utopian plan for total authority and control. This is not confined to religion as venue or to older times. Veblen described the beginnings of technocracy. This utopian moment of professionalist style proved (Bailes 1978) to have as wide a resonance in the USSR as in the USA, the two contexts in which engineering has provided a frame for extensive professionalist claims.

Engineering has since lapsed into a corporatist guild mold. Between corporatism and professionalism there is no clear divide. Neither has or can have some unique architecture, each is a historically contingent reality recognized in incidence of species of discipline, as well as in joinings by networks. All are similar in blocking action through concern with meanings and with concrete strings to realize them.

Much the same counterpoint can be seen building up around the modern medical field for professionalization. The Ehrenreichs (1971, esp. pp. 44–48) and Alford (1975) are early observers for New York of the gloving of the AMA (American Medical Association) variety of medical professionalism in the mystiques of management technocracy. Arrow (1972) gives a gloss of the actual social organizational process using the rhetoric of economics.

As Abbott (1988) has made clear, these developments should be seen and can best be interpreted as part of an unfolding and sheathings of the very many sorts of professions with their many demarcations and competing inner layers of interpretation. Authority is coin of the realm of professions and, as in other realms, whether corporatism or clientelism, authority osmoses through any putative spectator. Authority oozes into and out of any one profession to extents shaped by the overall pattern of struggles for jurisdictions among changing fields and subfields.

It is helpful to analytic development to consider this style, professionalism, in remote contexts. The model of professionalism has similarities to the institution in the previous chapter for research science in American academia and caste in India. The layering of purity as professional ideology can be imagined parallel to the tangible layering between castes in public social interaction.

Within the village caste institution of chapter 4, it is caste ideology to which professional style has analogy. Meaning is asserted and even calibrated, in direct coordination with strings of ties to be recognized and asserted. Professional jurisdiction is not a monovalent matter of tasks; nor is jurisdiction within caste institutions, which ramify into kin and marital networks across regions, and into ideas beyond religion. And jurisdiction permeates within castes: "My central theme is that the caste is ordered internally by the same principles which govern relations between castes" (In Parry 1979, p. 6).[40]

Demerits of Merit Systems

Take an extended example of careers in formal organization, and how they interpenetrate style. Modern civil service recruitment in Britain, for its upper levels, was shaped by a major change in style to a "merit" system in the 1880s, the famous Northcliffe reforms (Kelsall 1952). This can be seen as a regression from career in the style sense back to an institution. Or it can be seen as the emergence of professionalism.

The ostensible core of the new system was an examination which was strenuously academic. Even the topic was sufficiently recondite to give a closed-corporate cast to candidacy. Classics (Greek and

[40] He is a follower and developer of Mayer and Dumont.

Roman) dominated in the early years when it could be studied effectively, at the highest level, only at the elite universities, at Oxbridge. As Kelsall shows with great care, the style of examination, partly *viva voce*, as much as the content made successful competition next to impossible for those not from the "right set."[41] Structural equivalence predominated here and shaded into closed corporation.

Earlier recruitment style had been much maligned as permitting a "spoils system" to operate and thereby often letting in unsuitable if not dishonorable candidates. This earlier system was very much a matter of networks. The Walpole era in the eighteenth century had had no pretense at a coherent civil service (Plumb 1967). Back then recruitment had seen a true spoils system.[42] By the mid-nineteenth century, the idea of coherent frames of paid offices in a bureaucratic mold was emerging, and the total number of positions was growing sharply. The result was pressures for episodic and ad hoc use of whatever network ties came to hand for recruitment. As Kelsall makes clear, and as he illustrates with vignettes, someone often got plumped into a civil service post in an arbitrary way through a tie that could be quite casual.

It should be noted that some of the most creative and notable members of British government came out of these casual networks. The actual choice often was not lightly made: able men had an eye for the novice "clark" or tradesman's nephew who showed remarkable wit and energy. And, on the other hand, Kelsall conclusively demonstrates that class bias in selection was enormously greater under the new "reformed" mode of civil service recruitment. Stories did and do not jibe with the facts, as a blockmodel, after adaptation, might be able to show.

Regimes

Professionalism involves structuring discourse about social networks and institutions as much as it does changes in them. The sources of larger views of explicit social order beyond the institution seem clear. Institutions and the rhetorics they come to agree upon both are open-ended and can be extrapolated beyond present local disciplines and networks. Call the product, which is a native statement combining styles around institutions, a regime. A regime is native theory for middle-range order. Social science theories may satisfy this definition; history certainly has, since Thucydides.

[41] It was of course possible, if one took aim early on, to achieve membership in the gate-keeping mechanism so that the ostensible fairness was not entirely bogus.

[42] Of the sort taken up under clientelism in the preceding chapter.

Social formation must sustain and regenerate itself from within itself. Although the wholistic context has as tangible an impact as do direct local forces, which can be fully accounted for only within its hegemony, neither gods nor Walras auctioneers provide the mechanism. "Middle-range" is a relative term. It is the smallest scope, in time and in actions for self-reproducing formations. It is also the largest scope which yields interpretable accounts in stories that do not require reference to outside named formations.

Styles generalize and frame types of tie and story lines, and so they encompass several levels of embedding. A regime is explicit native identification of how style articulates to institution in that rhetoric. A regime includes only some among the very many homomorphisms which as analysts we can compute in blockmodels as being possible (Boyd 1989); sometimes social science and sometimes other professions are more assiduous in working out possible homomorphisms. Just as story-sets go with the endless struggle to sustain the viability of one and another identity, so perceived styles come in sets sufficient to maintain the viability of a regime. And there is the same sort of trade-off between ambage and ambiguity.

The simultaneous existence of a set of stories concerning any hunk of social reality is a necessity because the sheer plasticity and chaos of actual events cannot be accommodated otherwise, either by native or observer. But identities and events become used in new ways as the original performances become embedded in further levels or later reenactments (for which see Griswold 1986). Control is always being sought by some persons, at some unpredictable times, and this overlays the emergence of identities. A regime is an ongoing accomplishment.

Soothing nostrum is what rhetoric and thus regime is all about, but nostrums also provide materials for effective intervention. A passion for critique and reform has misled otherwise percipient observers on this score. Consider this assessment by Foucault:

> Each society has its regime of truth, its "general politics of truth": that is, the types of discourse which it accepts and makes function as true; the mechanisms and instances which enable one to distinguish true and false statements, the means by which each is sanctioned; the techniques and procedures accorded value in the acquisition of truth; the status of those who are charged with saying what counts as true . . . we cannot raise the banner of truth against our own regime . . . there is no common measure between the impositions of the one and those of the other . . . each regime is identified entirely with its imposed truth. (Foucault 1980, p. 131)

One must instead assert that there are a whole set of such truths simultaneously in operation, each as a rhetoric for a regime, more tangible than Foucault's society. Much in professional sports, as seen either today or long ago in Roman arenas, can be accounted for similarly, and Leifer has done so (1988, 1992). Much of the ranking of experts in public walks of life can be accounted for similarly; for example, generals and their reputations in war.

Embedding and control are the most difficult issues for regimes. Embedding and control are where all the puzzles of social reality impose themselves at once. But they are especially tricky when they interact with the concrete space of geography and the like, in buffering conflict or brokering dependencies (Chay and Ross 1986; Crozier and Thoenig 1976; Eccles 1981c; Porter 1976; Schwartzmann 1990; Tarrow 1977) or local jurisdiction (Ashford 1982). Uncertainty proper remains a key indicator because it reflects impact from meshing into the environing biophysical world.

Identities remain central in regimes. Irregularity-based identities call forth and propose alternate frames of interpretation which become known across actors; these are alternative story lines. Distinctive persons are a product as much as a cause of diverse overlays of different interpretive frames in a regime.

Influences from larger and more inclusive levels down to smaller ones explain how human social formations differ from those among animals. Human struggles for control are not settled once-and-for-all in a dominance order embracing the single social setting, as for an animal which has the flock as total world. A human being is spread out across different network populations, which are integrated at least by institution. The character of a person is induced in participations across several populations, though not as much among hunter-gatherers (Howell 1979; Rose 1960) as in more elaborated social formations. To many, all this means that language is a level and context by itself. Language can be seen as the prime medium and recorder of specifically human construction of social realities and their spaces (Culicover 1987; Culicover and Wexler 1977).

Language shapes the forms of stories. But audience is commonly given while ostensibly being denied, in practical human interaction. Language is as commonly being denied to any effective end, even as there is much talk (Garfinkel 1967; Goffman 1963). For purposes of analyzing the structuration underlying social action, perhaps language as such can be bracketed. Human social organization may require language,[43] but social grammar goes much beyond that of lan-

---

[43] As Gumperz argues in his survey, much of the communication in social settings requires only bare bones from language (1982, pp. 71–72): "The speech of closed net-

guage, and social options exceed the "choices" presupposed by the language. Stories are integral to social organization, and stories do presuppose language, but they are not predetermined by linguistic structure and practice.

It makes some sense to treat linguistics as a mystification, to remain resolutely skeptical of its explicit guidance about social formations. This still permits one to follow the guidance of a Labov (1966, 1971) on how parole (ordinary speech) shifts in accordance with segregation and dominance processes among social formations. And this treatment is consistent with the guidance of anthropologists since Morgan (1877; see Trautman 1987) on how kinship terminologies are both chips in and rules of the games of domestic lives and economic continuities (White 1963, pp. 146–47; Rose 1960). The trick is to gain as many cues as possible from words, syntax, and language, but to do so without giving up perspectives independent of and in tension with those built into the language as parsed by its scholars. This is but to follow the lead of great field anthropologists such as Fortes (1949, pp. 10–11) and of some linguists (Talmy 1984).

---

work groups is marked by an unusually large number of truncated, idiomatic stock phrases and context bound deictic expressions . . . exclusive interaction with individuals of similar background leads to reliance on unverbalized and context bound presuppositions in communication, and that the formulaic nature of closed network group talk reflects this fact . . . because of its reliance on unverbalized shared understandings, code switching is typical of the communicative conventions of closed network situations . . . switching strategies serve to probe for shared background knowledge . . . motivation for code switching seems to be stylistic and metaphorical rather than grammatical. The processes by which meaning is conveyed must be studied in terms of the stylistic interrelationship of sentences or phrases within the passage as a whole, not in terms of the internal structure of particular sentences."

SIX

GETTING ACTION

SOCIAL ORGANIZATION appears in two modes. On the one hand is the challenge of blocking larger waves from the endless upsets and contingencies that are inseparable from normal life. From this blocking comes some sense of coherence among everyone, as well as some continuity for some locales. This has been the face examined in the chapters thus far.

The other face is cutting open the Sargasso Sea of social obligation and context to achieve openness sufficient for getting fresh action. This is action the effects of which can be more cumulative and on a larger scale than from the routines of disciplines, institutions, and also styles. Annealing is a metaphor for this. Annealing shapes its own boundaries. This chapter ends with a section on annealing.

There may be elites, circles of "movers and shakers," who have special location and abilities which yield them insights about integrating both these openings and these shuttings in social life (but see the national case study by Bonilla 1970, pp. 92, 99, 104, 112–13, 240–46). They may jointly go about maneuvering the future. But even for them proleptics is an art of paradox. There has to be a peculiar flavor to "principles" for intervening in social organization, for getting action.

Social organization is just the perceivable traces left from contentions for control in social action, so that efforts at fresh action already are discounted in such social organization as survives to be observed. Getting action requires maneuvering choice by indirection to obtain intervention. Getting action can make use of prolepsis; that is, getting action may proceed by inveigling others to take an anachronistic view of the future.

Interventions have to deal with the underlying disciplines and their cumulations through networks. Disciplines suppress or transform some contingencies, but disciplines also, in the process of emerging, enlarge the spaces of possible social action. Each new discipline helps to generate occasions for novel control efforts, which can be less subject to counteraction and thus yield fresh action.

Intervention also is in institutions and styles, which tend in different ways also to block fresh action. Institutions and styles sustain and elaborate meanings through reenactments; so getting action has to take account of meanings, and to rely upon them, but yet a principal task it has is staying ahead of meaning and stripping away meaning.

Getting action becomes a higher-order project playing off disciplines and their embeddings into still further levels of networks and institutions, making use of decoupling. Take a fresh look from the standpoint of game theory:

> Strategic decoupling is also in evidence when money is used to decentralize the organizational decision process . . . devices such as overhead percentages, and department budgets. . . . Money, the decoupler, smooths away many of the difficulties that arise in dealing simultaneously with several independently motivated sources of strategic decision. . . . Chamberlin represented a mathematical step backward from the clarity and precision of Cournot, but a considerable step forward in modelling and economic insight concerning competition among the few. . . . The natural way to imbed oligopolistic competitions into a closed economy is to invent money and markets. (Shubik 1984, pp. 10, 50, 162)

Specific position within larger institutions can affect getting action. For example, final appeals court can be distinguished from lower appeals courts—as well as each from courts of primary jurisdiction—just through their leverage for fresh action (Shapiro 1980). Another example is how venture capitalist circles may quite consciously manipulate, through superficially neutral changes in money markets, the careers of large firms and even entire industries. Style for, and insights by, particular identities also are important, as Weber (e.g., 1978) insisted in his account of charismatic leadership.

Yet control and getting action can initiate at any level. And the ways that perceptions form, partly rooted in physiology, remain such as to sustain self-similarity across levels. It is for this reason that stories can operate as gears, as transcribers between actors and action on different levels as they maneuver for control. Analysis should be universal, or self-similar, so that the same terms and analyses apply at various scopes.[1] Failure and other forms of decoupling are the lubricant that permit self-similarity, and style is a positive mechanism for self-similarity across levels.

Multiplicity in social organization is the key to getting action, with stories being only mediators. Getting things done, getting choice given control becomes, on any scale, a self-contradictory and bizarre problem when one goes beyond the surface stories which suffice for

---

[1] For similar arguments on self-similarity, restricted to a macro scale, see Ashley (1980); Bergesen, Fernandez, and Sahoo (1987); and Caporaso (1989).

routine reproduction. Having anything to do—being subject to routine and responsibility—may interfere with getting action. Sticking to preset boundaries also interferes with getting action.

Getting action and control both can require ingenuities of decoupling and agency which crosscut the stories of disciplines and the larger institutions and styles into which they may cumulate. Getting action may be indirect and delayed. More direct and timely efforts are better described as control.

Further Control in Time

Disciplines become the main site for focused efforts at control within the networks that are social space. Identities from their formation are struggling for control. But identities form up social structures, in which control projects participate. Thereby controls become entangled in ways that cannot be visualized as projects of individual actors: In the words of Chanowitz and Langer (1980, p. 120), "Control is not something that we possess. It is some way that we *are*. . . . The exercise of control is a whole situation that cannot faithfully be fully reproduced as a number of parts or measures." Thus, search for further control, which is unending, keeps digging within complex social formation back into disciplines.

Production, social and material, comes through disciplines and relies on specialization. Specializations of three kinds index the embedding ratios for disciplines. Production by disciplines is always at the same time reproduction, that is, renewed implementation of that known social form. Control must rely upon disciplines and assess their locales and scopes, but the search for further control somehow must use or put them together in new contexts or in new exemplars.

Sometimes a new variety will be created of one of the three species of discipline, and then getting choice may be working toward further control from below in the embedding common to all disciplines. Effective control search views a discipline from the context into which its production is being embedded. Further control usually is found at embedding from the upper side, the numerator of the embedding ratio that indexes specialization.

These embedding ratios, from chapter 2, are extreme abstractions from direct description of a discipline in concrete operation. Each ratio is only of tendencies. The analogy in visual perception would be the gradients of illumination thrown off by texture and pattern in a curving surface of the three-dimensional field outside the eye. But these embedding ratios are the key abstractions, they index which forms of specialization can reproduce in that context and point toward possible intervention for fresh control.

Disciplines Mixed

Disciplines are locally overawing expressions of social control, but within a population there is no simple mapping of discrete form onto discrete effect. For example, a council discipline is a prime way to embed action and make it effective, and yet also it is a species of discipline with which to obfuscate action: Which predominates depends upon "context," upon environing networks of disciplines. But context is more than static cross-section, it includes those processes of forgetting and of historical referent which are always being invoked in various crisscrossing projects of control.[2]

A network population is a stew of disciplines. A network evolves, like disciplines themselves, under the social pressure of contending control efforts. These efforts play out over time in physical space, geographically, and also under pressures of material production, of work—subject, that is, to ecological pressures.

Interfaces are the easiest species to visualize fitting in among a mixture of discipline species.[3] An explicit map of stability was derived, in figure 2-2. This map is indexed for moderate complementarity, neither completely involuted nor turned entirely to delivery. Such maps can help suggest limitations and possibilities of concatenation with other disciplines.[4]

The question is where and how there are the most openings for fresh control—which may also suggest the most likely routes for evolution of more complex social formations up through institutions. Detailed results of models for a given species can show that for a given point in index space there is no viable variant of the species to construct. The black hole is the central region of index space, where the conjecture is that no variety of any species is viable. But indexed

[2] Lily Ross Taylor (1949) lays out the latter for contending senatorial factions during a period in the late history of the Roman Republic over two millennia ago: such basics of action in social organization do not change with period, scale, cultural realm, or strata. The values invoked to color action change, but not the species of discipline involved.

[3] As well as in self-cumulation, as in the tree of hierarchy discussed earlier in chapter 2.

[4] Others (Bales 1970; Breiger and Ennis 1979) have modeled what is, in my terms, the constitution of interfaces when complementarity ratio is nil, e.g., for free discussion groups, which do not concatenate.

situations in much of the space may sustain two, or even all three species.

What is not clear and will take extensive development is how to model interaction between species if coexistent: How can embedding of identity forms into network, in parallel and crossing arrangements, be modeled explicitly as population? Or alternatively, how can one predict and represent the suppression of one alternative discipline by another? The general issue is how congeries of disciplines, indexed in entirely different locations in the space, are invoked and fit together in larger populations—and what slippage there remains for further control. We return to this in the section on agenda for agency.

Across Levels

Control is achieved across levels too, but only disciplines generate and provide the endogenous social energy without which control is mere facade. Disciplines lead into a spreading out into networks in which each tie is a balance of gamings for control. Stories are always being spun into ties, and then whole sets of stories, that can keep up with whatever happens. And it is this that leaves opportunity for fresh control attempts.

Control efforts are attempted every which way across levels resulting from embedding. The idea of levels comes with embedding, but social spaces are not tidy layerings, and actors on presumably different levels can relate directly through control projects. Levels build up in social formations as by-products of interacting control struggles. "Actor" can become anything from a multinational giant firm to a Goffman creature of the brief encounter.

The playground networks of the first chapter imply, but they also presuppose, some larger social environment. Control must build from others' ties and disciplines. Results of control cumulate beyond networks to weave varieties of locality into larger social formations, institutions that prove their robustness by persisting. Style in control can characterize larger social formations and guide further efforts at getting action by personal actors. Such further control is achieved only across levels. Levels are not just an analytic convenience of aggregation. Levels are by-products of the turf war between getting action and blocking action. New levels of social structure emerge from and only from efforts at control, whereas coercion and the like exist on the same level. Further control, being across levels, presupposes embeddings for disciplines.

Engineering Control as Prototype

Mundane production control on the factory floor is an obvious parallel to and model for triage, and it leads into the deliberate engineering of control as a process.[5] Governments, like factories, can be surveyed as to whether they are "bang-bang" control systems, or instead more advanced systems. Lurching from crisis to crisis, with engineering controls not cutting in until the window shade has banged against the wall, or the temperature against its floor, is a bang-bang style of control. Washing machines are another example of this bang-bang control, which seems all too familiar from social life in general and formal organization in particular. The controls can be preset but they are not responsive at all to the process as it unfolds—a mimicry of elections perhaps.

Such classical engineering control systems, even if feedback loops are added, do not seem promising as analogues for analyses of social and management phenomena. For these phenomena are not only erratic in time but also reflect assessments and efforts made within the system. Control efforts among actors that are always struggling for identities among changing contexts are what generate the space of possibilities. Then after World War II, more advanced approaches to control theory were introduced, beginning with Wiener (1949).[6]

[5] Control theory in engineering has a long history, and many independent origins (Bennett 1979, and see the appendix below). So far it has been referred to social and managerial systems only vaguely and half-heartedly. Although strategic gaming can be present within such systems, too often it is just ignored (for a recent survey, see Shubik 1984a,b). Classical control theory, with emphasis upon mechanical systems and time-path analyses, is particularly associated with the Russian tradition. Control theory with emphasis upon electronic elements and upon frequency-spectrum dissection is associated with the American tradition (Dorf 1967).

[6] The conceptually important version for present purposes was introduced (as "dynamic programming") in this country by Richard Bellman (1957) and in Russia by Pontryagin.

An operationalization of "policy" is Bellman's signal contribution. He establishes a new way to operationalize for explicit computation the reality that policy is effective only through particular embeddings in time. Bellman construes a system as a convolution of successive stages, the representation being in a calculus of nested integrations. These yield computations of dependent variables vis-à-vis control goals, which themselves are able to shift and be influenced by intervening outcomes. The computations are thus partly decoupled from one another and yet at the same time one embeds the next through setting its boundary conditions. Realistic policy is modeled, as opposed to preset engineering instructions.

This deserves expanded comment. A limitation of classical control theory, from the social system perspective, is its focus on an explicit goal, often one to be maximized. Bellman retains this but in an attenuated form, where policy supplants goal. In the

Advanced control theory resembles the actual operation of social formations in blurring the line between structure and operational system. Control theory, beginning at least with Bellman, offers insights into how to conceptualize structure and system together. A major purpose of such control implementations is to decrease the sensitivity of outcomes to the parameters of the structure. Sensitivity is also cut to outside disturbances, which decreases the significance of the distinction between "outside" and "inside."[7]

The obverse approach also is used in control applications: One may introduce further structure in order to decrease sensitivity to system discipline.[8] The recent study by Eccles and Crane (1988) of the rapidly evolving world of investment banking is vivid on the intertwining of system with structure in attempting to maintain control in a structure bouncing too rapidly for architecture to be of much help.

Style and Control

Efforts to achieve further control consist in unpredictable action.[9] Identities are the source of social action and thus of seeking control, including control of social action. Identities are the only source of intentional efforts, which is to say of potentially unroutine action. These efforts contribute to uncertainties until interlocked in social formations by interaction with other such efforts.

---

solution space of classical theory the curve of constrained optimums, the extremum, is conceived as a locus of points. Bellman's decisive step was to reconceive of the extremal as an envelope of tangents. That is, the optimal approach is decoupled into a sequence of explicitly definable policies, each simplified to be made operational; so the optimal approach is broken down into an evolving profile of choices among a family of possible stances. Analytic machinery is developed, despite the exceptional complexities, to a point permitting generation of at least numerical solutions. More important here, the machinery is sophisticated enough to capture the frequent occurrence of abrupt and discontinuous policy changes (cf. the material on federal budget changes in this chapter, p. 277).

Against the background of Bellman's innovations, classical control theory can be milked for further insights and perhaps it can then furnish heuristic guidance in social situations. Bellman's perspective can be used to enrich the vast range of example solutions from classical engineering applications (Leigh 1987) available for these heuristics. This constitutes enriching a system in order to simplify structure!

[7] This conceptualization is developed further in the appendix section on Kalman filters.

[8] For instance, cascade compensation networks are introduced within feedback loops (Dorf 1967, chap. 10).

[9] This is developed further at the level of pair ties in the subsection "Leifer Ties" in chapter 3, and with respect to game theory in this chapter.

Gaining further control cuts across a mix of self-reproducing social organization, and hence does the same with meaning and its reproduction. Meaning is simply another face to blocking action through obtaining coherence in social organization. In one sense, therefore, there can be no particular type of organization associated with additional control. But there are styles conducive to shaking up for fresh control, as will appear in examples developed in the next section.

Styles can embrace sibling identities which project from much the same physical creatures, but which are nonetheless distinct. Styles then decouple between network populations which overlap in physical space. These multiple populations come into existence only with and through the induction and construction of new and specifically social space-times. Styles, in short, loosen institution and open it for control, though they need not solve and may complicate achieving control.

Control is endemic at all scopes and levels, yet it can be unpredictable because it emerges out of identities which are by-products of irregularities and mismatches. Control plays as large a part in blocking action as in getting action, and distinctive styles of control are observed among regimes of blocking action. Getting control at any time tends to lay a social track of tangible organization, as it requires some mixing of disciplines and embeddings across networks—and as efforts at blocking control begin coterminous with the laying of tracks.

Hieratic Styles

There are two logics of cumulation that are accompanied by frequent, open efforts at control. Designate one such logic as "segmentary," from the tribal kinship pattern which exemplifies it. Another logic is found in the "hieratic" style. The hieratic style is one of generalist oversight forced up out of the clash of specialized committees. Action is got and fueled by the magic of successive levels of actors entering the scene to culminate in a precise elite.

Both logics reflect processes of guiding others' perceptions into relatively few, and relatively segregated equivalence sets, or clusters. These are clusters both in reflexive analyses of ongoing actions and control attempts, and in similarities of perspectives as observed by outsiders. But these clusters cannot be such minimal units as discipline and tie. Reaching through to gain control cannot be pinned down as occurring in some one species of discipline, say the interface.

The hieratic is a generalization of any attempt at control which recognizes and makes intentional use of decouplings. In hieratic style events segregate out into equivalence structures comparable to and parallel with partition of actors into structural equivalence sets. Autocracy is but the utopian extreme of the hieratic; autocracy is an attempted solution without intermediaries to the problem of wresting control. This extreme can furnish a basis for story lines whereby control efforts feed into broader effort at getting action.

Army and Church

The classic general example of the hieratic is in separate social formations committed to fighting: the military. Active fighting requires control over friend and foe alike. It is common across a wide range of contexts, historically, regionally, and culturally, to find segregated levels within a military body, with formally distinct production tasks. Analysis of this example suggests that interchangeability, or structural equivalence of all within a level, is as important as the hierarchic ordering between levels, for getting action.

Fighting requires unpredictable alignments and changes of neighborhood and cooperation; it requires constant respecification of information and of the interconnections of actions. Equivalence within a rank, with attention focused on invidious comparisons to other ranks, opens up connectivity within the rank to a much closer approximation of all the possibilities inherent in complete interconnection. There is more freedom of maneuver to string together coalitions, because of equivalence within a level, and thus more leverage for overall control, given strict precedence between levels.

A singular example is the Roman Catholic Church (cf. Greeley 1979). In common thought, the church's hieratic flavor is associated with quietude, but this mistakes the reality. Recognition and engrossment of partitions of events and of actors into absolutely distinct levels of purity and power, tend to cut or atrophy the otherwise endless strings of interconnection within the concrete functioning of the church. Such truncation of chains of contingencies make interventions more calculable. And this segregation makes all attempts to reach for control more visible, and the end result is that only those from high up in levels, or from very far down, have legitimacy, are seen in the story lines of all as consistent with identities.

The obvious view is that hieratic form is asymmetric, unidirectional, from the top down. This is to mistake formalism in story line for the underlying likelihoods given the concrete organization. A detailed study of ethnicity and revolts within the Nigerian military

(Luckham 1971), for example, suggests that hieratic segmentation into a few structurally equivalent sets is also easily exploitable by insurgents from lower ranks. Numerous similar ethnic turbulences within that and other armies since then, led sometimes by noncommissioned officers, confirm the suggestion. The arousal and conduct of such insurgence is not predicted simply by this, but the hieratic style in itself is exploitable symmetrically, exploitable from below as well as from above. In either direction, hieratic style can open a way to obscure and to break up the endless recurrences to the inertia of blocking action which are endemic in social organization.

Committee Styles

Extreme ostentation has gone out of style; so in the current world the hieratic comes in new guises, but it yields the same impacts in getting action, even without gorgeous uniforms. Committee lattices are designations for what ostensibly are organizations and actually are new story lines in which the hieratic style can be embodied in today's world. Follow Vancil and Green (1983) in their contrast of committee style in conventional firm governance with that in the governance of International Business Machines (IBM), pre-1990.

IBM runs on the story line of being a single business, and its management committees bring together functional specialties. Conflicts and disagreements within and between initial committees are not just inevitable but encouraged, as the vehicle for getting action. Action stirs first in flows of appeals in what turns out to be a hieratic structuring of committees into clusters by level. Getting action can come both via pruning the appeals as well as via developing them. The initiative is coming from below, much as in the Japanese management style of "ringi" (Yoshino 1968; Yoshino and Lifson 1988).

The employees all wear shirts of the same color at IBM, just as Japanese managers differ little in dress, but the impress of the hieratic is of magic, and it is as easily coded by trifling differences in pay as by velvet over fustian on office furniture. One decisive point is that a few distinct levels of magic are the shelves into which all IBM committees are sorted both by themselves and by others. The second is that there are no unique individual identities, either of actors or of events, but rather a structurally equivalent set of magicians.

An important indicator is the development at IBM, as in many other large firms, of a collegial Chief Executive as committee. At IBM this is a three-man Chief Executive Office. The hieratic style is not an architecture, a set of rules, or the like, rather the committee clustering system is a style, is a flexible lattice of constraints and leads for making action possible.

It is not the committee in isolation but an arraying of committees that is crucial. The looseness of agenda, the flexibility of mobilizing issues and timing interests to which March has drawn our attention (March and Olsen 1976; Cohen and March 1974), depends on there being a flexible field of occasions for, meetings of, and attendance at, committees, who also can cite and call one another. By contrast, fully settled committees become opaque, turn into council disciplines that block action. Unsettling committees requires not just conflicts, and jurisdictional and appeals interfaces for sustaining unsettling, but also some such longer-range influence as emerges from hieratic style.

Colonialisms, Old and New

There is an analogy between this hieratic lattice of committees in a business corporation and the style and format of British colonial rule, evidenced in prewar Burma (Furnivall 1948). "Natives" and British expatriates, specialists and generalists by background, all were mixed up together throughout a lattice of governance which was partly by courts and advisory councils and partly by district executives. The elite, the "fair-haired boys" in this as in the IBM example, could thereby mingle throughout layers and networks of the rest, enabling reaching through to an underlying population that could easily become very opaque. To be a generalist was the finest thing, in the British scheme, and its lattice of committees kept being regrown on structural equivalence lines of recruitment which dovetailed with the hieratic form of stratification emphasis.

Now consider parallels in style of controls to Dutch East Indies colonialism. Successful searching for control is prominent in both of them, whereas it is difficult to find in functionally departmentalized governments or firms, as Chandler (1963) underlined. Dutch colonialism, in the East Indies, evolved a different form of committee system from the Burma one. Yet both Dutch and British systems evinced a hieratic style (Furnivall 1948). Every manager in Burma was a magistrate, while every manager in the Indies was an official: judge versus cop, that was the difference.

Both hieratic styles had emerged where small sets of outsiders had better be reaching through if they were to maintain control, much less get action, but the actions sought were different. Burma was to be directly productive, a sort of tributary economy. The Indies were conceived as a self-sustaining entity composed of innumerable productive sectors which could flourish in a context that made them transparent to the colonialists. A second American company can complete a balanced parallelism.

General Electric, as laid out in Vancil (1979),[10] has a remote sector of general management which, like Dutch colonialists, disdains hands-on production and its functional specializations, but which, again like the Dutch, uses a subtle lattice of committees to reach through to production interfaces. At GE, as apparently in the Indies, there is an elaborate cycling of draft strategy reports through committees over time that provides flexibility. Also both administrations in historical fact were endemically changing their exact arrangements in "one last change that will really get it right." The hieratic style was reflected in the scope of autonomous time between meetings, for the importance of which consult Jacques (1956). It was also reflected in the dependent dovetailing at GE of one layer of meetings on another. And finally, the hieratic was reflected in the undoubted use of diacritical symbolism of residence and office, dress, and the like. The same held among Dutch colonialism.

Dutch and British styles were nothing new, and there are other variants. Roman imperialism operated through municipality, through a lattice crafted from preexisting committees, namely the notables of respective preexisting city-states (Garner and Saller 1987; Reid 1913). Republican Rome actually forced and coaxed Italian tribes of all descriptions into the formation of cities (Stevenson 1939), and a hieratic style in lattice of cities and tributaries and provinces resulted. The state of Rome itself was a sort of General Office from which Alfred Sloan of General Motors (GM) would have learned new wrinkles, but both showed tendencies toward hieratic lattices of committees which were conduits for reaching through (Eckstein 1987).

On a much smaller scale the same style persists in many traditional American cities: Crain and others (1961, 1968) lay out civic contentions where invocation of a cascade of committees of higher and higher status is the only way that action was obtained. In other cities they studied, where hieratic layers could not be energized, paralysis stymied proposed action.[11]

Hieratic style can be episodic, and thus not be registered as long-lived lattices. Turn to the example of the War Industries Board. Cuff

[10] On GE one should also consult the Harvard Business School case studies done under his aegis that underlie Vancil and Green's analysis reported in the previous subsection.

[11] These actions were variously on school desegregation and on fluoridation.

(1973) lays out the emergence of a shifting hieratic style of committee mobilization, in the eighteen months or so of America's leap into World War I with full industrial weight. Dupont, GM, GE, and the like do not figure prominently as actors. They figure through agents, persons drifting and popping in and out of the Washington venue for their industrial, trade association, and commodity networks. There are literal committees, set up under the WIB, with memberships always at least dual between military procurement fiefdoms of long standing and variously defined opposite numbers from the civilian side. There was a public story line, from Bernard Baruch, which prefigured the Tennessee Valley Administration story line of David Lilienthal two decades later (Selznick 1955). This story line of "grass roots" exactly avoided any mention of the hieratic style.

Eisenhower Style

Dwight Eisenhower's initial months as President gives an analogue to the WIB, but one explicitly concerned only with policy, not with production. National security policy had settled into containment in the Cold War; Eisenhower and Dulles had campaigned in part on a theme of roll-back, on seizing initiative from the "communist world." After the fact it became clear that Eisenhower had no belief in any such change. But there was a vast array of officials and politicals out there which needed some kind of policy-nesting consistent with hieratic style if blocking action were not to remove entirely any presidential initiative (Greenstein 1982).

Recently declassified security documents permit inferring a masterly hieratic strategy on Eisenhower's part (Project Solarium, 1988). He convened a large and mixed set of dignitaries of security, in and/or out of political or official offices, into an intensive, total-institution setting for one month. This conference was factored out into three parallel committees, ranked by magical powers, though not formal status. One was for "yes" to the campaign promises, one for "no," and one for "maybe."

These committees for scenarios, or hypothetical policies, became a lattice in which, during later joint sessions and discussions, the foolhardiness, by their own respective standards, of the change policies was born in on each committee by the others, and on each member by the hieratic structure of consideration. Once again a set of committees permitted shakeup of ongoing production and expertise, and to an outcome structured more by the sociologic of the committee assignments and contrasts than by explicit intellectual contents.

Catholic and Communist as Structuralist

The structuralist conjecture is exemplified as pure organization by Wallerstein's world system theory (1974, 1980; and see Culler 1975 for cultural analysis), in which our entire world becomes the successive unfolding of a unique system. It also is illustrated by Lévi-Strauss's theory (1969; and see Culler 1975) of marriage alliances in which the whole social organization of a tribe plays out within one of a few overall structuralist schemes of balancing among splits and alliances.

Genesis is always the problem with the structuralist conjecture in pure form: By what staggeringly unlikely concatenation of constituents did some such marvelously singular system of integration come into being? The timing metric is interaction exposures, not physical seconds, but under no reckoning is the metric comparable to actual evolutionary scales. This structuralist conjecture is best reformulated as one about style rather than complete system.

The hieratic style is in fact one version of the structuralist conjecture. It does make an observable difference whether the overall configuration is constrained in hieratic fashion, a difference that should vary with some measure of violation of the structure. The difference is part of the impetus from many identities to push configuration toward hieratic form. But one must expect great exaggeration of the story line over the measured network configuration. And the hieratic is usually a middling affair, which at a period stretches over some, but not all, neighborhoods.

It was Gregory VII in the twelfth century who had the possibility of showing and did in fact show most dramatically in Western history the action potential of the hieratic style. This former German monk reflected a dual hierarchy within the church between monastic orders and regular clergy. He induced the same duality with the outside secular powers, so that the account joins this section to the section below on dual hierarchy (p. 267):

> Prior to the late eleventh century ecclesiastical jurisdiction in the broad sense of legislative and administrative as well as judicial competence . . . lacked precise boundaries. . . . It was the Papal Revolution, with its liberation of the clergy from the laity and its emphases upon the separation of the spiritual from the secular that made it both necessary and possible to place more or less clear limits upon, and hence to systematize, ecclesiastical jurisdiction. (Berman 1983, p. 221)

Gregory VII saw the potential for getting action and control which was latent in the hieratic structure. This was a structure of separate orders or estates in social organization, and of regulations, laws, and doctrine which were parallels in cultural guise. A degree of Europe-wide jurisdiction had already stumbled into being, but had not been taken at face value until Gregory made this an explicit and daring innovation. The many hieratic clusters within formal hierarchies and territorial organization demonstrated resonance to Gregory out of all proportion to the resonance obtained by secular rulers.

Gregory was the first in Europe to see how to and did in fact create an absolutist state on hieratic style. He was thus able to reach through levels in a way not comparable to the secular side. And this was scale-invariant: bishop, pastor, and monastery head each could invoke hieratic clustering in reaching through bewildering strings of commitments and localizations.

The Investiture Controversy between Emperor and Pope was the preeminent issue of an era, a classic mobilization of ongoing inter-face productions into events. An issue emerged from what had been only forms of words. The obverse of this was the suppression of identity formation among actors. Striking individuality of cleric, and flaunting of kinship with and dependency upon secular elites, was dampened. Canon law became more prominent, and it was built up around events (Berman 1983).

Soviet Communist governments, pre-1990, have been strikingly similar to the Catholic Church in underlying architecture of control (Brzezinski and Huntington 1964). Both presuppose corporatist poli-ties. The Party was shaped in hieratic style, with successive layers of purity, offices and committees within each layer being treated as pools of interchangeability. And the Party was also a second govern-ment parallel to state hierarchies of offices. Schurmann (1968) lays this out for the China of the 1950s, with attention to the additional double vision induced by attention to preceding USSR practices. The importance of network context may be reflected in the lack of success in the Chinese exemplar. Like the early Church, the Russian Soviet formation emerged initially out of a city-based movement, outside the established order of story lines, but bound into the loosely cou-pled ties of urban situations. "Red versus expert" is like "clergy ver-sus laity," and even more like regular clergy versus religious. Purity stories provide access for strings of connections reaching through large formations by skipping between hieratic clusters.

Purges in hieratic settings are said to eliminate heresies, but since at least the time of the Donatist heresy, against St. Augustine, it has been clear that, on its cultural face, the side of heresy may well be the orthodox side (Newman 1876; Willis 1950). The important point is that heresies are defined *after* the social organization shifts which make them necessary. Heresies are the type-case of forming issues out of events in reconciling troubles over identities of actors. Schisms, in church (Gill 1959, 1966; Williams 1982), Party, or government, are a converse. Schisms are mobilization into interests as part of reconciling divergent identities of process, of events. More generally, when hieratic style fails, strategy must be created and continually renewed to deal afresh with the problematic of control.

Agenda for Agency

Attempts at fresh control must aim to sidetrack the blocking action that is inherent in social organization. Yet decision-making structures are devices for enforcing custom, just as scalar organizations are devices for resisting change. Hegemony seems to be from stasis, whether or not authority speaks of change. These are implications of the analysis so far.

Fatalism need not follow. It is true that within any institution, following any style or profile, attempts at control tend to counteract one another and thus to engender new disciplines instead of fresh control. The same is true even within a tie. Blocking action is an endemic project, as common for the high and mighty as for challengers. Yet such control efforts which block action can be an important initial leverage for somebody's managing, by yet further impulse for control, to generate some action not to be anticipated. Control for fresh action thereby can be achieved, and even to some degree be routinized within various styles and institutional systems.

Agency resulting from control has been the principle theme, agency as by-product of control. From it derive first identities and simple social organization, and eventually persons as agents between populations in complex social organization. Now the principal theme becomes agency for control.

Shape this new theme as a contrast with the previous chapters, which concerned tendencies of action to freeze into an institution or other social organization, thereby denying innovation and blocking action. In contrast with this stasis are ways of using agency to upend institution and initiate fresh action in the course of seeking control. This contrast, at highest scope, is expressed elegantly: "Human societies have a very strong tendency to impart a certain rigidity to any new social organization and to crystallize themselves in any new form. Hence it often happens that the passage from one form to another is not by continuous movement but by leaps and jerks . . . for example, in language, in law" (Pareto 1937, p. 160).

Agency may be kept immediate; for example, in the study of Italian city-states: "The real state, the state felt all around one in the form of potent commissions or as a source of income (via speculation on the Monte), existed in the corporate and individual holder. . . . Nothing in the Florentine constitution emphasized the principle of indirect representation. . . . The contact with power was direct, immediate, sensory" (Martines 1966, pp. 391–92).

Agency abstracted from particular agents and goals is not control by agenda. Agenda cannot even be conceptualized independent of the social organizational context, whether the context be profiles across populations or only networks. The context supplies basis for discriminating control within a set of such constructs as power and authority.[12]

Means of Agency

Agency may loosen up mobilization, so that agency can work as delegation. That is, agency can apply through a direct tie which can be inserted exactly arbitrarily so far as the otherwise existing network context knows. Consider an example. The Medici recognized a vulnerability which had crept into their corporatist city-state. To all appearances, this corporatist institution had locked in the social formation of Florence in the early Renaissance. Taking for given the corporatism which existed amidst all but the lowest strata, the few score of leading families had come to perceive control as only a matter of factions among themselves as an elite, with merely some mirroring to control as a show among guilds and lower-level corporates.

Then came Lorenzo to consciously spin down strings of patronage, systematically cutting across the range of banking, business, social, and kinship activities of himself and associates (Padgett and Ansell 1988; DeRoover 1965). The factionalized style of patron-client politics took over nearly in a flash and then proved to be stable. After all, it was but a resuscitation of the sort of party politics which Lily Ross Taylor pinned down as central to the late Republic of Rome (Taylor 1948; and see Syme 1949).

Agency may instead turn control mechanisms from primary focus on network context to taking identity as important and as transposable. The extreme special case of agency is the *shaliach*, the Old Testament term for one who is but a shadow, or plenipotentiary agent,

---

[12] For an analogous, but more culturally oriented discussion see Fligstein (1990, pp. 10–11); the two approaches come together in the section General Management below. For background see Pratt and Zeckhauser (1985), especially the introduction and the chapter by White.

designed solely to carry out the implications of another's identity for concrete action.

An agenda denotes the outcome of more or less conscious shaping of issues and interests, within rhetorical forms, by projects of control. Agenda also describes the sequence of issue-interest pairings agreed for a specific meeting. Exotic examples are helpful in bringing out the formation and effects of agenda and agency. It is, after all, easier to discern the role of an agenda when the observer has no personal investment in the content of interests and issues. Then a result is to decrease the degree of exoticness perceived! And this process helps us to be as clear-eyed as March is about agendas in our own time and context (Cohen and March 1974; March and Olsen 1976).

Through agency, events can be framed via agenda into issues; actors can be framed into interests.[13] In many tribal contexts (Fortes 1940; Evans-Pritchard 1940; Hart and Pilling 1965) the emphasis is reversed: Issues are imputed in order to achieve coherent strings of actors by interests. And, from an advanced society, accounts of Thai society and government, in provinces as well as capital, offer an extreme example of issues being concocted to generate coherence among interests:

> Heavy reliance on oral, therefore secret, communications for much of the real business of government combined with a proliferation of paper work designed to maintain appearances . . . little or no serious attention is given to documents by overworked higher officials (p. 319). Inadequate scheduling of time leads to alternate periods of under-occupation and furies of last minute work (p. 113). Over-centralization is a vain hope, a groundless aspiration and pretence, masking the actual dispersal and localization of control . . . the formalism effect (p. 282). All the conspicuous doors cannot move, and egress must be sought through moving panels controlled by hidden buttons. (Riggs 1966, p. 7)

The fascination of Barth's Pathans (1965) is that they appear to be an intermediate case where issues and interests are being imputed and perceived more on the same footing (Skvoretz and Conviser 1971), so that agendas are more complex. Events concatenate into issues and actors into interests and factions by social negotiation. There is an active, manipulative aspect to the resulting mechanisms.

---

[13] These framings are an activist alternative to their being seen as part of the regular operations of styles and institutions among networks from the preceding chapters. Issues and interests are not attributes, not passive categories of perception by persons, instead they are by-products of efforts at control. They come out of projects of control, often through agencies, as these interact into larger dynamics through cumulation and specialization in a population of networks.

Cumulation of ties is a substantive social process of its own, rather than being a matter of sheer stipulation from sequence of ties in some representation of a network. Consider how cumulated agency can occur.

Calculus of Agency

Interests are socially imputed to actors in such a way as to reduce ambage in social organization, to make it less ambagious. This is the process of story lines. Issues are imputed to events in such a way as to minimize ambiguity of interpretation. This is the process of rhetoric. But one imputation tends to interfere with the other in actual contexts of networks among disciplines.[14]

Construction of an agenda deals with implications of this interference. It requires considering more complex, three-body interactions in real time.[15] What is missing is calculus of agency.

Joint perceptions of networks require articulation, as much as do perceptions for disciplines. Identities are aware of the connections coded as ties in a network and they are even aware of some of the topological parameters that are the scientific motivation for introducing networks. For example, actors have a sense of whether they are sociometric stars and of how connected-in they are. Actors also may sense how inbred their space is, how "weak" the ties are in Granovetter's sense (1973).

Once there are identities—and by hypothesis where and when these appear is chancy and erratic—not only do ties spin out from their nodes, but identities may perceive and thus activate ties among other nodes, especially as part of control projects. Types of tie can become coordinated in phenomenology with story lines, that is, sufficiently differentiated to supply minimum notation for story lines, along with issues and interests.

An example is the adaptation of clientelist ties for individual Romans to use in binding larger corporate actors (Badian 1958; Garnsey and Saller 1987). Or one can have the story lines differentiated on the basis of the types of ties. As examples, take the ways the Roman republic built up military leadership doctrine by cobbling together existing sorts of relationships (Suolahti 1955). One can start with how the Senate delegated military authority in various forms to senators

---

[14] In the extreme form of *shaliach*, of plenipotentiary, agency cuts ambage toward zero but with no limit on ambiguity (White 1985). In another extreme, with agency extended as onto surgeon or investment banker, ambage is high and ambiguity low (Johnson 1967; Eccles and Crane 1988).

[15] This is fleshed out in the case studies in Riker (1986).

and others as generals for campaigns of different types (Eckstein 1986).

Agency shades down from more complex maneuverings and interpretations to binary imperatives, all of which deal with meanings as much as with social patternings. Agency generates both perception and analysis, and defines a duality between event and actor. In interaction of agencies comes control. Even the simplest exemplar of agency, on the smallest scale, presupposes settings both for events and for actors. Mismatches can be shifted from one setting to another, but not eliminated.

Agency calculus is the computation of trade-offs, among ambage, ambiguity, and contingency, to suggest fresh ways to gain control. Agency calculus needs developing for specific disciplines and their combinations. Two examples of council and interface combinations are Barth's classic studies of men's clubs as political systems in a mountain valley (1970), and Prince's descriptions (1970) of putting together Broadway productions. They differ on size and on institutional background and so presumably also on locations in the index space. Figure 6-1 repeats just the three planes of mobilizer-council discipline from figure 2-5, and suggests index locations for these examples.[16]

One of the varieties of mobilizer discipline is the extreme of zero differentiation ratio; autocracies can be described here. When they occur embedded in the upper caste in the valley, Barth's mobilize disciplines can be seen as approximating this. Prince's mobilizing, by contrast, is among sets whose differentiation is to be seen as very high viewed from the outside. The WIB examples of mobilizer discipline, by contrast, will be clustering around an intermediate ratio of differentiation; presence of the military assures that outcome.[17]

The next steps are various and depend on context. The WIB situations below involve matchings with high dependency ratios sometimes, but not always. How disciplines would mesh depends on specific context. Barth's wheeling and dealing over dependencies and land rights would, one supposes, be at intermediate levels. And the Prince matchings are at low levels. But each combination would require the kind of treatment of context that is given in Barth's monograph to identify a population. And each is articulated in terms of values.

[16] Each is a region, since each example comes in variants.

[17] In much the same way, the presence of East Tennessee mountain Republicans assures that V. O. Key's "one-and-a-half party" system functions in that Southern political system (Eccles and White 1987).

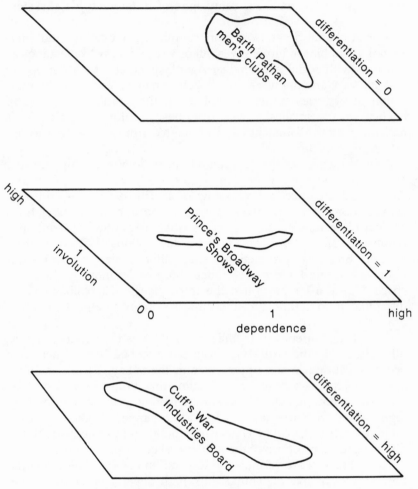

Fig. 6-1. Locales in the 3-D space

Crisis Regimes

A crisis regime is where by common agreement a rapid transition is sought through rearranging an existing complex that is, at least for the moment, not viable. In crisis regimes, networks decouple and committees embed. Two examples will flesh this out, wherein agency has to be traced through measurements capable of showing changes in both ambage and ambiguity: Agencies are both ambagious and ambiguous in their weaving together of interests and issues via actors, events, and delegation. Retrospective measures can be derived from episodes that are important enough to generate many contemporaneous accounts and intense investigation.

Fifty years after World War I, Cuff (1973) traced that war's emergency mobilization process. The initial system was dichotomized between private and public, with clear rules and high ambage. Then it was overlaid with a novel set of rules which were quickly reduced to nullity: agency was invoked to maintain unchanged existing systems in the face of proposed delegations. Ambage went to zero.

Bailey (1984) was much quicker, indeed contemporaneous, with measurement for his New York City bankruptcy crisis. And Bailey has a different sort of case from Cuff: a case of striking change in a system conceded to be a mix of pluralist and bureaucratic, one with high ambiguity and low ambage. The change was overridden by a set of rules which was defined with striking clarity. Operationalization of the rules in cash flows resulted in a system with low ambiguity and considerable increase in ambage of social patternings—measured across both the pluralist politics and the functionally departmentalized bureaucracy:

> The Great War produced an unparalleled expansion of the state in the United States. . . . An administrative army marched into Washington. . . . Networks of agencies spanned the nation and cut deeply downward through the country's social structure. . . . This book is about . . . the War Industries Board . . . established at the end of July 1917, almost four months after America entered the war, it was the outgrowth of a number of earlier, less satisfactory arrangements. (Cuff 1973, p. 1)

With these words begins what should apparently be a straightforward tale of cumulation, one that in fact unravels midway: "The WIB and its administrative program were a bundle of paradoxes where decentralization vied with centralization, competition with combination, individualism with integration, freedom with coercion" (p. 149). Underneath seas of rhetoric, the basic plot line is conflicts of established military purchasing agencies with businesses newly come to Washington. These businesses embed themselves into a succession of committee forms—mobilizer and arena disciplines in present terms—and thus gain a kind of control, albeit one contingent among competitors, over a new bonanza customer, the military.

The businessmen, particularly the industrialists, used networks, or more exactly the filling out and further growth of networks, to pick apart the defenses against their assumption of control. These defenses were in joint advisory committees for purchasing by the military. These defenses were manned not only by military officers but also by experienced civilian bureaucrats and tough-minded members of Congress, notably Senator McKellar of Tennessee. McKellar,[18] for example, successfully sponsored a rider amendment that put the businessmen on the embedded committees at legal risk when offering recommendations (that often verged on inducements).

Business immediately spun further network interconnections and remobilized along preexisting ties. So business reappears in yet another dual structure of committees. That is, there was a second embedding. The recently created chambers of commerce, seeking distinction beyond their localist origins, were pressed into service to set up committees more openly appointed and explicitly representative of the respective trades and industries. These committees became the official interfaces to the WIB from the respective military purchasing agencies—the latter still advised by much the same elite committees as before.

Was President Wilson the one who gained fresh control from this complex process? Cuff sees it differently:

> Until he appointed Baruch to the WIB chairmanship and enlarged the tools of priority planning, President Wilson exercised a meaningful control over the whole process. But once he officially delegated his authority to Baruch and the WIB in March, he assumed an essentially passive role in the policy area, for he remained true to his habit of relying upon the judgment and actions of trusted lieutenants. (p. 192)

But I claim that Cuff misses the point of how control is achieved by a sort of jujitsu, by using the strong forces of existing structures against themselves, via reliance on second-order efforts among networks and committees themselves to decouple diverse projects and inconsistent ends, all to the end of control.

Cuff himself summarizes earlier (p. 165): "The WIB's commodity sections are less a victory for WIB mobilizers than one result of a successful fight waged by military institutions to maintain a wide area of discretion for themselves in the face of bureaucratic invasions by emergency agencies." The same processes of decoupling and embedding are played out again and again in idioms of competing committee systems and network engendering, played for different projects which then interact and cumulate toward still other and more indirect control results.

---

[18] Who later, during the TVA era, showed the same disdain for songs of organic unity and innocent corporatist cooperation from David Lilienthal (Selznick 1965).

A parallel conclusion results for a more recent crisis regime, in the 1975 New York City bankruptcy crisis, where Bailey (1984) argues, "The fact is, however, that the powers of the mayor have been reinforced as a result of the financial crisis . . . his legal powers have been circumscribed, his political powers enhanced . . . the financial controls imposed by these statutes . . . shed new light on management systems as political resources within the political process" (p. 139).

Bailey also supplies a cogent definition of regime consistent with the one above: "recurring and sustained values, norms, decision rules and authority structures . . . the general matrix of regularized expectations within the limits of which political actions are usually considered authoritative" (p. 9). Mayor Abe Beame was a hapless and transparent mayor. Unlike the enigmatic President Wilson, Beame was bereft of insight and active agency for grasping the control engendered by the crisis shift in regime.

Apparently, the WIB crisis regime and the New York City regime faced utterly different problems. The core of the New York City crisis was financial in the tangible sense of cash flows: The private money markets, normally invisible in and to the city polity, suddenly refused to continue funding. These markets thereby set off the creation of MAC and EFCB and other acronymic authorities able by statute to reset policy with the operational goal of restarting flows from ostensibly private money markets.

Money flows were the least of the problems of the WIB. Underneath, however, both crises rested upon interaction among dual organizational systems of policy and action brought into close interplay for the first time. The crisis in each case takes the mode of successive embeddings in systems of committees—largely arena disciplines in our analytic terms—which were cut across by decouplings of ongoing structures. The mechanism attempted on each dual side was penetration by networks of mobilizer disciplines.

Networks decouple, committees embed. This formula runs opposite to the previous, classical contrast in which inertial status fixed by networks of traditional ties was set off against crisp change possible in contractual arenas, of which committees can be a modern embodiment. The new formula cannot be a fixed or pure truth any more than the old one. Social arrangements endlessly respin themselves in counterpoint to whatever the existing arrangements and competitive control projects are.

Crisis regimes show starkly that control is about the sheer existence of arenas in which to recognize the existence of issues hitherto nullified by hegemonic perspective. Just as networks and committees are but one tangible form in which decoupling and embedding processes can materialize, so financial flows are only one form of signal.

In 1950 Simon, Smithburg, and Thompson (p. 294) introduced the everyday counterpart to the duality that sets off the crisis regimes. They speak of "counterpart units" as inevitable defensive formations by organizations being subjected to control (from "higher" or from the "center"), control in the guise of specialized or professional advice by overhead units. In New York, the city bureaucracy, organized by authority or by agency, has now feverishly built up defensive expertise in cash-flow finance to counter dissection by computerized intervention networks. But the WIB's war ended just as the WIB was becoming sufficiently ensconced so as to induce counterpart units within the military contracting agencies.

Control is a matter of pattern and process engendered as a potential by decoupling and embeddings among social formations. Events were much more important identities in the New York City crisis network than for the WIB. But delegation of active agency was exhibited in both regimes.

Getting Action

The reality frame implied by the way I am presenting this analysis is troubling. A certain tidiness, a sense of order and regularity in social process is being generated which is, for better or worse, just not true. For one thing there is some implication of fixed genetic sequence in chapter 3 and later. But in fact there is no irreversibility in movement from one form, level, and scope of social organization to another.[19]

In addition, in the examples given earlier of successful control or manipulation, there is an unfortunate implication of inevitability. The material of control is social relations. Control in social context must simultaneously see to reproducing reliable responses while having also to track context just like an engineering system, and all the while searching for openings to change. Each of the many examples of institutions and styles earlier is also an ensemble of potential paths through to fresh control, but also to lockstep or devolution.

[19] On this issue I differ from Boyd (1989), who has done so much to put the formal analysis of blockmodels on sound footing, but who tends to take the formalism as causal.

Getting action, not control, thus is the general problem. Sheer complexity and interconnectedness, not to speak of raw scale, can vitiate implicit or explicit projects of control, with or without attributable goals. Any social formation whatever, complex or not, tends to settle into blocking action over time.

On a basis of routine, not emergency, accounting conventions are used at higher levels of business and government to generate streams of events which can be used to formulate decouplings of actors in aid of control projects. Events are crafted into localities of explanation. Events are crucial in the realization and elaboration of projects of control, and of the accompanying decouplings and embeddings of production from disciplines. But there is no definite architecture, no overarching system explicitly articulated, in which one can continue to reach through and get action. What then of getting action?

Four Claims

Getting action will override particular species of discipline, particular institution, and particular style, and will tend to mix together contexts. This is the *first general claim*. By contrast, institutions and styles variously interlock network populations made up of discipline species. Institutions are concrete and styles are floating anchors of frames of interpretation by story.

In short, getting action tends to invoke and bring about generality which crosscuts all specializations. Specializations are ineluctable because they are the dynamics of discipline production, but getting fresh patterns of action requires cutting across and overriding both specializations and larger social organization.

One example of this first claim is the growth of engineering as a learned profession. Industrial production, both with and without advanced machinery, had tended to be subject to control or at least veto by numerous groups of craftsmen who shared skills and were permanently committed to their respective specialties. Engineers were in part a deliberate creation by owners, a new form of generalization of the particular skills of craftsmen actually engaged in production. The production disciplines, and the craftsmen communities of role and position, were all crosscut thereby, though not destroyed. Owners sought to get action.

Getting action, or for that matter control, is not reserved for designated "positions," say elites of some sort. On the contrary, any particular designated position is by that very character likely to become part of blocking action. Nor is getting action a new form of specialization. On the contrary. This is *the second general claim*.

Consider an illustration. In educational systems there is a tendency for actors to opt for training "more general" than is suitable to them—for example, training in law or other paperwork as opposed to specific manual arts. One aspect of this tendency is a realistic perception that the more general and abstract training is more likely to fit with getting action and hence with surviving through changes of opportunity. There are counterexamples, such as the extreme specialization within Soviet education, that may tend to prove the rule.

Getting action must invoke changing concrete patterns, attaining new varieties and combinations of discipline, role, and position, and the changing must always continue. This is the *third general claim*. Illustrations here must deal with getting action continued over periods of time. And this claim suggests how it is that control must be a two-edged concept. Control may be realized in stopping change and thus blocking action, as well as in getting action via changing and mixing specializations, roles, and the like. Similarly, decoupling, which pairs with control, is two-valued: decoupling can be as central in blocking action as in getting action.

An example will best illustrate that it is change in more than content of organized arrangements that gets action:

> The change in [Athens's system], when it came, was sharp and sudden, following the overthrow of the tyranny in 510 with Spartan help and a two-year civil war which ensued; and the architect of the new type of government was Cleisthenes, a member of the noble family of the Alcaemonids. Cleisthenes was no theorist, and he seems to have become a democrat virtually by accident, turning to the common people when he urgently needed their support in the confused struggle to fill the vacuum left by the deposed tyrant, Hippia, the son of Peisistratus. . . . Having committed himself to a major innovation, Cleisthenes with his advisers, whoever they may have been, created the institutions which they thought their new objective required, retaining what they could, but not hesitating to demolish and to invent boldly and radically. (Finley 1977, p. 76)

This example at the same time illustrates the first general claim, of getting action as always crosscutting existing specializations.[20]

---

[20] The example also illustrates a practical limitation in my exposition. Only historically prominent and otherwise famous or significant instances of action are familiar to enough readers for brief exposition to be effective (if still not sufficient). I have been and will continue to cite studies without substantial description in hopes that the source monographs will be consulted. But even these studies tend to concentrate on

What getting action does generate unfailingly is inequality: this is *the fourth general claim*, which also is illustrated by the previous example. This claim may explain why interpretations as diverse as Marxism and functionalism give so much attention to systems of stratification. This fourth claim implies, however, that these other approaches have gone at the study of stratification wrongly. There are not classes cleanly differentiated by relations to the means of production, nor strata rationally arrayed according to worth of their occupations. On the contrary.

The central point about inequality is exactly that it is the only systematic regularity one can adduce from the continuing operation, within social spaces, of getting action seen as an observable drive widely present and with quite various and changing sources. Inequality is the by-product of attempts to get action and gain control: Inequality, the most pervasive idiom of blocking action, is the cumulative product of attempts to get action.

The implication is that stratification is the inevitable direction taken as institutional systems become removed increasingly from ecological constraint. Stratification is the destination, at least the interim destination, of the purely social evolving under pressures of getting action.

Tangible examples quickly cure the tidiness of general claims. First comes a topical example. Then in the remaining subsections come several brief illustrations of getting action from each of three perspectives. To try for some control by reaching through social formation is the animus of the first set of illustrations. This is followed by a set for reaching down through social formation, and then come examples from counterelite perspectives, on reaching up. Subsequent sections develop more extended analysis through case study of each perspective.

Glasnost as of 1989

Careers appear to have multiplier effects, to trigger and be triggered by other chains of contingency. Careers can in doing so induce boundaries of populations as a perceptual overlay (Stewman 1975,

---

larger scale and more prominent examples such as feudal England (Lachmann 1985) and Soviet Russia (Urban 1987)—or at least on the prominent as judged within the horizons of that world, say of highland New Guinea (Strathern 1971). Yet built into my whole approach is the claim that the same sort of generalities apply to getting and blocking action across very diverse scopes, at various levels of the complex cumulations and concatenations of embeddings of disciplines across various forms of specializations and identities in networks.

1988). But careers are anticipations, or careers are retrospections; what corresponds to career not over time but at a given time? Vacancy chains do: see White (1970b). Their importance is appreciated best in systems of control which focus on careers.

Firms and industries as well as governments engage in effective indirect controls over careers of themselves and other corporate actors and persons. The principle can be extended by analytic continuity to other scopes. Congestion profiles in flow systems, for example, also can be interpreted as supporting a control which is indirect in fashion and analogous to career (Feller 1949; Kleinrock 1967; Riordan 1962).

Careers often have been viewed from a passive observer stance. However, careers can be active counters in efforts at changes in regime. This can be seen for example in the USSR (Baker 1982; Urban 1987) as in Mexico (Herredia 1989). Glasnost and economic liberalization are parallel attempts in the two countries to reduce centralization and government participation in flows of goods and services. The attempts are parallel despite the great differences between the larger societies. Each is in serious trouble which on the surface looks like effects from some sort of turbulence from below as constraints and coercive disciplines are loosened.[21]

A fresh explanation of Glasnost can be suggested in terms of career systems as boundaries. Glasnost decoupling is, in the first instance, a shift in the expectations of the relatively small numbers, thousands rather than hundreds of thousands, of high-level social engineers. These are the professionals of Simirenko (1982) who have kept reproducing the hegemony of the regime. Their engineering of vast collocations of networks and levels are based upon an intricate but rather clearcut structuring of disciplines among themselves (Granick 1967, 1972, 1975). A key to any binding together of this upper control apparatus is the panoply of careers which this population of high-level (but not elite) actors has come to expect. It is a corporative ensemble which they expect.

As long as the career panoply below remains unchanged, elites may rely upon mutual competition for perceived, complex career possibilities to keep individual social engineers isolated vis-à-vis the elites, just as was so in the Sung dynasty in China. The USSR has a system of personnel placement, the *Nomenklatura*, which explicitly concretizes this situation. There are informal parallels in the Mexican main party, the PRI (see Herredia 1989). But Glasnost suggests the simultaneous dissolution of a large chunk of the panoply of careers

---

[21] In 1989, when this section was written.

being anticipated by the social engineers. Their identities, and their control projects nourished in endless professional gossip, are disrupted, not for one or another but for all at once.

The identities have been accounted around story lines concerned with broad political issues. These are the envelopes of endless concrete fixings of particular anomalies by these same high-level social technicians. Some will perceive their career crisis more explicitly than others, and this will spread through the endless gossiping.

Some sense of alienation must mount among exactly this group whose task is to keep reducing alienation in others. Yet their story lines do not encourage explicit discussion of the career disruptions. Instead one would expect, and does begin to see, the appearance of dissident splinter groups, factions public or not, whose ostensible causes will be highly diverse and variable. They may even appear to be an intensification of exactly the Glasnost process which is the real irritant. This speculative example serves also to suggest that careers, whether of individuals or of disciplines, cannot be discussed fully except in the context of networks of other careers involved in the larger social setting.

Career is anticipated memory. When the time is short, career shades into the present and memory which contains the present. Career systems can then verge on being pure institutions rather than sophisticate overlays among style and institution. Careers, both as anticipation and as observed tracks, couch into concrete networks and so crosscut the ostensible specializations which divide up, or rather attempt to divide up, actual social organization into coherent abstractions. In our time and place one way to see this is by recognizing how much careers are bound up with committees, systems of which are presently the common way to concretely bridge abstractly incommensurable specialties.

Reaching Through

Reaching through to other levels and neighborhoods, ones other than those of the disciplines of current routine social action, is a main strategy for the conundrum of getting action. It cannot however be meant as a technical term. The argument has been that beyond a particular scope or level of discipline embedded in network of identities, beyond that immediate scope and context of production and action there is an endless variety of nestings, concatenations, and aggregations. The physical analogies urged from the beginning have been to minerals, gels, glasses, and other forms intricately historied and packed.

It is only in the clusters of story lines evolved in some society that apparently regular macro-structures have appeared. Reaching through is a phenomenological term about strategic efforts to get action and control through and despite these complex deposits of social organization. And also despite the orderly stories invoked by them.

Reaching through is a matter of occasion and process as much as of structuration. Crisis is always associated both as cause and as product with reaching through. Crisis is as much a labeling to help make action possible as it is a report forced into the perceptions of disparate actors and events by configurations of network contingencies. Reaching through is as much selectivity as it is persevering through multiple connections.

Whether vertical or lateral, reaching through embedded social organization can be facilitated by kinds of formal organization whose prime story line is exactly preventing violations of orderly authority! Turn to the unique case of getting action given by British entrepreneurship. Bythell argues (1978, p. 198) that the putting-out system, the informal network style in which English manufacturing had evolved (discussed in chapter 4), remained attractive "in industries with a more stable pattern of demand, or with only modest and irregular growth over long periods," whereas if demand for some particular item grew dramatically over a period of a year or two it would "force some entrepreneurs towards technical innovation and new forms of organization."

Mergers and acquisitions in the present setting of Western industry can be argued to be similar covers for the introduction of shake-ups and disorders. These practices reach through on a more extensive scale than is easy to effectuate within a context defined as a continuing single formal organization. This fits with surveys such as Salter and Weinhold (1979, pp. 4, 27), who report that good diversification deals occur suddenly and are not planned and smooth, and the goodness can only be explained in terms of huge variances in returns on equity. Or take a particular case, normal in its bizarreness—American Express's adventures:

An odyssey of corporate decision making that would destroy Roger Morley's career, make James Robinson's, and culminate months after the debacle of (attempted acquisition of) McGraw-Hill with the celebrated acquisition of the brokerage house of Shearson Loeb Rhoades—an acquisition that appeared a daring masterstroke, but which, in reality, came as the result of miscalculations, opportunity and just plain luck, an acquisition no one at Amexco would have dreamed of or wanted when the process began in 1977. (Grossman 1987)

Another prime illustration of reaching through by mergers and acquisitions can be found in the Eccles and Crane account (1988) of changes in the U.S. investment banking industry. The predominant relation in earlier decades between an issuer of equity and an investment banker was an analogy to the family doctor. The same few people within the bank were the long-term trusted advisers of company management, with friends among directors and executives. These few nurtured their being the expert and informed guides to a dangerous and weird universe of capital—the source of which was decoupled from the advice relation, in the hands of more routine officialdom within the bank which serviced investment trusts of all sorts. Almost complete control was thereby achieved over the client corporation, except for the very largest handful of corporations daring and large enough to be sophisticated in a context set up to deal only with trusting naivete.

Cozy and profitable this traditional agency relation became—to the agent. The reversal of control into the hands of the agent is, after all, an old story, begun by "factors" of commodities, who likewise eased into exclusivity with client (Schwartz 1976). Getting action it was not; on the contrary, the context was one of protection and guardedness just as with the family doctor. "Doing deals" emerged as a kind of virus dissolving this peace into a febrile atmosphere of not wanting to miss one of the endlessly possible new sorts of financing. Why stick with the family doctor when there is a slew of glittering specialists thinking of new ways of reslicing reality to sell it yet again?

At the same time the buyer side was being integrated into a troika network binding issuer companies together with a range of specialists within investment bankers. This was reaching through with a vengeance. Action was being gotten so obsessively there was never even time to worry about organization charts or to cultivate trust. Why cultivate trust when glamor would trump you anyway?

Structural equivalence is the underlying guide in this recasting, and not just in the search for parallel agents and equivalent targets for nostrums. Structural equivalence was the very genesis of the successive banking nostrums, the successive waves of new ways to partition and reassign ownership and debt. Stringing had been the core of the old agency. And now the agents corporately, and their shifting kaleidoscope of self-defined experts individually, were being harshly stratified by success defined along "show biz" lines (Faulkner 1983). Timing becomes all—a week late with an idea, and it is dead.

Mergers and acquisitions assume, induce, and impose stratification by revaluations made unusually abrupt. These revaluations at the same time intend to and do generalize across the large-scale specializations indexed by industry and market. Also, as anticipated in my argument on getting action, structural equivalence is a key to the searches, erratic as they are, for targets of these takeovers.

Reaching Down

An earlier example of reaching down was the Padgett and Ansell account of the Medici strategy. More examples are needed. The triage seen in a hospital emergency room is a prototype for reaching down on a much larger scale. Getting action can never be any sort of universal; it is always a moment of, and interlude in, ongoing social life. Without selectivity even a moment of getting action disappears. Triage can be seen as the timely reaching through of disciplines, in layers or levels, in order to get action.

Reaching down to get action is not some mechanical predictable matter. An entrepreneur combining ownership and control to elide a level is getting action, but so is the same entrepreneur bringing in troubleshooting in various staff guises in order to scan and sample in testing for where crisis is appearing or can be coaxed into existence. Identities would never have been triggered in the first place if there were no uncertainties or contingencies. Once formed they encounter other identities, each defining further contingencies for the others, eventuating in the full panoply of ambage and ambiguity in addition.

Eliding levels helps to reach down through. British entrepreneurs of the previous century must be regarded as paragons of getting action. They showed tenacity throughout the nineteenth century in marrying together ownership and management as completely as in the industrial revolution itself: "Entrepreneurs with exceedingly little technical knowledge were prepared to risk large sums of money in manufacturing ventures and . . . to build a factory the size of which was determined not by rational calculations . . . but by the capital available for investment . . . and the maximum output the entrepreneur thought he could obtain" (Payne 1974, p. 32).

This is getting action, not blocking action. Nor were these entrepreneurs settling into quietude through family descent:

In 1830, of the 135 firms in Leeds engaged in the sale and manufacture of woolens, worsteds and blankets, for example, a long-established industry in the industrial city, only twenty-one houses had partners who could provide a direct link with those in 1782, only fifty years before. But this small scope under direct entrepreneurship made outreach limited: they could not engage in vigorous selling effort in world markets by means of a salaried force of commercial travelers.

Reaching down is seen as a positive opportunity for action in that it allows for the continued outreach to wider and changing scopes which is indispensable to continuing to get action.

Lateral relations as such are irregular, just as is reaching down through vertical layers, according to Sayles (p. 81). They are irregular because they interfere with routines, require iteration, are ambiguous. "Management thus becomes in large part a process of working interfaces. . . . Rough-and-tumble reality with its stops and starts and many cross-interrelationships and bargains thus seems disorderly and political" (pp. 90–92).

At very different scopes and in very different institutional contexts one can recognize similar strategies in reaching down to untie knots in congealed structures. Compare Gorbachev in the USSR of 1988 with Alfred Sloan in the staggering GM of the 1920s. Gorbachev's industrial reform calls for an expanded role for managers of industrial associations and enterprises, and a steep decline in the role of economic and administrative bureaucracies in day-to-day supervision of managers' activities. Gorbachev's plan did not envisage an increase in the direct responsibilities of the (Communist party) "apparat," which however would still expect to guide industry's transition to the new methods of planning and management.

The parallel is striking to Sloan's reaching down into the complexly specialized federation of the old GM, which was a haphazard throwing-together of a host of diverse industrial entities through merger and acquisition. Sloan relied on a new, removed formation of general managers in a central office. In both situations the control structure of routine information flows became more abstract, and yet actual accounts show that eruptions of central agency into concrete enactments of production became much more common and yet unpredictable (Hopwood 1978). In both cases the newly abstract central oversight came to be housed in an apparatus (*Nomenklatura* and general office, respectively) that focused on and decided personnel moves at all levels whence elite careers may emerge (Bialer 1987, p. 77; Chandler 1969, chapter 3; Sloan 1963).

Forms of state terror had characterized versions of reaching down the Soviet economy in earlier decades, and they had substantial effect. The analogue at GM was in economic terror, in bankruptcies and destroyed positions. Reaching down is not painless or neat; as in simpler forms of control the only real fuel there to support reaching is from excitation of grievances and fractures in the motivations of existing networks, identities, and disciplines embedded through many levels.

The moral is that autocracies induce structural equivalence. Both Gorbachev and Sloan rely on structural equivalence effects from their pulling up selected personnel to be in central, generalizing offices, whose idiom is the flexibility of being able to operate effectively across diverse units. Both faced some tension between this accomplishment of generality on the one hand, and orientation to change, technical and social, on the other. Innovation is not the same as getting action, and requires some stable embodiment of social support, some structure which allows the obsessive degrees of specialization which always attend successful technical innovation. It is hard to read through layers of obfuscation to check if the same is true of innovations in social organization, but it seems likely.

Yet streams of innovation are as necessary for keeping alive the option of getting action as they are for their ostensible missions to yield better fits to technical and competitive environments. Identities of both events and actors are reshaped and re-created more given a flux of innovations, and these reshapings provide the material for getting action. In the sphere of events, to reach-through or reach down is to invoke and create local history in hopes of getting non-Markovian impact on the inevitably stochastic process which is unfolding.

Issues and interests are engendered out of events and actors whose identities are being shaped among contending efforts at agency. Getting action must continue to break up the hardening crust of issues and interests which continually congeal to block action. Turn back to GM's early evolution. In 1913, the regime of the banker Storrow was seeking to block action in a scramble to bring coherence to a business then understood only by its creator-entrepreneur, William Crapo Durant. General Motors was centralized into three offices by this regime. One of these was purchasing, an apparently logical choice since half the product valuation was in purchased parts. The other two departments were changed when Durant regained control for a few years, and then, when Sloan was brought in from his own Hyatt Bearings to run the whole, purchasing fell back into organizational insignificance. Control was needed over disciplines to purchasers, not the ones to suppliers, since the former were still inchoate aggregates where action could not be gotten.[22]

Take in parallel the earlier evolution of Soviet industrial reforms

[22] Burt (1983) has developed and exploited this logic in his analyses of current American industry.

before Gorbachev. Here too events were induced and issues thereby generated because they were necessary for getting action, for reaching down into impacted layers. But here too earlier reforms, creating regional decentralizations, proved arbitrary, unrelated to the actual balances of ambiguity and ambage in the architecture of agencies which had been built up (cf. Granick 1967, 1972).

Reaching Up

There are special features to getting action when oneself and collaborators are not perceived as already the high and mighty. V. I. Lenin is credible as an expert on reaching up, through a complex social fabric, to get action on a large scale (Lenin 1902). On a similar scale, first- and second-century Church Fathers are also credible (von Campenhausen 1955; Dix 1946).

Lenin speaks for specialization; this apparently is the opposite of my claim that generalists are the path to action:

> Lack of specialization is one of our most serious technical defects. . . . The smaller each separate "operation" in our common cause will be, the more people we shall find capable of carrying out such operations (people, who, in the majority of cases, are not capable of becoming professional revolutionaries), the more difficult will it be for the police to "catch" all the "detail" workers . . . in order in breaking up functions to avoid breaking up the movement, and in order to imbue those who carry out these minute functions with the conviction that their work is necessary and important . . . it is necessary to have a strong organization of tried revolutionaries. (Lenin 1902; part D in 1976)

But Lenin goes on to link to elite and hieratic themes:

> Specialization necessarily presupposes centralization, and in its turn imperatively calls for it . . . our duty to assist every capable worker to become a *professional* agitator, organizer, propagandist . . . he is encouraged to widen the field of his activity, to spread it from one factory to the whole of his trade, from one locality to the whole country . . . his outlook becomes wider, his knowledge increases, he observes the prominent political leaders from other localities and other parties, he strives to rise to their level.

Then he connects back to the special problems of reaching up: "We must arrange that he be maintained by the Party, that he may in due time go underground . . . otherwise . . . he will not be able to stay in the fight against the gendarmes for at least a few years . . . *all distinctions as between workers and intellectuals,* and certainly distinctions of trade and professions, must be obliterated . . . of people whose profession is that of revolutionary."

Examples of reaching up need not be on such a scale, and they need not wear political or economic dress. Changes in art forms appear to come about more often from reaching up than do politically or administratively garbed changes. Reaching up can also be from intermediate locations in a complex formation.

Consider P. Kuhn's account of Chinese gentry response to the Taiping rebellion in the nineteenth century (Kuhn 1970). The Taiping itself was rationalized by a syncretism of Western religion with Chinese secret society. And the Taiping itself acted much as a reaching-down operation elsewhere would do. The Taiping could be seen either as Nazi forerunners, or as descendants of the astonishing Swiss peasant-city alliance that established its independence (T. Brady 1985).

The gentry were imbedded throughout China's provinces, yet they tied into the city network of empire by the shifting minority actually in office, from the larger pool certified to having passed the classics exams. The gentry waited and waited for the Taiping to be suppressed. But it was an empire in the last throes of involuteness through blocking action. Dual hierarchies pervaded the system; there were whole parallel sets of armies. On paper there was a rationalistic registration and surveillance system down through a village headman level that paralleled the informal local-notable networks of the gentry. The dynasty, like the Taiping usurpers, were from ethnic fringes disdained by the main Han.

Kuhn pieces out many threads of mobilization for defense and counterattack induced among dispersed gentry in desperation as the Taiping tide spread up the river valleys into core provinces. It is a bewildering kaleidoscope of crossing projects of control. It is a classic account of social process at the middle range of order which is, arguably, the only one possible of tangible realization on the ground. Action is gotten by astute juxtapositions of disciplines and skeins of social formations which normally served to block action.

The Charles Tilly school of social science has engendered a whole literature (see Tilly 1978 for review) on contentious gatherings, what used to be called riots, informed and stimulated by earlier dissection of the mechanics of riots (Milgram 1977; Granovetter and Soo 1983). These studies bring out the rationality of riots, the ways and extent to which they get action, reach through from below. There is never in social fact such a thing as an absolute bottom so that the thought of reaching up from the bottom of society necessarily is romanticized.

Tilly's accounts of Western European riots can be juxtaposed to

Kuhn's tracing of gentry countermobilization to the Taiping (1970). Abstracted from cultural overlays and scale, the essential similarities of gaining action by reaching up become clear. Events have to be generated and polished as identities so that issues can be forged. Hand in hand, new identities of actors are disgorged in the turbulence of mobilizing action. Structural equivalence is and has to be the key to an even greater extent than in reaching down. Generality is achieved in the organizers, the initiators who become central not to just one but to many facets of events of mobilization. Generalization is sought also across the events. In Europe often it was change in the price of bread that served as the catalyst.

Dual Hierarchy and Servile Elite

Attempts at control and getting action can themselves interact and cumulate into important changes in social organization, especially at elite levels. Parallel hierarchies have made their appearance several times.

Servile Elite

An elite is a heavily interconnected set of actors whose identities are so pronounced that all obfuscations about interests are suppressed. Thereby issues are suppressed as well. An elite is a particular social formation, not segregated in network from a broader population, a formation that is structured so as to get action among the broader set in part by being socially immunized against blocking processes endemic to social organization.

A servile elite is an elite induced and shaped from recruits arbitrarily introduced to a network, and so manipulable at least initially, but with the flexible social structuring common to spontaneous elites. The recruits' own networks of origin are diverse and dispersed. Reaching through for control is as much a horizontal problem of bridging sheer numbers of neighborhoods in social space as it is of bridging embedded levels and cumulated rankings, together with their stories.

The clear sign of a servile elite is the appearance of a distinction between public and private, in the meaning-accounting schemes. Elites proper have no need of such:

In the eleventh century the key position in Italian society came to be held by the class immediately below that of the greatest landowners. Of varied origins, these men were gradually caught up into the knightly class. . . . In 1037 the Milanese *vavassores* (subvassals) after a long and bitter struggle finally obtained from the Emperor Conrad II security in the tenure of their benefices and freedom to appeal to the emperor . . . in effect abolished the feudal dependence of the vavassores on the capitanii (tenants-in-chief) and had wider and more lasting effects in Italian society. . . . It consolidated the various ranks of the feudal hierarchy into a single legal class. (Hyde 1973, p. 28)

This managerial class crosscut the network of Italian city communes, making possible the functioning of "national" factions such as Guelphs and Ghibbelines.

More extreme versions of servile elites appear for example in the Managerial Revolution of Berle and Means (1932), in which ownership was separated from control in bringing firms public. The same variant is identifiable in Germany centuries before and contemporaneous with the Italian developments:

In Germany the lack of close feudal ties forced all lords, the king among them, to turn to the servile classes for such administrative officers and for armed knights; and so in Germany there rose a class of *ministeriales*. . . . They seem to have been employed in the first place by the great churches . . . because bishops and abbots were loath to enfeoff their lands to free vassals, against the performance of such duties, for fear lest their property might be appropriated. . . . And German kings, especially with Henry IV, soon use them to run kingdoms . . . developed a ministerial administrative class. (Barraclough 1946, p. 80)

During the Investiture Contest with the Pope, the *ministeriales* were able to throw off personal bondage which became accounted a differentiation into the ranks of the aristocracy. This was the same period which saw the rise of the fantastic map of German local particularism, held together only by the crosscutting of this servile elite.

Dual Hierarchy

A dual hierarchy is interspersed among these servile elite situations. Dual hierarchy arises from and for intervention in networks within corporatist institution. A dual hierarchy goes beyond any particular device for control in one locale.

From the early example of dual sovereignty between church and state following the Papal Revolution (Berman 1983), variants of a dual hierarchy evolve in Europe. Dual hierarchy may be modeled, as in world system theories, by the semi-periphery. Thus a dual hierarchy is a special phase leading up to the formal organization. After a beginning in hostile confrontation, dual hierarchies came to be perceived by the subtle as affording helpful avenues to overall projects of control.

A dual hierarchy makes several devices available. The collegium of bishops is a device of the hieratic style which makes it easier to penetrate through an equivalence set to a wide diversity of networks.[23] From another viewpoint, the collegium can be a resonance structure for bringing together local tendencies into sufficient correspondence so that events can be defined across and among them, and thence actions induced. The inspector general corps or function of an army exemplifies another device, having a chain of agents reaching all levels of a bureaucracy. The agents are bundled together and set apart.

Servile elite commonly co-occurs with dual hierarchy. The Italian pattern of servile elite can be found everywhere throughout history. Japan is not so different, nor is it only the well-known period of the Tokugawa that exhibits dual hierarchy:

> In the twelfth century the ruling families failed to give social recognition and security of tenure to the "Intermediate elite" in the countryside. Some members of this group came from the bureaucratic families of the center, had served as tax collectors, and opted to stay; others were descendants of pre-seventh-century landowning families who had commended their land to the bureaucratic families but remained in possession . . . together, . . . and entrenched, indispensable managerial class, partly literate and always accustomed to wielding arms. . . . In 1180 a rising of this class—a managerial revolution in the strictest sense—took place under the leadership of Minamoto no Yorimoto. Its success led to the establishment of a warrior government or bakufu in Kamakura which made the Kyoto government subservient. . . . This Kyoto Kamakura dyarchy continued until 1333. (Steenstrup 1987, p. 73)

The dual hierarchy is often mirrored in a preference for separate legal systems, separation of public from private, in contradistinction to a normal elite merger of law into administration. This same Japanese era supplies an example.

> In 1203 the in-laws of the Minamoto, the Hojo, ousted the Minamoto from power and for the next 130 years ruled through puppet shoguns . . . in continuous rivalry between the hereditary housemen of the Minamoto (the *gokenin*) and the hereditary housemen of the Hojo . . . [who] hung onto power for so long [through] . . . their ability to build

---

[23] Developed in an earlier section of this chapter.

a system of arbitration courts in which the landowning elites busily liti-
gated for rights over land. (Steenstrup 1987, p. 79)

For a parallel English case see Bearman (1989).

The Papacy showed endless ingenuity in use of dual hierarchy.
First the religious orders help penetrate diocesan and parochial ob-
scurantism; then mendicant orders penetrated both to reach the lay
publics. Another time a particular new order will be set up as the
backbone of reform, to be superseded by another, or by a reinvigora-
tion of a particular specialism among the ordinary clergy.

There are many variants of dual hierarchy. The Verzuiling or pil-
larized forms, called clects in studies of multicommunal, multiethnic
societies (Riggs 1965), began as simultaneous dual hierarchies re-
sponding to mobilization threats. For example, the Dutch case
(Lijphart 1968; Bank 1981), hardened out of a countermobilization to
massive general strikes in the early 1900s (Windmuller 1969). This
intervention was by a Dutch state that had lost Belgium by not intervening a couple of generations before (Kossman 1978).

What is lost over time by intervention, because of the hardening
which results, may be made up by greater horizontal reach through
of the servile elite which comes to crosscut the pillar headings. The
Prussian civil service as described by Rosenberg (1958) was in itself a
hieratic formation in which, however, resistance to arbitrarily in-
jected new officials kept them segregated and so responsive to royal
authority. As in any real example, the principle of dual hierarchy
was reused again and again, often with an issue crafted out of events
within the existing hieratic to extenuate the introduction of another
specialism.

The same tendencies hold on a smaller scale and at a humbler
level. One sign of reaching through by dual hierarchy is a flip in
tasks between the segregated pillars. Heclo (1969), Crozier and Thoenig (1976), and Ashford (1982), from different perspectives for
different countries, settle on a formulation of change in local government. In Heclo's formulation (p. 18) the official has become the poli-
cymaker and the councillor carries out routine administration.

The venerable conundrums of staff and line can quickly be disentangled as a variant of dual hierarchy. Various staff departments of
course do have much of the magic of authority, despite formal disa-
vowal, as seen in operational terms in behavior subject to disputes.
MacMahon et al. (1955) are especially lucid on this reality in their
account of the creation of the Works Project Administration during
the Depression. The difference is that collegiality, assumed in hier-

atic style, is not enhanced at higher levels, but on the contrary decreased, so that in order to get action other, random, often media-mediated communication must be forthcoming.

On a comparable scale, large business firms are sites for dual hierarchies of new sorts. These go beyond the staff-line dualities which have been established long enough to lose effectiveness as contexts for reaching through. Eccles and White (1985) identify one version: corporations are split into self-contained divisions each of which operates in a different market, jousting for a niche with a set of other corporations' divisions. A curious situation: markets are here functioning like hieratic levels or committees in a managerial control scheme of dual hierarchy. A chief executive office, individual or collective, has dual paths to reach through: either the market discipline context, or the conventional financial control context of the home corporation. Many of these messy dual hierarchy situations also have horizontal spread into servile elites.

Temperatures of Colonialism

Another formulation of the calculus of regimes is possible, one analogous to a thermodynamics (de Boer and Uhlenbeck 1962; cf. Leifer and White 1985). Most of both the preceding accounts were devoted to the particular ripostes of gamings and countergamings which were the particular paths by which the results came about in that crisis. Direct cumulation of and prediction from the outcomes of gamings has proved exceedingly difficult, even under simplified trial conditions without crises, and despite a wide variety of approaches (Axelrod 1984). Instead, a better path is specifications of feasible institutions, made up of networks of disciplines, which can result from such detailed dynamics. One then relies on measures of decoupling and embedding processes which reflect the net aggregated results from gamings.

Two sorts of "temperatures" or disorders, ambage and ambiguity, are to be estimated as averages or correlations across a system. The right illustrative case is one where the levels and kinds of disorder are generally agreed, there is no concealment of them, and there is a long time-series of relatively undisturbed observation. Colonial administration is a natural candidate for this new formulation.

Return to the major comparative study used earlier which compared the Dutch Indies to Burma, over a century or more preceding World War II. Furnivall focuses on the institutions and styles of rule at concrete middle-range, disdaining changing ideological fashions:

Our fathers and grandfathers . . . the generation of the Ethical leaders who aspired to build a brave new world in 1900 . . . put forward similar pretensions (to those) in Java at the onset of the great depression of the thirties. They in turn succeeded the Liberals who had thought to introduce a golden age in 1870 on the principle of freedom. The Liberals condemned, as rooted in unrighteousness, the systems by which Van den Bosch had expected to restore prosperity to a country ruined by the reforms that Raffles, a generation earlier, had claimed would bestow liberty and welfare. (Furnivall 1948, p. 281)

What is striking is how persistent through all these changing ideological climates were the styles of middle-range order. Also persisting were their contrasting balancings of uncertainties. He summarizes:

On the Dutch system even the European officials are policemen, agents of policy; on the British system even native officials tend to become magistrates and judges, servants of the law. . . . Burma represents in its purest form a system of direct rule. In Java, on the contrary . . . the purest type of indirect rule. In both countries there has evolved a social structure comprising distinct racial sections with an elaborate western superstructure. (Furnivall 1948, p. 229)

Ambiguity and ambage interchange roles between the contrasting forms of indirect and direct rule in Burma and Indonesia. In Indonesia, "Indirect rule through a local chieftain is the simplest and cheapest way by which . . . land and labour can be provided most readily by the local ruler, governing his people on traditional lines, and there tends to evolve a dual system of administration, half western and half tropical" (p. 276). Onto a preexisting patrimonial traditional system, with low ambiguity and high ambage, is grafted a dual system of particularistic, policing control without explicit new rules, but with explicit new partition by race. Race becomes a new set of rules conflicting with the preexisting ones, and this is in balance with the reduction of ambage through reinforced punitive controls.

Burma was different:

There is indeed hardly anything in common between the character and functions of the civil servants of the two countries. In Burma there is one service divided into three grades, there are no Europeans in the lowest grade but even the highest grade is open to natives. . . . In Java, instead of a single service, there are two separate services, one European and one native, each with its own functions, and in neither service does any officer perform either of the two main functions of the civil servant in Burma. There is a separate judicial service and a separate treasury service. . . . The European civil servant has magisterial or judicial powers, and no administrative responsibilities of any kind . . . his function is to watch over and help the native civil servants . . . (who) are not servants of the law but officers of police or policy. (p. 237)

In Burmese colonial practice, an explicit layer of rules was superposed on secular native culture—and the more elaborated monastic aspect of governance suppressed—to yield much higher ambiguity despite attempts at interleaving the rules, like the races, of administrators.

In both colonialisms the element of getting fresh action, of control as we define it, remains despite seeming permanence of regime because of the explicit exploitation. The briefest of Japanese incursions would dissolve both systems.

General Management

Getting action implies continuing to change and expand but also to contract and to otherwise elide efforts at coherence, which is to say to elide efforts at blocking action as they come along in the name of *ex post* stories. Management consultants today, in the USA, come to this same judgment. Consider this injunction:

The good manager can function effectively only in an environment of continual change. . . . Only with many changes in the works can the manager discover new combinations of opportunities and open up new corridors of comparative indifference. . . . In the day-to-day operation of a going concern, they find the milieu to maneuver and conceptualize. (Wrapp in Hamermesh 1983, pp. 491, 496)

The amazing swathe of sorts and examples of organizations we perceive around us should be interpreted as shells from previous getting-of-action. These shells block action. There are a huge number of organizations, many inactive, a sort of new fossil record for social forms. An active population of organizations compounds style, for justifying not getting action, with institution to sustain routine. Getting action always does continue to some extent, and it manages to have organizations, like other actors, involved. Those getting action also are perforce making use of organizations, but usually only parts and aspects are activated of what the common story says to be the organization.

Western Businesses

Narrow the focus to Western business of the recent past. As other sociologists have argued (Coleman 1973, 1990; Laumann and Knoke 1987), this is distinctively a world in which organizations are common and central as actors (cf. Burt 1978 for measurement). These populations of organizations are a new phenomenon not duplicated in other complex social contexts. All the styles described in chapter 5 are synthesized within a system that generalizes corporatism.

"General manager" is used to designate those expected to cut through organization style to get action in this world. "Administrator," in contrast, can designate orchestration of blocking styles. We should be able to find some recognition of each, and of the basic distinction between them, in the classic modern literature on business management.

An early Dean of the Harvard Business School, Wallace Donham, expressed both sides well but is not himself conscious of the contradiction between them. Himself a former Chief Executive Officer who had gotten action, Donham emphasizes situations and questions which involve both policy and action. He argues for this joint conception being peculiarly difficult (p. 9), but in his words "consciously or unconsciously it is the subject matter around which the lives of all our leading men in the world of affairs revolve." This is what was termed general management earlier when quotes from Wrapp and others showed it to be an endlessly unpredictable practice of dealing with contingencies to achieve action.

Yet he goes on:

> Ours is a professional school . . . business administration should be treated as a profession depending, to the same extent as other professions, on developing and constantly improving an intellectual framework the implications of which can be studied and taught . . . (including) acceptance of responsibility by each member of the group to the group as a whole . . . (with) special standards . . . of the relation of the whole group (of administrators) to the society. . . . Social change, which follows technological change, disintegrates the social group upon which our factories must depend . . . the difficulties of management increase almost geometrically. (Donham 1952, pp. 16, 34)

The modern organization is confusing, and its ostensible management is conflicted, because several styles are being lumped, and combined into an institution across populations of organizations.

One can conjecture that business organizations are primarily concerned with blocking action. Sets of stories elaborate these organizations, claim boundaries and integrality for them, argue jurisdiction, and spell out chains of influence. These stories are all aspects of striving for meaning. This striving can be observed to block action. Exactly by codifying what is to be done, into skeins of the allowable in sequence, and of the assignable in tie, the effect of formal organization is to block fresh action.

Blocking action is not the opposite of getting action, and it does not mean the mere absence of efforts at control. Blocking action achieves continuance of some social formation with some degree of coherence. Blocking action is induced, and sometimes motivated, in projects to maintain some coherence and some effectiveness of production.

The pressures for blocking action are enormous, in a sea of recurrent but uncoordinated disciplines for production. Inconsistent story lines are packaged in order to account for the events and actors whose identities are generated thereby. That was argued earlier to be universal. What is not universal is the growth in density of production and action over time, and the cumulation of networks of disciplines into organizations.

Thirty years ago "Management in the 1980s" was the topic for predictions by two respected social scientists in American business schools; and see the follow-up in 1989 in the *Harvard Business Review*. They took a very professionalist line: conceptualizing and measuring information would provide the growing core of management as a discipline. They say:

> Within ten years . . . a digital computer will be the world's chess champion. . . . We expect top management to become more abstract . . . and correspondingly less directly involved in the making of routine decisions . . . many middle management jobs may change in a manner reminiscent of (but faster than) the transition from shoemaker to stitcher, from old-time craftsman to today's hourly worker. As we have drawn an organizational class line between the hourly worker and the foreman, we may expect a new line to be drawn heavily, though jaggedly, between "top management" and "middle management". . . . There will be many fewer middle managers . . . depersonalization of relationships within management and the greater distance between people at different levels. (Leavitt and Whisler 1958)

In this statement they mirror the professionalist style but yet also build in corporatist assumptions. The utopian technocrat tone is there, professionalist, yet there also is awkward recognition of clientelism and corporatism: "The committors' . . . role of approving or vetoing decisions may be forced increasingly to have the top men operate as a committee, which would mean that the precise individual locus of decision may become even more obscure than it is today."

Their central substantive prediction, and its derivation, are what is wrong. They predict recentralization, with top managers having a bigger percentage of "creative functions," and much more structured jobs for middle management. "Decentralization has, after all, been largely negatively motivated. Top managers have backed into it because they have been unable to keep up with size and technology." Nonsense. Top managers embraced decentralization to enhance control and ease in getting action (Eccles and White 1986, 1987), and those tasks remain as urgent to them as ever.

Rhetorics of Organization

Modern organizations bedevil administration, and induce increasingly elaborate educational processes for management, because, under a cloak of technical rationality, they combine tensions from several quite different styles of coping by blocking change around meaning. Up to three quite different rhetorics of meaning are floating around in the soup of organizational disciplines. Administrators know this intuitively, however much they may be irritated by it. There are patron-client strings, there is a nascent ordering of purity or depth of expertise, there are jealous partitions into corporatist turfs of differential registration. Administrators are trying to maintain coherence but across different systems of rhetoric; general management is there to keep breaking up coherences and getting action, and is aided by multiple coherences.[24]

In parallel, the business firm administered well will not be in, but rather out of any wave of change. This is so of DuPont in America as chronicled by A. DuPont Chandler (1963). One Western nation is as apt an illustration as another. This is so of ICI in England, so well chronicled by a succession of astute historians (Reader 1975; Pettigrew 1985). And period per se is not magic. For the end period of Dutch hegemony, which Kossman (n.d., p. 157) describes, merchants and industrialists grew so much less in size and wealth than those in banking because, perhaps, the former were reduced to administration, whereas the latter had plenty of chance at broad inter-

---

[24] The same argument can be made and illustrated from the government realm. To quote Ashford (1982, p. 20), "As political and administrative hierarchies become less effective, national government turns toward spending and investment controls."

ventions, at general management. This was in the context of an economy of forms that had evolved from clientelist and professional roots
over a long period.

There follows from all this a proposition that general management
will be easier where administration is harder, and the reverse. The
rationale is clear, though measurement and operationalization is not.
General management, getting action through the complex web of
disciplines—whose groupings into designations as this or that organization are the coin of maneuver rather than neutral facts—is easier the more complex is the mixture of styles of blocking. By contrast,
administration is more difficult with three styles together than when
it deals with some fairly pure clientelist, or professionalized style—
or corporatist system.

The Federal Budgetary Process

Rhetoric of organization is as much an obfuscation in government as
in business. Levels mount up dizzyingly in the U.S. Federal government, the scope of which is huge no matter how tallied; so Washington should be a challenge for any theory which claims that self-similarity permits the same analytic devices to function at various levels.
An obvious focus in government—for contending efforts at control,
stratagems of decoupling, and efforts at reproduction—is the construction of the budget, and much of the process has already been
modeled successfully by Padgett (1980a, 1980b, 1981).

Padgett's key ideas fit well with the theoretical approach laid out
in this book.[25] He portrays all constituent processes, whether routine
reproduction or episodic control, as stochastic processes. Sufficient
decoupling into subprocesses is assumed that historical dependencies (in mathematical terms, non-Markovian features) are not needed
within particular subprocesses. There is an initial wave of relatively
predictable claims for budget resources called up from operational
programs within units, within departments or subdepartments.

The main action is in cutting down these initial requests. According to his analysis a dual hierarchy emerges, centered around the
Office of Management and Budget (OMB). Within the federal government, the OMB organization parallels, like an inspector general, the
higher levels in all operational departments. The latter tend to freeze
up and be incapable of conceiving further cuts in their own programs
as, over time, they become enmeshed in the blocking style of self-

---

[25] Padgett and I jointly taught a seminar on complex organization in the early 1980s
and we considered together writing a book such as this one.

reproducing social organization. Cuttings, as a result, follow a complex interactive pattern between dual authorities, as well as vis-à-vis operative units. In Padgett's words from the last of his series of analyses, "Thus macro fiscal targets, derived on grounds having little to do with detailed programmatic priorities, tip the lower-level bureaucratic politics 'balance of power' between organizations and among institutional levels" (1981, p. 121).

It is the OMB which can be likened to a semi-periphery, as between presidency and operational departments, as well as being in dual hierarchy as seen from lower units.

Padgett's approach was to model, from the grounding of actual program cuts and additions, for individual programs. He traced through the detailed archives of budget changes, both within the departments and the OMB. The departments and the OMB can be seen together as the dual hierarchy of authority through which a presidential elite exerts control pressure downward.

Padgett's key was to follow each single cut and confrontation in a series for a given unit program. It is this grounding that permits us to analyze even such a huge system as a congeries of interfaces which has evolved into an institution. The Federal budgetary process brings together into a common concrete organization an enormous variety of role frames with their story-sets and story lines.

Padgett's Stochastic Model

There are two radically different processes at work in shaping the huge accretion of requests into a budget, according to Padgett's model. One is serial judgment, in which program authorities and departmental superiors both consider, in turn, various substantive bases for cutting, or enlarging, a program request. The other is selective attention, in which the dual hierarchy chooses what individual program requests, at what stage in serial judgment, to examine for pruning or drastic cuts. This strategic program of cuts is the key part of shaping the total, as well as the profile, of programs, and later of whole departmental budgets, to a policy. The policy may or may not realize ostensible presidential goals, depending on competence and attention balances (Padgett 1980b).

Padgett successfully models the first process by negative exponential distributions. Here averages reflect degree of process controllability allowed by "the environment." The immediate conduits expressing the environment are legal and like constraints from Congress (a tertiary hierarchy).

Sequential attention, the second process, is deciding when serial judgment is to be invoked. Padgett models it as the columns of cuts, within a matrix of cuts by programs, which sum over time into a Poisson distribution of cuts for programs. The Poisson is the form into which cumulate the constituent distributions, each separately of negative exponential form. These are commit interfaces, the disciplines where it is the shapes that determine the processes, with the means reflecting accidents of environment.

An institution is not inconsistent with gaming and manipulation, but on the contrary builds on and presupposes them. Each stochastic process in Padgett's model also can be seen as modeling a tangible series of perceptions, and of gamed counter perceptions. The perceptions are socially constructed ones generated by disciplines. While at the unit program level the disciplines are interfaces, at the departmental level they appear to be mobilize disciplines, and at that level also the OMB dual hierarchy disciplines are select arenas.

Padgett's search for the distributional form that accommodates the observed distributions of cuts is thus a search for the generative principle of the process. The stochastic process is a mapping of very complex and various perception formations into an outcome that balances different control effects in the guise of different sources of uncertainty. Padgett brings it all together into a striking new insight into the process.

His principal finding is that there are, indeed there must be, occasional catastrophic budget cuts, including dissolutions of programs, because of the ways in which the dialectic of control with reproduction is structured within this institution. The programs, even at the finest recognized gradation, are themselves rhetoric devices in terms of which to recognize events and identities. An institution is a self-reproducing balance of control efforts from perspectives which are not mutually comparable with each other much less other institutions. A control process which cuts across and reaches into disparate institutions must generate occasional jagged, erratic cuts.

Most program units are incrementalist in their initial requests. At an even further disaggregation into locales, these requests, innocuous at the national scope with which Padgett's model starts, may prove to be generated variously in select or mobilize disciplines. Further control would require further decoupling, as is well realized by congressmen and other program supporters who devise couplings and imbeddings, as in the "entitlement" provisions. This is especially apparent when it comes to successive exposures to cuts, and, given an exposure, the considerations of how much cut to make on that particular go-round. Programs not coupled into other programs are the prime turf for cutting by a strategy which is openly independent of programmatic considerations, which is a second-order fiscal strategy.

Comparing Budget Stories

The conventional *ex post* story about budgets usually has concerned aggregation, which, until Padgett, was the apparently logical and unavoidable way to construe the shaping of budgets. Padgett's model, in contrast, operationalizes control problems from a self-similar theory, the point of view of middle-range order: According to it, results are more a matter of horizontal essays at agency, and at decoupling programs from their ostensible aggregate housings.

Embedding to a higher level, of new identities functioning in a different network of refashioned identities, can occur without any substantive aggregation whatever. And conversely, formal aggregation into larger partitions need have no impact on level of operation, on being perceived and perceiving in terms of more sophistication. Program units never touched by fights and confusions may have no standing whatever, no identities to generate bases and directions of action. Identities rear out of frictions along networks of productions and events whether or not these are being shaped by disciplines.

Putting together disciplines into some stratification process is building a tower of Babel. From an external observer's viewpoint, generality can be obtained only by a framework loose and flexible enough to accommodate concatenations of partly consistent schemes. Padgett's stochastic model of U.S. Federal Budget construction can be seen as an apt description. This stochastic model makes sense for observers of what is going on when numerous and diverse disciplines are competing and being put together into unified streams of claimants for flows of resources.

The other school of budget models (Wildavsky 1975) has urged that only the outside envelope of budgets be examined. From the incremental changes thus attended to they argue that inertia is the main "dynamic" in the accommodation of disparate organization units, the accommodation that is the substance of budgeting. No stochastic elements need be introduced.

But Padgett has demonstrated very much better fits from his models. They are in the spirit of Tuck's (earlier in chapter, p. 178). His models also conform better to the accounts of participants, and furthermore they provide bases for predicting secular changes. Above all, Padgett's models predict occasional dramatic shifts in allocations, which indeed are the crux of the real historical process observed.

Another model parallel to Padgett's, but for the private business economy, can be found in Burt (1983). Unlike Padgett, Burt did not have access to inside documents, here documents for sequences of market share and profits across industries and firms. So Burt infers dependencies and contingencies from a black-box analysis which predicts to the variation across firms and industries in rates of return. It bases these predictions upon measures of the range of alternatives in sourcing and the range in selling. These ranges can be construed as measures of feasible decoupling and therefore of likely control and autonomy.

One could draw a stochastic analogue for industry to Padgett's analysis. Congress and the other government presences operate so disjointly that the parallel to government from market economy may be worth drawing. Padgett's and Burt's aggregation paradoxes are solved at about the same scale, in government and business, respectively.[26]

Annealing

Successive waves of reform as strategy, as in the preceding examples, can be reinterpreted not as some detailed scheme of rational action predictable in its course, but rather as annealing, intentional but indirect and opportunistic. Annealing is a term from metallurgy. To anneal is to heat and thus shake up the mineral insides, hard but more or less at random, and then to cool and encourage resumption of normality with attendant hopes that the new formation will have more desirable properties. A mineral is a complicated mess with crystal bits and gels twisted together in historically unique configurations. Social formations of institutions, classes, and the like seem analogous.

Temperatures of colonialism suggest annealing when they rise high. Popular rebellion is another prototype for annealing, one which can be accomplished in many forms. Annealing need not always depend upon privileged location for its instigators. Annealing is an important prototype for gaining control to get action. Annealing disrupted is countercontrol and blocking action.

Envelopes from contingencies describe the effective boundaries of a social mineral. Such population envelopes (chapter 5) decouple, passively or via explicit perception, which is the reason these envelopes can trigger and be used in action projects. This is getting action

---

[26] Both are much smaller than Wallerstein's world system (1974, 1980), which encompasses both governments and economies, but there is some parallelism. One can argue that the OMB of Washington, D.C., is the analogue to semi-periphery, that is, to nations in the world system which factor between core economies and the huge peripheral regions (Wallerstein 1980, chap. 6; Nolan 1983), a classic example being Schwartzman's Portugal (1989).

conceived on a population base, rather than control concerned with disciplines, identities, and embedding. Such action cannot be targeted or focused as implied by the usual connotations of the term control in ordinary discourse. Annealing is the proper metaphor for action attempts on a population basis (Leifer and White 1988), for such generalized control.

In social as in metallurgical settings, annealing may need to be repeated a wearying number of times for substantial improvements to show up out of the throw of the dice. The social agency is not as cut-and-dried as heating: it may be media floods of information, or inflationary fiscal flows, or a new cohort, or a split in an existing age grade (cf. studies of the Galla: Prins 1953). The social analogue of heating is not singular, but in any form must, like heating, consume some resources and requires some coupling to other larger populations.

Cooling down may be less automatic in the social case. The distinctive fact of social organization is that, at any level and scope of population, there can be independent control attempts not predictable from routine analysis. Conjecture that it is easier to smother such other projects in an increased level of activity than it is to dampen them once freshly exacerbated. Social annealing is less controllable than the metallurgical variety, itself notoriously unreliable without extensive repetition. Agency is therefore more problematic and important in the social analogue of annealing. The annealing metaphor should be restricted to where the agency concerns population rather than disciplines and the like.

A principal agent for annealing action may be surrounded by an entourage. The entourage are the hangers-on who account for viscosity in flows of control action, which serves to cool down much more reliably than to activate the principal. Hull (1982) details the development of such an entourage around Kaiser Wilhelm. It obfuscated but did not suppress his erraticness which short-circuited attempts at control that might have aborted World War I. There have been parallel accounts of a Hitler entourage.

Institutions Mate to Change

Hardest to verify is annealing on the largest scale. Gorbachev's actions in the USSR through 1988 were analyzed earlier. One cannot tell yet (1990) whether Gorbachev will in the end prove to be an annealer—perhaps not by choice but by the exigencies of his situation. *Ex ante* coding is difficult.

Changing or shifting some institution is the weightiest kind of task for annealers. The specific conjecture to be explored is that a new institution requires an intermediate period of overlay and melding between preexisting institutions, followed by rejection as they become separate again, possibly leaving a newborn institution. Short of enormously detailed surveys, or a rare revolutionary period, it is hard to measure some institution such as caste with enough conviction to be sure about the when and what of a change. One needs a study with explicit reports of intent for annealing. And it makes sense to look for some cultural product in a visible interpretive genre, to use as a signature for the institution.

Ennis (1992) has supplied an enormously detailed and persuasive account of the breaking through of what he calls Rock 'n' Roll music as a seventh wave within the genre of American popular music. The first six waves fall into two groups: three smaller, deeper, and purer source streams (jazz, gospel, and folk) and three larger commercialized popular genres (country, black, and mainline pop). Each of these also has several synonyms, variants, and historical tracks. As they become well established, styles such as these each come to be the signature of an institution (H. Becker 1982; Hirsch 1972; Peterson 1976).

One can discriminate for each style of song a distinct complex of production together with audience, distribution, and critic. The complexes vary in how much they tie to broadcasting, to records, and to live performances, and as to commercial versus nonprofit sponsorship. The principal split is between the first three and the last three, but Ennis can make a case for a separate institution for each of the six.

To qualify as annealing there must be evidence about intentional agency. The evidence is extensive and clear in Ennis's case. Among the many important (musical) "agents" per se there were one or two disc jockeys who proved to have great insight.

Rock 'n' Roll Story

Rock was a scene of "reaching up" to get action, in many different respects at once. Rarely have so many streams of critical discourse, tutored or not, popular or not, agreed so emphatically as to the lack of value of an innovation! In part this was because rock music evolved out of resonances with the concerns of a depressed minority, adolescent youth.

Ennis tracks how the initial songs of what in hindsight is a new style struggled into limited acceptance. One key was new technology that permitted much more audience differentiation, and tapped newfound purchasing power of adolescents in the mid-nineteen-fifties. Another key was the generation of a looser kind of local circle of performances that supplied enough base for new technical resources, with which novel items could be broadcast without gatekeeping by established centers.

Intelligent and conscious maneuvering was there, from agents and disc jockeys marginal to the existing circles of self-supporting professionals in administration (agentry) as well as production and performance. But the key was spontaneous pickups crossing one stream of popular music into another, without necessarily leaving imprint on the established lists of top sellers. Only this endless crosscutting, protected by obscurity, between different streams brought enough artistic resources to bear to sustain a new form which by the nature of its audience had scope of motifs more limited than usual.

The maneuverings were reachings-up into established—and highly irritated—scopes of distribution and critique. New social forms were created. Local circuits of dispersed small clubs sustaining local stations of radio were sufficient to sustain existing separate streams and generate trial crossbreeds (of which rock 'n' roll was but one). But the seventh wave would have subsided unless producers reached-up into the broadcast network level of a Tin Pan Alley, and unless the creators of seventh-wave music brought new musical resources to bear to make the limited substantive content of lyrics less limiting.

The evolution of rock 'n' roll was a paradigm of searching by structural-equivalence. From the beginning it generalized across styles, it self-consciously cut across boundaries, including the basic black-white split of American popular culture. A new sense of stratification came into play; adolescents for the first time asserted a standing, even a preeminence on important perception dimensions.

The Lemma

Ennis's dissection supports a lemma: a major new style can be created in a two-step process. First, some two (or more) of the existing styles must be mobilized through the institutions producing them into an intensive program of hybrid examples, which are from a temporarily hybrid institution. This implies merging social carriers (creators, performers, critics, and the like) who are previously mutually specialized. Second, the reaction to the melding and to the new direction must become so intense as to cauterize the initial mixture.

That is, the initially separate institutions again fall apart. This can leave the incipient new wave to sustain itself—or fail—as a separate style and institution.

This is a lemma worth exploring in other cultural venues. An earlier study of change of institution in the French painting world, from Academy machine to dealer-critic system (White and White 1965), fits the Ennis paradigm well. There a single person, Durand-Ruel, who created a new sort of dealer role, was essential. Durand-Ruel had the exploratory and experimental approach of an annealer. Baxandall (1980) traces a major impetus to German sculpture in the early Renaissance, in which a new high style went hand in hand with the emergence of a new crossbreed of previous commercial and guild institutions. He traces lines compatible with the lemma, though across a dispersed field of small cities rather than for a primate ecology like that of French culture.

Many significant changes, called advances, in science appear to follow the Ennis paradigm of change. The annealing agents here are conscious of their agency and indeed insistent on credit (but see Merton 1985). The Ennis lemma appears to be a useful specification of Kuhn's argument (1970) about paradigm shift in science.

The great treatise by Spencer and Gillen (1903) on cultural-social evolution among a swathe of Aborigine tribes (at a period before their disintegration) also can be parsed in much the same way as Ennis dissects change in the pop music world. The populations respectively involved are even comparable in size and in focus on artistic aspects of life. Early developments of Christianity as a missionary, yet rooted, gospel within our own civilization can also be modeled similarly (White 1991a), and indeed on at least two levels: A newly invented Judaism overlaid for a while with nascent Christianity in its Jerusalem mode (Segal 1986), and a Pauline missionary church and theology struggled across the Roman imperium with the Jerusalem mode (von Campenhausen 1969; Dix 1949). The Catholic Church was the new institution resulting, and the religion of the Church Fathers was the new style.

Institutions, associated genres, and their possible changes come in many scales. The Puritan strand of English history, without which the United States would not have come to be, provides two contrasting examples. Both are of abortive changes. Both examples are from periods which are neither too familiar nor too remote in idiom to be accessible.

Here is one assessment: "History, indeed, has a further warning for the advocates of the 'historic episcopate' divorced from 'theories' as an administrative solution of troublesome dogmatic differences. . . . The treatment of the Puritans by the English episcopate from the reign of Elizabeth onwards must be sorrowfully admitted to have been as stupid as it was Erastian and wicked, whatever the provocation of factiousness on the other side" (Dix 1946, pp. 302–5).

Here is an assessment of a related struggle across the Atlantic:

> In *The Anglican Episcopate*, Professor Cross concerned himself with the history of an abortive institution and with a detailed analysis of the pamphlet literature for and against American bishops . . . [subsequent discoveries] now enable us to describe the backstage maneuvers of individuals and organizations, which were unknown to Arthur Cross. . . . This contest was, in truth, far more than the customary religious strife: it was a *Kulturkampf* between the dissenting bodies—already well entrenched in New England . . . —and the Church of England—few in numbers, new, aspiring, and contriving. The Anglicans aimed at nothing less than the complete reordering of American Society . . . in a great struggle for power which ceased only with American independence. For eighty-five years. (Bridenbaugh 1962, pp. ix, xix)

Here we see the same riddle about the relations of control to institution and style. The two cases are nicely converse as to churchly dominance, despite sharing exactly the same clash of styles. Neither exhibits accomplished change, and yet both fit the preconditions of the lemma. Change can come only through effective superposition, followed by hostility of each toward their cross product, which may but need not then spin off as separate. There was no effective annealing here.

SEVEN

RHETORIC AND THEORY

ACTION AND ORGANIZATION each derives from identity and control. Yet each also presupposes while counteracting the other. Thus the apt phrase is a conundrum: action versus organization. Melding action and organization should be the focus for a conclusion. This melding for the observer requires theory, as it does also for participants. But rhetoric is the older and more basic term which describes theory in action, theory for participants.

Two myths, I have argued, characterize rhetoric of social organization. One is the myth of the person as free-standing entity. The other is the myth of society as an embracing whole. Both myths permeate our culture, and to this day they still permeate our social science.

Effective theory of social relations is hindered by the presupposition that social action comes exclusively from particular biological creatures who yet, somehow, also are distinctive human personalities. I argue that social action instead comes out of all sorts of identities triggered initially by chance and mismatch. Accompanying the myth of the person is the rhetoric of rationality. This book instead pursues the implications of recognizing that identities—and thus social action—are being generated in contingent disruptions, in search of control.

Accompanying the myth of society is the story of social order. The worry this master story expresses is, how does it all fit together? How does it couple? But the real puzzle is the opposite: how is any flexibility kept in a field of social plumbing, among institutions and styles—how does decoupling come about? How do you get action?

Getting action dominates contemplation. The previous chapter explored approaches to getting action, within the complex polymer goo that is social organization, over and beyond the schema of routines that support and obscure all social organization. The present chapter points to dilemmas of reflexivity that are peculiar to any theorizing of social action, and examines how they may inhibit getting action. Getting action, like building theory, both go further when they take myth and all its progeny obfuscations into account, and even into use.

The next section places social science theories as rhetorics among other rhetorics. Rationality is then singled out for special attention for its scientific as well as its rhetorical importance. Then we contrast historians' insights with those derived from natural science approaches, in an abstract perspective of space and system.

Rhetorics and Systems

The task which rhetorics confront is daunting.[1] There is nothing neat about social organization. Building and maintaining word-scaffoldings for use around the messy actual social constructions is not easy. The scaffoldings themselves settle into further structure beyond just the story lines and story-sets of earlier chapters. Rhetorics are such further structure.

Social action tends to build into a self-similar system, to the extent there is system at all in social messes. There may be differences among levels in some sense, but there is no proper basis for defining crisply distinct levels. Much of our high culture does its best, however, to impose just such distinct levels, partly by imposing coherence within levels. Social science contributes.

The favored rhetoric of social science is system. System can reflect either or both the everyday phenomenology of a Goffman (1967) and the millennial phenomenology of a Gottwald (1979). System can only exist, if it does, because of decoupling, and then it can be analyzed using the calculus of uncertainty which applies between social and cultural aspects of populations, whose dynamics are self-similar across levels. System as perceived is expressed in rhetoric.

Micro and macro are familiar current examples of putative levels that tend to be reified in social science. Unbundling of relations is called for by rhetorics (e.g., Eccles and Crane 1988), and indeed natives use networks in their rhetorics. How these rhetorics operate can be calculated by factoring networks reporting actual complex and historical ties into several analytically distinct types of ties. That is what blockmodel algebras attempt (cf. chapter 3 and Romo 1992). Both independences and fits between rhetorics and networks are thereby captured, for a given set of identities.

Current world-system analysis in social science (Wallerstein 1974, 1980) pushes the macro level to an extreme. It is not a new extreme, on the contrary, its interest resides in its being but a relabeling and modernization of the Thomist worldview of orthodox Catholicism.

---

[1] For a recent commentary upon and elucidation of the term rhetoric along with related terms of discourse, evaluation, and interpretation see Lentricchia and McLaughlin (1990); an older version is Barnet, Merman, and Burto (1960). From the social sciences, Schanck and Abelson (1977) provide one scheme of representation.

Social science parallels metaphysics. Neuropsychology (Nadel et al. 1989), on the other end, carries the micro level to an extreme.

The real crux for analysis by system constructs in social science are the messy intermediate regions where it is hard to project crisp levels in rhetoric. There are a few prototypes, such as Thompson (1963) on formal organization as system. That, like micro and macro levels, gains plausibility only from kinship to lay constructs. These latter underwrite the valuations that help embed decouplings to enable fresh action in otherwise overdetermined systems.

Levels build up as social actors—whether personal actors or other identities—in turn become perceived as mere constituent nodes in larger formations. Each actor and network is defined by and helps shape still larger social settings, many of which have taken on identities of their own and directly figure in control efforts. As struggles for control across nested scopes reproduce themselves, institutional systems can be discerned. An institutional system, in combining institution with style, articulates different valuations into specific organization: System then combines style with institution as a rhetoric which contrasts with boundary.

System should be a protean term. System permeates configurations of process and structure, so that it is recognizable even when not articulated. System embraces social, cultural, and ecological; it is reflected in persons and in war alliances, and as well in the games of children (Opie and Opie 1969). Systems express the degrees to which, and the ways in which, different scopes and levels of social action and structure can be perceived as compatible. Systems reflect matters of planning or control, but the reflection is as net impacts from the astronomical numbers of combinations that co-occur between different levels of social organization. System is indeed protean if real, and could be expected to generate some powerful interpretive accounting. It could be that there is indeed an accounting of system, as a rhetoric for culture, without analysts being independently able to establish any reality for such system.

Culture as Basis for Social Science

There is also what can be called a snakeskin view of culture. In this view social formation must at any given time have a carapace which, however, is outgrown and drops off as a new one comes into place. Antiquarians, aesthetes, dictionarians, and university librarians all cherish and collect the snakeskins. But surely a culture should be seen as a continuously interacting population of interpretive forms articulated within some social formation.

In Swidler's terms (1986), culture is made up of practices. One can view culture as the interpretive contexts for all social actions so that it can be computed as an envelope from them, as well as shaped by them. Effective practices have evolved which thus precede, preface, and anticipate social sciences.

Kinship was the first social science. All the paradoxes and difficulties are there, in various peoples' own native constructions (cf. e.g., Blackwell 1927; Spencer and Gillen 1904) of their kinship edifices, constructions in formats that mix observation with analysis and with proclamation. Only a few of these formats have proved able to sustain and reproduce themselves. This first science was lost for a while. Its phenomena are too close and too involving to encourage recognition of abstract similarities in cultural content. Lewis Henry Morgan (re)discovered kinship;[2] it may well be the only preexisting and discoverable social science.

Social scientists today may see challenges to their authority from ordinary persons, but only with respect to the phenomenology of everyday life, which most social scientists would concede to them anyway. Yet even this can confound and obfuscate research. "Networks" are the outstanding example today. Ambitious MBAS, upwardly mobile yuppies, executives, social workers, journalists, all agree on the importance of networks. Since sources this diverse all urge the advantages of "networking" as social process, the term must confound many interpretations, and thus it confounds much social science fieldwork attempting to use network terms and concepts.

But, one may object, these lay persons are mere mechanics, clinicians rather than professionals; so their joint endeavors surely cannot be confounding codified scientific results as to more recondite aspects of social organization. Since the laity are no status threat, surely they cannot be besting scientists! However, the "laity" includes the jurists, bankers, all sorts of groups and persons preeminent over social scientists within existing social stratification. And sometimes, perhaps, the preeminence is because their professions' and professional insights are superior, especially for the aspects in which they specialize, whether or not a parallel specialty science, a political science, a sociology, or an economics, is split off.

Whatever the outcome of any such particular argument, the very discussion concedes the basic point, since the discussion is, literally, in lay terms. The language of the present work embeds, and makes as invisible as they are effectual, an enormous array of assumptions

---

[2] Consult Trautman (1987) for a recent history.

about social action. Social science is impregnated with existing culture.

Actual social orders and cultures are much messier and more interesting than are particular rhetorics, or embeddings of rhetorics into utopian schematics. But even utopian schematics do capture aspects of how actors try to perceive their social context, and these schematics do so across a wide range of historical contexts. Berman has argued (1983) an extreme form of this view, in his sweeping canvas of the evolution of legal systems for the whole Western era since the emergence of the Papacy. The point is that continual reshaping of meanings to maintain semblance of coherence in social action requires explicit and reliable interconnections between the framing of sets of stories and the structure of institution. It is these mappings that make rhetoric possible.

Conscious and proclaimed cultures are sets of rhetorics that encapsulate attempts, often inept, at regularizing social spaces from the perspectives of different populations and institutions. Hegemony (Williams 1977; Keohane 1984) reflects the success of a family of such attempts which exhibits some coordination and expertise in an autochthonous theory. A stochastic mode of perception, analysis, and reality is so omnipresent now just because of the feebleness of the hold of culture on the patchy social realities erecting and reerecting themselves upon continuing biosocial realities. Hegemony nonetheless testifies to the importance of some order being imposed: the transposable order that is supplied by basis sets of story lines which can account for whatever happens. Social science theories are recent attempts at hegemony.

A task of social science is to construe boundaries and environments. All analytical sciences work from boundaries: boundary conditions are preeminent. Social analysis is peculiar only in that it must seek out the generation of its own spaces as part of the environment. Since the spaces are plural—and irregular, temporary, and ill-connected to boot—the boundaries are difficult to find, subtler than in other sciences.

Completion of the task requires systematic measurement and modeling, both of which may be confounded by existing local insights of elites and professionals. There is a tension between the stories produced and ties counted by a social formation and the analytic technique believed by the analyst. Padgett and Ansell put the conundrum well:

> For the case of the Medici at least, behavioral "reality" was quite at variance with clear contemporary cultural self-understandings. . . . Now

our general position on the interrelation of social attributes and social networks can be clarified. Obviously (contra some occasionally over-stated polemics by network afficionados), we do not believe that social attributes are irrelevant: The particular way in which the Medici recombined social attributes through networks is the heart of the story here. What we object to is the arraying of them discretely as groups or spatially as grids. . . . Of course actors in the system, as well as researchers, do exactly these procedures mentally when they analyze their own social structure; this is what "boundedly rational" cognitive classifications are all about. But there is a widely underappreciated gap between these macro cognitive (or "cultural") operations and micro-behavioral "local action," taken by concrete individuals in very particular, heterogeneous and often cross-pressured circumstances. Simplifying social reality into homogeneous subsets "with common interests" rips individuals out of their (often contradictory) multiple network contexts and obscures the very heterogeneity and complexity that organizations like the Medici party are constructed out of. (1989, p. 1 and p. 33 n. 45)

The hardest task will be to unravel the constitutions of the numerous social times which exist. This requires overcoming the lingering astrology in our thinking which leads us to merely consult watches, or centuries, to infer social order.[3] Only Marxism among classical strands of theory has a central role for problematics and dynamics of time and thence of development in the large. And only Pareto among classic theorists has a central role for attempts at control which go beyond discipline and social routine, and so turn on timing.

Most early theorists were not able to convert sketches and conjectures on social organization into operational measure and theory. There were heroic attempts, from Marx through Ricardo (consult Morishima 1973, 1989) and on through Sorokin (1927), as well as some measures and models still current, mainly of Pareto (1966). Further steps in this direction are timely, steps which presuppose not only these earlier contributions but also the enormously expanded range of measurement, of mathematics, and of analogy from natural sciences, which are available today.[4] It is especially impor-

---

[3] It is a vain presupposition that the watches on our wrists give us "the" time which orders social life in some self-evident way. There are leads in Abbott (1983, 1984).

[4] Some possibilities for models are suggested in Appendix 2. Modern analytic and quantitative techniques can be applied both to existing native accountings and to data freshly garnered. These techniques can yield answers to questions and support for conjectures, such as the examples below, but explicit formal models will be called for. One can use stochastic processes, for example, to model bruises from ties as triggers of identities. Combinatorial and stochastic analyses also can model the cognitive proc-

tant to operationalize the terms which have been heretofore primitive, mythical, and invisible, such as society and person. Burt in a work (1992a) quoted in chapter 5, has shown the many payoffs from full operationalization, there in a software package (Burt 1991).

Evolution of Rhetorics

Inequalities commonly are by-products of getting action, and thus of the elaborate structures associated with blocking action. Rhetorics emerge along with stratification. Social class is where valuations from molecular disciplines come together with networks of stories into larger, compelling formations of stochastic order, with rhetorics as their by-products.

Planned repartition of rights and duties does invoke and induce inequalities. But planned inequalities are never as large as inequalities that emerge as unplanned by-products. Inequalities are largest just at the disjunctions between social formations. These occur in liminal zones (Turner 1969, 1974) and marginal areas with the least elaborated culture. This explains why it is so very hard to shift inequalities and the rhetorics associated with them.

One can also view native rhetorics as explicit articulations among concepts for use in control, articulations which correlate styles with institutions. Rhetoric goes with a network of institutions so that thetoric, unlike its concrete messages, is not easy to change. A rhetoric is a robust abstraction from linguistic practices generated by the intersection of style together with institution as tendencies in networking networks of disciplines. Social sciences have emerged partly in this tradition of rhetorics.

It matters a good deal whether the extrapolation to perceived order is down from higher or upward from lower levels of embedding. Vichniac (1985), for example, draws an elegant contrast between British and French (metalworker) unions based on the respective realities perceived by lower and by higher level officialdom and the resulting mismatch at any particular level. A classic rhetoric is the exclusive use of individualist and dyadic concepts by people-changing organizations when their effectiveness depends essentially on the extreme wholism of a total institution (cf. e.g., Street, Vinter, and Perrow 1966, p. 73).

Rules of thumb are a primitive rhetoric. Ethnic minorities tend to be at a disadvantage in blocking action, but they can be at an advan-

---

esses implicated in the generation of stories. Citations to examples of computations have been woven into the text.

tage in getting action because their ties do not connect as densely into central groups. Thus ethnic groups may be less credulous of standard rules of thumb, which are transmitted along traditional strings.

Rules of thumb (Simon 1945) come in packages, a simple form of the multiple stories that accompany embeddings of values. But rules of thumb are very widely transposable across concrete social contexts and across role frames of interpretation. Rules of thumb applied *here* affect the application of rules of thumb *there*, or their application here at other times. It is not an accident that rules of thumb are transmitted and vouched for along strings of interconnection. Rules of thumb have the property that they are unlikely to generate events; thus they keep simpler the field of identities being rationalized.

Formation of rhetorics out of joint perceptions, and conversely, thus has an evolutionary logic. Objectively odd but strongly held beliefs can result. For example, there is a strong prejudice against venality in our society. This seems an accidental by-product of evolutionary course, a still feudal assessment. Venality simply states that there is a payment flow to an actor in some discipline or more complex social formation, which is not calibrated to participation in that formation. Bribe is certainly a case but it is only a special case. Any salary is to some approximation an example of venality, with only the details varying, say between a research professor's salary for "teaching" and a general executive's salary for "planning."

Corruption and venality also take on social forms not keyed to market systems (Mousnier 1971; Swart 1949). They epitomize style, and at the same time characterize institution in a more abstracted form, as rhetoric. Then they are a solution to the search for decoupling from social embeddings. The stigma attached to them is to be expected, since their basis is exactly interference with accepted functioning of social embeddings. When Stone's Tudor magnates exhibit obsession with corruption and venality (1965, pp. 296–97), this sudden perception reflects their heightened attention to their own new forms of decoupling in an era of rapid change, and their alertness to others' cognate attempts; certainly this perception is not due to any novelty of actual violation of the codes of honesty which are so hazily intertwined with embedded systems. Such styles are interpretive duals to concrete middle-range orders.

Any of the general forms of explanation—stories or pragmatics or types of tie and story lines—comes about through evolution. Evolution always will occur among packages which each contain multiple versions. There is some fit to what happened, but what happened also is subject to contingency and also to control manipulations. What has eventuated are sets which can account after the fact for whatever happens. The set for identities was termed a convention earlier; rhetorics is the general term for sets of such sets of explanations. In both vertical dramas and horizontal gossip-stories, actors come to condense out just a particular aspect of total ties as being a relation of a given sort, say friendship on animosity. Often a means-ends schema underlies the particular rhetoric and this schema requires distinct types of ties to go with the calculus of motives. Kinds of network ties are prominent in Riggs's account of Thailand quoted earlier.

Particular meanings themselves move and are confirmed along personal ties (Granovetter 1973, 1982). Meanings are a vehicle in which control initiatives are turned into blocking action. "Standards being maintained" is the theme song for blocking action. Standards select which stories to apply to concrete situations. Attention is attracted to the story contents, but application as meaning is via ties.

The values that are at play within an institution need not cause what is happening, but the package of values are a medium sufficient for accounting what happens, if taken together with style to form a rhetoric. Actions may be erratic and zany under the usual pressures of contingency and chance from physical as well as social context, as well as by the flukes of maneuver for advantage. But the rhetoric that accounts those actions, by invoking a fixed set of values and institutional arrangement thereof, induces perception of regularity: that is its chief attribute, which supposes some mapping from rhetoric to underlying system.

From Status into Contract?

Social science is shaped conceptually as well as practically by its social organization. This past half-century has been dominated by social science from American universities, whose social organization has been laid out in some detail in the first section of chapter 4 as being a variant of corporatism. Anachronisms result from this shaping, in particular a preoccupation with values that is native to corporatist institution. Structuralism in the work of Talcott Parsons, a master of American academe, is a notable exemplification.

Structuralism in most of its varieties is set over against economic theory because structuralism dissolves the person (Culler 1975, p. 28), but economic theory is merely a variant of structuralism, a variant which is not clear-sighted enough to perceive its own dissolution of the acting person. Economic theory appears to emphasize persons, but in fact the person invoked is just an abstract construct, a bracketing.

Examine what structuralism has to say about a massive social phenomenon. Its story will turn out to dovetail with a rationalist argument, which I am claiming is really just an obverse or variant form of
structuralism. Concern with tangible social organization has so far
turned this book away from evolution-of-civilization perspectives
across centuries or millennia, the supposed big pictures. I have put
aside the *gemeinschaft* and *gesellschaft* of introductory texts. But my
focus on control suggests a critique of such macro-perspectives derived from classical theory.

Since at least Sir Henry Maine's *Ancient Law* (1861), a major theme
common across the social sciences has been modernization (cf. Inkeles 1991). This is just Maine's postulated universal evolution away
from status, which is conceived as nexus of reciprocal obligations
enmeshing all persons and actions in traditional bonds ultimately
derived from kinship, toward contract, which is conceived as free-
standing adults running around a cosmic beach playing some generalized tag in which coup is counted.[5] Inside each of Maine's adults is
presupposed an apparatus of preferences, together with a hidden
god enforcing the rules. As C. B. MacPherson has pointed out (1962),
this contract theory of possessive individualism was only believable
by, and so was contingent upon, the real social context of an emerging class. More precisely it was dependent, in the England of its genesis, upon the gentry as a fraction of a class unable to fully realize
itself as the dominant formation.

Accounting for the putative trend from status to contract was the
classical puzzle which, more than any other, generated sociological
theory. It was in part an argument about identity, its sources and
changes. Disentangling how order is created by competing agencies
of control can yield understanding both of identity formation at the
micro level and of macro-level trends. Generalization of identities is
necessary to both enterprises. Institution is one such generalization.
An institution generates identities in the course of integrating disparate frames onto the same population. In doing so it gains its own
identity.

Analogous puzzles have kept being posed at smaller scales, in less
global form and with the polarity interchanging. This is true since
Maine's time, but also earlier: see the cites from Steenstrup on early
Japan in the previous chapter. The classical status-to-contract argument has been brought down to middle-range scope in organization-

[5] The same issues bedevil evolutionary arguments about periods long predating our
modernization, as in the discussion of changes from moiety systems to cross-cousin
marriage (Homans and Schneider 1955; Needham 1962; White 1963). The issues are
ones of universal analysis as much as historical periodization.

versus-market arguments. Today in the economic realm the special form is "from hierarchy to market" (Williamson 1975), whereas a generation ago it was the reverse "from ownership to management" (Berle and Means 1933). In the political realm it used to be from political-machine to reform politics (Banfield and Wilson 1963), but now is from budget allocations to cash flows as governing controls (Kaplan 1982; Wildavsky 1975). But all such putative wholistic trends have ambiguous implications for identity, and they have proved to be mare's nests, both in empirical studies and in theory, from macroscale on down.

Exactly what Berle and Means (1933) proposed half a century ago was that there had been a turning back from the contract pole and toward stronger and stronger hierarchical formations within American big business. This institutional polarity, contract versus market, is reassessed by modern legal scholars also. They have done so for tangible embodiments within particular settings of law. In these reassessments, the polarity can get blurred: market converts partly into hierarchy, and status converts partly to contract: see for example Horwitz (1977) on nineteenth-century U.S. commercial law.

Macneil (1978) has reformulated the whole set of presuppositions about contract, in his relational theory of contract, by intertwining them with aspects of status reciprocities. So, at middle-range scope, some theorists are arguing that status and contract as concepts cannot be seen as unmixed poles; and others are arguing for contingency rather than unilinearity in movement between the two poles. Rational choice approaches deserve criticism exactly when they elide the decisive impact of context, which generates the very identities which rational choice takes as preset and unproblematic. But persons, and historical periods to boot, are reified by institutionalist grand theory, also.

Rationality

Work gets done. Decoupling, not rationality, is the prerequisite. The decouplings must take endlessly different specific forms and be endlessly repeated, because decouplings go in tension with solving social equations of relative arrangement. Each work group, each slash-and-burn settlement, each metalworker circle in a city, in short each production-setting inherits, each day and each generation, a strangling embedding in social arrangements computed on other grounds than work; each such inheritance must in some fashion be decoupled. Choice of one or another technical path of production is of subsidiary importance. Even choice of goals is secondary because illusory.

Ends and goals are a pattern of deposits from social process. Rationality comes into play only after this deposition. Ends appear exogenous, but instead of being a constraint on, they are a dependent part of the social process that is unfolding. In this sense, ends are endogenous. Yet it should be possible to allow for this. Proper structural theory should fold in but reinterpret rational choice. The kind of social formation must be uncovered, and this in turn should lead to prediction of the specific sort of means-end schema commonly used within that formation, as adapted to specific locales, and at specific points in social calendars. Rational choice does not drive social action, but neither is it epiphenomenal.

As causal guides, means-ends schema can lead afield, but the impetus to rational choice theory is natural in a scientific theory. Means-ends schema do accommodate to dynamics. Means-ends schema are at the root of calculi of motivation which at present supply almost the only systematic theory in social science (MacPherson 1962; Parsons 1937) that is also quantitative (Coleman 1990). And a convincing case can be made for the importance of these schemas in particular contexts, as, for example, Pocock (1975, p. 309) does concerning Italian Renaissance settings.

It is silly to treat rational choice theory as the basic or general theory of social organization. It is just as silly to carp at any particular approximations it uses, and then refer to the carping as an institutional theory. All theory is simplification; scientific theory simplifies so as to uncover new phenomena. Rational choice theory has suggested new phenomena and the present task is to determine contexts in which it is likely to be productive.

Contexts for Rationality

Rational choice theory as presently in vogue is modeled on neoclassical microeconomics (e.g., Mansfield 1968, 1975). It focuses on the "individual." But individuals come out of relations, out of skills in relations that are disdained by the theory. "You" and "I" and others are gotten together by, as much as we construct through social action, our contexts of practical production and control. The economist Kreps's (1988) hero Totrep (Trade-Off Talking Rational Economic Person) is a straw man.[6] Rational pursuits along means-ends chains

---

[6] Some versions of rational choice (e.g., Dahl and Lindblom 1953; Shubik 1984) are not so myopic.

remain important, but such pursuits are secondary to engenderment of ends.

A main goal or end of action is control, and control need not have explicit intermediate goals anymore than does some feedback control system in engineering (Bryson and Ho 1969; Leigh 1987). The history of some effort at control is all concerned with sequence in finding and sustaining leverage. Even long-term goals of much explicitness are inapt for control in social context, and at the extreme, say in a teenage hang-around context, control may not refer to any goals even indirectly, since means-ends schema may not capture any of the variation there.

Ends, and means-ends chains, are perfectly sensible constructs, but they are of only tactical help in uncovering social action: That is the practical objection to rational action theory and also to many other role theories. An actor's social existence comes to pass only through embeddings which specify ends as well as support identity, embeddings which are matters of friction and mismatch rather than of induction into roles. Rationality should be seen primarily as a by-product from reading larger-scale patterns.

The real danger is that means-ends schema stand in the way of proper observation by social scientists, the more particularly because these schema have trained our perceptions of existence. To use goal and means as a guide to observation and analysis is to mislead one-self, to turn away from the sources of action toward by-products of the glossing, the explaining away which is natural to social process. Explicit ends may be built up, with difficulty, together with means, out of stray materials to hand, but they may just as well be bypassed, with meanings coming from colorings of action by stories. And among the identities rubbed up from mismatched productions, events are as ineluctable as actors. Both goal and personality as con-cepts miss the central point. Not just degree of rational pursuit, or efficiency with respect to, but the independence and thus reality of goals in processes over time must be questioned. Similar strictures apply to concepts of means which also abstract from events.

Structuralism in the form of role theory takes embedding seri-ously. But structuralism treats embedding as decisive by itself in isolation, and so structuralism is misled through inattention to con-tingency. Structuralism is as much a danger to observation as is indi-vidualist rational choice. Embedding should not be confused with rhetoric, with wishes encapsulated as justice (Zajac 1985). One suc-ceeds or not, and now rather than then, according to position in con-crete context, and that is in part an aspect of embedding in identities as well as being a network matter.

Goals are the problem with rational choice theory. Not just degree of rational pursuit, or efficiency with respect to goals, but also the independence and thus reality of goals in themselves must be questioned. Ends are supplied stochastically by the shifting embeddings in which actors are caught up over time. These same embeddings also frame means-ends chains, which can be important in much the way presumed by rational-choice theorists, although more care is needed in specifying the dual embeddings in physical and social space. But such chains are limited in scope by their embedding; they show dependencies not causalities.

Rationality as Style

The significance of rationality is misapprehended. Rationality cannot be discarded as a concept, as an explanatory heuristic, any more than the reader and I can deny our quite sturdy identities as persons. Rationality follows in the train of identity. Pressure for control comes from identities, themselves triggered often by pressures from other identities.[7] Chance in the realm of work and practical production also triggers identities. Styles may emerge in complicated contexts that result, and it is exactly as such a style that rationality gains its relevance.

Begin with a critique of everyday epistemology for the personal relation. Courtesy, as Goffman long ago observed, grants to the other in an encounter some "face," which becomes a facade concealing disparities among fragments of identity. Many of these fragments get displayed in stories across locales of networks and ranges of disciplines. It is through grabbing hold of, and dropping, identities that stories come about to begin with, and it is through stories that identities can be connected into persons. The way in which courtesy grants face is through story-sets able to furnish explanations for any action and which thereby loosen constraints upon the actor. "Ends," "preferences," goals, and the like, as are found in one or another story, are thus partly afterthoughts, traces of manipulation and rationalization. Yet rationalization is a style and like any style is valuable to selves and observers in patching together action.

Rational choice is one preferred style today among us as natives. Theory of rational choice is also a style for us as theorists. In the previous section this theory was shown to complement the structuralist

---

[7] The tradition of experiments on self-justification contain elegant exemplifications of rationality following from identity: see the witty review by Weick (1968). And for revealing case studies at three different scopes see Allison (1971), Eccles (1981d), and Powell (1985).

theory of values, upon which instead critique might appropriately have focused forty years ago.[8] These theories are, respectively, micro and macro explanations which share in an underlying ontology of "spirits." If carried to an extreme as utilitarian and utopian explanations, respectively, each theory rests upon angels, that is, upon spirits both disembodied and independent.[9]

There is an absurdity here. To be interesting, rational choice theory should concentrate on possible new decisions, on change. But explicit goals or preference orderings, which are essential to the means-ends schema of rational choice, are appropriate and relevant only to entities which are inertial as well as isolate—angels, in short. The situation for the theorist is bewildering, which is just the context in which one expects styles to loom large, for native or theorist.

The central paradoxes in current social science concern rationality, person, and contract, all of which presuppose stratification and other stigmata of embeddings in a complex world. Similar paradoxes involve the structuralist conjecture. Above it was noted that both try to deny the independent reality—which is both enabling and constraining—of an indefinite number of intermediate levels of control. They also both bypass the reality of several different frames of interpretation and accountings. Rational choice theory needs revision so as to be able to accommodate varying styles to varying contexts.

[8] Comparison with alternative theories of social action helps prepare the ground for a new approach. Each theory tends to erode others. Rational choice theory erodes value theory in many forms. For a variety centered on culture (e.g., Swidler 1986), the erosion is assessed by Rieder (1990, p. 204) as follows: "Recasting moral values and rhetorics in terms of selection dilemmas does not entirely undermine the explanatory status of culture. But notions of repertoire and use, by diminishing culture as a constraint, tend in this direction. To the extent that culture is rendered malleable, its particular manifestation 'selected out' by situational contingencies and strategic purpose, it loses its coercive quality. Culture becomes a dependent variable, fickle and lambent, that changes in rhythm with the structural realities that impinge on it and the changing incentives and costs that accompany them." Much the same erosion follows from my approach.

[9] Both descend through the *philosophes* from medieval theology. In the words of Carl Becker (1932, pp. 30–31): ". . . at every turn the *Philosophes* betray their debt to medieval thought. . . . They dismantled heaven, somewhat prematurely it seems, since they retained their faith in the immortality of the soul . . . there is more of Christian philosophy in the writings of the *Philosophes* than has yet been dreamed of in our histories . . . the underlying preconceptions of eighteenth-century thought were still, allowance made for certain important alterations in the bias, essentially the same as those of the thirteenth century." I only wish Becker's judgment of us moderns was true for social science: "The rise of history and of science were but two results of a single impulse, two aspects of the trend of modern thought away from an overdone rationalization of the facts to a more careful and disinterested examination of the facts themselves."

Where, as in ties of romantic love, change and subtle calculation are all, the apparatus of preference orderings and "goals" seems mal-apropos, but style with rationality can be observed. Performance skill involves more subtle interactions than are entertained in the main traditions of rational choice theory (Coleman 1990), but it sub-sumes that turf too. Ties in such settings are of the nature of reso-nance modes within social echo-chambers among characters that call for and induce validations in a ritual of style. The temptation to by-pass rationality should be resisted even though it is subsidiary to meaning.

When rationality is seen as a style, it becomes more useful. Mac-neil is, appropriately enough for a law professor, judicious in his ap-proach to rational choice theory, which he has as being but one phase, or style, of an overall theory of exchange:

> Only the most aberrant social behavior, if that, ever appears altogether lacking in some element of exchange, direct or indirect, short-term or long-term. As many views of exchange and its nature exist as there are viewers, but two in the non-Marxist world stand out as apparent polar opposites. One is the utilitarian position that exchange enhances the individual utilities of the participants respecting the goods being ex-changed. The other is that certain patterns of exchange—categories of reciprocity—enhance social solidarity and *not* individual utility respect-ing the goods being exchanged, whereas other patterns enhance such individual utility and harm solidarity. . . . Man is both an entirely self-ish creature and an entirely social creature. . . . Man is, in the most fundamental sense of the word, irrational, and no amount of reason-ing, no matter how sophisticated, will produce a complete and consis-tent account of human behavior, customs or institutions.

Which all leads to a compromise solution: "Getting something back for something given neatly releases, or at least reduces, the tension . . . and solidarity—a belief in being able to depend on another—permits the projection of reciprocity through time" (Macneil 1986, p. 569). Macneil states the individualist objection to individualism: "in-dividualist" because this "solidarity" is like a taste or mood of indi-viduals.[10]

Few analysts are so foolish as to invoke a means-ends schema as universal. That would deny inconsistency and passion in intentional

---

[10] Some sociologists make this elision too: "If we know the categorical identities of the person that are relevant to his or her society we then, as W. Lloyd Warner often asserted, know all we need to know about the person as a member of the society" (Warriner 1981).

action.[11] But even if one conceded the universal use of means-ends schema, rational choice theory would be of limited validity. Action—what is to be explained about social formations—comes from ignorance and incoherence as much as from their opposites. Halevy writes: "The historian, that latecomer, is a fortunate man: he knows everything and does not waste his time on unwarranted apprehensions. His objective detachment distorts his accounts, for the riddles and unknown quantities of the moment are lacking" (1974, p. 36).

It is meaning, not rationality, that is the focus of most social organization. Identities are rafts cobbled together out of leftovers to face cross-tides of circumstance. Sustenance of identities requires comparability of and meaning between identities, so that meaning is the focus of insight for projects of control. The useful way to treat rationality is as but a special case of meaning, a case of limited scope. Meaning only comes into being as accommodation to patterns of social action which have been able to reproduce themselves. Meaning comes as a single structure only in an institution like corporatism.

History and Natural Science as Guides

History stands for what is unforeseen, which only therefore is of historical interest. So, paradoxically, history stands for action. Network can stand for the analytic and transposable approach of social science, and therefore network can also stand for social organization in general. Sociology needs to meld both into its foundations. Then action and organization separately, and thus action versus organization, can be derived from identity and control.

One can get only so far with the Simmelian soup of strangers that is often used for initial bracketing in both social science and everyday public life. This milieu is lacking in physical siting, as well as in the social siting which ultimately is a by-product of the physical. To trace the siting in detail sufficient for explanation is not feasible, usually. Even when it is, the natural sciences provide only partial guidance because observation has to allow for the perceptions shaping action and thus organization.

---

[11] Pareto (1935, 1966) is the preeminent expositor of the nonrational assessed alongside the rational or logical; for further development see Levy (1948).

Histories

Embedding and decoupling both are processes which fade and re-appear in perception, and which do so in terms of each other. Embedding and decoupling describe enactments and so are distinguishable from status and contract, which describe merely claims or reflections of enactments. They also apply for smaller scopes than classical theorists claim for status and contract. Embedding and decoupling assert a duality between interpretive and assertive moments, between ambiguity and ambage. On the one side, decoupling is the basis of size distributions and other profiles which can describe style, and without decoupling tangible social formation would be too rigid to reproduce as institution. On the other hand, without embedding there would not be the successive appearances of new actors and new sorts of actors.

History folds into itself assumptions about perception that are presumed to suit the time. History is the largest, most embracing rhetoric for accounting action, and as such it is the folk theory of embedding and decoupling, or rather of their results. Folk-theory is what stories grow into; myth is what values grow into. Both trace descent from mere disciplines: theory from ordering as it transmutes into story, while myth traces from valuation as it transmutes into value.

As folk theory of social action, history must concern ad hoc initiatives from entities generated unpredictably by social turbulence. The central paradox of action versus context is vastly extended by recursion, and social systems are self-similar only in part. Some sort of theory there can and must be, ordered perception and formulation that goes beyond descriptive particularity. But theory for social phenomena must express the congested, which is to say the erratic and the contingent.

History taken seriously concerns policies and their effects, so that it is especially concerned with what was observed. A policy is a preset pattern in counteractions to interactive contingencies.[12] Policies are often developed but only sometimes applied. Policy may enlarge control, but like all paths to control it may encourage blocking action. Policy is a rhetoric polished for and specialized to application.

Policies assume observation and they may subsequently be modified by observation. For actor, "observation" is a problematic con-

---

[12] Game theory develops a framework for and then explores the resulting perceptions and interactions (Peleg 1987; Shubik 1984). Game theory considers coalition formation, but in isolation from the matrix of ecological and social constraints.

cept. Policy analysis has the actor in scientific stance. There is no independent base for observation, no magical status for social scientist in ontology and epistemology. Observation is universal, it permeates social formations, it is built into the phenomenology generating social spaces and sustaining social formations. Solipsism intrudes when scientists speak of interviewing or empathizing or other observations as if by putting on white coats they can pull out of the social taffy. Solipsism bedevils strategy.

It becomes clear that history always comes as histories. Further, histories are but one kind of folk-theory, so that history, like policy, is a bracketing term for other ways of disciplining stories into sets. The most explicitly articulated exemplars of story-sets are in the law, and the use of story-sets is most clearly seen in legal systems built on precedent, so-called common-law systems. According to Llewellyn, a noted theorist and expositor of the American context for common law, "The doctrine of precedent is itself two-headed, providing one technique for narrowing an unwelcome precedent and another for expanding a welcome precedent." For Llewellyn, these contradictory techniques are *each* "correct," and, in fact, their coexistence is necessary for the viability of the case-law system. Furthermore, as Llewellyn argues in his brilliant discussion of concurring and dissenting opinions, there is leeway in deciding "what 'the' facts are" and how they are classified for purposes of legal analysis, with "each way of construing the facts containing a degree of violence to either the fact situation or the classifying category" (Llewellyn 1989, pp. xviff.).

Stories as Accounts

The accounts available, all too available, are the problem as well as the only basis for solving riddles of policy, as of history. Actors, persons or compounds, are embedded in seas of accounts and are generating accounts constantly. In observation, there are difficulties about coverage, recording, biases, and reliabilities, but these are ordinary difficulties of workmanship. The real problem is validity. Some even argue that there is no meaning among the accounts available from social formations, just because many participants are caught up in strategies.

Distortions by self-interest are but one niggle, one minor and modernist niggle, in the problem of observation. Frameworks for accounts are thrown up universally and diversely within social formations wherever observed. And there are multiple accounts, as has been emphasized from the first chapter. Leach (1945) is a particularly vivid parsing of this sad truth for would-be scientific observers.

New rhetorics have always accompanied joint creations of yet more complex social reality, including whole institutions, for which the rhetorics provide matrices of supple explanation. There is some rhetoric in each field of scholarship too, as a doctoral candidate facing comprehensive examinations should be able to testify. All these rhetorics are extraordinary languages which provide additional ways to conceal as they explain away social reality.

There is no such thing as pure behaviorist observation; observers cannot avoid dependence on "native" frames and accounts. The same is true of actors. And the accounts being in multiple frames merely shows recognition, even within institutions, that social action is sometimes strategic. It is naive to think that all strategic uncertainty is generated from identities confounding one another.

Participants are insisting upon accounting schemes consistent with the perspectives they variously bring. Each such scheme has some accountability, reports some piece of sense about what is going on. And each such scheme has to take some account of some of the others. One example, Axelrod's tracing of the Munich talks (see chapter 3, n. 18), can be generalized to the growth and furnishing of social spaces for political worlds more generally. Forment (1989b) has the right line in his talk of political discourse as rhetoric interacting with power to the effect of generating social spaces and times out of events and story lines. He has demonstrated how this comes about over centuries in a continent and for shorter periods in specific regions of a country.

Contexts in Natural Science

Analogues from natural science are instructive. Consider a phase transition: it could be in patterns of electric-dipole order, or in antiferromagnetism, but just take a liquid-to-solid transition (DeGennes 1979; Ma 1973; Ziman 1979). Temperature is important, analogous to how the larger context induces level of activity in a social example, and temperature calibrates level of order and disorder. But the existence of phases, here liquid (Gray and Gubbins 1984) and solid, is a statement that "order and disorder" as a congeries of local arrangements must be referred to a wholistic context. This wholistic context, or phase, has a direct and overwhelming bearing on the topology of order, indeed the phase is defined by the topology. This helps us rethink the status-to-contract arguments.

Transition from one phase, one wholistic context, to another is a radical disjunction which yet must take some tangible form of intermediate behavior. Only in the past few decades has there emerged cogent observation of this, and also modeling of the process as distinct from mere endpoint thermodynamics. The transition, although indeed typically narrowly bounded in terms of relevant parameters, is a system state of its own, in which physical space, which heretofore seemed all-determining, loses its absolutely sharp character. The main line of theory, initiated by K. Wilson (1979), introduces a metrical measure of dimensionality ranging continuously—not discretely!—from at least one to four and more in various contexts. Spatial correlations almost disappear in the form of local orders. But spatial correlations reemerge as long-range; they do so through vague bindings of actions and particles over here with actions and particles over there—and there and there—from "nearby" to previously far-off. For vivid physical descriptions see Sengers and Sengers (1968).

The central point from this analogy is to refer contract to the phase transition itself, with "status" referred to the phase regimes on either one "side" or the other of the transitional regime. Adam Smith himself never subscribed to naive notions of free atoms contracting at will in some abstract arenas, which are common caricatures of his thought. But even the caricatures can be seen as real possibilities if hedged in sufficiently as being delicate, as being poised on a cusp of transition. This cusp lies between immanent and contending wholistic contexts.[13] The analogy argues against the usual markets-to-hierarchies theorizing (Williamson 1975).

Control and production, not temperature and force-gradients, are the impetuses to social process. Both the social analogue to space and the analogue to molecule are emergent and negotiable, identities established by chance. Yet another, a wholly new possibility emerges: the analogues to two different phases in a physical material may coexist not in the narrowly circumscribed sense of phase transitions, but rather as two emergent and negotiated contexts of possibility, which might co-occur.

Self-Consistent Field

Contingencies are the origin of identities and of identities' searches for control. Contingencies are thus the sources of social organization and its spaces—which are not pregiven Cartesian spaces but build as networks. Indeed social spaces are continually being rebuilt and torn down, over and over again, with everyday and demographic contingencies at the root of both tearing down and reproducing. Careers can combine with networks to represent that. The puzzle is what

---

[13] As in catastrophe models, for an overview of which see Fararo (1978).

sorts of spaces and combinations thereof can coexist, what spaces and array of spaces are self-consistent.

Identities do not appear in preexisting spaces but rather induce social spaces as well as themselves by and in their interactions. The central problem is that these spaces are simultaneously the environment for and the result of social action. The conundrum is how to stipulate a context in social action for disciplines and ties and values which by their cumulation produce just that stipulated order. Call this the "self-consistent field" conundrum, by analogy to the like problem of order within matter in physical space.[14]

To have talked about disciplines is to have presupposed that they can embed themselves into formations with whose larger processes they are consistent. Social networks are a first analogue to Euclidean space as matrix for the context of physical process. The parallel question is whether and how varieties of disciplines map into some common accounting scheme. Three species were specified and an accounting scheme of three distinct embedding ratios developed in chapter 2. It is not clear how, in general, to predict and understand which disciplines will and which won't fit together further—which will or will not cumulate or aggregate. And there are further questions beyond the preliminary ones. Social spaces are partial and multiple, not some Euclidean totality.

Pressures from production and for control are unending and self-breeding. Ever larger scopes and higher levels build on networks and disciplines. Populations interpenetrate even as they become recognizable, and new levels of identity compound out of previous ones. No single self-consistent field will do.

Self-Consistent Space

Theorists of social process commonly assume that their space resembles the planetary heavens as a vast playing field in being regular, continuous, neatly measurable, and controlled by precise rules or even by clockwork. However, liquids, polymer gels, minerals, or coral reefs provide more appropriate metaphors. Metaphors they are, since the social generates its own distinctive spaces of possibilities, even though they are ones somehow intertwined with physical-biological spaces.

[14] The term is borrowed from the physics and chemistry of matter, where the conundrum is subjected to increasingly elegant solutions: as to process, by statistical mechanics (Huang 1963), and as to architecture by various Mean Field Approximations (Ziman 1979; deGennes 1979) and see Appendix 2, and also chapter 1.

The physical spaces needed as metaphors are crowded spaces.[15] It is not the empty heavens but rather crowded insides of matter or coral reefs that are called for. Social spaces are contexts in which identities and interactions locate in the unfolding of projects for control, which ricochet off continuing impacts of physical events. Isotropy does not exist but rather levels, catenations, and interlockings.

Before those whom we take for granted as distinct actors impinge upon our everyday consideration, there is already being constructed and perceived much social space. Whatever the level or scope of the actors involved, counteractions have interacted to generate the sense of structured possibilities for further interaction which is just social space. Ties make up, together with disciplines and their embedding mechanisms, social spaces. Continuations through some form of signaling elicit the corresponding possibilities of social time.

Pragmatics

Space, social or physical, requires and yields three pragmatics of analysis. Space operationalizes distance and closeness, which we all find indispensable for orienting ourselves and our analysis. Second, location is the resulting matrix for closeness, which is at the same time the matrix for dynamics, which embeds time in space for and from a system of actors. Third, space-time can be made to represent and explain context.

Developing a public account for how we view and locate ourselves even in physical space has proved very difficult. In the European histories of engineering and art, satisfactory perspective renderings in plane projections were achieved only a few centuries ago. In the modern psychology of perception, Gibson (1950, 1979; and see Restle 1980) and Shepard (1984, 1987, 1989) are still wrestling with these problems.

It should be no surprise that social scientists are as yet groping toward analogous effectiveness in communicable representations of how we see ourselves in and operate in social space(s), which in any case cannot be divorced from representations in biophysical space, where production resides. In whatever portrayals finally prove effective for them, social spaces will be multiple in an extreme, with very fragmentary and scrappy topology.

[15] Economic theory as contextualized by Samuelson (1947) made the regressive step to homogeneous and isotropic field constructs, as in gravity or electromagnetism, a step back from the institutionalist perspective of Marshall (1891) or Chamberlin (1933), which latter induces perception of crowded, irregular, and scrappy spaces.

Guidance can be sought in mathematics and also in mathematical formulations of natural science. Examples given in Appendix 2 demonstrate that a science need not construe even physical space either as unique or as a matter of human phenomenology. Hypothetical spaces are vital in natural sciences too, such as a two-dimensional Cartesian space for physical phenomena, in which, for example, wave motion would be impossible (Weyl 1949). And abstract spaces, so-called state spaces, are constructed for particular processes and problems. These state spaces are aids to our perceptions rather than putative arenas of causal contingency.[16] The only state spaces which prove indispensable are those adduced from already successful portrayals of cause.[17] We can learn from principles of perception that spaces are as much the consequences as the "real" arenas of causal action.

Conundrums

Boundaries are matters of context, as are units also. Social organization exhibits historical particularities, but, within it as context, control efforts yield as joint result a continued tendency toward self-similarity and self-consistency across levels and time. One can draw both parallels to and divergences from the contexts of natural science, which are spaces. Conundrums result which become paradoxes if not dealt with explicitly.

Attempts to specify self-consistent space lead to conundrums. Recapitulate the constituents: Any two disciplines may be joined by a tie or ties, so that networks cross between as well as within species, and each discipline has a story-set. There are further possible concatenations of embeddings among these identity-disciplines connected by networks of various types of tie. The resulting social space-times are storied and are catenations of incidences, and of embeddings and other operations. The problematics are set by operations unlike those of homogeneous physical space-times.

---

[16] Some natural scientists also are dismissive of spatial texture; e.g., the biologist Gold who believes that (1977, p. 49) "A dimension is a label attached to a number that gives the information 'number of what.'"

[17] In the spirit of this dictum are some exploratory efforts in sociology such as those concerning social mobility (e.g., Sorokin 1927; Levine 1966; Hauser and Featherman 1977) or social influence (e.g., Levine 1972; Mizruchi and Schwartz 1988). Thermodynamics comes close to being a model for this dictum, with the prior causal discoveries being those by Count Rumford (S. Brown 1962; Huang 1963; Ziman 1979). Furthest from the causal are "spaces" generated in routine factor analysis, psychometrics, and much econometrics (Leamer 1978).

The whole ensemble must survive being buffeted by chance junctures with work and biophysical space-time as well as by distinct but indeterminate efforts at control at various levels in social space-times, where, however, "level" is well defined only with respect to a given discipline, there being no assured mechanism to separate distinct levels as aggregates. Even the juncture between biophysical and social is somewhat arbitrary. And there is no mechanism for locking social space-times into some unified totality, except vaguely through ricochet off biophysical space-time.

Thus arises a chicken-and-egg conundrum: disciplines and ties generate social space-times, the shape(s) of which however predetermine(s) what disciplines and ties there can be. This is the principal difficulty of analysis for social structure and process.

There is an auxiliary self-similarity conundrum—if approximately separate levels coagulate out will the "laws" be the same at each "level"?[18] The conundrum can be approached analytically: For example one may conjecture that arenas tend to come in larger contexts where self-similarity obtains, leading to the hieratic style explicated in chapter 6.

· · · · ·

History, like every social rhetoric, is for explaining away, which shapes some of further action. Social sciences confront weirder combinations of existing rhetorics with own rhetorics than do other sciences (cf. Gergen 1982). It should not be surprising to now conclude that there is no clear distinction between, on the one hand, history and other rhetorics, as folk theories, and, on the other, social science. Indeed, social science must have evolved primarily to fill needs for rhetoric.[19]

A sure litmus test for whether a given social science is more rhetoric or more science can be borrowed from Llewellyn's analysis of common law, quoted above. He observes, "When there are no precedents from a judge's own state, he is quick to rely on the larger legal

---

[18] For example, in the study cited earlier (Eccles and Crane 1988) of change in investment banking, the shift from sole-bank model for client to competitive multi-tie model also proved to be associated within each bank with decentralization to network form and thus to "flat" organization. But, by contrast, in Key's (1945) study of Southern politics, the South as a whole region held as a monolith in national politics despite radically different, and differently decentralized, party systems across the constituent states.

[19] For a recent overview of some of the paradoxes lying between social science and rhetoric, consult S. Baker (1990).

encyclopedias. These are often enough under capable enough editorial supervision, but responsibility for sorting through the gigantic masses of material and for painstakingly working through the details of individual cases—on which everything hangs—is assigned to a low-paid, indeed an inferior, work force" (Llewellyn 1989, p. 7). The litmus test is whether it is high status members of the field who delve into reality situations with obsessive care and attempts at precision—or instead lower status ones.

The principal product of theory in social science can be seen as the topics unearthed for investigation. One hundred are given, as examples, in Appendix 1. All these concern, in one way or another, networks of disciplines across levels. Such are the only social patternings which robustly survive the inhomogeneous and contingent which are at the root of social action. Systematic accountings, such as those urged in Appendix 2, are required for networks and disciplines before they can be used to settle questions and develop topics.

Identity and Control

The theory presented in this book grows around a rhetoric of identity and control, and it is fitting to end with a restatement. Identity concerns fury and fear as well as sweetness and light because identity seeks control. Identity is urgent, and its expression is urgent. The former aspect implodes and the latter explodes the greatest of energies.

Layers of Identity

Identity begins as and from a primordial and continuing urge to control, which can be seen always, in all contexts. For example, a new child on a playground has an overriding need to find some sort of stable social footing so that he or she can know how to act in an otherwise chaotic social world. Only occasionally does this lead to bullying, to some physical attempt at dominance. Identity in this first sense is the expression in social context of the same urge for secure footing which also leads to behavioral patterns of posture in physical settings.

A second, more elaborate and quite distinct sense of identity is as "face." This is identity achieved and expressed or operationalized as part of a distinct social discipline: A discipline is some sort of grouping in which each member has face just because it is a social face, one of a set of faces together making up that discipline.

It follows that identity always is a matter of levels, it induces distinct levels. One's own identity is achieved only as dual to, as part of, and induction to a larger identity of which it is a reflection. Identity in this second sense appears to be a sufficient base for our everyday construct for the person, which is as an actor in a role which supplies preferences that may guide him or her toward goals, and into rational action.

The larger identity of the social discipline exists only through and as realization of the dovetailing of "faces." Thus this second sense of identity carries a strong implication: Having goals actually locks one into others' control. This implication gives perspective on, for example, how artworks can be so charged with importance. In expressing and celebrating identities, artworks such as dances may also be announcing ways in which identities are subject to control.

Both these first two senses of identity, however, might already apply in wolf packs, or hen flocks, or monkey bands and other such nonhuman social settings. No one is sufficiently expert to be sure. One test would be whether some examples of what we call artworks can be discerned in such settings.

There is an additional, a third, and distinctively human sense of identity, which builds upon the first two. This is identity from frictions and errors across different social settings and disciplines. This third sense of identity arises from the central fact of human social organization: Whenever and wherever social organization has been observed, each human is in more than one continuing discipline, in more than one social molecule. That is, each human participates in each of several distinct realms, such as family and village, and job and secret society, so that actions and thence selves crosscut these realms. Human lives are not lived in a single pack or band but rather are mixed in with different bands in different realms. This is so even with children.

Utopias acknowledge this central fact. They may be utopian in imagining individual humans to be not just in roles but in prescribed and consistent packages of roles. In such a utopia each human is assigned an embracing super-role. There are many literary examples, and there are religious evocations such as by Savonarola or by Cotton Mather. Some theorists, such as Talcott Parsons and Claude Lévi-Strauss, have come close to arguing that the real world is like that. Or the utopia may go to the other extreme and suppose there are no cross-pressures at all between roles in distinct realms, as in Marx's classless state.

The third, and crucial, sense of identity has no application in utopias, because this third layer of identity arises exactly from contradictions across disciplines, from mismatches and social noise. There is nothing unusual or esoteric about this third layer of identity. Consider a homely example. The child on the playground above may pick up a new way of wearing (or tearing) its clothes as being the proper thing (an aspect of the second meaning of identity). But then the child finds, upon arriving home, that peer-proper is not family-proper. Such contradictions—all the screwups, mistakes, errors, and social noise—in life are just what brings about identity in this third sense, achieved even as a child.

One can even speak of a fourth layer of identity, a sense which is close to what is usually meant by identity in ordinary talk. This is identity as more-or-less coherent accounts, as biography. This is identity after the fact as presented in accounts which may become woven into some unique narrative story. More commonly, however, such accounts are built from and stored in sets of stories and story lines. These sets are standard, and are held in common within some social world, the ubiquity contributing to their usefulness. Indeed their incidence provides a way to map boundaries within social worlds. These sets of stories are the stuff of daily socializing, they are used in daily reconstructions by interpretation of selves and of social organization.

Layers in Expression

Action gets sited differently with respect to these different senses or layers of identity. The fourth sense of identity is all about rationalization and about failures of action. In this fourth layer of identity, action and its agency are suppressed. The third layer is where social action centers.

Consider a particular realm. Works of art by artists are action once removed, they are expressions of identity by agency. Since artworks are displacements of identity celebrations, they get sited differently in action according to the layer of identity being expressed. Turn to an example of some complexity. When William Paley builds a magnificent modern painting collection, he is doing so neither as Paley the trustee of the Museum of Modern Art (MOMA) nor as Paley the founder of the CBS broadcasting network, nor as yet other more personal Paleys. It is exactly the uneasy intersection of these faces of Paley which induced Paley as identity in the third sense. Riding the irregular combination was what made Paley most Paley and called forth, along with exceptional energies and vitality, a commensurate hunger for its celebration.

Now turn to a simpler example. A bedroom farce on Broadway is also artwork. A farce also celebrates identities (by somewhat roundabout agencies that run through stereotyping mechanisms which we have not explicitly considered). But these are identities in the second sense. That is the import of farce. Farce extracts humor by obvious twists on just those identities which are most confining. These are identities in the second sense, identities that absolutely straitjacket one through enforcement in everyday social disciplines. No doubt Paley also could enjoy farce—although there are no chuckling little Klee sketch-oils in his collection of paintings—but the Paley who did so would be from just one setting, say Paley resenting a confining mother-son bond.

Yet all four senses of identity come wound together in the same constructed reality. They are wound up in ways that may change constantly. Nor is there any simple correlation between medium of expression and the layer of identity being celebrated. A painting can reflect a second or fourth (and boring) sense of identity, and some story or play may reflect the interesting third (or first) senses; but the reverse occurs as well. It would therefore be silly to reify the four senses of identity, to set them up as separate personae. This book has not followed that path.

Agency and Identities

Agency is social, not personal, both in its roots and in its main realizations. Chickens in the pecking order of a flock do have agency even though they do not have personhood. Agency is about relations. Agency is the dynamic face of networks.

Agency can be dissected in terms of the four senses of identity. Agency is confined, from the principal's perspective, to the third or fourth senses, whereas from the agent's perspective agency concerns either the second or the third senses of identity. But when some set of agents captures control, when agents wrest control away from their principals, the anatomy of agency is changed thereby: the agents tend to move into identities of the third sense, whereas the principals are being put back on the interpretive shelf in being confined to the fourth sense of identity. This turnover of control in agency is the common theme in evolution of social organization.

Consider the realm of art. In case studies of collectors, one can see the artist slipping the noose of agency once held by some patron, now held by some more remote principal, a buyer or dealer. The mark of success for this slippage is moving the artist's own self into the seat of signification. This can be helped by the presence of some fourth party to agency, a witness, in particular a critic as witness. The critic as witness can be an ideologue of generalities. The dominant individual critic of the nineteenth century, John Ruskin, was such. We then begin to see a new sort of critic emerge. The critic as witness can be a lackey, a promoter of individual career, as Clement Greenberg was for those who came after New York Abstract Expressionism. In either case such a critic moves into new prominence and invades the very production of art, as if in lieu of the patron. The critic becomes a new sort of agent because of a new sort of principal. This new principal is a patron as the compound (the fictional compound) of a host of viewers. There is a sort of double slippage of agency and thus a double displacement of identity.

Until the modernist developments in arts, first in elite arts and today also in arts of the media, only religious, political, and military heroes were accepted. Only such heroes were legitimate for displacements of and thus alienations from identities. Identities of larger collectives often build themselves in the first place around such traditional heroes. That was a first but only partial reversal of agency as we define it. It was a real coup to first establish the idea that a beholder could gain benefit in his or her own identity by deferring to an artist's expression of that artist's own identity. That is what the Avant Garde myth and the genius myth are really about. Their implications for broader patterns of control in social formations have yet to play out.

The example of William Paley as art collector is again instructive. Paley was a principal who used many agents in art matters, and these agents were sufficiently differentiated from one another that he could keep control as principal. Paley could keep getting his own action. He was not an artist according to our conventions, yet Paley did create among artworks, he created by putting together. A collector such as he is akin to an artist who creates those artworks called "constructions" in today's idiom. Paley created rather in the same way as does the director of a play or movie, the "auteur." The director creates if and only if sufficient space is being left between his "agents," the stars and author. Similarly, Paley created in space he uncovered between painter and dealer, or between painter and MOMA curator.

What I have tried to achieve in this book is analogous to Paley's collection. A great deal of my text consisted of quotes, and many of the ideas are borrowed from others. I hope that my collection, like his, develops an identity of its own.

APPENDIX 1

ONE HUNDRED TOPICS

IN ORDER to fill out and test the theory-sketch offered in this book, many research topics must be pursued. Conversely, the chapters above can suggest for research many topics that are of interest independent of the theory. Three lists of topics are offered, in successively less specified form. Altogether there are one hundred. Most are by the author; a source is attributed to each of the others.

Conjectures 1–27

1. Mathematics became, around 1900, inward-turned and obsessed with purity, at the cost of its ties to empirical science, because of its being institutionalized into an American academic science system akin to the Indian caste system—with mathematics, like Brahmins, in the highest rank. Rationale: cf. chapter 4 and see White (1992a) commenting upon Kline (1980).

2. Universities in the United States in the 1990s will be under severe budget and demographic pressures. As a result they will selectively eliminate disciplines. They thereby may move toward less overlap in the set of disciplines between one university and another. If so, parameter values in the underlying institution (modeled in chapter 4 above) will move closer to those for Indian castes-in-villages, that is, toward rigidification. One may conjecture that each separate university's prestige order and administration will have more (local) authority and that the overall split as by humanities, social science, and natural science will become hegemonic.

The autonomy of particular "invisible colleges" will not suffer but their influence within that science will, and sciences will ossify. There will be less room for change and thus less potential for "getting action" (as in chapter 6 above) in the institution as a whole, and more authority in the local administrations.

Simultaneous elimination of the same disciplines across universities might prove more beneficial to creative autonomy in sciences.

3. Democracy is a superb control device, in that:

There are no clear-cut goals.
It is hard to identify who is in authority.

It is hard to rebel. (A comparative count of rebellions from inside shows
that democracies are the most robust form.)

Nor is democracy restricted to political institutions: A commercial "factor" coming to control its principals is a prototype for democracy.

4. Any discipline is a pronouncement of style whose effect depends upon the extent to which it frames perceptions.

A formal organization to be effective must appear as a nesting of
similar forms on successive scales. In present terminology, it appears
from the outside as a set of interfaces which is in turn disciplined
within an embracing interface, and so on, with each constituent discipline having the ethos of a pecking order. Examples include units
within departments within a firm, and they perhaps extend to firms
within a production market or states within an international system
of war.

5. Conversely to #4, any mobilizer species presupposes its constituents are of *different* species. For example, a political campaign organization is to have as constituents, first, interfaces of rational bureaucratic order focused on specialized tasks, and second, arenas
wherein persons sort out on degrees of purity on various issues, and
in addition mobilizations of preexisting networks, as of ethnic group
and community.

6. Types of tie appear, and die or consolidate as triggered by-
products of continuous evolution in the profile for the incidence of
discipline species.

7. Multiplex connections invoke and are invoked by privately enacted organization, whereas a separate type of tie invokes and is
induced by ceremonially enacted public organization.

8. Major crises (at whatever level and scope of social formation)
invariably are associated with a change in the distinct types of tie
which are recognized.

9. Types of tie are more independent of one another in a network
among nodes established as an elite than they are elsewhere. Pareto
(1935) furnishes a different phrasing which is also a rationale: because sentiments of elites are more differentiated and independent.
Among elites, enmities in particular are not transferred from oneself
to a partner nor from one context to another. Business is business,
for elites especially.

10. The volume of social action, which is also the volume of social
space-times, is proportional to the density of stochastic eruptions.
This density reflects first, unpredictable fluctuations in biophysical

ecology, and second, extensiveness of interconnections between this ecology and social space-times—which latter interconnections can be grouped principally as work or war. Internally, social space-times exhibit isotropic, though stochastic, connections which permit short-circuiting biophysical distances.

11. It follows from #10 that the new in the social becomes so at a new level of complexity and intricacy. It becomes so always on a small scale: for example, a medieval city of a few thousand within a huge feudatory empire. And the new comes at a crevice, nook, or cranny, one out of sight of the existing big shots. The rise of Holland along with new form of economy is a classic illustration, which brings out the third requirement—some actor, like the DeWitt and Oldenbarnevelt entourages of chapter 5 above, who senses enough of the new to be its midwife.

12. Engineering in the capitalist context should tend to be more generalized than in a socialist one. Rationale: Engineering emerged as a profession in the West to subsume and generalize and thence control the specialized technical skills of craftsmen, to the benefit of owners/managers, in the period when putting-out systems are being pulled into factories.

13. General managers should tend to remain less specialized in the West than are executives in the socialist orbit. Rationale analogous to that for #12: General managers evolved to control the various professions.

14. The enterprises which are most effective in a given context are those which mix the styles known in that context. For example:

   a) in our day and locale, the nonprofits and quangos (quasi-autonomous nongovernmental organizations);
   b) in the medieval West, the knightly religious order;
   c) in the medieval Middle East, the slave army.

15. Inside a firm, processes of forming prices generate confusion and yield information; outside the firm, its activities with respect to prices reduces information and simplifies social relations. Rationale: See Eccles (1981c, 1985).

16. General management will be easier where administration is harder, and the reverse. Rationale: Intervention, the getting and shaping of action, should be somewhat easier and more common in formal organizations than in other institutions, whereas routine administration should be more difficult. Routine administration is the blocking of fresh action together with the keeping of some sense of

coherence in a self-reproducing social formation. This is nothing esoteric: custom is less effective and getting action is easier in formal
organization than in traditional social organization, whether the ambiance in the latter be primarily clientelistic, or corporatist, or from
professionals.

17. Churches, especially the Catholic Church, will become wealth-
ier as a by-product of demographic changes in kinship patterns. Rationale: Fewer children per couple mean more childless marriages
and hence more inheritances not earmarked; also there will be fewer
nephews and nieces, to the same effect. However, if sufficient attention is paid to higher education for the fewer children, colleges may
benefit instead.

18. (Philip Ennis) Styles must mate temporarily in order to be able
to engender change in style, which however becomes a new style
only through subsequent mutual rerejection by the initial pair,
which resume separate identities. Thus, for instance:

a) Rock'n'Roll resulted from the merger then split of white with
black streams of popular music (Ennis 1990);

b) Feminism emerged from the overlay of the black civil rights movement with white radicalism subsequent to their mutual rejection
(McAdam 1988).

19. (Kathleen Schwartzman) A social formation which operates as
a semi-periphery within a larger system will itself be disarticulated
internally. Rationale: The semi-periphery is, in terms from chapter 6,
a sink for ambage at large, at the price of being a peak of internal
ambiguity. Thus, for instance:

a) Portugal, semi-periphery for centuries, is an inert collection of incomparable subunits (Schwartzman 1989);

b) the deanships of colleges within universities are incoherent internally as organizations;

c) Parent Teacher Associations are never able to "hold it together."

20. (Ilan Talmud) "The more identity is a mixture of web of affilia-
tions with criss-cross groups, the more difficult it is to anticipate
events and to control systems of complex, interrelated events." Rationale: See DeTocqueville and Federalist Paper #10.

21. (J. Kocka in Chandler and Daems 1980, p. 108) "A low degree
of division of labor in the economy as a whole led to a high degree of
division of labor within the new enterprises . . . if they get off the
ground at all."

22. (Scott A. Boorman) Network systems which exhibit high vari-

ance and can yield novel traits also have a strong tendency to self-concealment: that is, the cross-section data on outcomes yields extremely little information on the actual earlier configurations which led to the present (and its new trait).

23. (Stark and Bainbridge 1979) Science as a practice is akin to magic, not religion, and so its style is analogous to the clientelist styles of magic.

24. (Carlos Forment 1990, pp. 58, 91) Colonialism as an example of the paradox of corporatism: "The ruling bloc, by keeping the dispossessed out of the political space, forces them to negotiate in private and in isolation from each other, . . . not able to effect changes in public life (p. 58) . . . . [But] the proliferation of special courts [thirty-two in Mexico City alone, each with exclusive jurisdiction over a specific area of public life] transferred judicial power from the state . . . strengthened civil society in its relations with the state (p. 91). [So] these regimes have highly stable institutional arrangements and constitutional guarantees, making it very difficult for state officials to trespass and gain control over the public realm (p. 58)."

25. (Stanley Udy 1990, personal communication) The units of observation in social phenomena are never the same as the units appropriate for analysis.

26. (Michael Mann 1986, pp. 1, 4) "Societies are not unitary. They are not social systems (closed or open); they are not totalities. . . . I operate at a more concrete, socio-spatial and organizational level of analysis. Societies are constituted of multiple overlapping and intersecting socio-spatial networks of power. Societies are much messier than our theories of them."

27. (Richard Lachmann) "Action is gotten where corporatism can be constructed to challenge clientelism or vice versa. Action is in a period of shift. . . . Indeed, corporatism may be the structural artifact of elite blocking action, while clientelism is the artifact of a chief's getting action."

Speculations 1–19

1. Events will supersede persons in stratification process, just as persons five hundred years ago came to replace positions within corporatist *standesstaat*, which in turn much earlier replaced identities within tribes.

2. The corporation comes in during the same period as the nation-state because each is a cause and by-product of the emergence of personal actors as modal source of action.

3. There are more stories in the set for a high dependency situation than there are in the story-set for an autonomous, low dependency situation, with both being disciplines of the arena species (Fig. 8).

4. The feminist revolution has decreased the decoupling between genders (averaged over all social networks) and thereby increased control exerted by male gender.

5. A discipline can continue and be observable only within operational ranges on separate valuations which are mutually restricted. These ranges are with respect to both upstream and downstream. The upshot is that observable social formations are characterized by variances and ratios.

6. Predictable control is achieved only through mutual efforts at control, which is to say through disciplines; so further control that is not predictable can be achieved only through sequencing and combinatorics of disciplines.

7. A human person is as large and complex an array of constituent disciplines and networks as is an aboriginal tribe that is parsed down to individual positions: this exemplifies the self-similarity of social analysis.

8. Scalar organization (Weberian hierarchy) interdigitates all three species of discipline. By contrast, collegial formal organizations, such as partnerships and cooperatives—"organic organization"—appear as some one species of discipline; namely, the select species exemplified by exchange markets as arenas, wherein role polarity may shift back and forth.

9. The more evenly distributed across biophysical space-time are the embeddings of social space-times, the greater the prominence of magic and of simple tales and of barter; the less evenly distributed, the greater is the prominence of religion, complex narrative, and media of exchange.

10. Inequality is the by-product of attempts to get action and gain control. Inequality is the most pervasive idiom of blocking action, but it itself is the cumulative product of attempts to get action.

11. Dominance across, and thus sense of membership in, a network population is induced through action patterns which indicate

high correlation between valuation status in social spaces and degree of autonomy in physical space.

12. Personalities parallel organizations in the paths by which they block action by their constituent identities.

13. Romantic love is triggered only by non-associative process.

14. Decision-making structures are devices for enforcing custom, just as scalar organizations are devices for resisting change.

15. The more decoupling mechanisms there are, the higher the number of identities.

16. Protestantism shifted with modernism (Kurz 1986) toward the kinds of cultural content which typify magic cults, so that one predicts a corresponding shift in Protestant institutions toward clientelistic hierarchies.

17. Decentralization is required only as an expedient to gain some measure of centralization.

18. Our daily walk-around life and casual acquaintance are temporary bubbles of social space-time which cohere with institution and person only through such devices as story lines.

19. Ties to a discipline are independent of, and may be as numerous as, the entities within it.

Questions 1–54

1. Why do shopping trades cluster, whereas convenience trades scatter?

2. Why has the translation of bishops, from one diocese to another, been a sin?

3. Why is there no institutionalized role of critic in the modern sciences?

4. What is the minimum size, in number of actors, for social formations that can sustain and define asymmetric ties for a subset of dyads?

5. In what ways are investors in a capitalist economy parallel to Apostles in the early Christian Church?

6. Why in some contexts is it gross flow that determines status (potlach system), whereas in other contexts (small business) it is net flow (revenue minus cost)?

7. Rather than one working on one's relationships, is it nearer the truth that a person's relationships work upon oneself?

8. Why has engineering never risen to the dominance that various technocratic movements have predicted (as well as proclaimed) in this century, here or abroad?

9. How does it happen that economic theory holds behavior in a market to be more predictable as the number of distinct actors increases, yet political theory has elections more predictable as the number of candidates decreases?

10. As the context of economic activity evolves toward more complexity, is there a direction of evolution in form of agentry going from factors (two-way) to brokers (one-way)?

11. Do production markets become smaller and more numerous and specialized, as firms become larger, and conversely?

12. Is franchising of businesses a return to the early modern system of venality, the purchase of jobs?

13. Does vertical integration induce further differentiation of products?

14. How does it happen that, within a market, control is imputed to be higher when concentration is higher, which means unequal size firms, and yet control within a firm presumes relatively equal size among constituent divisions?

15. Why are equal shares in production markets so uncommon?

16. Why are sunk costs included in prices of manufactured products but not in pricing by merchants in exchange markets?

17. What are the minimum scopes of institution and style required to permit and sustain the concepts and behaviors surrounding notions of privacy?

18. Are cartels easier to form in markets for producers' goods than in consumers' markets?

19. Why does sales now dominate procurement within at least the U.S. economy?

20. Are we heading for resurgences of the outwork production and mercantile network systems that spread across the West before industrialism?

21. Do prices link one market to another rather than linking producers to buyers?

22. Do observable markets enter and exit from an economic sector more commonly than do firms? Do firms do so less commonly than individual persons?

23. Why this similarity? The top four in open primary elections typically garner 75% of the vote, while the top fifth of products in an industrial sector typically gain 80% of the total sales.

24. Why this contrast? In government today persons buy highest level jobs from party organizations, whereas in the economy firms buy the careers that lead to top jobs from persons.

25. Why are reported bribes so small compared to ordinary commercial markups, whether at a city inspector level or a Supreme Court Justice level? Is it because truly large bribes are designated as profit or other legitimate category?

26. In what structural contexts do foreign conquerors ally with native priests?

27. Why were city-states uncommon in the Far East, but common elsewhere?

28. When do executives operate in "corridors of indifference," and when, on the other hand, do they induce controversies and disputes in order to control?

29. Why are equal shares in votes between political candidates reputed to be both good and normal, whereas equal shares among firms in a production market are reputed abnormal and unstable?

30. Why are wealth distributions always more concentrated than income distributions?

31. Is mismatch in timing, especially as between operations and supervision, the crux of turf wars in organization? Should this be construed as a matter of identities' embeddings—and decouplings?

32. Does effective social mobilization entail switchings between rooted and traveling foci, between large and small assemblies, between passive and active modes, between single-issue and broad-spectrum programs?

33. Why now are universities closer to high government than to high business circles in their main activities, whereas the medieval analogue to universities, the walled cities, were the opposite?

34. Why is it that the more numerous the entities making up a molecular discipline, the fewer will be the stories in a story-set accounting the discipline?

35. How did it happen that the Papacy never went bankrupt in the medieval era, whereas the Absolutist European monarchies commonly did?

36. The early Christian movement achieved enormous success while in a dual structure of traveling ministers vis-à-vis settled presbyters: why, in continuing the church, was the apostolic wing dropped?

37. Why are movies an average two hours in length? and books 200 pages? Can these be clues to how story lines, and sets of stories, work?

38. Why has the practice of setting prizes in science for solving outstanding problems almost died out, compared to its peak during the Enlightenment?

39. Do newspapers follow any rules in how they constantly adapt identities of actors being reported from one story to another by changing their embeddings?

40. Does subjecting many authors to one editor yield as coherent a story-set as does a common theme?

41. What will be the impact on institutions from the great decrease in the incidence of uncles and aunts among European groups by A.D. 2000?

42. Why do people keep attitudes which are losing, that is, are neither confirmed by events nor helpful directly to the holder?

43. When does control over money require identity, for example, as in bookkeeping, through assignment of debit, and when does it require anonymity, as in agency?

44. Does the top executive layer of large modern firms constitute a servile elite which is analogous to the government *ministeriales* of the early-modern mosaic of German principalities, and analogous to the estate managers for English magnates in Stuart times and for magnates in present-day Thailand?

45. Why were the entourages of Hitler, Mao, and Kaiser Wilhelm (Hull 1982) stable, whereas Stalin's entourage was not?

46. Why does a fight induce one-to-one matching, whereas mobilization induces many-to-one?

47. What are men doing with the time and attention that women are conventionally supposed to be devoting to shopping?

48. Will the new prominence of skilled around-the-clock shift work lead to new social formations?

49. Is it only persons who have become intimate who can generate the intensity to really become antipathetic and fly apart violently, or to the contrary is it only persons split into two blocs in polar opposition who can do so?

50. As more people understand social organization on a broader scale better, via, for example, network metaphors, will there be a shift of ambiance in social organization such that control, while not being denied or overturned, is subjected to negotiation, explicit as well as implicit, of its terms?

51. What social formations at what junctures are predatory with respect to what target social formations?—as for example the Norman vis-à-vis the English in 1066 (Searle 1988).

52. French Protestants (Hugenots, Calvinists, etc.) were neither an ethnic nor a regional cluster, and they contributed much in taxes and leadership from their economic success; so why did so gifted a strategist as Cardinal Richelieu revive as conscious policy a centuries-long persecution?

53. The most significant biographies of all time—Mohammed, Jesus, Buddha—are drawn from records which are purely partisan; so maybe impartiality in observers is exactly wrong for getting the truth for social spaces and action?

54. Sometimes it seems that business firms hardly ever die; sometimes it seems that sovereignties—ethnic or local—never die; do the styles which underlie these two impressions tend to go with institutions that make one, both, or neither true?

APPENDIX 2

SOME MODELS

N EW LINES of observation do not develop without the stimulus of new theoretical representations, especially of mathematical models, which help break open conventions, which are linguistically embedded representations of social formations. For example, let social institutions be seen as approximations to the Kalman filter, with custom as the mechanism of inertial extrapolation. Then gossip can be modeled as an indigenous way, now supplemented by polls, to get through surface indicators at possible real changes in structure. By this analogy, to be developed in part C below, long-standing social institutions are analogous to engineering that is of a new post-lunar sophistication. But Kalman filters do not have, with present scopes of computation, either the combinatorial scope or the layered depth to deal with embeddings as disciplines in the networks of social spaces, even if we began to have assembled sufficiently systematic data.

There have been many prior such openings by models. Some of these (e.g., Samuelson 1949) were straight transcriptions of the physics spaces of field theory expanded upon in part C below. Others (e.g., Arrow 1950; Burt 1989; Coleman 1957; Kleinrock 1964; Landau 1968; March and Olson 1976; Rapoport 1983; Scarf 1973; Simon 1957; von Neumann and Morgenstern 1944) came out of the formal logic of biology, philosophy, and other fields. They have sparked novel perspectives on patterns of interrelations, from diffusion and conflict on through exchange, social computation, and purification.

Also important have been new statistical theories of inference (Leamer 1978; Tukey 1977) and techniques for assessing data (e.g., Bishop, Holland, and Fienberg 1975; Goodman 1979, 1984; Heil 1989; Hubert 1987; Levine 1992; Spilerman and Singer 1976; Tufte 1987; Tuma and Hannan 1984; Wasserman and Faust 1991).

A. Disciplines and Networks

Perceptions of disciplines will be affected by the systematic impacts they have on participants' outcomes, effects that are by-products of the social logic of the discipline mechanism. Is it the outside of the participants, and how skewed, who engross outputs of disciplines?

Does niche in one discipline give basis for selectivity for niche in another? Is control effort more effective if directed at one discipline from simultaneous location in another?

Disciplines can be appraised in balance-theoretic terms (Davis 1967, 1970; and see review by Freeman 1991) as applied to network interconnections among constituent niches. Interfaces for persons would come close to the early formulation of balance theory by Abelson and Rosenberg (1958). And the Heider ideas (1946) can also be applied to an embedded level. Balance now concerns relations among aspects of a system, a discipline as embedded. Turn to the earlier figure of the social triangle and apply it to siting three species of disciplines in terms of specializations for network, identity, and production. Balance is stipulated here, but not some simple balance between dichotomized corners of the triangle. On the contrary, the whole point is that mechanisms are articulated which express how two sorts of specialization balance each other in enabling reproduction of the whole discipline.

Models are most usefully grown in connection with observation. One main venue has been field studies of networks, which were touched upon in chapter 3 above (and cf. Burt 1980; Freeman, D. White, and Romney 1989; Pappi 1987; Romo 1992; Ziegler 1990; Wellman and Berkowitz 1988). Networks implicate disciplines or their equivalents, which is to say networks may run among congeries of actors that go much beyond the ego and alters implied in normal speech (Boyd 1989; Reitz and D. White 1989; H. White 1964, 1988a). A purpose of this book is to extend and integrate network approaches with embeddings in disciplines and associated story lines. Exceptionally lucid overviews by Granovetter (1973, 1985), Bott (1957), and by Key (1949) suggest how such generalization of networks to new views of spaces can permit derivation of economic, domestic, and political institutions, respectively.

Interpretive Models

An illustrative task for application of interpretive models comes from trying to relate ties with disciplines in terms of stories. One result can be explaining variation across a species of discipline.

Chapter 2 showed monochromatic dominance in pecking order factoring out into several valuations, each of which structures a species of discipline. Within a discipline, within an identity, valuation need only be implicit. Social pressure within a discipline may be intense enough and interlocked enough, as in a pecking order, to establish valuation ordering without explicit articulation in stories.

Chapter 3 traced networks as ties only between disciplines. Yet within as well as across disciplines, particular pairs host now one and now another of the menu of stories, so that pairs within as well as between disciplines may map into the types of tie. A discipline as a mechanism could then be seen as the endless recurrence of these virtual ties in rapid succession across the interior of the discipline. In this sense, even within a discipline there are types of tie.

One basis for variations within species of discipline, such as those indicated in figures 2.2 through 2.7, is correlation between story-set and specialization in behavior. Within a discipline, the pattern of incidence of stories is induced by and tends to support the transitive order on valuation which is predominant in that species. One story or type of tie may tend to become predominant within each discipline.

Take each species of discipline in turn. The type of story-tie which is likely to engender ordering for quality valuation is business (earlier the technical, or sibling tie). The type of story-tie for prestige valuation as the shadow of dominance is the honor tie (earlier the patriarchal tie). And the type of story-tie for purity value is, in today's everyday parlance, the professional tie (analogous to the merchant tie of centuries ago, and to parent-child ties).

A story-set is a reflection of a mutual structure that implies and induces a valuation ordering which shadows dominance, but may go beyond dominance. The three terms for discipline valuations connote the respective themes around which a genre of explanatory stories for that species of discipline collects, stories sufficient to account for happenings for that discipline. The narrative content of the constituent stories must as a set cover all the possibilities of action (that continues to be subject to endless stochastic eruptions and contextual pressures), so as to provide a sufficient explanation ex post to constituent entities.

This can be elaborated further in the roles as developed in chapters 3 and 4: Particular story-ties are configured with respect to each other across a set of entities in a package that proves robust and transposable across concrete instances—as in mother role, vis-à-vis son, daughter, husband, etc., repeated in a whole population. They concern interdigitated instances of valuations such as purity, quality, and prestige.

The basis of variation for species can also be expressed as variations in types of tie. The specifics of implementation may be historical, but the same three sorts of valuations can be discerned and tied in with stories and with types of ties. In, say, the interface species of molecular discipline, production array and tie types adjust to preserve particular story-set. Within a second species, variation in production array plays off against variation in story-set. And in a third species, some production array can be reestablished by sophisticated variation in type of tie for change in story.

Putting these considerations together yields further characterizations of the three species of discipline:

1. Interface—differentiation ratio (prestige) balances dependence (purity) ratio, with accompanying story rationale, for the particular quality intensity of commitment maintained by an interface. The (above/below) ratio on differentiation plays off the like dependence ratio in interfaces which prove to reproduce (in the given context). Low commitment is exemplified by a self-absorbed group, a prototype being a troupe rehearsing (and even putting on) a play, a T-group of the 1960s, or a domestic group "at home relaxing." Medium commitment is exemplified in a production market, within an input-output set of connections; a career exemplifies high commitment intensity.

2. Arena—membership ratio (quality) balances differentiation ratio (prestige) so as to sustain a specific exclusion intensity on purity. Low purity (operationalized as low exclusion ratio) is exemplified by a Pure Theory of Exchange system of trade markets; medium purity is exemplified by professions or a *parlement* system; highest purity is for religious interfacing, as in a caste system.

3. Council—here membership ratio (quality) balances dependence ratio (operationalization of purity as recessive valuation) in an interface mechanism that stabilizes intensity of prestige. For the council mechanism, Nadel's (1955) role-summation is always high, even with the different levels of differentiation fixed, since the differentiation refers to the representatives, with each of whom the fates of their dependency strings are bound.

One can also sort from the other side. One expects that stories take on characteristically different guises for each distinct range of intensity of valuation for a discipline and thus for the contexts loosely coupled to that species' predominance. These guises are to be in alignment with the operational mechanisms reflected in embedding ratios corresponding to the two secondary valuations. For a preliminary assessment of the correspondence see Hunt (1984).

4. Tales—for ratios between the two extremes, what was treated earlier as the normal situation: here the onus is explaining incremental realignments of constituent segments by coherent ex post interpretation via a balanced set of stories;

5. Romance—for infinite valuation, where identity formation is the onus so that a historical and unique pattern over supposed time epoch is emphasized, with minimal spread in the stories; call it *prefiguring;*

6. Epic—for zero valuation, where preemptive assertions of control are the onus in the absence of valuation fixation vis-à-vis the context (the embedding ratio is zero for above/below, which is context over mechanism): this engenders concern to amplify the multiplexity, the many-strandedness of ties.

Structural Models

Multiplex social networks have been represented and interpreted in a very large and flexible variety of ways (Burt 1982, 1985, 1989; Holland and Leinhardt 1979; Freeman, D. White, and Romney 1989; Romo 1992; Wellman and Berkowitz 1988). Networks can be turned inside out into duals in several ways; measures can be imposed upon links, and stochastic variability added; the notion of ordered set can be generalized to allow for three-body interaction; and so on (Harary 1977).

Linguistic structures suggest new kinds of models for embedding disciplines in networks; for example, kinship role structures as sketched in the section on blockmodeling in chapter 3. A variety of modern algebras furnish powerful formal frameworks for this, although much needs to be done to develop computational capacity.

John Boyd's book in press (1989) is the decisive mathematical development for blockmodels. Others, notably Breiger and Pattison (1986), Reitz and White (1989), and Wasserman and Faust (1991) have worked to integrate the two divergent perspectives on blockmodels, the graph-theoretic and the algebraic. But before Boyd no one has adequately grounded the approach in the mathematics.

Boyd offers mastery in the use of the finite representation theory of semigroup algebra: in particular the use of the Schutzenberger representation for decompositions into subdirect products (also foreshadowed in Pattison 1983), and of Green's relations. The full potential of ideal theory for idempotents is brought to bear, guided by lattice-theoretic considerations. In principle the mathematical material has long been available to all, as in the classic Clifford and Preston two-volume treatise on semigroups (1961, 1967), and in Fuchs's survey of partial order algebras (1963). But in practice it is an enormous step, and essential to applied work, to have such an integrated and informed development of the basic research as Boyd's.

Boyd's second contribution is equally important. He has shown how to bring the full power of real number operations to bear, replacing Boolean operations where appropriate. This is directly helpful in producing more robust and interpretable multiplication tables for semigroups. It also permits him to bring more powerful and gen-

eral computing algorithms to bear, so as to be closer to definitive resolution of questions of fit. Boyd shows how to obtain both smallest-
space results and discrete solutions.

Boyd reports as prototype a full analysis of one population,
Sampson's monastery (1969) on the brink of fission. The top panel of
figure 10 reproduced Boyd's multiplication table of a semigroup for
the Sampson data. The bottom panel reports a splitting of the actors
and networks, into two moieties in kinship terms, which is consistent with the algebra of multiple networks.

Combinatoric and Stochastic Models

Some sort of distance and locale for social relations are being generated in perceptions and assertions of network. But the topology, the
interconnectedness and twistedness, of a corresponding space remains open. It should depend upon the network's being spread
across a skein of actors (Laumann and Knoke 1985). "It" probably
should be plural and should draw upon other developments in psychology and related behavioral sciences. Shepard scalings have become a major technique for computing and representing mappings
which can give body to the notion of social spaces: cf. chapter 2 and
part B below.

Multiplex networks of social relations come embedded into and
embed such social formations as survive contending attempts at control. There emerges some order, at least middle-range order. It is as
if a social learning is taking place, and the question is how to theorize
and model this. There is a tradition of learning models (e.g., Bush
and Mosteller 1955), all stochastic, but they presuppose minds as the
learners, though the minds are treated as black boxes.

"Mind" has been dissolved by the new cognitive science (Wickelgren 1979) into a congeries of biological substrates, neurological
patternings (Nadel et al. 1989; McClelland and Rumelhart 1986), and
perception interfaces (Shepard and Cooper 1982). This dissolution
prepares the ground for thinking of persons themselves as interactive outcomes of continuing social patterns. These new directions in
neuro-cognitive psychology (discussed in the next section) seem
more promising than learning theory models as guides to stochastic
process modeling. They relate back to combinatoric traditions in
modeling.

Combinatorics (Riordan 1958; Ryser 1963) in much of natural science and statistical theory has been referred primarily to distributions of monads—of colored balls into boxes—with identifiability
being a chief issue. And it has been used so in some social science:

see Ijira and Simon (1977), White (1963b), and Zipf (1949). Consider the insistence upon individuation by a great mathematical scientist in his book on philosophical foundations:

> The philosophically most relevant feature of modern science is the emergence of abstract symbolic structures as the hard core of objectivity behind—as Eddington puts it—the colorful tale of the subjective story-teller mind. . . . The present appendix deals with some of the simplest structures imaginable, the combinatorics of aggregates and complexes . . . this primitive piece of symbolic mathematics is so closely related to the philosophically important problems of individuation and probabil-ity. . . . Our decision as to what is to be considered as equal or different influences the "counting" of different cases . . . it is through the com-binatorial theory of aggregates that these things find their exact mathe-matical interpretation. (Weyl 1949, Appendix B)

This "subjective storyteller mind" is itself but a colorful tale dress-ing up the reality of identities triggered by mischance. These identi-ties subsist in and come out of social networks, in ways which we should be able to model.

Understanding of social networks can be greatly enhanced by combinatorial analysis of skeletal structures, as was shown early in social science by Cliff and Robson (1978); Flament (1963); Ford and Fulkerson (1962); Holland and Leinhardt (1976); Howell (1979, 1988); Kemeny, Snell, and Thompson (1957); Luce (1953); Schelling (1978); and by Tuck (1955), among others. There are many unexplored avenues.[1]

Mathematicians like Erdos (1974) and Moon (1968) have published extensively on probabilistic approaches to large graphs. An early and useful physics survey of linear graphs, with topological and combi-natorial tables for small graphs, is Uhlenbeck and Ford (1962); and see Ziman (1979) for a recent survey. Feynman's sophisticated use of graphs (Hofstadter 1979, pp. 142–46 is the most accessible introduc-tion) to study dynamical transfigurations marked a new era in com-putation. The much more advanced analyses of matter which were set off (for a comprehensive survey cf. Ma 1973) have contributed to the new understanding of physico-chemical space treated earlier.

---

[1] A number of these were explored for dual mobility models in an earlier mono-graph of mine (White 1970b): e.g., match-making counts in section 8.6 and Systems of Distinct Representatives in section 11.3. Take another example: the family of theo-rems associated with Ramsey and Turan (Ore 1965). These curious discoveries, of a meta-logic, are that if only one keeps looking one always can see in any formal net-work structure some basis for arguing particular instances of cliques, fully connected corporates.

There are other combinatorial and stochastic lines of modeling network phenomena. One is the Davis-Holland-Leinhardt-Johnsen line of statistical/topological models for social structure as built out of triads. Like balance theory, these can be applied within persons also.

1. *Times*—For social phenomena at least, existing ideas of clock time must be greatly enlarged. Time is constructed by and in social formations; it is not some outside constraint imposed except to the limited, and variable extent that the biophysical is controlling. Explicit models will be crucial to developing this idea. perhaps the Feller arcsin law (Feller 1968; and see White 1963c for articulation to social setting) could be turned around to be an induction *of* time rather than a dependent *from* time. That is to say, identities interacting in some cumulative reputation fight may simply induce perception of time such that a "fair and just" frequency of predominance reversals take place.

We can suppose from having read Merton (1968), Mullins (1973), Crane (1972), and other sociological analyses of research that a dozen or so social scientists must be writing accounts parallel to this one. New ways of theorizing identity and choice among networks are coming onto the scene. There is a corresponding need to key into new ways of observing, recording, and analyzing—and thus recognizing and paying attention to—social action in social space-times.

2. *Parallel Distributed Processing*—Good leads for combinatorial aspects of social modeling can come from models of parallel distributed processing (PDP). They were developed by cognitive scientists in the faith that "Software rules on various levels can change, hardware rules cannot—in fact, to their rigidity is due the software's flexibility! Not a paradox at all, but a fundamental, simple fact about the mechanisms of intelligence" (Hofstadter 1979, p. 686).

Detailed accounts of PDP network models can be found in McClelland and Rumelhart (1986), McClelland (1985), and Feldman (1985). There is also a growing, rigorous technical literature (e.g., Newman 1987) to back up the impressionistic PDP models.

There are discouraging precedents. Kauffman (1969) heralded a wave of excitement about network models in the evolutionary genetics literature, but with little concrete result. However, the PDP approach unlike Kauffman's has definite mechanisms which are intuitively plausible as realizations of cybernetics. And after all, it took a long time for the anticipated impact of the McCulloch and Pitts piece and of Hebb (1949) to become manifest.

Outside experts see deep potential:

Connectionism provides a uniform framework within which diverse performances and competencies arise from a small set of general principles . . . the major appeal of the connectionist approach has been that, through error-driven tuning of their own weights, connectionist networks manifest a capability of "programming" themselves . . . however . . . only if sufficient knowledge about the world in which the system is to learn is already built into that system . . . there are general constraints that have uniformly governed the form and transformation of all terrestrial objects and situations throughout evolutionary history . . . space is locally Euclidean and three-dimensional. (Shepard 1989, pp. 105–7)

The core idea is that the strength or carrying capacity of connections, of ties in a network, can themselves be shaped and evolved by the passage of initial flows. There is a literal physical basis for learning. In PDP models this assumption can be modeled as an unobservable intermediate layer of nodes. This core idea seems similar to the independent idea of Boorman (1974; and cf. Boorman and Levitt 1980, chapter 5) for the evolution of sociality in animal populations: High variance in local connectivities is the key to the trait's establishing itself from some initial chance toehold, and the new trait does better if it is breaking out from a border peripheral location in the ecology of sites.

The real problem is that the PDP thinkers have underestimated the problematics of space. The creatures they wish to model live not just in biophysical space but in exfoliating sets of social network spaces: The Boorman work just cited on cascade diffusion is one model for attending to network spaces—in the context of island archipelago ecologies for various animal species. Another model is the Winship line leading to positional analysis in chapter 5 above.

Perception and cognition in social species must be dealing with and situating within multiple and Escherian compendia of spaces. Strategizing brings in yet further complexities. These are briefly discussed in chapters 6 and 7.

These PDP models may be more suited for social networks than they will prove to be for the neural networks to which it is hoped they apply! The advantage of social terrain over psychological for use of connectionist models is implied by Shepard's warning: "even if such a (connectionist) system were to exhibit intelligent behavior, its workings might remain as inscrutable and unspeakable as the workings of the mind itself" (1989, p. 108). The chapters above lay out examples which may be seen as manifestations of cybernetic networks in tangible social formations and processes. Burt's STRUCTURE programs can hook up with Davis's General Social Survey (Davis and Smith 1988) to provide general scans of networks around specific locales studied in organizations (Baker 1984; Laumann and Knoke 1987; Walker 1985), in communities (Fischer 1982; Wellman 1981), and so on.

There is a parallel earlier irony: balance theory was created by psychologists (Heider 1946; Abelson et al. 1968), and yet its most effective uses have been in the treatment of networks of affections among persons (Barnes 1972; Burt 1980; Cartwright and Harary 1956; Mitchell 1969, 1974; White 1961).

B. Space-Times

Somehow, "spaces" of social action must be specified to provide the foundation and core of effective models. There exist purely technical approaches: two examples are Atkin's (n.d.) operationalization of topology for city planning, and the survey of statistical assessments of social network models by Wasserman and Faust (1991). But there is a need for substantive theoretical guidance.

Social Spaces

The most straightforward theoretical attack on this is still Parsons and Bales (pp. 85–89, chapter 3 in Parson, Bales, and Shils 1953). On the suggestion of the mathematical psychologist R. R. Bush, they assumed a conventional Euclidean space, but it is "a" space rather than "the" physical Cartesian space or any enlargement of it. Their space is a context for and arrangement of indexes. They are lucid about its ontological status: "The unit which is the particle of the system then is a 'hypothetical' entity . . . [*footnote in original*: It is at least close to the concept of unit act developed in Parsons 1937], not to be confused with the units of observation. It is *this* to which location and change of location in action space must be attributed" (p. 87).

1. *Messiness*—is the first problem, the sheer messiness of the social contexts which are to be rendered into spaces with topologies. But physical space may have seemed as messy to the precursors of Descartes. We are creatures living within social goos, shards, and rubbery gels made up by and of ourselves. We, like gels, may dissolve into a different order under some heat. Even the frozen shards

exhibit only limited orderliness, and even then an orderliness lacking in homogeneity, and an orderliness made more problematic through its dual relation to physical space.[2]

Contrast the perception of social space as messy with the crisp intricacy yet uniform orderliness of physical space as reported earlier in the century, for example by Herman Weyl (1949). His was the era of crystalline views of matter (Seitz 1940) before natural science learned to pay attention to and do much with "gup." Social scientists should celebrate and exploit the current ability of natural sciences to take as serious topics exactly the gels, goos, and shards (DeGennes 1979) which seem at present the natural analogue to human social contexts with their conundrums of decoupling and embedding.[3] One can simply impose an abstract space, in the spirit of Shepard, as for example Winship (1977) does for sociometry and Levine (1991) does more generally.

2. *Rhetorics*—are the second problem: social spaces come from social reality as joint recognitions (however partial and flawed) across some array of identities triggered by happenstance. Even in being born, identities seek control and induce accountings, stories which circulate. Social space thus also must be mixed up with meanings, which are one sort of vehicle for decouplings.[4]

Stories come in sets and thereby do not constrain outcomes, either as to motives or by environment. Social spaces must accommodate stories and pertain to style. There are several beginnings within sociology (Abell 1987; Skvoretz, Fararo, and Axten 1980), some of which draw on the resources of comparative literature (Auerbach 1953; Ricoeur 1977; for a recent introduction see Lentricchia and McLaughlin 1990).

Larger meanings, styles, and valuations, become carriers of historical effects or what in technical jargon are called non-Markovian processes, and of localities—as well as of obfuscation. For example, each cohort of persons to some extent lives in its own time-bubble of

[2] Gibson and Shepard (see chap. 6 above) say we impose and must impose some orderliness on physical space just out of our psychological construction through evolutionary survival. We do not yet seem to have found such orderliness in perception of social life; we have not yet found the perspective points and scales and particular contexts which would render the view limpid.

[3] The current dissolution of space by quantum field theories is also instructive, as are contingency paradoxes in the spatial structuring of galaxies (Ferris 1982). I do not share the artificial-intelligence vision of spaces (Hofstadter 1979, perhaps because I first programmed in octal on the early vacuum-tube computer Whirlwind at MIT in the late '40s, long before automata theory and automation of recursion!).

[4] As well as of obfuscation: see presuppositions in the preface.

meanings, with appropriate signifiers of song, dress, and career, just as to some extent it fragments into other meaning-bubbles for ethnicity, profession, clique, and so on.

The sharpest dilemmas within this second problem are how to deal with times and how to deal with languages, both everyday language and high languages, permanent verbal languages and short-lived fashions. We must resist obfuscation by existing formulations; yet they are woven in as part of any social reality. On the mutual construction of narrative and time see Abbott (1983, 1984) and Ricouer (1988).

Physical and Formal Space-Times

Two major, successive sophistications from mathematical science of this century prepare us for new views of space for social action. One advance is topology. The second is the notion that "space is as space does," a notion which springs up independently in molecular biology (Lewontin 1974; Watson 1969), in ecology (Levins 1966), and in condensed matter physics (K. Wilson 1979). This second advance has also appeared, independently, in psychology (Gibson and Shepard as cited in chapters 1 and 4). The two are bridged by the Wiener-Kolmogorov developments of probability for Banach spaces.

Begin with philosophical insights from Albert Einstein:

> How would the ascent of a mountain be possible, if the use of hands, legs and tools had to be sanctioned step by step on the basis of the science of mechanics? And yet **in the interests of science it is necessary over and over again to engage in the critique of these fundamental concepts, in order that we may not unconsciously be ruled by them**. . . . Now as to the concept of space, it seems that this was preceded by the psychologically simpler concept of place. **Place is first of all a (small) portion of the earth's surface identified by a name**. . . . Simple analysis shows "place" also to be a group of material objects . . . by a natural extension of "box space" one can arrive at the concept of an independent (absolute) space, unlimited in extent, in which all material objects are contained. Then a material object not situated in space is simply inconceivable; on the other hand, in the framework of this concept formation it is quite conceivable that an empty space may exist. . . . These schematic considerations concern the nature of space from the geometric and from the kinematic point of view, respectively. They are in a sense reconciled with each other by Descartes' introduction of the coordinate system. . . . The concept of space was enriched and complicated by Galileo and Newton, in that space must be intro-

duced as the independent cause of the inertial behavior of bodies if one wishes to give the classical principle of inertia (and therewith the classical law of motion) an exact meaning. To have realized this fully and clearly is in my opinion one of Newton's greatest achievements. In contrast with Leibniz and Huygens, it was clear to Newton that the space concept of a group of objects was not sufficient to serve as the foundation for the inertia principle and the law of motion. He came to this decision even though he actively shared the uneasiness which was the cause of the opposition of the other two: space is not only introduced as an independent thing apart from material objects, but also is assigned an absolute role in the whole casual structure of the theory. This role is absolute in the sense that space (as an inertial system) acts on all material objects, while these do not in turn exert any reaction on space. It required a severe struggle to arrive at the concept of independent and absolute space, indispensable for the development of theory. . . . It seems to me that the atomic theory of the ancients, with its atoms existing separately from each other, necessarily presupposed a "box" space, while the more influential Aristotelian school tried to get along without the concept of independent (absolute) space. . . . The victory over the concept of absolute space or over that of the inertial system became possible only because **the concept of the material object was gradually replaced as the fundamental concept of physics by that of the field.** That which constitutes the spatial character of reality is then simply the four-dimensionality of the space. . . . there is no space without a field. (In his foreword for Jammer 1954)

1. *Mathematical sophistications*—Turn to mathematical authority for the modern discoveries about the hard core within any consistent conception of "space." "Space" long was conceived in the dimensions insisted upon by Descartes:

Poincaré had penetrated very deep, in stressing the inductive nature of the geometric meaning of dimension and the *possibility of disconnecting a space by subsets of lower dimension* . . . "to divide space, cuts that are called surfaces are necessary; to divide surfaces, cuts that are called lines are necessary; to divide lines, cuts that are called points are necessary" (Poincare 1912) . . . . Before the advent of set theory . . . a configuration was said to be *n*-dimensional if the least number of real parameters needed to describe its points, in some unspecified way, was *n*. The dangers and inconsistencies in this approach were brought into clear view by two celebrated discoveries of the last part of the 19th century: *Cantor's 1:1 correspondence between the points of a line and the points of a plane.* . . . The new concept of dimension clarified considerably the entire structure of topology. . . . Topology consists essentially in the study of the connectivity structure of spaces . . . the root-concept from which is derived . . . homology . . . dimension . . . etc.: *a space is connected if, except for the empty set and the whole space, there are no sets whose boundaries are empty.* . . . Any set of real numbers containing no interval is 0-dimensional . . . as is every non-empty finite or countable space. (Hurewicz and Wallman 1948, emphases added)

Identities seem discrete, however numerous, but perceptions of ties, controls, and moods arguably can be continuous, which leaves us confused as to whether social spaces must be 0-dimensional. Intricacy and thus interest is developed by mathematicians mainly for continuous spaces:

Starting from the Euclidean plane, we created topologically different surfaces by adding points at infinity in different ways. When a single point at infinity was added, the result was a sphere. If there is a line at infinity with one point at infinity on each family of parallel lines of the Euclidean plane, the surface is a projective plane . . . many theorems of Euclidean plane geometry are simplified, for there is no need to consider separately cases in which lines of the theorem are intersecting or parallel. (Blackett 1967, p. 45)

Every continuous surface is combinatorially equivalent to a sphere with a finite number of patches replaced by Mobius bands, cuffs, and handles. If there is at least one Mobius band in the "canonical equation," the surface contains a nonorientable piece and hence is nonorientable. If there are no cuffs on a surface, every edge occurs twice and the surface is closed. Orientability, the genus, and the number of cuffs are intrinsic properties of the surface which are invariant under combinatorial equivalence.

The concept of embeddedness, however, not only is crucial even to this case of continuous surfaces but also should generalize to discrete spaces (pp. 32–33): "One-sidedness and two-sidedness are not topological properties of surfaces . . . they are embedding properties that depend not only on the surface but also on the space in which the surface is located and the way in which the surface is embedded in this space."

So it turned out that the structure of a space is best built up by recognizing intercalations of neighborhoods, giving a new and subtler sense to dimensionality. We would do well to try to emulate this sophistication process: "The notion of a topological space . . . is a natural product of a continuing consolidation, abstraction and extension process . . . testing . . . by comparing the abstractly constructed object with the objects from which it derived" (Kelley 1955).

Topology is not the only part of mathematics that bears on spatial models. Mathematics can teach us an enormous variety of alternative formulations of space, which may be better suited to embedding the social. Mathematical combinatorics (Ryser 1963) and algebra (Kurosh 1965) host a very large number of alternative conceptualizations. There are new fields of metamathematics, such as category theory (Bucur and Deleanu 1968; Maclane 1971) which can join lattice theory (Birkhoff 1967) in establishing some order among the possibilities. Graph theory offers some richnesses (Harary 1977; Ore 1965):[5] Networks can be turned inside out into duals in several ways; measures can be imposed upon links and stochastic variability added; the notion of ordered set can be generalized to allow for three-body interaction; and so on. Nodes can be operationalized quite variously, as can multiplex ties.

2. *Dimensions from natural science*—A major recent advance in spatial understanding in natural science has been in biology, with DNA (Lewontin 1974), where, to the surprise of many,[6] Cartesian space proved the key to so-called "ordinary" space and separable time. Ironically, in just this era Cartesian space is being superseded in physics where it began: at macro-scope by Einstein's general relativity, at micro-scope by quantum chromodynamics, and recently at meso-scope by phase transition theory (Ma 1973; K. Wilson 1979).

The second major sophistication of recent vintage has come, however, from physics and chemistry of matter. Natural science studies of order/disorder have led to process-oriented approaches to topology, space becoming what it does:

> It can be shown under rather general conditions concerning the range of the forces that spontaneous crystalline order should not exist in one or two dimensions . . . a one-dimensional system cannot be topologically disordered. . . . We have begun to see the great importance of dimensionality in all theories of spatial order and disorder. . . . This fundamental topological characteristic may show its influence either through the convergence of a volume integral of some continuous func-

---

[5] It may be a painfully slow process to develop maximum likelihood statistical inference for such new structures. It has been a slow process for networks: see e.g., Marsden (1989) on use of Goodman (1979); Holland (1976, 1978, 1983; and with Bishop and Fienberg 1975); and see Fienberg and Wasserman (1981). But now Hubert (1987) has developed an ingenious new approach (see also Krackhardt 1988, who has later pointed to some biases in the approach).

[6] E.g., Lwoff (1966), Pattee (1979), and see Levins (1966) and Wilson (1979); Watson (1969) is vivid on the discovery of DNA.

tion, or through some combinatorial factor in the counting of steps along lattice paths. (Ziman 1979, p. 40)

One sees from this path too how "dimension" per se is an oversimplified and crude guide to a more general idea of imposing neighborhood structure on a family of sets. "Networks" have proved useful impositions for social spaces (White et al. 1976), and their topology is well known in a general way (Blackett 1967, chapter 6): "The topology of networks revolves around two operators, the boundary and the coboundary—which change numerical functions of edges into numerical functions of vertices, and conversely." Nontrivial topology which is not referred to dimensions is the needed direction for the spaces of social networks, which are combinatoric rather than continuous.

Physical systems can be abstracted and interpreted as networks in a variety of ways, some of which parallel existing models for social networks. There are clear leads in solid-state theory to appropriate models for social network spaces:

> A *Bethe Lattice* is an infinite regular tree . . . important in the theory of disordered systems as an artificial mathematical model for which some theoretical techniques give exact solutions. But . . . it cannot be realized as a physical system: to preserve the geometrical homogeneity of the structure and the equivalence of the z branches from each vertex, one would have to think of each branch as a step along a new dimension in a regular lattice of an *infinite* number of spatial dimensions. On the other hand, topologically speaking, a tree has many "one-dimensional" characteristics; it is simply connected and there is only one path between any two vertices. But it is not so restricted "locally" as a linear chain and has some of the combinatorial properties of a lattice of higher dimensionality . . . for example, the number of chains of length L that may be traced from a given vertex is exactly $z(z-1)^{L-1}$ . . . . This is a convenient model for the number of *self-avoiding walks* in a regular lattice. . . . But the dimensional ambivalence of this model can give rise to disturbing paradoxes. (Ziman 1979, pp. 152–54)

From such natural science developments of topology come suggestive leads for the enterprise of modeling social process. For example, here are important abstract discriminations among diffusion concepts—which evolved only in tandem with very extensive empirical work:

> The *site percolation* problem . . . of *"atoms" distributed at random on the sites of a regular lattice is the probability that a given atom belongs to an infinite*

cluster; . . . has much wider applicability, to problems as diverse as the percolation of a fluid through a porous medium and the spread of disease through an orchard. The companion problem of *bond percolation* applies to a lattice where a fraction of the "bonds" are . . . open to traversal. . . . This is none other than the problem of gel formation in a polymer solution. Numbers derived by laborious computations and Monte Carlo calculations . . . conform quite closely to a few simple empirical rules . . . *percolation occurs in a regular three- (two-) dimensional network if there are on the average more than 1.5 (2) favorable links to any node* . . . *site percolation occurs in a regular three- (two-) dimensional assembly when favorable regions occupy about 15 per cent (45 per cent) of the total volume* . . . these formulae remain tantalizingly approximate and empirical. . . . There is a subtle mathematical difference between a *diffusion process*, where the transition probabilities are re-randomized after each step, regardless of the position of the particle, and a *percolation process*, where the branching probabilities or restrictions are associated with the actual node reached by the particle at any given moment, and do not otherwise vary with time. (Ziman 1979, pp. 370–77, 481, italics his)

Granovetter and Soong (1983) and Schelling (1978) are among the few social scientists who have exploited these parallels.

The richness of the physical contexts encompassed are suggested by the following excerpts. First, accounts of polymer phenomenology which suggests how valuable formal modeling of even a crude sort can be:

> In three-dimensional polymer melts, the chains are essentially ideal and move freely. In two dimensions they should be slightly swollen and strongly segregated. . . . In a dense system each chain is gaussian and ideal. This was first understood by Flory, but the notion is so unexpected that it took a long time to reach the community of polymer scientists. . . . The notion of blobs. . . . Inside one blob the chain does not interact with other chains. the solution is essentially a closely packed system of blobs. (DeGennes 1979, pp. 61, 81)

And in more detail:

> A polymer gel is a network of flexible chains, with reticulation point (junctions) and with loops on some chains too, plus dangling end, and knots. . . . It is also possible to imagine a gel which would be made without any chemical bonding between the constituent chains; all the attachments being realized by suitable knots. We call this an "olympic gel" in analogy with the Olympic rings. . . . When we get to the gel phase . . . a finite fraction of the chains belong to an infinite network, and the system can resist stresses. Gels (very much like glasses) must

be described in terms of two ensembles, the preparative ensemble and the final ensemble. This is much more complex than the usual equilibrium systems, where a single ensemble ruled by Boltzmann exponentials is required . . . cross-links in a system of chains tends to induce a segregation between chains and solvent. . . . However because solvent expansion is slow in the gel phase . . . have the formation of very small pockets which have strange heterogeneities . . . ribbons, fibrils, nodules and so forth with sizes in the range of 200 to 1,000 angstroms . . . often have discouraged the experimentalists. . . . The classical picture for the transition to a strong gel is a "tree approximation" for the growing clusters . . . the essential simplification is . . . no closed cycles and no steric hindrances. The chain is assumed to branch off freely, the branches never being limited in their growth by the existence of other branches in the same cluster: the trees are taken to be ideal . . . clearly a gross oversimplification. . . . However, the tree approximation has been accepted by polymer scientists because it gives good values for the threshold, for the fraction of reacted bonds which is reached when the sol-gel transition takes place. (DeGennes 1979, pp. 128, 136)

The quote brings out the essentially historical nature of these physical phenomena, where there is no question of gaming and the like. The quotes are extensive to also bring out how centrally the natural phenomena, suggestive as they are for modeling the social, depend upon dimensionality. We cannot expect this basic aspect of physical space to be the same as for social spaces, anymore than biologists can for their analysis of systems (cf. Pattee 1979). An introduction to the latter, which is both lucid and requires no mathematical prerequisites, is Gold (1977).

Polymer plastics are not an isolated or peculiar kind of matter. The ways in which apparently totally different forms of matter share basic organization is suggestive for our task of modeling social configurations. In the words of Edwards (1981, p. 216): "The basic theoretical physics of quenching appears in its clearest form in the process of the cross-linking of polymers, and, in as much as from a mathematical point of view a rubber is a glass . . . a simple glass will betray the nature of its quenching." In the same volume proceedings, Kovacs has glass as disequilibrium of long duration, with nonlinear and asymmetric recovery and pronounced memory effects, and Robertson emphasizes that glasses are combinations of localized environments. The details of glass are brittle but its macro properties are robust—it sounds very like Mayer's caste India, taken up in chapter 6. Separation of process from structure models no longer seems cogent.

C. Persons as Kalman Filters

The root distinction of the social as system is that it engenders and functions in social space-times that are dual to and alongside bio-physical space-time. Persons are contingent by-products which are traceable to this distinction. There should be an epistemology for systems, some sort of multiple cybernetics suitable to persons. I shall argue for an engineering epistemology.

Persons

Specification of models for formation of persons out of identities has not proceeded far. This is in part because of difficulties with robustness and reliability, once outside highly restricted contexts such as tournament chess (Leifer 1991).

One possibility is a general model of bruising. This would be stochastic, setting encounters in heterogeneous kinds of arenas, so that its predictions can be decoupled from details about social formations of embedding. Such a model can capture a central insight that correlative and interactive mechanisms shape as they create identities. One can draw upon a wealth of epidemiological (Bailey 1957, 1982) and of social psychological (Brown 1965) models.

In parallel, one can model ties as generated stochastically as by-products of struggles for control (cf. Grusky, Bonacich, and Peyrot 1988). Introducing network context explicitly should help to model identity formation as a tangible process. It is natural to have self-similar, level-invariant uses of such models. By setting the interaction intensity at which bruising occurs, for example, one can accommodate wholly different substantive ideas. These may range from the most discontinuous triggering notion, just on/off, to a gradualist accretion model which begins to shade into an essentialist one from classical philosophy.

A second possibility is adaptation of game theory. Identity was paired with control in the text, and perhaps game theory can be turned around to help model formation of players as robust identities (Putnam 1988; Shapley and Grofman 1984; Shubik 1984 a,b). In the paradigms of objective phenomenology available from existing culture, the closest parallel to identity formation are the analysis of strategic doctrines (Clauswitz 1976), which pertain to compound actors. Although such compounds are more complex, they are easier to map (Boorman 1974), and it may be that the theory of simple games could model their formation.

A third approach is through natural system models. I question whether the functional/structural system properties of biological creatures and systems[7] are a useful guide to persons. I am inclined to deny analogy between social system and biological organism as system.[8] The main distinction of the biological organism, too often elided in social science borrowings from it, is the existence of a dual, zygote population which alternates with population of organisms. This book does not attempt to incorporate biological substrates: nor the neurology and physiology of the human organism;[9] nor the genetics of social behavior, except for analogies to island-cascade models (cf. Boorman and Levitt 1980); nor comparative biosociology of species[10] (E. Wilson 1979); nor population ecology[11] (Hannan and Freeman 1977); nor behaviorism[12] (Skinner 1953). However, in developing the duality with physical spaces, I have endeavored to avoid inconsistency with approaches through biological substrates.

Kalman Filters

Process and how it refounds network structures and social spaces are the core issues. The modern theories of quantum electrodynamics and of sloppy matter have each modeled process refounding structure.[13] How can it be done for social spaces from identities seeking control?

A first step is to consider engineering theories of control and how they might be applied to individuals as actors:

> The advantages of distributed control are (a) the autonomy of local controllers allows the reliability and simplicity of generation 1 schemes [local analogue controllers operated independently, in parallel] . . . (b) Intercommunication via the data highway allows integrated control as in generation 2 systems [large computers, centralized operation] . . . (c) The complete system configured, commissioned and operated without

---

[7] See e.g., Lwoff (1962) for micro level, Levins (1966) for meso level, and for population level see Simpson (1960).

[8] Even the primitive numbers are way off—Ns of 10^4 as opposed to 10^8 discriminable units; evolution over 10^6 versus 10^9 years.

[9] Except for a brief excursus on neural net models below.

[10] Except for treatment of pecking orders (Chase 1990) in chapter 2.

[11] Except for Tuck's triangle and some other size distribution arguments in chapters 3 and 5.

[12] Behaviorism is not individualism, in the social science sense (contrary to Homans 1958); rather, it relates to the biology of individuals as ecology does to the biology of populations.

[13] See note 10.

extensive software effort. Algorithms called from manufacturers are interconnected by programs resident in local RAMS [softwiring] using a control-oriented high-level language. The system is readily expanded and modified. (Leigh 1987, p. 110)

A basic idea, decoupling, is missing from standard engineering. Standard control theory is analogous not to control as defined in this book but rather to "social discipline," because explicitly given goals are assumed. Decoupling is then at most a device interjected so that different interlocking control loops can be adjusted independently. I argue that in getting action in social contexts it works better to change goals than to pay heavy costs of predetermined control goals; or rather it works better to float with and adjust goals, maintaining a sort of overall control: a delicate balance!

Space exploration was one impetus for more advanced systems for engineering control, which go beyond the classic theory (Bryson and Ho 1969). Kalman filters are core models for these systems. Persons' uses of control, as construed in the present work, can be assimilated to Kalman filters.

The person becomes a Kalman filter to the extent s/he goes with the social tide. A Kalman filter is an engineering system which is self-instructive as to the principles which it should use (Leigh 1987; Kailath 1974). An ideal Wall Street denizen would be a Kalman filter, in that s/he would shift from being a technician—a chart reader and extrapolater of the preceding market traces—to being a fundamentalist probing the substance of business changes, according to reading signals as to whether there was some real information in the fundamentals.

A person is one coupling between distinct populations, as shown in chapter 5. Distinct populations are the human settings of alternate principles. A person is induced as a Kalman filter which shifts in process between distinct populations according to online reading of signals.

There are many sources on Kalman filters. Leigh (1987) explains the phenomenology of the engineering; Kailath (1974) surveys the more general conceptual and mathematical context. There is also a recent account by an economist (Harvey 1989), who however misses the central ideas. They all go back to cybernetics, in some sense, to the initial ideas about extrapolation and filling-in of time series developed by the mathematician Norbert Weiner that merged with the development of recursive function applications as surveyed in Hofstadter (1979).

The Kalman filter also could be an appropriate analogue to a dynamics for the models of how actors made up of identities work, discussed in the preceding section and in chapter 2. The actor is in fact a compound, a discipline built out of triggered identities, built according to alternative plans. Others have argued much the same: "Societies everywhere must mobilize their members as self-regulating participants in social encounters. One way is through ritual. . . . Universal human nature is not a very human thing. By acquiring it, the person becomes a kind of construct, built up not from inner psychic propensities but from moral rules that are impressed upon him from without" (Goffman 1967, p. 43). Coleman (1990, chapters 19, 20) shares much the same view.

Discipline species should apply as well within persons as they do to larger exemplars of disciplines, since persons too are mutual balancings that amount to embeddings of constituents which themselves are triggered by-products of social pattern and shared interpretation schemes. Persons consisting in disciplines ties us back to a literature from cognitive and perceptual psychology. Shepard (1989, p. 105) is proposing, in effect, the Kalman filter as a model for human performance. Disciplines also apply at much larger scales, such as markets and parties, quite as well as they do at the personal level. Larger congeries, institutions, may also function as Kalman filters. Consider plea-bargaining in the courts, analyzed as a system by Padgett (1989). Leigh's diagram can be transposed directly there.

The Kalman filter thus can serve as model both for the person as seen from "above," as intersection of populations, and from "below," as integrator of identities. Many of the assertions and conjectures in Appendix 1 can be specialized to apply to persons in one or the other of these modes. Together they imply that personal complexity goes down as cultural schemes are elaborated. In Goffman's words (1955; and see Weick 1968), "The person as a ritually delicate object has special license to accept mistreatment at his own hands." This is an issue for the person as strategizer of control.

APPENDIX 3

LIST OF SOFTWARE

J. Atkins (U. Essex, UK)—Grafik: a multipurpose kinship metalanguage

P. Bonacich (UCLA)—Membership interlock algorithms

R. L. Breiger (Cornell University)—CONCOR (APL language) for blockmodels and nested fits of partitions

R. L. Burt (Columbia University)—STRUCTURE (general network analysis package)

K. Carley (Carnegie-Mellon University)—CONSTRUCT1 (transportable simulation model)

M. G. Everett (UC-Irvine)—EBLOC (graph-theoretic blocking algorithm)

L. Freeman (University of California-Irvine)—UCINET (general network program package)

G. H. Heil (Toronto)—COBLOCK; SR PROGS (Network algorithms in APL)

P. Holland (Educational Testing Service, NJ)— Triad distribution statistics

E. R. Leifer (Columbia University)—Markets for Managers (APL language, DOS environment)

F. U. Pappi (University of Manheim)—SONIS (general network analysis package)

P. Pattison (University of Melbourne)—Blockmodel algebras (transportable, in FORTRAN)

F. Stokman (University of Groningen)—GRADAP (flexible object process programming language)

WORKS CITED

Aarts, E., and J. Korst. *Simulated Annealing and Boltzmann Machines*. New York: Wiley, 1989.

Abbott, Andrew. "Status and Status Strain in the Professions." *American Journal of Sociology* 86(1981): 819–836.

———. "Sequences of Social Events: Concepts and Methods for the Analysis of Order in Social Processes." *Historical Methods* 16(1983): 129–147.

———. "Event Sequence and Event Duration: Colligation and Measurement." *Historical Methods* 17(1984): 192–204.

———. *The System of Professions*. Chicago: University of Chicago Press, 1988.

———. "The New Occupational Structure: What Are the Questions?" *Work and Occupations* 16(1989): 273–291.

Abbott, Andrew, and John Forrest. "Optimal Matching Methods for Historical Sequences." *Journal of Interdisciplinary History* 16(1986): 471–494.

Abdul-Jabbar, Kareem. *Giant Steps*. New York: Bantam Books, 1983.

Abell, Peter. *Social Syntax*. Oxford: Clarendon Press, 1987.

Abelson, Robert P., and M. J. Rosenberg. "Symbolic Psychologic: A Model of Attitudinal Cognition." *Behavioral Science* 3(1958): 1–13.

Abelson, Robert, Elliot Aronson, W. McGuire, T. M. Newcomb, M. J. Rosenberg, and P. H. Tannenbaum, eds. *Theories of Cognitive Consistency: A Sourcebook*. Chicago: Rand McNally, 1968.

Abolafia, M. "Structured anarchy: formal organization in the commodities futures market." In *The Social Dynamics of Financial Markets*, edited by P. Adler and P. Adler. Greenwich, CT: JAI Press, 1984.

Acquaviva, S. S., and M. Santuccio. *Social Structure in Italy: Crisis of a System*. Translated by Colin Hamer. London: Martin Robertson, 1976.

Adler, Judith. *Artists in Offices*. New Brunswick, NJ: Transaction Books, 1979.

Alchian, A., and H. Demsetz. "Production, Information Costs and Economic Organization." *American Economic Review* 62(1972): 777–795.

Alexander, Jeffrey C. *The Modern Reconstruction of Classical Thought: Talcott Parsons*. Berkeley and Los Angeles: University of California Press, 1983.

———. *Action and its Environment: Towards a New Synthesis*. New York: Columbia University Press, 1988.

———. "Parsons' Prolegomena to a Theory of Social Institutions: Commentary: Structure, Value, Action." *American Sociological Review* 55(1990): 339–345.

Alexander, Jeffrey C., and Steven Seidman, eds. *Culture and Society: Contemporary Debates*. New York: Cambridge University Press, 1988.

Alexander, Jennifer, and Paul Alexander. "What's a Fair Price?: The Cultural Construction of Information in Javanese Markets." Manuscript, Anthropology Department, University of Sydney, May 1990.

Alexander, Michael. *Cicero's Letters*. London, 1935.

Alford, Robert R. *Health Care Politics*. Chicago: University of Chicago Press, 1975.

Allen, Patrick M. "Power and Privilege in the Large Corporation." *American Journal of Sociology* 86(1981).

Allison, Graham T. *Essence of Decision*, Boston: Little, Brown, 1971.

Alonso, William. *Location and Land Use: Toward a General Theory of Land Rent*. Cambridge, MA: Harvard University Press, 1964.

Aminzade, Ronald. "Party Formation, Social Class and Suffrage Reform." In *Political Power and Social Theory: 6*, edited by Maurice Zeitlin, 1987.

Anderson, Lisa, "States and Regimes." Political Science Department, Columbia University, manuscript, May 1989.

Anderson, M. S. *Europe in the Eighteenth Century: 1713–1783*. London: Longmans, 3d ed., 1987.

Anderson, Michael. *Family Structure in Nineteenth Century Lancashire*, Cambridge: Cambridge University Press, 1971.

Anderson, Perry. *Lineages of the Absolutist State*. London: New Left Books, 1974.

Andreassen, Paul B., and Stanley Schachter. "The Effects of Price Variability and News on Volume of Trading and Profits." Department of Psychology, Columbia University, 1984.

Andrews, P.W.S. *On Competition in Economic Theory*. London, 1964.

Antal, F. *Florentine Painting and its Social Background: The Bourgeois Republic before Cosimo de Medici's Advent to Power: XIV and early XV Centuries*. London: Routledge and Kegan Paul, 1965.

Apter, David. *The Politics of Modernization*, Chicago: University of Chicago Press, 1965.

Arabie, Phipps, and Scott A. Boorman. "Blockmodels: Developments and Prospects." In *Classifying Social Data*, edited by H. C. Hudson, 177–198. San Francisco: Jossey-Bass, 1982.

Arabie, Phipps, Scott A. Boorman, and Paul R. Levitt. "Constructing Blockmodels: How and Why." *Journal of Mathematical Psychology* 17(1978): 21–63.

Arensberg, Conrad M., and D. Macgregor. "Determination of Morale in an Industrial Company." *Applied Anthropology* 1(1942): 11–34.

Argyle, M. *Bodily Communication*. New York: International University Press, 1975.

Arrow, Kenneth J. *Social Choice and Individual Values*. New York: Wiley, 1951.
———. "Problems of Resource Allocation in United States Medical Care." In *The Challenge of Life*, edited by R. M. Kunz and H. Fehr. Basel: Stuttgart: Birkhauser-Verlag, 1972.

Arrow, Kenneth J., and Frank H. Hahn. *General Competitive Analysis*. San Francisco: Holden-Day, 1971.

Arthur, W. Brian. "Competing technologies and lock-in by historical small events: The dynamics of allocation under increasing returns." Center for Economic Policy Research, Pub. #43, Stanford University, January 1985.

Ascher, Marcia, and Robert Ascher. *Code of the Quipu: A Study in Media, Mathematics and Culture*. Ann Arbor, MI: University of Michigan Press, 1981.

Ashford, Douglas E. *British Dogmatism and French Pragmatism*, London and Boston: Allen Unwin, 1982.

Ashley, Richard K. *The Political Economy of War and Peace*. London: Pinter, 1980.

Atkin, R. H. *Research Report #1*. Urban Studies Research Project, Department of Mathematics, University of Essex, n.d.

Aubert, Vilhelm. *The Hidden Society*. Totowa, NJ: Bedminster Press, 1965.

Auerbach, Erich. *Mimesis: The Representation of Reality in Western Literature*. Princeton, NJ: Princeton University Press, 1953.

Auerbach, Joel D., Robert Putnam, and Bert A. Rockman. *Bureaucrats and Politicians in Western Democracies*. Cambridge, MA: Harvard University Press, 1981.

Austin, William W. *Music in the Twentieth Century: From Debussy through Stravinsky*. New York: Norton, 1966.

Axelrod, R. *The Evolution of Cooperation*. New York: Basic Books, 1984.

———, ed. *Structure of Decision: The Cognitive Maps of Political Elites*. Princeton, NJ: Princeton University Press, 1976.

Aylmer, G. E. *The King's Servants: The Civil Service of Charles I in 1625–1642*. New York: Columbia University Press, 1961.

Bachnik, Jane M. "Recruitment Strategies for Household Succession." *Man* 18(1983): 160–182.

Bachrach, P., and M. S. Baratz. "Two Faces of Power." *American Political Science Review* 56(1962): 947–952.

Badian, E. *Foreign Clientelae, 264–70 B.C.*, Oxford: Clarendon Press, 1958.

———. *Publicans and Sinners: Private Enterprise in the Service of the Roman Republic*. Ithaca, NY: Cornell University Press, 1982.

Bailes, Kendall E. *Technology and Society Under Lenin and Stalin*. Princeton, NJ: Princeton University Press, 1978.

Bailey, N.T.J. *The Mathematical Theory of Epidemics*. London: Griffin, 1957.

———. *The Biomathematics of Malaria*. London: Griffin, 1982.

Bailey, Robert W. *The Crisis Regime: The MAC, the EFCB and the Political Impact of the New York City Financial Crisis*. Albany, NY: State University of New York Press, 1984.

Bailey, William, and Calvin Morrill. "The Skinhead Threat: Power, Identity and Social Style." Department of Communication, University of Arizona, December 1989.

Bain, Joe S. *Barriers to New Competition*. Cambridge, MA: Harvard University Press, 1956.

Baker, R. H. "Clientelism in the post-revolutionary state: The Soviet Union." In C. Clapham, ed., 1982.

Baker, Scott. "Reflection, Doubt and the Place of Rhetoric in Postmodern Social Theory." *Sociological Theory* 8(1990): 232–248.

Baker, Wayne. "The Social Structure of a National Securities Market." *American Journal of Sociology* 89(1984): 775–811.

———. "Floor Trading and Crowd Dynamics." In *The Social Dynamics of Financial Markets*, edited by P. Adler and P. Adler. Greenwich, CT: JAI Press, 1985.

Baker, Wayne. "What is Money?: A Social Structural Interpretation." Chap. 4 in Mizruchi and Schwartz, 1987.

———. "Market Networks and Corporate Behavior." *American Journal of Sociology* 96(1990): 589–625.

Bakhtin, M. *Rabelais and his World*. Cambridge, MA: MIT Press, 1968.

Baldwin, David A. "Money and Power." *Journal of Politics* 33(1971): 578–614.

———. "Power and Social Exchange." *American Political Science Review* 72(1978): 1229–1242.

Bales, Robert Freed. *Personality and Interpersonal Behavior*. New York: Holt-Rinehart-Winston, 1970.

Ballonoff, Paul, ed. *Genealogical Mathematics*. Paris: Mouton, 1974.

Banfield, Edward C., and James Q. Wilson. *City Politics*. New York: Random House, 1963.

Bank, J. "Verzuiling: A Confessional Road to Secularization, Emancipation and the Decline of Political Catholicism, 1920–1970." In *Britain and the Netherlands*, edited by A. C. Duke and C. A. Tamse, 207–231. The Hague, 1981.

Barber, Bernard. "Case Materials and Case Analysis in American Professional Training." Manuscript circa 1953.

———. "Absolutization of the Market." In *Markets and Morals*, edited by G. Dworkin, G. Bermant, and P. Brown. New York: Halsted Press, 1977.

———. *Effective Social Science: Eight Cases in Economics, Political Science and Sociology*. New York: Russell Sage Foundation, 1987.

Barnard, Chester. *The Functions of the Executive*. Cambridge, MA: Harvard University Press, 1938.

Barnes, J. A. *Social Networks*. Reading, MA: Addison-Wesley, 1972.

Barnet, Sylvan, Morton Berman, and William Burto. *A Dictionary of Literary Terms*. Boston: Little, Brown, 1960.

Baron, James N., and W. T. Bielby. "Bringing the Firms Back In." *American Sociological Review* 45(1980): 737–765.

———. "The Organization of Work in a Segmented Economy." *American Sociological Review*. 49(1984): 454–473.

Barraclough, Geoffrey. *The Origins of Modern Germany*. Oxford: Blackwell, 1946.

———. *The Medieval Papacy*. New York: Harcourt, Brace and World, 1968.

Barth, Fredrik. *Political Leadership Among Swat Pathans*. University of London, Athlone Press, 1965.

Baumol, William J., John C. Panzar, and R. D. Willig. *Contestable Markets and the Theory of Industry Structure*. San Diego, CA: Harcourt Brace Jovanovich, 1988.

Baxandall, Michael. *Painting and Experience in Fifteenth Century Italy*. New York: Oxford University Press, 1975.

———. *The Limewood Sculpture of Renaissance Germany*. New Haven, CT: Yale University Press, 1980.

Bearman, Peter. "The Eclipse of Localism and the Formation of a National Gentry Elite in England, 1540–1640." Ph.D. thesis, Department of Sociology, Harvard University, 1985.

———. "The Social Structure of Suicide." *Sociological Forum* 5(September 1991).

Beato, Paulino. "The Existence of Marginal Cost Pricing Equilibria with Increasing Returns." *Quarterly Journal of Economics* 97(1982): 669–687.

Becker, Carl L. *The Heavenly City of the Eighteenth-Century Philosophers.* New Haven, CT: Yale University Press, 1932.

Becker, Gary S. *A Treatise on the Family.* Cambridge, MA: Harvard University Press, 1981.

Becker, Howard. *Art Worlds.* Berkeley, CA: University of California Press, 1982.

Becker, Howard, and Charles Ragin, eds. *The Logic of Social Inquiry: What is a Case?* New York: Cambridge University Press, 1992.

Bell, Daniel. *The Cultural Contradictions of Capitalism.* New York: Basic Books, 1978.

———. *The End of Ideology: On the Exhaustion of Political Ideas in the Fifties* (reissue of 1965 original). Cambridge, MA: Harvard University Press, 1988.

Bellman, Richard. *Dynamic Programming.* Princeton, NJ: Princeton University Press, 1957.

Bendor, Jonathan, and Piotr Swistak. "The Evolutionary Stability of Cooperation." Manuscript, University of Maryland Collective Choice Center, College Park, MD, 1991.

Bennett, S. *A History of Control Engineering, 1800–1930.* New York: Peter Peregrinus, 1979.

Bensman, Joseph, and R. Lilienfeld. *Craft and Consciousness.* New York: Wiley, 1973.

Benson, J. K. "The Interorganizational Network as a Political Economy." *Administrative Science Quarterly* 20(1975): 229–249.

Benston, George. "Required disclosure and the Stock Market." In *The Development of SEC Accounting*, edited by Gary J. Previts. Reading, MA: Addison-Wesley, 1981.

Berge, C. *The Theory of Graphs and Its Applications*, Translated by A. Doig. New York: Wiley, 1962.

Berge, C., and V. Chvatal. *Topics on Perfect Graphs.* Amsterdam: North-Holland, 1984.

Bergesen, Albert. "Art Styles and Linguistic Codes." Sociology Department, University of Arizona, 1983.

Bergesen, Albert, Roberto M. Fernandez, and Chintamani Sahoo. "America and the Changing Structure of Hegemonic Production." Chap. 8 in *America's Changing Role in the World System*, edited by Terry Boswell and Albert Bergesen. New York: Praeger, 1987.

Berkowitz, S. D. *An Introduction to Structural Analysis: The Network Approach to Social Research.* Toronto: Butterworths, 1982.

Berle, Adolf A., and Gardiner C. Means. *The Modern Corporation and Private Property.* New York: Macmillan, 1933.

Berman, Harold J. *Law and Revolution: The Formation of the Western Legal Tradition.* Cambridge, MA: Harvard University Press, 1983.

Bernal, Martin. *Black Athena: The Afroasiatic Roots of Classical Civilization.* New Brunswick, NJ: Rutgers University Press, 1987.

Bernard, Paul. "Association and Hierarchy: The Social Structure of the Adolescent Society." Ph.D. thesis, Sociology Department, Harvard University, 1974.

Bernheim, B. D., and Michael D. Whinston. "Common Agency." *Econometrica* 54(1986): 923–942.

Betts, Richard K. *Surprise Attack.* Washington, D.C.: Brookings, 1982.

———. *Nuclear Blackmail and Nuclear Deterrence.* Washington, D.C.: Brookings, 1987.

Bialer, Seweryn. "Gorbachev's Move." *Foreign Policy* 68(1987): 59–87.

Biddle, Bruce. "Recent Developments in Role Theory." *Annual Review of Sociology* 12(1986): 67–92.

Bidwell, Charles E., and John D. Kasarda. *Structuring in Organizations: Ecosystem Theory Evaluations.* Greenwich, CT: JAI Press, 1987.

Bilous, Frances R., and Robert M. Krauss. "Dominance and Accommodation in the Conversational Behaviours of Same and Mixed-Gender Dyads." Manuscript, Department of Psychology, Columbia University, 1989.

Birkhoff, Garrett. *Lattice Theory,* 3d ed. Providence, RI: American Mathematical Society, 1967.

Birkhoff, Garrett, and S. Mac Lane. *A Survey of Modern Algebra.* New York: Macmillan, 1953.

Bishop, Yvonne, Stephen E. Fienberg, and Paul W. Holland, *Discrete Multivariate Analysis.* Cambridge, MA: MIT Press, 1975.

Bjerstedt, Ake. *Interpretations of Sociometric Choice Status.* Lund: Gleerup, 1956.

Black, Duncan. *The Theory of Committees and Election.* Cambridge, UK: Cambridge University Press, 1958.

Blackett, Donald W. *Elementary Topology: A Combinatorial and Algebraic Approach.* New York: Academic Press, 1967.

Blau, Peter M. *Dynamics of Bureaucracy.* New York: Random House, 1956.

———. *Exchange and Power in Social Life.* New York: Wiley, 1964.

Blau, Peter M., and Otis Dudley Duncan, *The American Occupational Structure.* New York: Wiley, 1967.

Blau, Peter M., and William R. Scott. *Formal Organization.* San Francisco: Chandler, 1962.

Blau, Peter M., and R. K. Merton, eds. *Continuities in Structural Inquiry.* Beverly Hills, CA: Sage, 1981.

Bloch, R. Howard. *Medieval French Literature and Law.* Berkeley, CA: University of California Press, 1977.

Block, Fred. *Postindustrial Possibilities: A Critique of Economic Discourse.* Berkeley, CA: University of California Press, 1990.

Bloom, David. "Is Arbitration *Really* Compatible with Bargaining?" *Industrial Relations.* 20(1981): 233–244.

Blum, Jerome. *Lord and Peasant in Russia.* Princeton, NJ: Princeton University Press, 1961.

Blunt, Anthony, *Artistic Theory in Italy, 1450–1600.* Oxford: Clarendon Press, 1958.

Blythe, Ronald. *Akenfield: Portrait of an English Village.* New York: Pantheon, 1969.

——. *The View in Winter: Reflections on Old Age.* London: Harcourt, Brace, Jovanovich, 1979.

Bogue, Donald J., and Calvin L. Beale. *Economic Areas of the United States.* New York: Free Press, 1961.

Bonacich, Phillip. "Using Boolean Algebra to Analyze Overlapping Memberships." In *Sociological Methodology,* edited by K. F. Schuessler. San Francisco: Jossey-Bass, 1977.

——. "The 'Common Structure Semigroup': An Alternative to the Boorman and White 'Joint Reduction.'" *American Journal of Sociology* 81(1980): 1384–1446.

——. "Power and Centrality: A Family of Measures." *American Journal of Sociology.* 92(1987): 1170–1182.

——. "What is a Homomorphism?" Chap. 8 in Freeman et al., 1989.

Bonacich, Phillip, and Maureen J. McConaghy "The Algebra of Blockmodelling." In *Sociological Methodology 1980,* edited by K. F. Schuessler, 489–532. San Francisco: Jossey-Bass, 1979.

Bonilla, Frank. *The Failure of Elites.* Cambridge, MA: MIT Press, 1970.

Boone, James L., and Charles L. Redman. "Alternative Pathways to Urbanism in the Medieval Maghreb." *Comparative Urban Research* 9(1982): 28–38.

Boorman, Scott A. *The Extended Game: A Wei-Ch'i Interpretation of Maoist Revolutionary Strategy.* Oxford: Oxford University Press, 1969.

——. "Island Models for Takeover by a Social Trait Facing a Frequency-Dependent Selection Barrier in a Mendelian Population." *Proceedings of the National Academy of Sciences* 71(1974): 2103–2107.

——. "A Combinatorial Optimization Model for Transmission of Job Information through Contact Networks." *Bell Journal of Economics* 6(1975): 216–249.

Boorman, Scott A., and Paul R. Levitt. *The Genetics of Altruism.* New York: Academic Press, 1980.

Boorman, Scott A., and Harrison C. White. "Social Structure from Multiple Networks: Part II, Role Interlock." *American Journal of Sociology.* 81(1976): 1384–1446.

Bott, Elizabeth. *Family and Social Network.* London: Tavistock, 1957.

Boudon, Raymond. *Educational Opportunity and Social Inequality.* New York: Wiley, 1973.

Bourdieu, Pierre. "Social Space and the Genesis of Groups." *Theory and Society* 14(1985): 723–744.

Bove, Paul A. *Intellectuals in Power: A Genealogy of Critical Humanism.* New York: Columbia University Press, 1986.

Bower, Joseph L. *Managing the Resource Allocation Process.* Homewood, IL: Irwin Press, 1972.

Boyd, John P. "The Algebra of Group Kinship." *Journal of Mathematical Psychology* 6(1969): 139–167.

——. "The Universal Semigroup of Relations." *Social Networks* 2(1980): 91–117.

Boyd, John P. *Social Semigroups: A Unified Theory of Scaling and Blockmodelling as Applied to Social Networks*. Fairfax, VA: George Mason University Press, 1991.

Bradach, Jeffrey L., and Robert G. Eccles. "Price, Authority, and Trust: from Ideal Types to Plural Forms." *Annual Review of Sociology* 15(1989): 97–118.

Bradfield, I., ed. *Ibn Khaldun: Collected Works*. London: Cambridge University Press, 1973.

Bradfield, Richard M. *A Natural History of Associations*, vols. I and II. London: Duckworth, 1973.

Bradley, Ian, and Ronald L. Meek. *Matrices and Society*. Princeton, NJ: Princeton University Press, 1986.

Brady, Robert A. *The Rationalization Movement in German Industry*. Berkeley, CA: University of California Press, 1933.

Brady, Thomas A. *Turning Swiss: City and Empire, 1450–1550*. New York: Cambridge University Press, 1985.

Brand, Myles. *Intending and Acting: Toward a Naturalized Action Theory*. Cambridge, MA: MIT Press, 1984.

Braudel, Fernand. *The Mediterranean and the Mediterranean World in the Age of Philip II*. Translated by Sian Reynolds, New York, 1972.

———. *The Wheels of Commerce*. Translated by S. Reynolds. New York: Harper & Row, 1982.

Breiger, Ronald L. "The Duality of Persons and Groups." *Social Forces* 53(December, 1974): 181–190.

———. "Career Attributes and Network Structure: A Blockmodel Study of a Biomedical Research Specialty." *American Sociological Review* 41(February, 1976): 117–135.

———. "Toward an Operational Theory of Community Elite Structures," *Quality and Quantity*, 13(1979): 21–57.

———. "Structures of Economic Interdependence among Nations." Chap. 12 in *Continuities in Structural Inquiry*, edited by Peter M. Blav and Robert K. Merton. Beverly Hills, CA: Sage, 1981a.

———. "The Social Class Structure of Occupational Mobility." *American Journal of Sociology* 87(1981b): 578–611.

———. "Social Control and Social Network: A Model from Georg Simmel." In Calhoun, Meyer, and Scott, eds., 1990.

———. *Explorations in Structural Analysis*. New York: Garland, 1991.

———, ed. *Social Mobility and Social Structure*. Cambridge: Cambridge University Press, 1990.

Breiger, Ronald L., Scott A. Boorman, and Phipps Arabie "An Algorithm for Clustering Relational Data with Applications to Social Network Analysis and Comparison with Multidimensional Scaling." *Journal of Mathematical Psychology* 12(August, 1975): 328–383.

Breiger, Ronald L., and James G. Ennis, "Personal and Social Roles: The Network Structure of Personality Types in Small Groups." *Social Psychology Quarterly*, 42(1979): 262–270.

Breiger, Ronald L., and Philippa E. Pattison. "The Joint Role Structure of Two Communities' Elites." *Sociological Methods and Research* 7(1978): 213–226.

————. "Cumulated Social Roles: The Duality of Persons and their Algebras." *Social Networks* 8(1986): 215–256.

Brewer, John. *Sinews of Power: War, Money and the English State 1688–1783*. New York: Knopf, 1989.

Bridenbaugh, Carl. *Mitre and Sceptre: Transatlantic Faiths, Ideas, Personalities, and Politics 1689–1775*. Oxford: Oxford University Press, 1962.

Brilliant, Elinor. *The United Way*. New York: Columbia University Press, 1990.

Brillouin, Leon, *Wave Propagation in Periodic Structures: Electric Filters and Crystal Lattices*. 2d ed. New York: Dover, 1953.

————. *Science and Information Theory*. 2d ed. New York: Academic Press, 1962.

Brown, D. *Executive Compensation*. Glencoe, IL: Free Press, 1959.

Brown, Donald J., and Geoffrey M. Heal. "Equity, Efficiency and Increasing Returns." *Review of Economic Studies* 46(1979): 571–585.

Brown, Roger William. *Social Psychology*. New York: Free Press of Glencoe, 1965.

Brown, Sanford C. *Count Rumford, Physicist Extraordinary*. Garden City, NY: Greenwood Press, 1962.

Brownstein, Larry. *Talcott Parsons' General Action Scheme: An Investigation of Fundamental Principles*. Cambridge, MA: Schenkman, 1982.

Brunt, P. A. *The Fall of the Roman Republic and Related Essays*. Oxford: Clarendon Press, 1988.

Bryson, Arthur, and Yu-Chi Ho. *Applied Optimal Control; Optimization, Estimation and Control*. Waltham: Blaisdell, 1969.

Brzezinski, Z., and S. P. Huntington. *Political Power USA/USSR*. New York: Viking Press, 1964.

Buchan, John. *Augustus*. Boston: Houghton Mifflin Co., 1937.

Bucur, I., and A. Deleanu. *Introduction to the Theory of Categories and Functors*. New York: Wiley, 1968.

Bueno de Mesquita, Bruce, and David Lalman. *War and Reason*. New Haven, CT: Yale University Press, 1992.

Burawoy, M. *Manufacturing Consent*. Chicago: University of Chicago Press, 1979.

Burgelman, Robert A. "Corporate Entrepreneurship and Strategic Management: Insights from a Process Study." *Management Science* 29(1983): 1349–1364.

Burke, Kenneth. *A Grammar of Motives*. New York: Prentice-Hall, 1945.

Burke, Peter. *Venice and Amsterdam: A Study of Seventeenth-Century Elites*. London: Temple-Smith, 1974.

Burke, Peter J. "Participation and Leadership in Small Groups." *American Sociological Review* 39(1974): 832–843.

Burling, R. *The Passage of Power*. New York: Academic Press, 1974.

Burns, Tom. "*Des Fins et des Moyens dans la direction des enterprises.*" *Sociologie du Travail* 3(1962).

————. *The BBC: Public Institution and Private World*. London: Macmillan, 1977.

Burns, Tom, and G. Stalker. *The Management of Innovation*. London: Tavistock, 1961.

Burns, Tom, and Elisabeth Burns, eds. *The Sociology of Literature and Drama*. London: Penguin, 1973.

Burt, Ronald S. "Positions in Multiple Network Systems, Part One: A General Conception of Stratification and Prestige in a System of Actors Cast as a Social Topology." *Social Forces* 55(1976): 93–122.

———. "Corporate Society: A Time Series Analysis of Network Structure." *Social Science Research* 4(1978a): 271–328.

———. "Cohesion versus Structural Equivalence as a Basis for Network Subgroups." *Sociological Methods and Research* 7(1978b): 189–212.

———. "Models of Network Structure." *Annual Review of Sociology* 6(1980): 79–141.

———. *Toward a Structural Theory of Action: Network Models of Social Structure, Perception and Action*. New York: Academic Press, 1982.

———. *Corporate Profits and Cooptation: Networks of Market Constraints and Directorate Ties in the American Economy*. New York: Academic Press, 1983.

———. "Social Contagion and Innovation; Cohesion versus Structural Equivalence." *American Journal of Sociology* 92(1987): 1287–1335.

———. "Kinds of relations in American discussion networks." In Calhoun, Meyer, and Scott, eds., 411–451. 1990.

———. "Measuring Age as a Structural Concept." *Social Networks* 13(1991): 1–34.

———. *Structural Holes: The Social Structure of Competition*. Cambridge, MA: Harvard University Press, forthcoming, 1992a.

———. *Social Contagion*. New York: Columbia University Press, 1992b.

Burt, Ronald S., and Debbie S. Carlton. "Another Look at the Network Boundaries of American Markets." *American Journal of Sociology* 94(1989): 723–753.

Burt, Ronald S., and Thomas Schotter. "Relation Contents in Multiple Networks." *Social Science Research* 14(1985): 287–308; also chap. 6 in Freeman et al., 1989.

Bush, R. R., and Frederick Mosteller. *Stochastic Models of Learning*. New York: Wiley, 1955.

Bushnell, G.H.S. *Peru*. New York: Praeger, 1963.

Bynum, Carolyn. *Holy Feast and Holy Fast: The Religious Significance of Food to Medieval Women*. Berkeley, CA: University of California Press, 1987.

Bythell, Duncan. *The Sweated Trades: Out-work in Nineteenth-Century Britain*. London: St. Martin's, 1978.

Calabresi, Guido. *The Costs of Accidents: A Legal and Economic Analysis*. New Haven, CT: Yale University Press, 1970.

Calhoun, C. J. "Community: toward a variable conceptualization for comparative research." *Social History* 5(1980): 105–129.

Calhoun, C. J., M. W. Meyer, and W. R. Scott, eds. *Structures of Power and Constraint: Papers in Honor of Peter M. Blau*. New York: Cambridge University Press, 1990.

Calvert, Peter, ed. *The Process of Political Succession*. Houndmills, Basingstoke: Macmillan, 1987.

Campbell, John L., J. Rogers Hollingsworth, and Leon N. Lindberg, eds.

Governance of the American Economy. New York: Cambridge University Press, 1991.

Campenhausen, Hans von. *Ecclesiastical Authority and Spiritual Power in the Church of the First Three Centuries*, 1955. Translated by J. A. Baker. Stanford, CA: Stanford University Press, 1969.

Cannadine, David. *Lords and Landlords: The Aristocracy and the Towns, 1774–1967*. Leicester, UK: Leicester University Press, 1980.

————. "The Last Hanoverian Sovereign?: The Victorian Monarchy in Historical Perspective, 1688 to 1988." Department of History, Columbia University, 1989.

Cannadine, David, and Simon Price, eds. *Rituals of Royalty*. Cambridge and New York: Cambridge University Press, 1987.

Caporaso, James A. "The State in a Domestic and International Context." 2d draft, Department of Political Science, University of Washington, February 1989.

Carley, Kathleen M. *Consensus Construction*. Ph.D. thesis, Sociology Department, Harvard University, June 1984.

————. "Knowledge Acquisition as a Social Phenomenon." *Instructional Science* 14(1986): 381–438.

————. "Growing Up: The Development and Acquisition of Social Knowledge." Department of Social and Decision Sciences, Carnegie-Mellon University, 1988.

Carlton, Dennis W. "Vertical Integration in Competitive Markets under Uncertainty." *Journal of Industrial Economics* 27(1979): 189–209.

Caro, Anthony. *The Power Broker: Robert Moses and the Fall of New York*. New York: Knopf, 1974.

————. *The Path to Power*. New York: Random, 1990.

Carr, Raymond. *Spain, 1808–1939*. Oxford: Clarendon Press, 1966.

Carroll, Glen R. "Organizational Ecology." *Annual Review of Sociology* 10(1984): 71–93.

————. "Concentration and Specialization: Dynamics of Niche Width in Populations of Organizations." *American Journal of Sociology* 90(1985): 1267–1283.

Carruthers, Peter. "Emerging Syntheses in Modern Science." Preprint LA-UR 85-2366, Los Alamos National Laboratory, 1985.

Carter, Anne P. *Structural Change in the American Economy*. Cambridge, MA: Harvard University Press, 1976.

Cartwright, D., and Frank Harary. "Structural Balance: A Generalization of Heider's Theory." *Psychological Review* 63(1956): 277–293.

Caves, Richard E., M. Fortunato, and P. Ghemawat. "The Decline of Dominant Firms, 1905–1929." *Quarterly Journal of Economics* 99(1984): 523–546.

Chaiken, J. M., and Richard C. Larson. "Methods for Allocating Urban Emergency Units: A Survey." *Management Survey* 19(1972): 110–130.

Chalmers, Douglas A. "Corporatism and Comparative Politics." Chap. 4 in *New Directions in Comparative Politics*, edited by Howard J. Wiarda. Boulder, CO: Westview, 1985.

Chamberlin, E. H. *The Theory of Monopolistic Competition*. Cambridge, MA: Harvard University Press, 1933.

Chambers, Frank. *Cycles of Taste*. Cambridge, MA: Harvard University Press, 1935.

Chandler, A. D. *The Visible Hand*. Cambridge, MA: Belknap, 1977.

Chandler, A. D., and Herman Daems, eds. *Managerial Hierarchies*. Cambridge, MA: Harvard University Press, 1980.

Chandler, Alfred. *Strategy and Structure*. Cambridge, MA: MIT Press, 1969.

Chase, Ivan D. "Social Process and Hierarchy Formation in Small Groups: A Comparative Perspective." *American Sociological Review* 45(1980): 905–924.

———. "Behavioral Sequences during Dominance Hierarchy Formation in Chickens." *Science* 216(1982): 439–440.

———. "Explanations of Hierarchy Structure." *Animal Behaviour* 34(1986): 1265–1267.

———. "Vacancy Chains." *Annual Reviews of Sociology* 17(1991): 133–154.

———. *The Emergence of Order in Human and Animal Behavior*. Cambridge, MA: Harvard University Press, 1991.

Chase, Ivan D., and Theodore H. DeWitt. "Vacancy chains: a process of mobility to new resources in humans and other animals." *Social Science Information* 27(1988): 83–98.

Chay, John, and Thomas E. Ross, eds. *Buffer States in World Politics*. Boulder, CO: Westview, 1986.

Cheney, D., R. Seyfarth, and B. Smuts. "Social relationships and social cognition in non-human primates." *Science* 234(1986): 1361–1366.

Chesneaux, Jean, ed. *Popular Movements and Secret Societies in China, 1840–1950*. Stanford, CA: Stanford University Press, 1972.

Chesnut, Glenn. *The First Christian Histories*. Macon, GA: Mercer University Press, 1986.

Chevalier, F. *Land and Society in Colonial Mexico*. Translated by A. Eustis. Berkeley, CA: University of California, 1963.

Chrimes, S. *An Introduction to the Administrative History of Medieval England*. Oxford, Blackwell, 1952.

Christian, William A. *Divided Island*. Cambridge, MA: Harvard University Press, 1969.

———. *Person and God in a Spanish Valley*. New York: Seminar Press, 1972.

———. *Local Religion in Sixteenth-Century Spain*. Princeton, NJ: Princeton University Press, 1981.

Chu, Moody T. "On the Continuous Realization of Iterative Processes." Department of Mathematics, North Carolina State University, 1986.

Church, William F. *Louis XIV in Historical Thought*. New York: Norton, 1976.

Cicourel, Aaron V. *Cognitive Sociology*. New York: Free Press, 1973.

———. "Three Models of Discourse Analysis." *Discourse Processes* 3(1980): 101–132.

Cipolla, Carlo M. *Before the Industrial Revolution: European Society and Economy, 1000–1700*. New York: Norton, 1980.

Clapham, C. *Private Patronage and Public Power*. London: Frances Pinter, 1982.

Clausewitz, Carl von. *On War*. Edited and translated by M. Howard and P. Paret. Princeton, NJ: Princeton University Press, 1976.

Clegg, Stewart. *The Theory of Power and Organization*. London and Boston: Routledge, Kegan Paul, 1979.

Cliff, Andrew D., and B. T. Robson. "Changes in the Size Distribution of Settlements in England and Wales, 1801–1965." *Environment and Planning* A10(1978): 163–171.

Clifford, A. H., and G. B. Preston. *The Algebraic Theory of Semigroups*, vols. I and II. Providence, RI: American Mathematical Society, 1961, 1967.

Coase, R. "The nature of the firm." *Economica* 4(1937): 386–405.

Cobban, Alfred. *The Social Interpretation of the French Revolution*. Cambridge: Cambridge University Press, 1964.

Cockcroft, Eva, J. Weber, and J. Cockcroft. *Toward a People's Art*. New York: Dutton, 1977.

Cohen, Joel. *Casual Groups of Monkeys and Men: Stochastic Models of Elemental Social Systems*. Cambridge, MA: Harvard University Press, 1971.

Cohen, Michael D., and J. G. March. *Leadership and Ambiguity: The American College President*. New York: McGraw-Hill, 1974.

Cole, Jonathan. *Fair Science: Women in the Scientific Community*. New York: Free Press, 1979.

Cole, Stephen, Leonard Rubin, and Jonathan R. Cole. *Peer Review in the National Science Foundation*. Washington, DC: National Academy of Sciences, 1978.

Coleman, James S. *Community Conflict*. New York: Free Press-Bureau of Applied Social Research, 1957.

———. *The Adolescent Society*. New York: Free Press, 1961.

———. *An Introduction to Mathematical Sociology*. New York: Free Press, 1964.

———. *The Mathematics of Collective Action*. Chicago: Aldine, 1973.

———. *Foundations of Social Theory*. Cambridge, MA: Harvard University Press, 1990.

Coleman, James S., E. Katz, and H. Menzel. *Medical Innovation; A Diffusion Study*. Indianapolis, IN: Bobbs-Merrill, 1966.

Collier, Ruth B., and David Collier. *Shaping the Political Arena: Critical Junctures, the Labor Movement and Regime Dynamics in Latin America*. Princeton, NJ: Princeton University Press, 1989.

Collins, Randall. *Conflict Sociology*. New York: Academic Press, 1975.

———. "Microfoundations of Macrosociology." *American Journal of Sociology* 85(1981): 984–1014.

———. *Theoretical Sociology*. New York: Harcourt, Brace, Jovanovich, 1985.

Comanor, William S., and T. A. Wilson. *Advertising and Market Power*. Cambridge, MA: Harvard University Press, 1974.

Conell, Carol. "Sophisticated Timing: Potential and Actual Gains in Late Nineteenth Century Strikes." Manuscript, Department of Sociology, Stanford University, August 1990.

Conell, Carol, and Samuel Cohn. "Environmental Variation and Diffusion in

Strike Waves: French Coal Mining, 1890–1935." Manuscript, Department of Sociology, Stanford University, October 1990.

Connolly, William E. *Politics and Ambiguity*. Madison, WI: University of Wisconsin, 1987.

Cook, Karen S., Richard M. Emerson, Mary Gilmore, and T. Yamagishi. "The Distribution of Power in Exchange Networks." *American Journal of Sociology* 89(1985): 275–305.

Cooper, Lynn A., and Dennis T. Regan. "Attention, Perception and Intelligence." Chap. 3 in *Handbook of Human Intelligence*, edited by Robert J. Sternberg. Cambridge, UK: Cambridge University Press, 1981.

Corey, E. Raymond. *Procurement Management*. Boston: CBI, 1978.

Cornell, Stephen. *The Return of the Native: American Indian Political Resurgence*. New York: Oxford University Press, 1988.

Corwin, Ronald G. "Patterns of Organizational Conflict." *Administrative Science Quarterly* 14(1969): 507–521.

Coser, Lewis A., Charles Kadushin, and Walter W. Powell. *Books: The Culture and Commerce of Publishing*. New York: Basic Books, 1982.

Coulborn, Rushton, ed. *Feudalism in History*. Princeton, NJ: Princeton University Press, 1956.

Coxon, A.P.M., P. M. Davies, and C. L. Jones. *Images of Occupational Stratification*. Beverly Hills, CA: Sage, 1986.

Cozzens, Susan E. *Social Control and Multiple Discovery in Science: The Opiate Receptor Case*. Albany, NY: State University of New York Press, 1989.

Crain, Robert L., Elihu Katz, and D. Rosenthal. *The Politics of Community Controversy: The Fluoridation Decision*. Indianapolis, IN: Bobbs-Merrill, 1961.

———. *The Politics of School Desegregation: Comparative Case Studies of Community Structure and Policy Making*. Chicago: Aldine, 1968.

Crain, Robert L., R. Mahaaud, and R. Narot. *Making Desegregation Work: How Schools Create Social Climate*. Cambridge, MA: Ballinger, 1982.

Crane, Diana. *Invisible Colleges*. Chicago: University of Chicago Press, 1972.

———. *The Transformation of the Avante Garde*. Chicago: University of Chicago Press, 1987.

Crowell, Richard H., and Ralph H. Fox. *Introduction to Knot Theory*. Boston: Ginn, 1963.

Crozier, Michel, and J. C. Thoenig. "The Regulation of Complex Organized Systems." *Administrative Science Quarterly* 21(1976): 547–570.

Cuff, Robert D. *The War Industries Board*. Baltimore, MD: Johns Hopkins University Press, 1973.

Culicover, Peter, "Situating Linguistics within Cognitive Science." Floppy disk, Department of Linguistics, Ohio State University, 1987.

Culicover, Peter, and K. Wexler. "Some Syntactic Implications of a Theory of Language Learnability." In *Formal Syntax*, edited by P. Culicover, T. Wasow, and A. Akmajian. New York: Academic Press, 1977.

Culler, Jonathan. *Structuralist Poetics: Structuralism, Linguistics and the Study of Literature*. Ithaca, NY: Cornell University Press, 1975.

———. *Framing the Sign*. Norman, OK: University of Oklahoma Press, 1990.

Curtis, Richard F., and James T. Borhek. *A Sociology of Belief*. Malabar: R. E. Krieger, 1975.

Cyert, Richard M., and James G. March. *A Behavioral Theory of the Firm*. Englewood Cliffs, NJ: Prentice-Hall, 1963.

Dahl, Robert A., and Charles E. Lindblom. *Politics, Economics and Welfare*. New York: Harper, 1953.

Dalton, Melville. *Men Who Manage*. New York: Wiley, 1959.

Dauber, Ken. "Claims, Identities and Multiple Logics." Department of Sociology, University of Arizona, September 25, 1987.

Davis, James A. "Clustering and Structural Balance in Graphs." *Human Relations* 20(1967): 181–187.

———. "Clustering and Hierarchy in Interpersonal Relations" *American Sociological Review* 35(1970): 843–852.

———. "The Davis/Holland/Leinhardt Studies: An Overview." In Holland and Leinhardt, 1979, pp. 51–62.

Davis, James A., and Tom W. Smith. *General Social Surveys, 1972–1988: Cumulative Codebook*. Chicago: National Opinion Research Center, 1988.

Davis, Stanley, and Paul Lawrence. *Matrix*. Reading, MA: Addison-Wesley, 1977.

Davison, W. Phillips., "Mass Media Civic Organizations and Street Gossip: How Communication Affects the Quality of Life in an Urban Neighborhood." *Working Paper*. Gannett Center for Media Studies, Columbia University, 1987.

de Boer, J., and G. E. Uhlenbeck, eds. *Studies in Statistical Mechanics*. Amsterdam: North-Holland, 1962.

DeGennes, Pierre-Gilles. *Scaling Concepts in Polymer Physics*. Ithaca, NY: Cornell University Press, 1979.

De Graaf, N. D., and H. D. Flap. "With a Little Help from My Friends." *Social Forces* 67(1988): 452–472.

Dehez, Pierre, and Jacques Dreze. "Competitive Equilibria with Increasing Returns." European University Institute, Florence, Working Paper #86/243, 1987.

Delaney, John. "Social Networks and Efficient Resource Allocation: Job Vacancy Allocation Through Contacts." Chap. 16 in Wellman and Berkowitz, 1988.

de Roover, Raymond. *The Rise and Decline of the Medici Bank: 1397–1494*. New York: W. W. Norton, 1966.

Desan, Philippe, Priscilla Ferguson, and Wendy Griswold, eds. *Literature and Social Practice*. Chicago: University of Chicago Press, 1989.

De Soto, Clinton B. "The Predilection for Single Ordering." *Journal of Abnormal and Social Psychology* 62(1961): 16–23.

De Soto, Clinton, and Frank Albrecht. "Cognition and Social Orderings." Chap. 49 in Abelson et al., eds., 1968a.

———. "Conceptual Good Figures." Chap. 45 in Abelson et al., eds., 1968b.

De Swaan, Abram. *Coalition Theories and Cabinet Formations*. Amsterdam: Elsevier, 1973.

Deutsch, Karl W. *Nationalism and Social Communication*. New York: Wiley, 1953.

Deutsch, Karl W., and Sidney Burrell. *Political Community and the North Atlantic Area*. Princeton, NJ: Princeton University Press, 1957.

Devore, Irven, ed. *Primate Behavior*. New York: Holt, Rinehart and Winston, 1965.

De Vos, Henk. "Altruism and Group Boundaries." In *Modellierung Sozialer Prozesse*, edited by H. Esser and K. Troitsch, 5–19. Bonn: Informationszentrum Sozialwissenschaften, 1991.

Dew, Mary A. "Small Groups as Markets." Department of Sociology, Harvard University, May 1982.

Dibble, Vernon K. "The Organization of Traditional Authority: English County Government, 1558–1640." Chap. 21 in James G. March 1965.

Diestel, Joseph. *Sequences and Series in Banach Spaces*. New York: Springer-Verlag, 1984.

Dietz, Frederick. *English Government Finance: 1485–1558*. New York: Barnes and Noble, 1964, 2d ed.

Dillon, J. M., and A. A. Long. *The Question of Eclecticism*. Berkeley, CA: University of California Press, 1988.

DiMaggio, Paul. *Non Profit Enterprise in the Arts: Studies in Mission and Constraint*. New York: Oxford University Press, 1986.

———. "Classification in Art." *American Sociological Review* 52(1987): 440–455.

DiMaggio, Paul, and Walter W. Powell. "The Iron Cage Revisited: Institutional Isomorphism and Collective Rationality in Organizational Fields." *American Sociological Review* 48(1983): 147–160.

Dix, G. "The Ministry in the Early Church." In *The Apostolic Ministry*, edited by K. E. Kirk. New York: Morehouse-Gorham Co., 1947.

Donham, Wallace B. *Administration and Blind Spots*. Boston: Harvard Graduate School of Business Administration, 1952.

Doreian, Patrick, and Norman Hummon. *Modelling Social Processes*. New York: Elsevier, 1976.

Douglas, Jack D., ed. *Understanding Everyday Life*. Chicago: Aldine, 1970.

Douglas, Mary. *Purity and Danger: An Analysis of the Concepts of Pollution and Taboo*. London: Routledge and Kegan Paul, 1966.

———. *Natural Symbols*. New York: Pantheon Books, 1970.

Douglass, Frederick. *Life and Times of Frederick Douglass*. New York: Bonanza-Crown, 1952 (reprint of 1892 ed.).

Drucker, Peter. *Managing for Results*. New York: Harper and Row, 1964.

Duby, Georges. *The Three Orders*. Chicago: University of Chicago Press, 1980.

Dumont, Louis. *Homo Hierarchicus*. Translated by Mark Sainsbury. London: Weidenfeld and Nicolson, 1970.

———. *A South Indian Subcaste*. Translated by M. Moffatt. New York: Oxford University Press, 1986.

Dunbar, R. M. *Primate Social Systems*. London: Croom-Helm, 1988.

Duncan, Starkey. *Face-to-Face Interaction*. Hillsdale, NJ: Erlbaum Associates, 1977.

Durkheim, Emile. *The Elementary Forms of the Religious Life.* Translated by J. W. Swain. London: Allen Unwin, 1915.

――. *The Division of Labor.* Translated by G. Simpson. Glencoe, IL: Free Press, 1933.

――. *Suicide.* Translated by J. Spaulding and G. Simpson. Glencoe, IL: Free Press, 1951.

Dweck, Carol S. "The role of expectations and attributions in the alleviation of learned helplessness." *Journal of Personality and Social Psychology* 31(1975): 674–685.

Dweck, Carol S., and Ellen L. Leggett. "A Social-Cognitive Approach to Motivation and Personality." *Psychology Review* 95(1988): 256–273.

Easterlin, R. A. *Birth and Fortune: The Impact of Numbers on Personal Welfare.* New York: Basic Books, 1980.

Eccles, Robert G. "Bureaucratic versus Craft Administration: The Relationship of Market Structure to the Construction Firm." *Administrative Science Quarterly* 26(1981a): 449–469.

――. "VISA International: The Management Change." Case 0-482-022, HBS Case Services, Boston: Harvard Graduate School of Business Administration, 1981b.

――. "The quasifirm in the construction industry." *Journal of Economic Behavior and Organization* 2(1981c): 335–357.

――. GENRAD, INC. (A-D). "The Pursuit of Renascence Under the Ambivalence Born of the Confluence of Nascence and Senescence." Harvard Business School, HBS Case Services, 0-482-029, -030, -107, -108, 1981d.

――. "Creating the Collaborative Organization." Harvard Graduate School of Business Administration, Division of Research, Working Paper 9-784-04, 1984.

――. *The Transfer Pricing Problem: A Theory for Practice.* Lexington, MA: Lexington Books, 1985.

――. "A Note on Control Systems." N9-491-084, Boston, MA: Harvard Business School Publishing Division, 1991.

Eccles, Robert G., and Dwight B. Crane. *Doing Deals: Investment Banks at Work.* Boston, MA: Harvard Business School Press, 1988.

Eccles, Robert G., and N. Nohria, eds. *Network Organization.* Boston: Harvard Business School Press, 1992.

Eccles, Robert G., and Harrison C. White. "Firm and Market Interfaces of Profit Center Control." In Lindenberg et al., 1986a.

――. "Concentration for Control?: Political and Business Evidence." *Sociological Forum* 1(1986b): 131–158.

――. "Price and authority in inter-profit center transactions." *American Journal of Sociology.* Supplement, 94: S17-S51, 1988.

Eckstein, A. M. *Senate and General.* Berkeley, CA: University of California Press, 1986.

Eckstein, Harry. *Internal War.* New York: Free Press, 1964.

――. "Case Study and Theory in Political Science." Chap. 3 in *Case Study and Theory in Political Science,* edited by L. Pye. Bloomington, IN: Indiana University Press, 1975.

Edelstein, J. D., and M. Warner. *Comparative Union Democracy.* New Brunswick, NJ: Transaction Books, 1979.

Edgerton, Robert B. *Rules, Exceptions and Social Order.* Berkeley, CA: University of California Press, 1985.

Edmonson, Munro. "Culture and Uncertainty." Social Relations Department, Harvard University, March 1965.

Edwards, S. F. *Annals of the New York Academy of Sciences* 371(1981): 216.

Eemeren, F. V. "Dialectical Analysis of Argumentative Discourse." *Text* 6(1986): 1–16.

Eemeren, Frans H. van, and Rob Grootendorst. *Speech Acts in Argumentative Discussions.* Dordrecht-Holland: Formi, 1984.

Ehrenreich, Barbara and John. *The American Health Empire.* New York: Vintage Books, 1970.

Eisenberg, Melvin. *The Structure of the Corporation.* Boston: Little, Brown, 1976.

Eisenstadt, S. N. *From Generation to Generation.* Glencoe, IL: Free Press, 1956.

———. *The Political System of Empires.* New York: Free Press, 1963.

Eisenstadt, S. N., and R. Lemarchard, eds. *Political Clientelism, Patronage and Development.* Beverly Hills, CA: Sage, 1981.

Eisenstadt, S.N., and L. Roniger. "Patron-Client Relations as a Model of Structuring Social Exchange." *Comparative Studies in Society and History* 22(1980): 42–77.

Elias, Norbert. *The Civilizing Process I: The History of Manners.* New York: Pantheon, 1978.

———. *Quest for Excitement: Sports and Leisure in the Civilizing Process.* New York: Blackwell, 1986.

Elliott, Philip. *The Sociology of the Professions.* New York: Herder and Herder, 1972.

Emerson, Richard. "Power-Dependence Relations." *American Sociological Review* 27(1962): 31–40.

Emmet, Dorothy. *Rules, Roles and Relations.* New York: St. Martin's Press, 1966.

Empson, William. *Seven Types of Ambiguity.* New York: Harcourt, Brace and Co., 1931.

Ennis, Philip. *The Seventh Stream: A History and Geography of Rock 'n Roll to 1970.* Middletown, CT: Wesleyan University Press, 1992.

Erasmus, Charles J. *Man Takes Control.* Minneapolis, MN: University of Minnesota Press, 1961.

Erdos, Paul, and Joel Spencer. *Probabilistic Methods in Combinatorics.* New York: Academic Press, 1974.

Erickson, Erik. *Young Man Luther.* New York: Norton, 1958.

Esping-Anderson, Gosta. *Politics against Markets: The Social Democratic Road to Power.* Princeton, NJ: Princeton University Press, 1985.

Etzioni, Amitai, ed. *Complex Organizations.* New York: Holt, Rinehart and Winston, 1961.

European Coal and Steel Community. *Management, Organizations and Methods in the American Iron and Steel Industry.* Fact Finding Mission to USA, March–April 1957.

Evans, Peter. "Multiple Hierarchies and Organization Control." *Administrative Science Quarterly* 22(1977): 364–385.

———. *Dependent Development*. Princeton, NJ: Princeton University Press, 1979.

Evans, Rowland, and Robert Novak. *Lyndon B. Johnson: The Exercise of Power, a Political Biography*. New York: New American Library, 1966.

Evans-Pritchard, E. E. *The Nuer*. Oxford: Clarendon Press, 1940.

Everett, Martin G. "EBLOC: A Graph-Theoretic Blocking Algorithm for Social Networks." *Social Networks* 5(1983): 323–346.

———. "Role Similarity and Complexity in Social Networks." *Social Networks* 7(1985): 353–359.

Fallers, L. *Bantu Bureaucracy*. Chicago: University of Chicago Press, 1965.

Fama, Eugene F., and Michael C. Jensen. "Separation of Ownership and Control." *Journal of Law and Economics* 26(1983).

Fararo, Thomas J. *Mathematical Sociology*. New York: Wiley, 1973.

———. "An Introduction to Catastrophes." *Behavioral Science* 23(1978): 291–317.

———. "Biased Networks and Social Structure Theorems." *Social Networks* 3(1981): 137–159.

Fat, F. E. Tjon Sie. *Representing Kinship*. Leiden: Faculty of Social Sciences, 1990.

Faulhaber, G. R., and W. J. Baumol. "Economists as Innovators." *Journal of Economic Literature* 26(1988): 577–598.

Faulkner, Robert R. *Studio Musicians*. Chicago: Aldine, 1971.

———. *Music on Demand: Composers and Careers in the Hollywood Film Industry*. New Brunswick, NJ: Transaction Books, 1983.

———. *Big Hollywood, Little Hollywood*. Manuscript excerpts, n.d.

Feldman, Jerome A. "Connectionist Models and Parallelism in High Level Vision." *Computer Vision, Graphics and Image Processing* 31(1985): 178–200.

Feller, William. *An Introduction to Probability Theory and its Application*, 3d ed. New York: Wiley, 1968.

Ferejohn, John. "Rationality and Interpretation: Parliamentary Elections in Early Stuart England." Manuscript, Stanford University, February 1990.

Ferguson, Priscilla. "Reading Revolutionary Paris." In Desan et al., 1989.

Fernandez, Roberto M., and Doug McAdam. "Multi-Organizational Fields and Recruitment to Social Movements." In *Organizing for Social Change*, edited by Bert Klandermans. Greenwich, CT: JAI Press, 1988.

Ferris, Timothy. *Galaxies*. New York: Stewart, Tabori and Chang, 1982.

Feynman, Richard P., Robert B. Leighton, and Matthew Sands. *The Feynman Lectures on Physics*. Reading, MA: Addison-Wesley, 1963.

Fichtenau, Heinrich. *The Carolingian Empire*. Translated by Peter Munz. Oxford: Blackwell, 1957.

Field, G. Lowell, and John Higley. *Elitism*. Boston: Routledge and Kegan Paul, 1980.

Fienberg, Stephen E., M. M. Meyer, and Stanley S. Wasserman. "Statistical Analysis of Multiple Social Relations." *Journal of the American Statistical Association* 80(1985): 51–67.

Fienberg, Stephen E., and Stanley Wasserman. "Categorical Data Analysis of Single Sociometric Relationships." Pp. 156–192 in Leinhardt, ed., 1981.

Findley, Carter V. *Bureaucratic Reform in the Ottoman Empire.* Princeton, NJ: Princeton University Press, 1980.

Fine, Ben, and Lawrence Harris. *The Peculiarities of the British Economy.* London: Lawrence and Wishart, 1985.

Fine, Gary A. "Small Groups and Culture Creation: The Idioculture of Little League Baseball Teams." *American Sociological Review* 44(1979): 733–745.

———. *Shared Fantasies: Role Play Games as Social Worlds.* Chicago: University of Chicago Press, 1983.

Finley, M. I. *The Ancient Economy.* Berkeley, CA: University of California Press, 1973.

———. *Aspects of Antiquity.* Harmondsworth: Penguin, 1977.

———. *The Ancient Greeks.* London: Penguin, 1977.

Fiorenza, Elisabeth, ed. *Aspects of Religious Propaganda in Judaism and Early Christianity.* South Bend, IN: University of Notre Dame Press, 1976.

Firth, Raymond. *We, The Tikopia.* London: Allen Unwin, 1957.

Fischer, Claude. *To Live Among Friends: Personal Networks in Town and City.* Chicago: University of Chicago Press, 1982.

Fitz, Virginia W. "Ralph Wormeley: An Anonymous Essayist." *William and Mary Quarterly* 26(1969): 586–595.

Flament, Claude. *Applications of Graph Theory to Group Structure.* Translated by M. Pinard, R. Breton, and F. Fontaine. Englewood Cliffs, NJ: Prentice-Hall, 1963.

Flap, Hendrik D. *Conflict, loyalty and violence: The effects of social networks on behaviour.* Bern: Peter Lang, 1988.

———. "Patronage: An Institution in its own Right." Chap. 10 in Hechter, Opp and Wippler, 1990.

Flap, Hendrik D., and Charles Goldenbeld. "Crossed Categorizations and Intergroup Discrimination." Faculty of Social Science, University of Utrecht, April 1989.

Fleck, Ludwik. *Genesis and Development of a Scientific Fact.* Translated by Fred Bradley and Thaddeus J. Trenn (from 1935 German text). Chicago: University of Chicago Press, 1979.

Fligstein, Neil. "The Multidivisional Form." *American Sociological Review* 50(1985): 377–391.

———. *The Transformation of Corporate Control.* Cambridge, MA: Harvard University Press, 1990.

Fligstein, Neil, and Roberto M. Fernandez. "Worker Power, Firm Power and the Structure of Labor Markets." *The Sociological Quarterly* 29(1988): 5–28.

Flusser, David. *Judaism and the Origins of Christianity.* Jerusalem: Magnes Press, 1988.

Foley, Duncan K. "Economic Equilibrium with Costly Marketing." *Journal of Economic Theory* 2(1970): 276–291.

Foner, Eric. *Politics and Ideology in the Age of the Civil War.* New York: Oxford University Press, 1980.

Forbes, Duncan, Introduction to G.W.F. Hegel. *Introduction to Lectures on the*

Philosophy of World History. Cambridge: Cambridge University Press, 1975.

Ford, Franklin. *Robe and Sword: The Regrouping of the French Aristocracy After Louis XIV*. Cambridge, MA: Harvard University Press, 1953.

Ford, L. R., and D. R. Fulkerson. *Flows in Networks*. Princeton, NJ: Princeton University Press, 1962.

Forment, Carlos A. "Political Practice and the rise of an ethnic enclave." *Theory and Society* 18(1989a): 47–81.

———. *The Emergence of Political Space in Spanish America: 1700–1830*. Department of Sociology, Ph.D. thesis, Harvard University, November 1989b.

Forster, Ken, et al. "Masked Priming with graphemically related forms: Repetition or partial activation." *Quarterly Journal of Experimental Psychology* 39A(2)(1987): 211–251.

Fortes, Meyer. *The Dynamics of Clanship among the Tallensi*. London: Oxford University Press, 1945.

———. *The Web of Kinship among the Tallensi*. London: Oxford University Press, 1949.

Fortes, M., and Evans-Pritchard, E. E., eds. *African Political Systems*. London: Oxford University Press, 1949.

Foster, C. C., A. Rapoport, and C. Orwant. "A Study of a Large Sociogram." *Behavioral Science* 8(1963): 56–66.

Foucault, Michel. *Power/Knowledge*. New York: Pantheon, 1980.

Franklin, Julian. *Jean Bodin and the Rise of Absolutist Theory*. New York: Cambridge University Press, 1973.

Freeman, John H., and Michael T. Hannan. "Niche Width and the Dynamics of Organizational Populations." *American Journal of Sociology* 88(1983): 1116–1145.

Freeman, Linton C. "Centrality in Social Networks." *Social Networks* 1(1979): 215–239.

———. "The Sociological Concept of 'Group': A Comparison of a Traditional and a Modern View." IRU in Mathematical Behavioral Science, University of California, Irvine, 1991.

Freeman, Linton C., Douglas R. White, and A. Kimball Romney, eds. *Research Methods in Social Network Analysis*. Fairfax, VA: George Mason University Press, 1989.

Frend, W.H.C. *The Donatist Church*. London: Oxford University Press, 1952.

Fried, Charles. *An Anatomy of Values: Problems of Personal and Social Choice*. Cambridge, MA: Harvard University Press, 1970.

Friedell, Morris. "Organizations as Semilattices." *American Sociological Review* 32(1967): 46–54.

Friedkin, Noah E. "Social Networks in Structural Equation Models." *Social Psychology Quarterly* 53(1990): 316–327.

Friedman, Debra. "Strikes and Uncertainty: A Multilevel Theory." Department of Sociology, University of Arizona, 1987.

Friedman, Debra, and Michael Hechter. "The Contribution of Rational Choice Theory to Macro-Sociological Research." *Sociological Theory* 6(1988): 202.

Friedman, Milton R. *A Theory of the Consumption Function*. Princeton, NJ: Princeton University Press, 1957.

Friedmann, Harriet. "Form and Substance in the Analysis of the World Economy." Chap. 11 in Wellman and Berkowitz 1988.

Friendly, H. J. *Federal Administrative Agencies*. Cambridge, MA: Harvard University Press, 1962.

Frings, Manfred S. *Max Scheler; A Concise Introduction*. Pittsburgh, PA: Duquesne University Press, 1965.

Froholk, F. *Rational Association*. Syracuse, NY: Syracuse University Press, 1987.

Frye, Northrop. *Anatomy of Criticism*. Princeton, NJ: Princeton University Press, 1957.

Fuchs, L. *Partially Ordered Algebraic Systems*. Reading, MA: Addison-Wesley, 1963.

Fuller, Lon. *The Morality of Law*. New Haven, CT: Yale University Press, 1964.

Funaba, Masatomi. "Japanese Local Finance and Local Autonomy." *Academic Publications of Hiroshima University*, 345–370, 1989.

Furnivall, J. S. *Colonial Policy and Practice: A Comparative Study of Burma and Netherlands India*. London: Cambridge University Press, 1948.

Fusfeld, Daniel R. "The Conceptual Framework of Modern Economics." *Journal of Economic Issues* 14(1980): 1–52.

Fuss, Melvyn, and Daniel MacFadden, eds. *Production Economics: A Dual Approach to Theory and Applications*. Vols. I and II, 1978.

Galaskiewicz, Joseph. *Exchange Networks and Community Politics*. Beverly Hills, CA: Sage, 1979.

Gans, Herbert. *The Urban Villagers: Group and Class in the Life of Italian Americans*. New York: Free Press of Glencoe, 1962.

―――. *Deciding What's News: A Study of CBS Evening News, NBC Nightly News, Newsweek and Time*. New York: Vintage, 1979.

Ganzeboom, Harry B. G., and Henk Flap, eds. *New Social Movements and Value Change*. Amsterdam: SISWO, 1989.

Garfinkel, Harold. *Studies in Ethnomethodology*. Englewood Cliffs, NJ: Prentice-Hall, 1967.

Gargiulo, Martin. "The Uruguayan Labor Movement in the Post-Authoritarian Period." In *Labor Autonomy and the State in Latin America*, edited by Edward C. Epstein. Boston: Unwin Hyman, 1991.

Garnsey, Peter, and R. P. Saller. *The Roman Empire*. London: Duckworth, 1987.

Gartrell, C. D. "Relational and Distributional Models of Collective Justice Sentiments." *Social Forces* 64(1985): 64–83.

Geertz, Clifford, and Hildred Geertz. *The Social History of an Indonesian Town*. Cambridge, MA: MIT Press, 1949.

Gelzer, Matthias. *The Roman Nobility* (1912). Translated by R. Seager. New York: Barnes and Noble, 1969.

Gerberding, Richard A. *The Rise of the Carolingians and the Liber Historiae Francorum*. Oxford: Clarendon, 1987.

Gergen, Kenneth J. *Toward Transformation in Social Knowledge*. New York: Springer-Verlag, 1982.

Germani, G. *Authoritarianism, Fascism and National Populism*. New Brunswick, NJ: Transaction Books, 1978.

Gersick, Connie J. G., and Richard J. Hackman. "Habitual Routines in Task-Performing Groups." *Organizational Behavior and Human Decision Processes* 47(1990): 65–97.

Ghurye, Govind S. *Caste and Race in India*. Bombay: Popular Book Depot, 1957.

Gibson, J. J. *The Perception of the Visual World*. Boston: Houghton Mifflin, 1950.

———. *The Ecological Approach to Visual Perception*. Boston: Houghton Mifflin, 1979.

Giddens, Anthony. *The Class Structure of the Advanced Societies*. New York: Harper and Row, 1973.

———. *Central Problems in Social Theory*. London: Methuen, 1979.

———. *The Constitution of Society*. Cambridge, UK: Polity Press, 1981.

Gierke, Otto. *Political Theories of the Middle Age*. Translated by F. Maitland. Cambridge, UK: Cambridge University Press, 1913.

———. *Natural Law and the Theory of Society, 1500–1800*. Translated by E. Barker. Cambridge, UK: Cambridge University Press, 1950.

Gies, Joseph, and Francis Gies. *Life in a Medieval City*. New York: Crowell, 1969.

Gill, Joseph, S.J. *The Council of Florence*. New York: Cambridge University Press, 1959.

———. *Personalities of the Council of Florence*. New York: Barnes and Noble, 1964.

Givnish, Thomas. "On the Adaptive Significance of Leaf Form." Manuscript, Harvard University, 1981.

Givon, Talmy. "Cause and Control: On the Semantics of Interpersonal Manipulation." In *Syntax and Semantics Vol. 4*, edited by J. P. Kimball. New York: Academic Press, 1975.

Gluck, Carol. *Japan's Modern Myths*. Princeton, NJ: Princeton University Press, 1985.

Goffman, Erving. "On Face Work." *Psychiatry* 18(1955): 213–231.

———. *Behavior in Public Places*. Glencoe, IL: Free Press, 1963.

———. *Interaction Ritual*. New York: Pantheon, 1967.

———. *Relations in Public*. New York: Harper, 1971.

———. *Frame Analysis*. New York: Harper and Row, 1974.

Goguel, Maurice. *The Primitive Church*. Translated by H. C. Snape. London: Allen Unwin, 1964.

Gold, Harvey J. *Mathematical Modelling of Biological Systems: An Introductory Guidebook*. New York: Wiley, 1977.

Goldberg, Victor. "Relational Exchange: Economics and Complex Contracts." *American Behavioral Scientist* 23(1980): 337–352.

Goldsmith, Raymond W. *Financial Structure and Development*. New Haven, CT: Yale University Press, 1969.

Goldsmith, Raymond W. *Premodern Financial Systems*. New York: Cambridge University Press, 1987.

Goldstone, Jack A., ed. *Revolutions: Theoretical, Comparative and Historical Studies*. New York: Harcourt, Brace, Jovanovich, 1986.

Goldthorpe, John H. "The End of Convergence: Corporatist and Dualist Tendencies in Modern Western Societies." In *Order and Conflict in Contemporary Capitalism*, edited by J. Goldthorpe. New York: Oxford University Press, 1984.

Gombrich, E. *Meditations on a Hobby Horse*. London: Phaidon, 1963.

Goodman, Leo A. "Some Multiplier Models for the Analysis of Cross-classification Data." Pp. 649–696. In *Proceeedings of the Sixth Berkeley Symposium in Mathematical Statistics and Probability*, edited by L. LeCam, J. Neyman, and E. L. Scott. Berkeley, CA: University of California Press, 1979.

———. *The Analysis of Data having Ordered Categories*. Cambridge, MA: Harvard University Press, 1984.

Goodman, Leo A., Nathan Keyfitz, and Thomas W. Pullum. "Family Formation and the Frequency of Various Kinship Relationships." *Theoretical Population Biology* 5(1974): 1–27.

Goody, John, ed. *Succession to High Office*. New York: Cambridge University Press, 1966.

Gottwald, Norman K. *The Tribes of Jahweh: A Sociology of the Religion of Liberated Israel, 1250–1050 B.C.E.* Maryknoll, NY: Orbis Books, 1979.

Gould, Roger V. "Power and Social Structure in Community Elites." *Social Forces*, 1989.

Gould, Roger V., and Roberto M. Fernandez. "Structures of Mediation: A Formal Approach to Brokerage in Transaction Networks." In *Sociological Methodology 1989*.

Grandmont, Jacques-L. *Nonlinear Economic Dynamics*. New York: Academic Press, 1987.

Granick, David. *Soviet Metal-fabricating and Economic Development: Practice vs. Policy*. Madison, WI: University of Wisconsin Press, 1967.

———. *Managerial Comparisons of Four Developed Countries*. Cambridge, MA: MIT Press, 1972.

———. *Enterprise Guidance in Eastern Europe: A Comparison of Four Socialist Economies*. Princeton, NJ: Princeton University Press, 1975.

Granovetter, Mark. "The Strength of Weak Ties." *American Journal of Sociology* 78(1973): 1360, 1380.

———. *Getting a Job: A Study of Contacts and Careers*. Cambridge, MA: Harvard University Press, 1974.

———. "Threshold Models of Collective Behavior." *American Journal of Sociology* 78(1978): 1420–1443.

———. "The Theory Gap in Social Network Analysis." In Holland and Leinhardt, 1979, pp. 501–518.

———. "A Network Theory Revisited." *Sociological Theory* 1, 1982.

———. "Economic Action and Social Structure: The Problem of Embeddedness." *American Journal of Sociology* 91(1985): 481–510.

———. "Labor Mobility, Internal Markets and Job Matching: A Comparison of the Sociological and Economic Approaches." *Research in Social Stratification and Mobility* 5(1986): 3–39.

Granovetter, Mark, and Roland Soong. "Threshold Models of Diffusion and Collective Behavior." *Journal of Mathematical Sociology* 9(1983): 165–179.

Grant, R. M. *Gnosticism and Early Christianity*. New York: Columbia University Press, 1966.

Gray, C. G., and K. E. Gubbins. *Theory of Molecular Fluids*. New York: Oxford University Press, 1984.

Greeley, Andrew. *The Making of the Popes, 1978: The Politics of Intrigue in the Vatican*. Kansas City, KS: Andrews and McMeel, 1979.

Green, Jerry, and Eytan Sheshinski. "Competitive Inefficiencies in the Presence of Constrained Transactions." *Journal of Economic Theory* 10(1978): 343–357.

Green, Jerry, and Nacy L. Stokey. "A Comparison of Tournaments and Contracts." *Journal of Political Economy* 91(1983): 349–365.

Greenstein, Fred I. *The Hidden-Hand Presidency: Eisenhower as Leader*. New York: Basic Books, 1982.

Gregory, Paul R., and Robert C. Stuart. *Soviet Economic Structure and Performance*. New York: Harper and Row, 1974.

Grether, David M., R. Mark Isaac, and Charles R. Plot. *The Allocation of Scarce Resources: Experimental Economics and the Problem of Allocating Airport Slots*. Boulder, CO: Westview, 1989.

Grieco, Margaret. "The regeneration and capture of opportunity: vacancy chains and family networks." Jesus College, Oxford University, November 1984.

Griffeth, Robert, and Carol Thomas. *The City-State in Five Cultures*. Santa Barbara, CA: ABC-Clio, 1981.

Griswold, Wendy. "American Character and the American Novel: An Expansion of Reflection Theory." *American Journal of Sociology* 86(1981): 740–765.

———. *Renaissance Revivals: City Comedy and Revenge Tragedy in the London Theatre, 1576–1980*. Chicago: University of Chicago Press, 1986.

Gross, Neal W., S. Mason, and A. W. McEachern. *Explorations in Role Analysis; Studies of the School Superintendency Role*. New York: Wiley, 1958.

Grossman, Peter Z. *American Express*. New York: Crown, 1987.

Groves, Theodore, and Martin Loeb. "Incentives in a Divisionalized Firm." *Management Science* 25(1979): 221–230.

Gruen, Erich S. *The Last Generation of the Roman Republic*. Berkeley, CA: University of California Press, 1974.

Grusky, Oscar, Phillip Bonacich, and Mark Peyrot. "Group Structure and Interpersonal Conflict in the Family." *Advances in Group Processes* 5(1988): 29–51.

Guilarte, Miguel G. "Semi-periphery in United Nations Parliamentary Process." Center for the Social Sciences, Columbia University, 1990.

———. "Delegitimation of the Colonial System after World War II." Ph.D. thesis, Dept. of Sociology, Columbia University, 1990b.

Gumperz, John J. *Discourse Strategies*. Cambridge: Cambridge University Press, 1982.

Habermas, Jurgen. *Legitimation Crisis*. Translated by T. McCarthy. Boston: Beacon, 1975.

Hackman, Richard J. "New Directions in Crew-Oriented Flight Training." Department of Psychology and Graduate School of Business Administration, Harvard University, January 1990.

Hagan, John, and Alberto Palloni. "Toward a Structural Criminology." *Annual Review of Sociology* 12(1986): 431–449.

Hagg, Ingemard, and Jan Johanson. *Firms in Networks—New Perspectives on Competitive Power*. Stockholm: Business and Social Research Institute, 1983.

Haggett, Peter, A. D. Cliff, and A. Frey. *Locational Models*, vols. 1 and 2. New York: Wiley, 1977.

Hahn, Roger. *The Anatomy of a Scientific Institution*. Berkeley, CA: University of California Press, 1971.

Haire, Mason, and A. P. Brief, eds. *Modern Organization Theory*. New York: Garland, 1987.

Hajnal, J. "Age at marriage and proportions marrying." *Population Studies* 7(1953): 11–36.

Halevy, Daniel. *The End of the Notables*. Translated by A. Silvera. Middletown, CT: Wesleyan University Press, 1974.

Hamermesh, R. G., ed. *Strategic Management*. New York: Wiley, 1983.

Hamilton, Gary G., and Nicole W. Biggart. "Why People Obey." *Sociological Perspectives* 28(1985): 3–28.

Hammack, David C. *Power and Society: Greater New York at the Turn of the Century*. New York: Russell Sage, 1982.

Hammel, E. A., and D. Hutchinson. "Two Tests of Computer Microsimulation." In *Computer Simulation in Human Population Studies*, edited by B. Dike and J. W. MacCluer. New York: Academic Press, 1974.

Hanagan, Michael P. *Class Formation and Workers' Families*. Oxford: Blackwell, 1989.

Hannah, Leslie. *The Rise of the Corporate Economy: The British Experience*. Baltimore, MD: Johns Hopkins University Press, 1983.

Hannah, Leslie, and J. A. Kay. *Concentration in Modern Industry*. London: Macmillan, 1977.

Hannan, M. T., and J. H. Freeman. "The Population Ecology of Organizations." *American Journal of Sociology* 82(1977): 929–964.

———. *Organizational Ecology*. Cambridge, MA: Harvard University Press, 1989.

Harary, Frank. *Graph Theory*. Reading, MA: Addison-Wesley, 1977.

Hareven, Tamara K. *Family Time and Industrial Time*. New York: Cambridge University Press, 1982.

Harmon, N. B. *The Organization of the Methodist Church*. Nashville, TN: Methodist Publishing House, 1962.

Harris, N. *Competition and the Corporate Society*, 2d. ed. London: Methuen, 1983.

Harrison, Roderick J. "Identifying Occupational Labor Markets in a National

Economy: A Blockmodeling Approach." *Research in Social Stratification and Mobility* 8(1989): 129–176.

Hart, C., and A. Pilling. *The Tiwi*. New York: Holt, 1960.

Harvey, Andrew C. *Forecasting, Structural time series models and the Kalman filter*. New York: Cambridge University Press, 1989.

Hatten, Kenneth J., Dan E. Schendel, and Arnold Cooper. "A Strategic Model of the U.S. Brewing Industry: 1952–1971." *Academy of Management Journal* 21(1978): 592–610.

Hauser, Robert M., and David L. Featherman. *The Process of Stratification: Trends and Analyses*. New York: Academic Press, 1977.

Hauser, Robert M., and David B. Grusky. "Cross-National Variation in Occupational Distributions, Relative Mobility Chances, and Intergenerational Shifts in Occupational Distributions." *American Sociological Review* 53(1988): 723–741.

Hawley, Amos. *Human Ecology: A Theory of Community Structure*. New York: Ronald Press, 1950.

Hawley, Ellis W. *The New Deal and the Problem of Monopoly*. Princeton, NJ: Princeton University Press, 1969.

Hearle, J.W.S. *Polymers and their Properties*. Chichester, UK: Ellis Horwood, 1982.

Hebb, D. O. *The Organization of Behavior*. New York: Wiley, 1949.

Hebdidge, D. *Subculture: The Meaning of Style*. London: Methuen, 1979.

Hechter, Michael. "Ethnic Political Structure in Britain." *American Journal of Sociology* 79(1974): 1151–1179.

———. *Principles of Group Solidarity*. Berkeley, CA: University of California Press, 1987.

Hechter, Michael, and Lynn Nadel, eds. *Toward a Scientific Analysis of Values*. Stanford, CA: Stanford University Press, forthcoming, 1993.

Hechter, Michael, K. D. Opp, and R. Wippler, eds. *Social Institutions: Their Emergence, Maintenance and Effects*. New York: Aldine de Gruyter, 1990.

Heclo, H. Hugh. "The Councillor's Job." *Public Administration* 47(1969).

Heclo, Hugh, and A. Wildavsky. *The Private Government of Public Money*. London: Sidgwick and Jackson, 1986.

Hedstrom, Peter. *Structures of Inequality*. Stockholm, Sweden: Almqvist and Wisksell International, 1988.

Heers, J. *Parties and Political Life in the Medieval West*. Translated by D. Nicholas. New York: North-Holland Publishing Co., 1977.

Heider, F. "Attitudes and Cognitive Organizations." *Journal of Psychology* 21(1946): 107–112.

Heil, Gregory H. "Algorithms for Network Homomorphism." Ph.D. thesis, Computer Science Department, University of Toronto, 1983.

———. "Empirical Blocking Methods." Chap. 12 in Freeman et al., 1989.

Heil, Gregory H., and Harrison C. White. "An Algorithm for Finding Simultaneous Homomorphic Correspondences between Graphs and Their Image Graphs." *Behavioral Science* 21(1976): 26–35.

Heimer, Carol A. *Reactive Risk and Rational Action*. Berkeley, CA: University of California Press, 1985.

Henderson, James M., and R. E. Quandt. *Microeconomic Theory*, 2d ed. New York: McGraw-Hill, 1971.

Heritage, John. *Garfinkel and Ethnomethodology*. Oxford: Polity Press-Blackwell, 1984.

Herlihy, David. *Medieval and Renaissance Pistoia*. New Haven, CT: Yale University Press, 1967.

Herredia, Blanca. "Economic Liberalization and Regime Change: Mexico in Comparative Perspective." Department of Political Science, Columbia University, February 1989.

Herrmann, T. *Speech and Situation*. New York: Springer-Verlag, 1983.

Hesse, Mary. *Revolutions and Reconstructions in the Philosophy of Science*. Bloomington, IN: Indiana University Press, 1980.

Heydebrand, Wolf V. "New Organizational Forms." *Work and Occupations* 16(1989): 323–357.

Hickson, David J. "Decision Making at the Top of Organizations." *Annual Reviews of Sociology* 13(1987): 165–192.

Higley, John, Michael G. Burton, and G. Lowell Field. "In Defense of Elite Theory." *American Sociological Review* 55(1990): 421–427.

Hinson, E. G. *The Evangelisation of the Roman Empire: Identity and Adaptability*. Macon, GA: Mercer University Press, 1981.

Hintze, Otto. *The Historical Essays of Otto Hintze*. Edited by Felix Gilbert. New York: Oxford University Press, 1975.

Hirsch, Eli. *The Concept of Identity*. Oxford: Oxford University Press, 1982.

Hirsch, Paul M. "Processing Fads and Fashions: An Organization Set Analysis of Culture Industry Systems." *American Journal of Sociology* 77(1972): 639–659.

Hirschman, Albert. *The Passions and the Interests: Political Arguments for Capitalism before its Triumph*. Princeton, NJ: Princeton University Press, 1977.

Hiskett, Mervyn. *The Sword of Truth: The Life and Times of the Shehu Usuman Dan Fodio*. New York: Oxford University Press, 1973.

Hobbes, Thomas. *Leviathan*. 1651; new ed. Indianapolis, IN: Bobbs-Merrill.

Hocart, A. M. *Caste; A Comparative Study*. London: Methuen, 1950.

Hochberg, Julian E. *Perception*. Englewood Cliffs, NJ: Prentice-Hall, 1978.

Hofstadter, Douglas R. *Godel, Escher, Bach: An Eternal Golden Braid*. New York: Basic Books, 1979.

Holdaway, A., and T. A. Blowers. "Administrative Ratios and Organization Size." *American Sociological Review* 36(1971): 278–287.

Holland, Paul W. "An Omnibus Test for Social Structure Using Triads." *Sociological Methods and Research* 7(1978): 227–256.

Holland, Paul W., K. B. Laskey, and Samuel Leinhardt. "Stochastic Blockmodels: First Steps." *Social Networks* 5(1983): 109–137.

Holland, Paul W., and Samuel Leinhardt. "Local Structure in Social Networks." In *Sociological Methodology 1976*, edited by D. R. Heise.

———, eds. *Perspectives in Social Network Research*. New York: Academic Press, 1979.

Hollingshead, S. *Elmtown's Youth*. New York: Wiley, 1949.

Holmstrom, Bengt R., and Jean Tirole. "The Theory of the Firm" pp. 61–133 in Schmalensee and Willig, eds., 1989.

Homans, George C. *The Human Group*. New York: Harcourt, Brace, 1950.

———. "Social Behavior as Exchange." *American Journal of Sociology* 65(1958): 597–606.

Homans, George C., and David Schneider. *Marriage, Authority and Final Causes: A Study of Unilateral Cross-cousin Marriage*. Glencoe, IL: Free Press, 1955.

Honsley, N. J. "Politics and Heresy in Italy." *Journal of Ecclesiastical History* 33(1982): 193–208.

Hopwood, Anthony G. "Towards an Organizational Perspective for the Study of Accounting and Information Systems." *Accounting, Organizations and Society* 3(1978): 3–13. .

Horwitz, Morton J. *The Transformation of American Law, 1780–1860*. Cambridge, MA: Harvard University Press, 1977.

Hotelling, Harold. "Stability in Competition." *Economic Journal* 39(1928): 467–484.

Hover, Julie, and Charles Kadushin. "Influential Intellectual Journals." *Change* 4(1972): 38–47.

Howell, Martha C. *Women, Production and Patriarchy in Late Medieval Cities*. Chicago: University of Chicago Press, 1988.

Howell, Nancy (Lee). *The Search for an Abortionist*. Chicago: University of Chicago Press, 1969.

———. *Demography of the Dobe !Kung*. New York: Academic Press, 1979.

———. "Understanding Simple Social Structure: kinship units and ties." In Wellman and Berkowitz, 1988.

Hsiao, Kung-chuan. *Rural China: Imperial Control in the Nineteenth Century*. Seattle, WA: University of Washington Press, 1960.

Hsu, Francis. *Clan, Caste and Club*. Princeton, NJ: Van Nostrand, 1963.

Huang, Karen Tsin. "The Integration of Organization Structure and Individual Networks." B. A. Honors thesis, Sociology Department, Harvard College, 1982.

Huang, Kerson. *Statistical Mechanics*. New York: Wiley, 1963.

Hubert, J. L. *Assignment Methods in Combinatorial Data Analysis*. New York: Marcel Dekker, 1987.

Hull, Isabel. *The Entourage of Kaiser Wilhelm II*. New York: Cambridge University Press, 1982.

Hummell, Hans J., and Wolfgang Sodeur. "Evaluating Models of Change in Triadic Sociometric Structures." Pp. 281–305 in Weesie and Flap, 1990.

Hunt, Lynn. *Politics, Culture, and Class in the French Revolution*. Berkeley, CA: University of California Press, 1984.

Hurewicz, Witold, and Henry Wallman. *Dimension Theory*. Princeton, NJ: Princeton University Press, 1948.

Hutchison, William. *The Modernist Impulse in American Protestantism*. Cambridge, MA: Harvard University Press, 1976.

Hyde, J. K. *Padua in the Age of Dante*. Manchester, UK: Manchester University Press, 1966.

Hyde, J. K. *Society and Politics in Medieval Italy*. London: Macmillan, 1973.

Ijira, Yuji, and H. A. Simon. *Skew Distributions and the Sizes of Business Firms*. Amsterdam: North-Holland, 1977.

Ingold, Tim, David Riches, and James Woodburn, eds. *Hunters and Gatherers I. History, Evolution and Social Change*. Oxford: Berg, 1988.

Inkeles, Alex, and David H. Smith. *Becoming Modern: Individual Change in Six Developing Countries*. Cambridge, MA: Harvard University Press, 1974.

Isenberg, D. J., and J. G. Ennis. "Perceiving Group Members." *Journal of Personality and Social Psychology* 41(1981): 293–305.

Ishida, Hiroshi, John H. Goldthorpe, and Robert Erikson. "Intergenerational Class Mobility in Post-war Japan: Conformity or Peculiarity in cross-national Perspective?" *American Journal of Sociology*, forthcoming.

Israel, Jonathan I. *The Dutch Republic and the Hispanic World, 1606–1661*. Oxford: Clarendon Press, 1982.

Jacobs, Jerry A. *Sex Segregation and Women's Careers*. Stanford, CA: Stanford University Press, 1989.

Jacobs, Jerry A., and Ronald L. Breiger. "Careers, Industries and Occupations: Industrial Segmentation Reconsidered." In *Industries, Firms and Jobs; Sociological and Economic Approaches*, edited by George Farkas and P. England, 43–64. New York: Plenum, 1988.

Jacques, E. *Measurement of Responsibility*. London: Tavistock, 1956.

Jakobson, Roman. *On Language*. Edited by Linda R. Waugh and M. Monville-Burston. Cambridge, MA: Harvard University Press, 1990.

James, John. "The Distribution of Free-Forming Small Group Size." *American Sociological Review* 18(1953): 569–570.

James, William. *Pragmatism, and Four Essays from the Meaning of Truth*. Edited by R. B. Perry. Cleveland, OH: Meridian World, 1955.

Jammer, Max. *Concepts of Space*. Cambridge, MA: Harvard University Press, 1954.

Jasso, Guillermina. "Methods for the Theoretical and Empirical Analysis of Comparison Processes." In *Sociological Methodology 1990*, edited by Clifford C. Clogg, 369–419. Washington, DC: American Sociological Association, 1990.

———. "Cloister and Society: Analyzing the Public Benefit of Monastic and Mendicant Institutions." *Journal of Mathematical Sociology*, 1991.

Jensen, Michael C., and W. H. Meckling. "Theory of the Firm: Managerial Behavior, Agency Costs and Ownership Structure." *Journal of Financial Economics* 3(1976): 305–360.

Jervis, Robert. *Perception and Misperception in International Politics*. Princeton, NJ: Princeton University Press, 1976.

Jevons, W. Stanley. *Money and the Mechanism of Exchange*. New York: Appleton, 1907.

Johnsen, Eugene C. "Network Macrostructure Models for the Davis-Leinhardt Set of Empirical Sociomatrices." *Social Networks* 7(1985): 203–224.

Johnson, H. T. "The Search for Gain in Markets and Firms: A Review of the Historical Emergence of Management Accounting Systems." *Accounting, Organizations and Society* 8(1983): 139–146.

Johnson, T. J. *Professions and Power*. London: Macmillan, 1972.

Johnston, J. *Statistical Cost Analysis*. New York: McGraw-Hill, 1960.

Kadushin, Charles. "Power, Influence and Social Circles." *American Sociological Review* 43(1968): 685–699.

Kahneman, D., P. Slovic, and A. Tversky, eds. *Judgment under Uncertainty: Heuristics and Decisions*. Cambridge, UK: Cambridge University Press, 1982.

Kailath, Thomas. "A View of Three Decades of Linear Filtering Theory." *IEEE Transactions on Information Theory IT-20*, pp. 146–181, 1974.

Kantor, Brian. "Rational Expectations and Economic Thought." *Journal of Economic Literature* 17(1979): 1422–1441.

Kantorowicz, E. H. *The King's Two Bodies*. Princeton, NJ: Princeton University Press, 1957.

Kapferer, Bruce. "Social Network and conjugal role in Urban Zambia: Towards a Reformulation of the Bott Hypothesis." In *Network Analysis*, edited by J. Boissevain and J. C. Mitchell, 83–110. Paris: Mouton, 1973.

Kaplan, Robert S. *Advanced Management Accounting*. Englewood Cliffs, NJ: Prentice-Hall, 1982.

Katz, Donald R. *The Big Store: Inside the Crisis and Revolution at Sears*. New York: Penguin, 1988.

Katznelson, Ira, and Aristide R. Zolberg. *Working-Class Formation*. Princeton, NJ: Princeton University Press, 1986.

Kauffman, S. A. "Metabolic Stability and Epigenesis in Randomly Constructed Genetic Nets." *Journal of Theoretical Biology* 22(1969): 437–467.

Kaufman, H. *The Forest Ranger*. Baltimore, MD: Johns Hopkins University Press, 1960.

Kaufman, Robert. "Corporatism, Clientelism and Partisan Conflict: A Study of Seven Latin American Countries." Chap. 5 in J. M. Malloy, ed. 1974.

Kearns, Doris. *Lyndon Johnson and the American Dream*. New York: Harper, 1976.

Kegan, Robert. *The Evolving Self*. Cambridge, MA: Harvard University Press, 1982.

Keilman, Nico, Anton Kuijsten, and Ad Vossen, eds. *Modelling Household Formation and Dissolution*. Oxford: Clarendon Press, 1988.

Kellett, J. R. "The Breakdown of Gild and Corporation Control over the Handicraft and Retail Trade in London." *Economic History Review* 10(1958): 381–394.

Kelley, Donald R. "Horizons of Intellectual History: Retrospect, Circumspect, Prospect." *Journal of the History of Ideas*. Pp. 143–169, 1987.

Kelley, John L. *General Topology*. Princeton, NJ: Van Nostrand, 1955.

Kelsall, R. K. *Higher Civil Servants in Britain*. London: Routledge and Kegan Paul, 1955.

Kemeny, John, J. L. Snell, and F. L. Thompson. *Introduction to Finite Mathematics*. Englewood Cliffs, NJ: Prentice-Hall, 1957.

Kent, D. V., and F. W. Kent. *Neighbours and Neighbourhood in Renaissance Florence*. Villa I Tatti, #6. Locust Valley, NY: J. J. Augustin, 1982.

Kent, Dale. *The Rise of the Medici: Faction in Florence, 1426–1434*. New York: Oxford University Press, 1978.

Kent, Davis, and D. Shapiro. "Resources Required in the Construction and Reconstruction of Conversation." *Journal of Personality and Social Psychology* 36(1978): 13–22.

Kent, Sherman. *Strategic Intelligence*. Princeton, NJ: Princeton University Press, 1966.

Keohane, Robert O. *After Hegemony*. Princeton, NJ: Princeton University Press, 1984.

Keohane, Robert O., and Joseph S. Nye, Jr. *Power and Interdependence*. Boston, MA: Little, Brown, 1977.

Kershaw, Ian. *The Nazi Dictatorship: Problems and Perspectives of Interpretation*, 2d ed. London: Arnold, 1989.

Key, V. O., Jr. *Southern Politics in State and Nation*, 1945; new ed. Knoxville, TN: University of Tennessee Press, 1977.

Keyfitz, N. *Introduction to the Mathematics of Population*. Reading, MA: Addison-Wesley, 1968.

———. *Applied Mathematical Demography*. New York: Wiley, 1977.

Kim, K. H., and F. W. Roush. "Two-generator Semigroups of Binary Relations." *Journal of Mathematical Psychology* 17(1978): 236–246.

———. *Mathematics for Social Scientists*. New York: Elsevier, 1980.

———. *Team Theory*. New York, 1987.

Kirkpatrick, S., C. D. Gelatt, and M. P. Vecchi. "Organization by Simulated Annealing." *Science* 220(1983): 671–679.

Kitto, H.D.F. *The Greeks*. Harmondsworth, UK: Penguin, 1958.

Kleinrock, Leonard. *Communication Nets: Stochastic Message Flow and Delay*. New York: McGraw-Hill, 1964.

———. *Queuing Systems*, vols. 1 and 2, New York: Wiley, 1975–1976.

Kline, Morris. *Mathematics: The Loss of Certainty*. New York: Oxford University Press, 1980.

Knight, Frank. *Risk, Uncertainty and Profit*. Cambridge, MA: Houghton Mifflin, 1921.

Knoke, David, and D. L. Rogers. "A Blockmodel Analysis of Interorganizational Relations." *Sociology and Social Research* 64(1979): 28–52.

Knoke, David, and James R. Wood. *Organized for Action: Commitment in Voluntary Associations*. New Brunswick, NJ: Rutgers University Press, 1981.

Knorr-Cetina, Karin, and A.V. Cicourel, eds. *Advances in Social Theory and Methodology: Toward an Integration of Micro- and Macro-Sociologies*. Boston: Routledge and Kegan Paul, 1981.

Kochen, Manfred, ed. *The Small World*. Norwood, NJ: Ablex, 1989.

Kohlberg, Lawrence. *The Philosophy of Moral Development: Moral Stages and the Idea of Justice*. San Francisco, CA: Harper and Row, 1981.

Kohn, M. L., and C. Schooler. "The Reciprocal Effects of the Substantive Complexity of Work and Intellectual Flexibility: A Longitudinal Assessment." *American Journal of Sociology* 84(1978): 24–52.

Kolb, David. *The Critique of Pure Modernity: Hegel, Heidegger, and After*. Chicago: University of Chicago Press, 1986.

Koopmans, Tjalling C. *Three essays on the state of economic science*. New York: McGraw-Hill, 1957.

Korte, C., and S. Milgram. "Acquaintance Networks between Racial Groups: Application of the Small World Method." *Journal of Personality and Social Psychology* 15(1970): 101–108.

Kossman, E. H. *The Crisis of the Dutch State, 1780–1813*. In *Britain and the Netherlands*, vol. 4, n.d.

———. *The Low Countries*. New York: Oxford University Press, 1978.

Kotter, John P. *The General Managers*. New York: Free Press, 1982.

Kotz, David M. *Bank Control of Large Corporations in the U.S.* Berkeley, CA: University of California Press, 1978.

Krackhardt, David. "Predicting with Networks: Nonparametric Multiple Regression Analysis of Dyadic Data." *Social Networks* 10(1988): 359–381.

Kramer, Stella. *The English Craft Guilds*. 1927. New York: Columbia University Press, 1922.

Krantz, David. "Tactical Decision-Making in Distributed Systems: Goals and Heuristics for Solving Decision Problems." Bell Laboratories, November 1983.

Krantz, David H., and Laura K. Briggs. "Judgments of Frequency and Evidence Strength." Manuscript, Psychology Department, Columbia University, February 6, 1990.

Krantz, David H., R. Duncan Luce, Patrick Suppes, and Amos Tversky. *Foundations of Measurement*, vol I. New York: Academic Press, 1971.

Krauss, Robert M., and Peter D. Bricker. "Effects of Transmission Delay and Access Delay on the Efficiency of Verbal Communication." *Journal of the Acoustical Society of America* 41(1967): 286–292.

Kreckel, Marga. *Communicative Acts and Shared Knowledge in Natural Discourse*. London: Academic Press, 1981.

Kreps, David M. *Notes on the Theory of Choice*. Boulder, CO: Westview, 1988.

Kriedte, Peter, Hans Medick, and Jurgen Shlumbohm. *Industrialization before Industrialisation*. New York: Cambridge University Press, 1981.

Krieger, Joel. *Undermining Capitalism*. Princeton, NJ: Princeton University Press, 1984.

Krieger, M. H. "Where do Centers Come From?" *Environment and Planning* 19(1987): 1251–1260.

———. *Marginalism and Discontinuity*. New York: Russell Sage Foundation, 1989.

Krumeich, Gerd. *Armaments and Politics in France on the Eve of the First World War*. Translated by Stephen Conn. Oxford: Berg, 1984.

Kuehn, Alfred. "Supermarket Layout." Unpublished.

Kuhn, Philip A. *Rebellion and its Enemies in Late Imperial China*. Cambridge, MA: Harvard University Press, 1970.

Kuhn, Thomas S. *The Structure of Scientific Revolutions*. Chicago: University of Chicago Press, 1970.

Kurosh, A. G. *Lectures in General Algebra*. Translated by Ann Swinfer. Oxford, UK: Pergamon Press, 1965.

Kurz, Lester R. *The Politics of Heresy: The Modernist Crisis in Roman Catholicism*. Berkeley, CA: University of California Press, 1986.

Kwoka, John E. "The Effect of Market Share Distribution on Industry Performance." *Review of Economics and Statistics*. 61(1)(1979): 101–109.

384 WORKS CITED

Labov, William. *The Social Stratification of English in New York City*. Washington, DC: Center for Applied Linguistics, 1966.

———. "The Study of Language in its Social Context." In Joshua A. Fishman. *Advances in the Sociology of Language I*. The Hague: Mouton, 1971.

Lachmann, Richard. "Feudal Elite Conflict and the Origins of English Capitalism." *Politics and Society* 14(1985): 349–378.

———. "The Cultural Bases of Legal Legitimacy: Edgerton's Pictures." *American Bar Foundation Research Journal*. 301–312, 1986.

———. *From Manor to Market*. Madison, WI: University of Wisconsin Press, 1987.

Lachmann, Richard, and Stephen Petterson. "Rationality and Structure in the 'Failed' Capitalism of Renaissance Italy." Department of Sociology, University of Wisconsin-Madison, 1988.

Lammers, Cornelis J. "The Interorganizational Control of an Occupied Country." *Administrative Science Quarterly* 33(1988): 438–457.

Lancaster, Kelvin, J. "A New Approach to Consumer Theory." *Journal of Political Economy* 74(1970): 132–157.

Landau, Hyman. "On Dominance Relations and the Structure of Animal Societies: I. Effect of Inherent Characteristics; II. Some Effects of Possible Social Factors." *Bulletin of Mathematical Biophysics* 13(1950–51): 1–19, 245–261.

———. "Development of Structure in a Society with Dominance Relation when new Members are added Successively." *Bulletin of Mathematical Biophysics* 27(1965): 151–160.

Landes, David S. *Bankers and Pashas*. Cambridge, MA: Harvard University Press, 1958.

Lang, Gladys, and Kurt Lang. "Recognition and Renown: The Survival of Artistic Reputation." *American Journal of Sociology* 94(1988): 79–109.

Lasswell, Harold D., and A. Kaplan. *Power and Society*. New Haven, CT: Yale University Press, 1950.

Lauderdale, Pat. "Deviance and Moral Boundaries." *American Sociological Review* 41(1976): 660–676.

Laumann, Edward O., and David Knoke. *The Organizational State: Social Choice in National Policy Domains*. Madison, WI: University of Wisconsin Press, 1987.

Laumann, Edward O., and P. V. Marsden. "Microstructural Analysis in Interorganizational Systems." *Social Networks* 4(1982): 329–348.

Laumann, Edward O., P. V. Marsden, and D. Prensky. "The boundary specification problem in network analysis." In *Applied Network Analysis*, edited by R. S. Burt and M. J. Minor. Beverly Hills, CA: Sage, 1982.

Laumann, Edward O., and Franz V. Pappi. *Networks of Collective Action: A Perspective on Community Influence Systems*. New York: Academic Press, 1976.

Lawrence, Paul, and Jay Lorsch. *Organizations and Environment*. Cambridge, MA: Harvard University Press, 1967.

Lawrence, Paul R., and Davis Dyer. *Renewing American Industries*. New York: Free Press, 1983.

Lazarsfeld, Paul F. *Latent Structure Analysis*. New York: Bureau of Applied Social Research, 1957.

Lazarsfeld, Paul F., and Morris Rosenberg, eds. *The Language of Social Research*. Glencoe, IL: Free Press, 1955.

Lazerson, Mark H. "Organizational Growth of Small Firms: An Outcome of Markets and Hierarchies." *American Sociological Review* 53(1988): 330–342.

Leach, Edmund R. *The Political Systems of Highland Burma*. Boston: Beacon, 1954.

————, ed. *Aspects of Caste in South India, Ceylon and W. Pakistan*. Cambridge Papers in Social Anthropology #2, Cambridge University Press, 1960.

Leamer, Edward. *Specification Searches: Ad Hoc Inference with Non-experimental Data*. New York: Wiley, 1978.

Leavitt, Harold J., and T. L. Whisler. "Management in the 1980s." *Harvard Business Review*, November–December 1958.

Lebretton, Jules, and J. Zeiller. *A History of the Primitive Church*. London, 1944.

Lee, Nancy Howell—see Howell, Nancy

Lee, Richard B. *The !Kung San*. Cambridge: Cambridge University Press, 1979.

Leffler, A. Gillespie, D. L. and J. C. Conaty. "The Effects of Status Differentiation on Nonverbal Behavior." *Social Psychology Quarterly* 45(1982): 153–161.

Le Goff, Jacques. *The Birth of Purgatory*. Translated by Arthur Goldhammer. Chicago: University of Chicago Press, 1984.

Lehmann, Donald R., and W. L. Moore. "On Hypotheses, Measurements and the Extension of Knowledge." *Journal of Consumer Research* 10(1983): 32–33.

Lehmbruch, G., and P. C. Schmitter, eds. *Patterns of Corporatist Policy-Making*. Beverly Hills, CA: Sage, 1982.

Leifer, Eric M. "Hierarchies of Ends: Uncertain Preferences in Strategic Decision Making." Department of Sociology, Harvard University, December 1982.

————. "Markets as Mechanisms: Using a Role Structure." *Social Forces* 64(2)(1985): 442–472.

————. "The Feasibility of Fairness." Department of Sociology, University of North Carolina, November 1987.

————. "Enacting Networks." 1990.

————. *Robust Action*. New York: Garland, 1991a.

————. "Organizing for Involvement: The Evolution of League Sports in America." Department of Sociology, Columbia University, May 1991b.

Leifer, Eric M., and Harrison C. White. "Wheeling and Annealing: Federal and Multidivisional Control." In *The Social Fabric: Issues and Dimensions*, edited by James F. Short. Beverly Hills, CA: Sage, 1986.

————. "A Structural Approach to Markets." in Mizruchi and Schwartz, eds., 1988.

Leigh, J. R. *Applied Control Theory*. 2d ed. London: Peter Peregrinus, 1987.

Leijonhufvud, Axel. *On Keynesian Economics and the Economics of Keynes*. Oxford: Oxford University Press, 1968.

Leik, R. K., and B. F. Meeker. *Mathematical Sociology*. Englewood Cliffs, NJ: Prentice-Hall, 1975.

Leinhardt, Samuel, ed. *Sociological Methodology, 1981*. San Francisco: Jossey-Bass, 1981.

———. *Sociological Methodology, 1983–1984*. San Francisco: Jossey-Bass, 1984.

Lenin, V. I. "What is to Be Done?" 1902. In *Essential Works of Lenin*, edited by H. M. Christman. Bantam, 1966.

———. *The Development of Capitalism in Russia*, vol. 3 in *Collected Works*. English trans. of fourth Russian edition, Moscow: Progress Publishers, 1976.

Lenski, Gerhard E. *Power and Privilege: A Theory of Social Stratification*. New York: McGraw-Hill, 1966.

Lentricchia, Frank, and Thomas McLaughlin, eds. *Critical Terms for Literary Study*. Chicago: University Of Chicago Press, 1990.

Leontief, Wassily W. *Input-Output Economics*. New York: Oxford University Press, 1966.

Lepenies, Wolf. *Between Literature and Science: The Rise of Sociology*. Translated by G. J. Hollingdale. New York: Cambridge University Press, 1988.

Levi-Strauss, Claude. *The Elementary Structures of Kinship* (revised edition). Boston: Beacon Press, 1969.

Levine, Joel H. "The Sphere of Influence." *American Sociological Review* 37(1972): 14–27.

———. *World Atlas of Director Interlocks*. Mathematical Social Science, Dartmouth College, 1989.

———. *Lectures on Method*. Boulder, CO: Westview Press, 1992.

Levins, Richard. "The Strategy of Model Building in Population Biology." *American Scientist* 54(1966): 421–431.

Levins, Richard, and Robert MacArthur. "The Maintenance of Genetic Polymorphism in a Spatially Heterogeneous Environment." *The American Naturalist* 100(1966): 585–589.

Levy, Hermann. *Retail Trade Associations*. New York: Oxford University Press, 1944.

Levy, Marion J. "A Note on Pareto's Logical-Non-logical Categories." *American Sociological Review* 13(1948): 756–757.

———. *The Structure of Society*. Princeton, NJ: Princeton University Press, 1952.

Lewontin, Richard C. *The Genetic Basis of Evolutionary Change*. New York: Columbia University Press, 1974.

Libecap, Gary D. *The Evolution of Private Mineral Rights*. New York: Arno Press, 1978.

Libecap, Gary D., and Stephen N. Wiggins. "Contractual Response to Common Pools: Prorationing of Crude Oil Production." *American Economic Review* 74(1984): 87–98.

Lie, John. "Social Origins of Natural Markets: England (1550–1730)." Department of Sociology, Harvard University, December 1986.

Lieberson, Stanley. "An Empirical Study of Military-Industrial Linkages." *American Journal of Sociology* 76(1971): 562–585.

Lijphart, Arend. *The Politics of Accommodation*. Berkeley, CA: University of California Press, 1968.

———. "Comparative Politics and the Comparative Method." *American Political Science Review* 65(1971): 682–693.

Lin, Nan. "Social Resources and Social Mobility: A Structural Theory of Status Attainment." In R. L. Breiger, 1982.

Lin, Nan, Walter M. Ensel, and John C. Vaughn. "Social Resources and Strength of Ties." *American Sociological Review* 46(1981): 393–405.

Lincoln, James R. "Analyzing Relations in Dyads." *Sociological Methods and Research* 13(1984): 45–76.

Lincoln, James R., and Kerry McBride. "Japanese Industrial Organization in Comparative Perspective." In W. Richard Scott and James F. Short, eds. *Annual Review of Sociology* 13(1987): 289–313.

Lindenberg, Siegwart. "Rational Repetitive Choice: The Discrimination Model versus the Camilleri-Berger Model." *Social Psychology Quarterly* 44(1981): 312–330.

———. "Sharing Groups." *Journal of Mathematical Sociology* 9(1982): 33–62.

———. "Choice and Culture: The Behavioral Basis of Cultural Impact on Transactions." In *Social Structure and Culture*, edited by Hans Haferkamp, 175–200. Berlin: DeGruyter, 1989a.

———. "Social Production Functions, Deficits, and Social Revolutions." *Rationality and Society* 1(1989b): 51–77.

Lindenberg, Siegwart, James S. Coleman, and Stefan Nowak, eds. *Approaches to Social Theory*. New York: Russell Sage, 1986.

Lindenberger, Herbert. *The History in Literature: On Value, Genre, Institutions*. New York: Columbia University Press, 1990.

Lipset, S. M., M. A. Trow, and James S. Coleman. *Union Democracy*. Garden City, NY: Doubleday, 1956.

Llewellyn, Karl N. "Agency." In *Encyclopedia of the Social Sciences*, vol. 1, p. 483, 1930.

———. *The Bramble Bush: Our Law and Its Study*. New York: Oceana, 1951.

———. *The Case Law System in America* (1933). Translated by Michael Ansaldi and edited by Paul Gerwitz. Chicago: University of Chicago Press, 1989.

Loasby, B. J. *Choice, Complexity and Ignorance*. Cambridge: Cambridge University Press, 1976.

Lorrain, François. *Reseaux Sociaux et Classifications Sociales*. Paris: Herman, 1975.

Lorrain, François, and Harrison C. White. "Structural Equivalence of Individuals in Social Networks." *Journal of Mathematical Sociology* 1(1971): 49–80.

Love, R. Geoffrey, "An Investigation of Block-Modeling Techniques Applied to International Trade Flows." B.A. Honors thesis, Applied Mathematics, Harvard College, May 1982.

Luce, R. Duncan. *Response Times: Their Role in Inferring Elementary Mental Organization*. New York: Oxford University Press, 1986.

Luce, R. Duncan, Josiah Macy, Lee S. Christie, and D. H. Hay. "Information Flow in Task Oriented Groups." Technical Report, MIT Research Laboratory of Electronics, 1953.

Luce, R. Duncan, and Howard Raiffa. *Games and Decisions: Introduction and Critical Survey*. New York: Wiley, 1957.

Luckham, Robin. *The Nigerian Military: A Sociological Analysis of Authority and Revolt, 1960–1967*. New York: Cambridge University Press, 1971.

Lukes, S. *Power: A Radical View*. London: Macmillan, 1975.

Lwoff, Andre. *Biological Order*. Cambridge, MA: MIT Press, 1962.

Lydall, Harold. *The Structure of Earnings*. Oxford: Clarendon Press, 1968.

Lynes, Russell. *The Tastemakers*. New York: Greenwood Press, 1955.

Lytle, G. F., and S. Orgel, eds. *Patronage in the Renaissance*, 1981.

Ma, Shang-keng. "Introduction to the Renormalization Group." *Review of Modern Physics*, 45(1973): 589–613.

McAdam, Doug. *Political Process and the Development of Black Insurgency*. Chicago: University of Chicago Press, 1982.

———. *Freedom Summer*. New York: Oxford University Press, 1988.

Macauley, S. "Non-contractual relations in business: a preliminary study." *American Sociological Review* 28(1963): 55–67.

McCarthy, John D., and Mayer N. Zald. "Resource Mobilization and Social Movements: A Partial Theory." *American Journal of Sociology* 82(1977): 1212–1241.

McClelland, James L. "Putting Knowledge in Its Place: A Scheme for Programming Parallel Processing Structures on the Fly." *Cognitive Science* 9(1985): 113–146.

McClelland, James L., David E. Rumelhart, et al. *Parallel Distributed Processing, Vols 1 and 2*. Cambridge, MA: MIT Press, 1986.

McCloskey, D. M. "English Open Fields as Behavior Towards Risk." *Research in Economic History* 1(1976): 144–170.

McConaghy, Maureen J. "The Common Role Structure: Improved Blockmodelling Methods Applied to Two Communities' Elites." *Sociological Methods and Research* 9(1981): 267–285, 303–312.

McCormack, Thelma, Presentation, Oct. 17, 1986, at annual Conference on the Sociology of Arts, held at University of California at La Jolla.

McFarlan, F. W., and J. L. McKenney. *Corporate Information Systems Management*. Homewood, IL: Irwin Press, 1983.

MacIntyre, Alasdair, and Paul Ricoeur. *The Religious Significance of Atheism*. New York: Columbia University Press, 1969.

MacLane, Saunders. *Categories for the Working Mathematician*. New York: Springer-Verlag, 1971.

MacMahon, A. W. et al. *The Administration of Federal Work Relief*. Social Science Research Council, 1941.

Macneil, Ian R. "Contracts: adjustment of long-term economic relations under classical, neo-classical and relational contract law." *Northwestern Law Review* 72(1978): 854–906.

———. "Exchange Revisited: Individual Utility and Social Solidarity." *Ethics* 96(1986): 567–593.

McNeill, William H. *The Pursuit of Power: Technology, Armed Force and Society Since A.D. 1000*. New York: Oxford University Press, 1983.

MacPherson, C. B. *The Political Theory of Possessive Individualism: Hobbes to Locke*. Oxford: Oxford University Press, 1962.

McPherson, Miller. "An Ecology of Affiliation." *American Sociological Review* 48(1983): 519–532.

Madsen, Richard. *Morality and Power in a Chinese Village*. Berkeley, CA: University of California Press, 1984.

Maier, Charles S. *The Unmasterable Past: History, Holocaust, and German National Identity*. Cambridge, MA: Harvard University Press, 1988.

Maier, Henry W. *Three Theories of Child Development*. New York: Harper's, rev. ed., 1969.

Maine, Henry. *Ancient Law*. 1861.

Major, J. Russell. *Representative Institutions in Renaissance France: 1421–1559*. Madison, WI: University of Wisconsin Press, 1960.

Malloy, James M., ed. *Authoritarianism and Corporatism in Latin America*. Pittsburgh, PA: University of Pittsburgh Press, 1974.

Mandel, Michael. "Local Roles and Social Networks." *American Sociological Review* 48(1983): 376–386.

Mandelbrot, Benoit B. *Fractal Geometry of Nature*. New York: Freeman, 1983.

Mann, Michael. *The Sources of Social Power: Vol. I A History of Power from the Beginning to A.D. 1760*. New York: Cambridge University Press, 1986.

Mansfield, Edward. "The Timing and Determinants of War." Ph.D. dissertation, Political Science Department, University of Pennsylvania, 1989.

Mansfield, Edwin. *The Economics of Technical Change*. New York: Norton, 1968.

———. *Microeconomics: Theory and Applications*, 2d ed. New York: Norton, 1975.

Maraffi, Marco. "State/economy Relations: The Case of Italian Public Enterprise." *British Journal of Sociology* 31(1980).

March, James G., and Johan P. Olsen. *Ambiguity and Choice in Organizations*. Bergen Universitetsforlaget, 1976.

———. *The Organizational Basis of Politics*. New York: The Free Press-Macmillan, 1989.

March, James G., and Herbert A. Simon. *Organizations*. New York: Wiley, 1958.

March, James G., ed. *Handbook of Organizations*. Chicago: Rand McNally, 1965.

Markovitz, A. S., and Karl W. Deutsch, eds. *Fear of Science—Trust of Science*. Cambridge, MA: Oelgeschlager, Gunn and Hain, 1980.

Marriott, McKim. "Interactional and Attributional Theories of Caste Ranking." *Man in India* 39(1959): 92–107.

———. "Caste Ranking and Food Transactions, a Matrix Analysis." In *Structure and Change in Indian Society*, edited by Milton Singer and Bernard S. Cohn. Chicago: Aldine, 1968.

Marsden, Peter. "Restricted Access in Networks and Models of Power." *American Journal of Sociology* 88(1983): 686–717.

———. "Methods for the Characterization of Role Structures in Network Analysis." Chap. 14 in Freeman, White, and Romney, 1989.

Marsden, P. V., and E. O. Laumann. "Collective Action in a Community

Elite." In *Power, Paradigms and Community Research*, edited by R. J. Liebert and A. W. Imershein. Beverly Hills, CA: Sage, 1977.

Marshall, Alfred. *Principles of Economics*, 1891.

Martines, Lauro. *Lawyers and Statecraft in Renaissance Florence*. Princeton, NJ: Princeton University Press, 1968.

Marwell, Gerald, and D. R. Schmitt. "Interpersonal Risk and Cooperation: Cross-cultural and Cross-procedural Generalizations." *Journal of Experimental Social Psychology* 8(1972): 9–32.

Mathews, Douglas W., and W. W. Parsons. "The Californiazation of Arizona Water Politics." Department of Political Science, University of Arizona, 1987.

Mayer, Adrian C. *Caste and Kinship in Central India*. Berkeley, CA: University of California Press, 1960.

Mead, G. H. *The Philosophy of the Act*, C. W. Morris et al., eds. Chicago: University of Chicago Press, 1938.

———. *On Social Psychology*. Edited by A. Straus. Chicago: University of Chicago Press, 1956.

Meeker, B. F. "Decisions and Exchange." *American Sociological Review* 36(1971): 485–495.

Meiss, Millard. *Painting in Florence and Siena after the Black Death*. Princeton, NJ: Princeton University Press, 1976.

Menard, Henry W. *Science: Growth and Change*. Cambridge, MA: Harvard University Press, 1971.

Merton, Robert K. *Social Theory and Social Structure*. New York: Free Press, 1968.

———. *The Sociology of Science*. Edited by Norman W. Storer. Chicago: University of Chicago Press, 1973.

———. *On the Shoulders of Giants: A Shandean Postscript*. New York: Harcourt, Brace, Jovanovich, 1985.

Meyendorff, John. *Orthodoxy and Catholicity*. New York: Sheed and Ward, 1966.

Meyer, Marshall W. "Organizational Design and the Performance Paradox." Chap. 11 in Swedberg, 1991.

Meyer, Marshall W., and Lynne G. Zucker. *Permanently Failing Organizations*. Newbury Park, CA: Sage, 1989.

Meyer, Marshall W. et al. *Limits to Bureaucratic Growth*. New York: de-Gruyter, 1985.

Milgram, Stanley. *Obedience to Authority: An Experimental View*. New York: Harper and Row, 1975.

———. *The Individual in a Social World*. Reading, MA: Addison-Wesley, 1977.

Miliband, Ralph. *Marxism and Politics*. Oxford: Oxford University Press, 1977.

Miller, George A. *The Psychology of Communication: Seven Essays*. New York: Basic Books, 1967.

Milner, Helen. *Resisting Protectionism*. Princeton, NJ: Princeton University Press, 1988.

Mintz, Beth, and Michael Schwartz. *The Power Structure of American Business*. Chicago: University of Chicago Press, 1985.

Mintzberg, Henry, D. Raisinghani, and A. Theoret. "The Structure of 'Unstructured' Decision Processes." *Administrative Science Quarterly*: 55(1976): 246–275.

Mischel, Walter. *Introduction to Personality: A New Look*, 4th ed. 1968.

———. "Personality Dispositions Revisited and Revised: A View after Three Decades." Chap. 5 in *Handbook of Personality Theory and Research*, edited by L. Pervin. New York: Guilford Press, 1990.

Mitchell, J. Clyde, ed. *Social Networks in Urban Situations*. Manchester: Manchester University Press, 1969.

———. "Social Networks." *Annual Review of Anthropology* 3(1974): 277–299.

———. "Algorithms and Networks: A Test of Some Analytical Procedures on Kapferer's Tailor Shop Material." Chap. 10 in Freeman, D. White, and Romney, eds., 1989.

Mitnick, B. M. *The Political Economy of Regulation*. New York: Columbia University Press, 1980.

Mizruchi, Ephraim M. *Regulating Society*. Chicago: University of Chicago Press, 1987.

Mizruchi, Mark S. "What is Class Cohesion? Sources of Corporate Political Power." *Power and Elites* 1(1984): 23–36.

———. "Urgency, Motivation, and Group Performance: The Effects of Prior Success on Current Success among Professional Basketball Teams." *Social Psychological Quarterly* 54(1991): 181–189.

Mizruchi, Mark S., and Thomas Koenig. "Economic Sources of Corporate Political Consensus." *American Sociological Review* 51(1986): 482–491.

Mizruchi, Mark S., and Michael Schwartz, eds. *Intercorporate Relations: The Structural Analysis of Business*. New York: Cambridge University Press, 1988.

Moe, Terry M. *The Organization of Interests: Incentives and the Internal Dynamics of Interest Groups*. Chicago: University of Chicago Press, 1980.

Mommsen, Theodor. *The Provinces of the Roman Empire* (1885). Translated by T. R. Broughton. Chicago: University of Chicago Press, 1968.

Moon, J. W. *Topics in Tournaments*. New York: Holt, Rinehart and Winston, 1968.

Moore, Basil J. *Horizontalists and Verticalists: The Macroeconomics of Credit Money*. New York: Cambridge University Press, 1988.

Moore, Gwen. "The Structure of a National Elite Network." *American Sociological Review* 44(1979): 673–692.

Moore, Sally Falk. *Power and Property in Inca Peru*. New York: Columbia University Press, 1958.

Moote, A. Lloyd. *The Revolt of the Judges: The Parlement of Paris and the Fronde, 1643–1652*. Princeton, NJ: Princeton University Press, 1971.

Morgan, G. *Images of Organization*. Beverly Hills, CA: Sage, 1986.

Morgan, Lewis Henry. *Ancient Society* (1877). Edited by E. Leacock. Gloucester, MA: Smith, 1974.

Morishima, Michio. *Marx's Economics*. New York: Cambridge University Press, 1973.

———. *Ricardo's Economics: A General Equilibrium Theory of Distribution and Growth*. New York: Cambridge University Press, 1989.

Morrill, Calvin. "Conflict Management Among Corporate Executives." Communication Science Department, University of Arizona, 1986.

Morse, Philip M., and H. Feshbach. *Handbook of Theoretical Physics, Parts I and II*. New York: McGraw-Hill, 1953.

Moss, Scott J. *An Economic Theory of Business Strategy*. New York: Wiley-Halstead, 1981.

Mosteller, Frederick F. *Sturdy Statistics*. Reading, MA: Addison-Wesley, 1973.

Mousnier, Roland. *La Venalite des Offices Henri IV et Louis XIII*. Paris: Press Universitaires de France, 1971.

———. *Institutions of France under the Absolute Monarchy, 1578–1789*. Translated by B. Pearce. Chicago: University of Chicago Press, 1984.

Muller, Gary J. "Administrative Dilemmas: The Role of Political Leadership." *American Political Science Review*, 1989.

Mullins, Nicholas. *Theories and Theory Groups in Contemporary American Sociology*. New York: Harper & Row, 1973.

Murdock, George P. *Atlas of World Cultures*. Pittsburgh, PA: University of Pittsburgh Press, 1981.

Murphy, Raymond. *Social Closure: The Theory of Monopolization and Exclusion*. Oxford: Clarendon Press, 1988.

Muth, John F. "Rational Expectations and the Theory of Price Movements." Office of Naval Research, Research Memorandum #65, Graduate School of Industrial Administration, Carnegie Institute of Technology, August 1959.

———. "Optimal Properties of Exponentially Weighted Forecasts." *Journal of the American Statistical Association* 55(1960): 299–305.

Myers, Milton L. *The Soul of Modern Man: Ideas of Self Interest: Thomas Hobbes to Adam Smith*. Chicago: University of Chicago Press, 1983.

Myrdal, Gunnar. *The Political Element in the Development of Economic Theory*. Stockholm, 1930. Translated by Paul Streeten. New York: Simon & Schuster, 1953.

Nadel, Lynn, Lynn A. Cooper, Peter Culicover, and R. Michael Harnish, eds. *Neural Connections, Mental Computation*. Cambridge, MA: MIT Press, 1989.

Nadel, S. F. *A Black Byzantium*. Oxford: Oxford University Press, 1946.

———. *The Theory of Social Structure*. London: Cohen and West, 1957.

Nagi, Saad Z. "Gate-Keeping Decisions in Service Organizations." *Human Organization* 33(1974): 47–58.

Najemy, John M. *Corporations and Consensus in Florentine Electoral Politics, 1280–1420*. Chapel Hill, NC: University of North Carolina Press, 1982.

Namier, Lewis. *The Structure of Politics at the Accession of George III*. London: Macmillan, 1961.

Napier, Augustus, and C. A. Whitaker. *The Family Crucible*. New York: Harper and Row, 1978.

Needham, Rodney. *Structure and Sentiment*. Chicago: University of Chicago Press, 1962.

Nelson, David R. "Recent Developments in Phase Transitions and Critical Phenomena." *Nature* 269(1977): 379–383.

Nelson, Richard R., and Sidney G. Winter. *An Evolutionary Theory of Economic Change*. Cambridge, MA: Harvard University Press, 1982.

Neusner, Jacob. *Judaism and Christianity in the Age of Constantine*. Chicago: University of Chicago Press, 1987.

————. *Judaism and its Social Metaphors*. New York: Cambridge University Press, 1989.

Newcomb, Theodore M. *The Acquaintance Process*. New York: Holt, Rinehart and Winston, 1961.

Newell, Allan, and Herbert A. Simon. *Human Problem Solving*. Englewood Cliffs, NJ: Prentice-Hall, 1972.

Newman, Charles M. "Memory Capacity in Neural Network Models: Rigorous Lower Bounds." Department of Mathematics, University of Arizona, 1987.

Newman, John Henry. *The Arians of the Fourth Century*. Miami, FL: Pickering, 1876.

Newman, Peter. *The Theory of Exchange*. Englewood Cliffs, NJ: Prentice-Hall, 1965.

Niebuhr, Reinhold. *The Structure of Nations and Empires*. New York, 1959.

Nissen, Hans J. *The Early History of the Ancient Near East: 9000–2000 B.C.* Translated by Elizabeth Lutzeier. Chicago: University of Chicago Press, 1988.

Nohria, Nitin. "A Quasi-Market in Technology Based Enterprises: The Case of the 128 Venture Group." Graduate School of Business Administration, Harvard University, February 1990.

Nolan, Patrick. "Status in World System." *American Journal of Sociology* 89(1983): 410–419.

North, Douglass C. *Structure and Change in Economic History*. New York: Norton, 1981.

North, J. A. "Democratic Politics in Republican Rome." *Past and Present* 126(1990): 3–22.

Oates, Wallace E., ed. *The Political Economy of Fiscal Federalism*. Lexington, MA: Lexington Books.

Oberman, Heiko. *Masters of the Reformation*. New York: Cambridge University Press, 1981.

Oberschall, A., and E. Leifer. "Efficiency and social institutions: uses and misuses of economic reasoning in sociology." *Annual Review of Sociology* 12(1986): 233–253.

Olafson, Frederick A. *The Dialectic of Action: A Philosophical Interpretation of History and the Humanities*. Chicago: University of Chicago Press, 1979.

Opie, Peter, and Iona Opie. *Children's Games in Street and Playground: Chasing, Catching, Seeking, Hunting, Racing, Duelling, Exerting, Daring, Guessing, Acting, Pretending*. Oxford: Clarendon Press, 1969.

Ore, Oystein. *Theory of Graphs*. Providence, RI: American Mathematical Association, 1965.

Ortega y Gasset, Jose. *The Revolt of the Masses*. Translated by A. Kerrigan. Notre Dame, IN: University of Notre Dame Press, 1985.

Ouchi, W. "Markets, bureaucracies and clans." *Administrative Science Quarterly* 25(1980): 129–141.

Padgett, John F. "Bounded Rationality in Budgetary Research." *American Political Science Review* 74(1980a): 354–372.

———. "Managing Garbage Can Hierarchies." *Administrative Science Quarterly* 14(1980b): 583–604.

———. "Hierarchy and Ecological Control in Federal Budgetary Decision-Making." *American Journal of Sociology* 87(1981): 75–129.

———. Lecture Notes #1–#6: Sociology 317/Political Science 373, University of Chicago, March 1982.

———. "Plea Bargaining and Prohibition in the Federal Courts: 1908–1934." *Law and Society Review*, 1989.

Padgett, John F., and Christopher K. Ansell. "From Faction to Party in Renaissance Florence." Department of Political Science, University of Chicago, September 1989.

Page, Benjamin I., and Robert Shapiro. *The Rational Public*. Chicago: University of Chicago Press, 1992.

Palmer, Donald. "Broken Ties: Interlocking Directorates and Intercorporate Coordination." *Administrative Science Quarterly* 28(1984): 40–55.

Panebianco, Angelo. *Political Parties: Organization and Power*. Translated by Marc Silver. New York: Cambridge University Press, 1988.

Panofsky, Erwin. *Renaissance and Renascences in Western Art*. Stockholm, 1960.

Panzar, J. C., and R. D. Willig. "Economics of Scope." *American Economic Review* 71(1981): 268–272.

Pappi, Franz Urban, ed. *Methoden der Netwerkanalyse*. Munich: Oldenbourg, 1987.

Parasuraman, Raja, and D. R. Davies. *Varieties of Attention*. New York: Academic Press, 1984.

Pareto, Vilfredo. *The Mind and Society*. Translated by A. Livingston and A. Bongiorno. New York: AMS, 1935.

———. *Sociological Writings*. Edited by S. E. Finer. New York: Praeger, 1966.

Parkes, James. *The Foundations of Judaism and Christianity*. Chicago: Quadrangle Press, 1960.

Parkin, Frank. *Class, Inequality and Political Order: Social Stratification in Capitalist and Communist Societies*. New York: Praeger, 1971.

Parry, J. P. *Caste and Kinship in Kangra*. London: Routledge and Kegan Paul, 1979.

Parsons, Talcott. *The Structure of Social Action*. New York: McGraw-Hill, 1937.

———. *The Social System*. New York: Free Press, 1964.

Parsons, Talcott, and Edward A. Shils, eds. *Toward a General Theory of Action*. New York: Harper and Row, 1951.

Parsons, Talcott, Robert F. Bales, and Edward A. Shils. *Working Papers in the Theory of Action*. Glencoe, IL: Free Press, 1953.

Pattee, H. H. "The Complementarity Principle and the Origin of Macromolecular Information." *Biosystems* 11(1979): 217–226.

Patterson, Nerys T. "Material and Symbolic Exchange in Early Irish Clientship." *Proceedings of the Harvard Celtic Colloquium*. Edited by James E. Doan and C. G. Buttimer. 4(1981): 53–61.

————. Ph.D. dissertation, Departments of Celtic Language and Literature and of Sociology, Harvard University, 1982.

Patterson, Orlando. *Slavery and Social Death: A Comparative Analysis*. Cambridge, MA: Harvard University Press, 1982.

Pattison, Philippa E. "The Analysis of Semigroups of Multirelational Systems." *Journal of Mathematical Psychology* 25(1982): 87–118.

————. "Network Models: Some Comments on Papers in this Special Issue." *Social Networks* 10(1988): 383–411.

————. *The Analysis of Semigroups of Multirelational Systems*. Melbourne, 1989.

Pattison, Philippa E., and W. K. Bartlett. "A Factorization Procedure for Finite Algebras." *Journal of Mathematical Psychology* 25(1982): 51–81.

Payne, P. L. *British Entrepreneurship in the 19th Century*. London: Macmillan, 1974.

Peleg, B. *Game Theoretic Analysis of Voting in Committees*. Cambridge: Cambridge University Press, 1987.

Perez-Diaz, Victor. "Economic Policies and Social Patterns in Spain during the Transition: The Two Faces of Neo-Corporatism." University of Madrid, 1984.

Perrow, Charles. *Complex Organizations*. Glenview, IL: Scott-Foresman, 1979.

————. *Normal Accidents: Living with High-Risk Technology*. New York: Basic Books, 1984.

Peterson, Richard A., ed. *The Production of Culture*. Beverly Hills, CA: Sage, 1976.

Petrey, Sandy. "The Reality of Representation: Between Marx and Balzac." Pp. 69–90 in Desan et al., 1989.

Pettigrew, Andrew. *The Awakening Giant: Continuity and Change in Imperial Chemical Industries*. Oxford: Blackwell, 1985.

Pettigrew, Joyce. *Robber Noblemen*. London: Routledge and Kegan Paul, 1975.

Pfeffer, Jeffrey, and Gerald Salancik. *The External Control of Organizations*. New York: Harper, 1978.

Pike, I., and T. Sritch, eds. *The New Corporatism*. London: University of Notre Dame Press, 1974.

Pirenne, Henri. *Early Democracies in the Low Countries: Urban Society and Political Conflict in the Middle Ages and the Renaissance*. 1915 (English trans: Norton, 1971).

Pitkin, Hannah. *The Concept of Representation*. Berkeley, CA: University of California, 1967.

Pizzorno, Alessandro, Notes for Seminar. "Identity and Social Structure." Sociology Department, Harvard University, 1984.

————. "On the Individualistic Theory of Social Order." Manuscript, Department of Political Science and Sociology, European University, Firenza, 1990.

Pletsch, Carl E. "The Three Worlds, or the Division of Social Scientific Labor, circa 1950–1975." *Comparative Studies in Society and History* 23(1981): 565–590.

Plumb, J. H. *The Growth of Political Stability in England, 1675–1725*. London: Penguin, 1967.

Pocock, J. A. *The Machiavellian Moment*. Princeton, NJ: Princeton University Press, 1975.

Poggi, Gianfranco. *The Development of the Modern State*. Stanford, CA: Stanford University Press, 1978.

———. "Clientelism." *Political Studies* 31(1983): 662–668.

Polanyi, Karl, Conrad M. Arensberg, and Harry W. Pearson. *Trade and Market in the Early Empires*. Glencoe, IL: Free Press, 1957.

Pooler, Victor H. *The Purchasing Man and his Job*. American Management Association, 1964.

Porter, Michael E. *Interbrand Choice, Strategy and Bilateral Market Power*. Cambridge, MA: Harvard University Press, 1976.

Posner, R. A., and K. E. Scott, eds. *Economics of Corporation Law and Securities Legislation*. Boston: Little, Brown, 1980.

Powell, Walter W. *Getting Into Print: The Decision-Making Process in Scholarly Publishing*. Chicago: University of Chicago Press, 1985.

———. "Hybrid organizational arrangements: new forms or transitional development?" *California Management Review* 30(1987): 67–87.

———. "Neither Market nor Hierarchy: Network Forms of Organization." *Research in Organizational Behavior* 12(1990): 295–336.

Powell, Walter, ed. *The Non-Profit Sector: A Research Handbook*. New Haven, CT: Yale University Press, 1987.

Powers, William J. "Control-System Theory and Performance Objectives." *Journal of Psycholinguistic Research* 5(1976): 285.

Pratt, John, and Richard Zeckhauser, eds. *Principals and Agents: The Structure of Business*. Boston: Harvard Graduate School of Business Administration Press, 1985.

Preston, Samuel H., ed. *Biological and Social Aspects of Mortality and the Length of Life*. Liege, Belgium: Ordina Editions, 1982.

Previts, Gary J., ed. *The Development of SEC Accounting*. Boston: Addison-Wesley, 1981.

Prince, Harold. *Contradictions*. New York: Dodd Mead, 1974.

Prins, A.H.J. *East African Age-Class Systems*. Groningen, NE: Wolters, 1953.

Project Solarium. "The Challenge of Leadership in Foreign Affairs." School of International Affairs, Columbia University, February 1988.

Putnam, Robert B. "Diplomacy and Domestic Politics." *International Organization* 42(1988): 427–460.

Putnam, Robert B., and N. Bayne. *Hanging Together*. Cambridge, MA: Harvard University Press, 1987.

Pzreworski, Adam. "Material Bases of Consent: Economics and Politics in a Hegemonic Regime." *Political Power and Social Theory* 1(1980): 21–66.

Radner, Roy. "A Behavioral Model of Cost Reduction." *Bell Journal of Economics* 6(1975a): 196–215.

———. "Satisficing." *Journal of Mathematical Economics* 2(1975b): 254–262.

Ragin, Charles C. *The Comparative Method: Moving Beyond Qualitative and Quantitative Strategies*. Berkeley, CA: University of California Press, 1987.

Rapoport, Anatol. *Mathematical Models in the Social and Behavioral Sciences.* New York: Wiley, 1983.

Rapoport, Anatol, and W. J. Horvath. "A Study of a Large Sociogram." *Behavioral Science* 6(1961): 279–291.

Ratcliff, R. E. "Capitalist Class Impact on Lending in Banks." *American Sociological Review* 45(1980): 553–571.

Rawls, Anne W. "The Interaction Order *Sui Generis*: Goffman's Contribution to Social Theory." *Sociological Theory* 5(1987): 136–150.

———. "Language, self and social order: A reformulation of Goffman and Sachs." *Human Studies* 12(1989): 147–172.

Reader, W. J. *Imperial Chemical Industries: A History, Vol. II.* Oxford: Oxford University Press, 1975.

Reid, James S. *The Municipalities of the Roman Empire.* Cambridge: Cambridge University Press, 1913.

Reiss, Albert J. *Occupations and Social Status.* Glencoe, IL: Free Press, 1961.

Reitlinger, Gerald. *The Economics of Taste: The Rise and Fall of Picture Prices, 1760–1960.* London: Barrie and Rockliff, 1961.

Reitz, Karl P. "Using Loglinear Analysis with Network Data: Another Look at Sampson's Monastery." *Social Networks* 4(1982): 243–256.

Reitz, Karl P., and Douglas R. White. "Rethinking the Role Concept: Homomorphisms on Social Networks." Chap. 13 in Linton et al., 1989.

Remmling, Gunter W., ed. *Toward the Sociology of Knowledge.* New York: Humanities Press, 1973.

Restle, Frank. "The Seer of Ithaca" (review of Gibson 1979). *Contemporary Psychology* 25(1980): 291–293.

Richards, I. A. *The Philosophy of Rhetoric.* London: Oxford University Press, 1936.

Richards, S. M. "The concept of dominance and methods of assessment." *Animal Behavior* 22(1974): 914–930.

Ricoeur Paul. *The Rule of Metaphor: Multidisciplinary Studies of the Creation of Meaning.* Translated by R. Czerny. Toronto: University of Toronto Press, 1977.

———. *Time and Narrative: Vol 3.* Translated by K. Blamey and D. Pellauer. Chicago: University of Chicago Press, 1988.

Rieder, Jonathan. "Rhetoric of Reason, Rhetoric of Passion." *Rationality and Society* 2(1990): 190–213.

Riggs, Fred. *Administration in Developing Countries: The Theory of Prismatic Society.* New York: Houghton Mifflin, 1964.

———. *Thailand.* Honolulu: East-West Center, 1966.

Riker, William H. "Implications from the Disequilibrium of Majority Rule for the Study of Institutions." Chap. 1 in *Political Equilibrium*, edited by Peter Ordeshook and Kenneth Shepsle. 1982.

———. *The Art of Political Manipulation.* New Haven, CT: Yale University Press, 1986.

Riker, William H., and Peter C. Ordeshook. *An Introduction to Positive Political Theory.* Englewood Cliffs, NJ: Prentice-Hall, 1973.

Riordan, J. *Introduction to Combinatorial Analysis.* New York: Wiley, 1958.

———. *Stochastic Service Systems.* New York: Wiley, 1962.

Roberts, David. *Executive Compensation*. Glencoe, IL: Free Press, 1959.

Robinson, Charles. "Reviewer Response to Novels about Race Relations Published in the 1950s." Honors thesis, Department of Sociology, Harvard University, May 1980.

Robinson, Joan. *The Economics of Imperfect Competition*. London: Macmillan, 1933.

Robinson, Thomas A. *The Bauer Thesis Examined: The Geography of Heresy in the Early Christian Church*. Edwin Mellen Press, 1988.

Roethlisberger, Fritz J. *The Elusive Phenomena*. Boston, MA: Harvard Graduate School of Business Administration Press, 1977.

Rogowski, Ronald. "Structure, Growth and Power: Three Rationalist Accounts." Chap. 9 in *International Organization*, vol. 37, 1983.

Romo, Frank. "The Omega Phenomenon: A Study of Social Choice." Institute for Social Analysis, State University of New York at Stony Brook, June 1991.

———. *Moral Dynamics*. New York: Cambridge University Press, 1992.

Rose, F.G.G. *Classification of Kin, Age Structure, and Marriage amongst the Groote Eylandt Aborigines*. Berlin: Akademie-Verlag, 1960.

Rosen, Sherwin. "The Economics of Superstars." *American Economic Review* 71(1981): 845–858.

———. "The Distribution of Prizes in a Match-Play Tournament with Single Eliminations." #84–89, Discussion Paper Series, Economics Research Center, Chicago: National Opinion Research Center, November 1984.

Rosenbaum, James E. *Career Mobility in a Corporate Hierarchy*. New York: Academic Press, 1984.

Rosenberg, Hans. *Bureaucracy, Aristocracy and Autocracy: The Prussian Experience, 1660–1815*. Cambridge, MA: Harvard University Press, 1958.

Rosenberg, Harold. *The Anxious Object*. New York: Collier Books, 1970.

Rosengren, Karl E. *Sociological Aspects of the Literary System*. Stockholm: Natur och Kultur, 1968.

Rosenthal, R. R., and Lenore Jacobson. *Pygmalion in the Classroom*. New York: Irvington Press, 1989.

Roseveare, Henry. *The Treasury: 1660–1870*. New York: Barnes and Noble, 1973.

Rossem, Ronan Van. "Trade Dependence in the World System." Department of Sociology, Columbia University, January 1989.

Rossi, Peter H. "Power and Community Structure." *Midwest Journal of Political Science* 4(1960): 390–410.

Rowen, Herbert H. *John de Witt, Grand Pensionary of Holland, 1625–1672*. Princeton, NJ: Princeton University Press, 1978.

———. *The Princes of Orange: The Stadtholders in the Dutch Republic*. New York: Cambridge University Press, 1988.

Roy, William G., and Phillip Bonacich. "Interlocking Directorates and Communities of Interest among American Railroad Companies, 1905." *American Sociological Review* 53(1988): 368–379.

Rueschemeyer, D. *Power and the Division of Labor*. Stanford, CA: Stanford University Press, 1986.

Rule, James B. *Theories of Civil Violence*. Berkeley, CA: University of California Press, 1988.

Runciman, Steven. *Byzantine Civilization*. London: Edward Arnold, 1933.

Runciman, W. G. *A Treatise on Social Theory*. New York: Cambridge University Press, 1989.

Ryder, Norman B. "The Cohort as a Concept in the Study of Social Change." *American Sociological Review* 30(1965): 843–861.

———. *Reproduction in the United States*. Princeton, NJ: Princeton University Press, 1971.

Ryser, J. *Combinatorial Mathematics*. Carus Monograph #14, Mathematical Association of America, 1963.

Saari, Donald, and S. R. Williams. "On the Local Convergence of Economic Mechanisms." *Journal of Economic Theory* 40(1986): 152–167.

Sachs, Sheldon, ed. *On Metaphor*. Chicago: University of Chicago Press, 1979.

Sailer, Lee D. "Structural Equivalence: Meaning and Definition, Computation and Application." *Social Networks* 1(1978): 73–90.

Saller, R. P. *Personal Patronage under the Early Empire*. New York: Cambridge University Press, 1982.

Salmon, E. T. *Roman Colonization Under the Republic*. Ithaca, NY: Cornell University Press, 1970.

Salter, Malcolm S., and W. A. Weinhold. *Diversification Through Acquisition*. New York: Macmillan, 1979.

Salzinger, Leslie. "The Ties that Bind: The Effect of Clustering on Dyadic Relationships." *Social Networks* 4(1982): 117–145.

Sampson, Frank. "Crisis in a Cloister." Ph.D. dissertation, Department of Sociology, Cornell University: #69-5775, Ann Arbor, MI: University Microfilms, 1969.

Samuelson, Paul. *Foundations of Economic Analysis*. Cambridge, MA: Harvard University Press, 1947.

Sarfatti-Larson, Magali. *The Rise of Professionalism*. Berkeley, CA: University of California Press, 1977.

Sattinger, Michael. *Capital and the Distribution of Labor Earnings*. New York: North-Holland, 1980.

Saussure, Ferdinand de. *Course in General Linguistics*. Translated by Wade Baskin. New York: McGraw-Hill, 1966.

Sayles, Leonard. *Leadership: What Effective Managers Really Do . . . and How They Do It*. New York: McGraw-Hill, 1979.

Sayles, Leonard, and George Strauss. *The Local Union*, rev. ed., New York: Harcourt, Brace, World, 1967.

Scarf, H. "On the approximation of fixed points of a continuous mapping." *SIAM Journal on Applied Mathematics* 15(1967): 1328–1343.

———. *The Computation of Economic Equilibria*. New Haven, CT: Yale University Press, 1973.

Scarrow, Howard A. "The Function of Political Parties." *Journal of Politics* 29(1967): 770–790.

Schachter, Stanley. "The interaction of cognition and physiological determinants of emotional state." *Advances in Experimental Social Psychology* 1(1984): 49–80.

Schachter, Stanley, Donald C. Hood, Paul B. Andreassen, and William Gerin. "Aggregate Variables in Psychology and Economics: Dependence and the Stock Market." In *Handbook of Behavioral Economics, Vol. B*, edited by S. Kaish and B. Gilad. Greenwich, CT: JAI Press, 1987.

Schama, Simon. *The Embarrassment of Riches: An Interpretation of Dutch Culture in the Golden Age*. New York: Knopf, 1987.

Schank, R. C., and Robert P. Abelson. *Scripts, Plans, Goals, and Understanding*. Hillsdale, NJ: Erlbaum, 1977.

Schauer, Frederick. "Authority and Indeterminacy." *Nomos* 29(1987): 28–38.

Schelling, Thomas C. *The Strategy of Conflict*. Cambridge, MA: Harvard University Press, 1960.

———. *Micromotives and Macrobehavior*. New York: Norton, 1978.

Scheppele, Kim L. *Legal Secrets: Equality and Efficiency in the Common Law*. Chicago: University of Chicago Press, 1988.

Scherer, F. M. *Industrial Market Structure and Economic Performance*. New York: Rand McNally, 1970. ·

Schieve, W. C., and P. M. Allen. *Self Organization and Dissipative Structures*. Austin: University of Texas Press, 1982.

Schmalensee, R., and R. Willig, eds. *Handbook of Industrial Organization I*. New York: North-Holland, 1989.

Schmitter, Phillippe C. "Still a Century of Corporatism?" in Pike and Sritch, eds., 1974.

Schmitter, Phillippe C., and G. Lehmbruch, eds. *Trends Toward Corporatist Intermediation*. Beverly Hills, CA: Sage, 1979.

Schoeps, Hans-Joachim. *Jewish Christianity: Factional Disputes in the Early Church*. Translated by D.R.A. Hare. Philadelphia, PA: Fortress Press, 1969.

Scholes, Robert, and Robert Kellogg. *The Nature of Narrative*. New York: Oxford University Press, 1966.

Schudson, Michael. "How Culture Works: Perspectives from media studies on the Efficacy of Symbols." *Theory and Society* 18(1989): 153–180.

Schurmann, F. *Ideology and Organization in Communist China*, 2d ed. Berkeley, CA: University of California Press, 1968.

Schusky, E. L. *Manual for Kinship Analysis*. New York: Holt, Rinehart, 1965.

Schwartz, Barry. *Vertical Classification: A Study in Structuralism and the Sociology of Knowledge*. Chicago: University of Chicago Press, 1981.

Schwartz, Joseph E. "An Examination of CONCOR and Related Methods for Blocking Sociometric Data." In *Sociological Methodology 1977*, edited by D. Heise, 255–282. San Francisco: Jossey-Bass.

———. "Penetrating Differentiation: Linking Macro and Micro Phenomena." Chap. 11 in *Structures of Power and Constraint: Papers in honor of Peter M. Blau*, edited by Craig Calhoun, Marshall W. Meyer, and W. Richard Scott. New York: Cambridge University Press, 1990.

Schwartz, Michael. "Introduction to Social Relations: Notes on Social Organization." Mimeo manuscript, Department of Social Relations, Harvard University, 1966, 1967.

———. *Radical Protest and Social Structure.* New York: Academic Press, 1976.

Schwartzman, Kathleen C. *The Social Origins of Democratic Collapse: The First Portugese Republic in the World Economy.* Lawrence, KS: University Press of Kansas, 1989.

Schweiker, Richard. *Environment by Design.* Cambridge, MA: Oelschager, 1986.

Schweizer, Eduard. *Church Order in the New Testament.* Translated by Frank Clarke. 1961.

Scott, John, and Michael Hughes. *The Anatomy of Scottish Capital.* London: Croom-Helm, 1980.

Searle, Eleanor. *Predatory Kinship and the Creation of Norman Power.* Berkeley, CA: University of California Press, 1988.

Searle, John R. *Speech Acts: An Essay in the Philosophy of Language.* New York: Cambridge University Press, 1969.

Segal, Alan F. *Rebecca's Children: Judaism and Christianity in the Roman World.* Cambridge, MA: Harvard University Press, 1986.

Seitz, Frederick. *Modern Theory of Solids.* New York: McGraw-Hill, 1940.

Sekulich, Dusan. "Socio-Economic Relations and Development in the Self-Management System." University of Zagreb, Paper at Karl Brunner Symposium, Interlaken, Switzerland, June 1990.

Seligman, Martin E. P., and J. Garber, eds. *Human Helplessness: Theory and Application.* New York: Academic Press, 1980.

Selznick, Philip. *The Organizational Weapon.* Berkeley, CA: University of California Press, 1952.

———. *The TVA and the Grass Roots.* Berkeley, CA: University of California Press, 1955.

Sengers, Jan V., and Anneke L. Sengers. "The Critical Region." *Chemical and Engineering News.* 104–118, 1968.

Sennett, Richard. *The Fall of Public Man: On the Social Psychology of Capitalism.* New York: Vintage, 1978.

Sewell, William H., Jr. Review (of Joan W. Scott. *Gender and the Politics of History.* New York: Columbia University Press, 1988) in *History and Theory* 29, 1990.

Shafer, Ingrid H., ed. *The Incarnate Imagination: Essays in Honor of Andrew Greeley.* Bowling Green, OH: Bowling Green University Popular Press, 1988.

Shapiro, Bennett, private communication.

Shapiro, Martin. "Appeal." *Law and Society Review* 14(1980): 629.

Shapiro, Robert Y., and L. R. Jacobs. "The relationship between public opinion and public policy: A review." In *Political Behavior Annual,* edited by Samuel Long. Boulder, CO: Westview Press, 1988.

Shapley, Lloyd, and Bernard Grofman. "Organizing group judgmental accuracy in the presence of interdependencies." *Public Choice* 43(1984): 329–343.

Sharpe, L. J., ed. *Decentralization Trends in Western Democracies.* Beverly Hills, CA: Sage, 1979.

Shepard, R. W. *Cost and Production Functions*. Princeton, NJ: Princeton University Press, Princeton, 1953.

Shepard, Roger N. "The Analysis of Proximities. Multidimensional Scaling with an unknown Distance Function. I and II." *Psychometrika* 27(1962): 125–140, 219–246.

———. "Ecological Constraints on Internal Representation: Resonant Kinematics of Perceiving, Imagining, Thinking, and Dreaming." *Psychological Review* 91(1984): 417–447.

———. "Evolution of a mesh between Principles of the Mind and Regularities of the World." In *The Latest and the Best: Essays on Evolution and Optimality*, edited by J. Dupre. Cambridge, MA: MIT Press, 1987.

———. "Internal Representation of Universal Regularities: A Challenge for Connectionism." Chap. 4 in Nadel, Cooper, Culicover, and Harnish, eds., 1989.

———. *Mind Sights*. New York: Freeman, 1990.

Shepard, Roger N., and Lynn A. Cooper. *Mental Images and their Transformations*. Cambridge, MA: MIT Press, 1982.

Shoda, Yuichi, Walter Mischel, and Jack C. Wright. "Intuitive Interactionism in Person Perception: Effects of Situation-Behavior Relations on Dispositional Judgments." *Journal of Personality and Social Psychology* 56(1989): 41–53.

Shorter, Edward, and Charles Tilly. *Strikes in France, 1830–1968*. New York: Cambridge University Press, 1974.

Shotland, K. Lance. *University Communication Networks: The Small World Method*. New York: Wiley, 1976.

Shubik, Martin. *Game Theory in the Social Sciences: Concepts and Solutions*. Cambridge, MA: MIT Press, 1984a.

———. *A Game Theoretical Approach to Political Economy*. Cambridge, MA: MIT Press, 1984b.

Shugart, W. F., and Robert D. Tollison. "Corporate Chartering: An Exploration in the Economics of Legal Change." *Economic Inquiry* 23(1983): 585–601.

Silver, Allan. "Friendship and trust as moral ideals: an historical approach." *European Journal of Sociology* 30(1989): 274–297.

———. "Friendship in Commercial Society: Eighteenth-Century Social Theory and Modern Society." *American Journal of Sociology* 91(1990): 1474–1504.

Simirenko, Alex. *Professionalization of Soviet Society*. New Brunswick, NJ: Transaction Books, 1982.

Simmel, Georg. *Conflict and the Web of Group-Affiliations*. Translated by K. Wolff and R. Bendix. Glencoe, IL: Free Press, 1955.

Simon, Herbert A. *Administrative Behavior*. New York: Macmillan, 1945.

———. *Models of Man*. New York: Wiley, 1957

Simon, Herbert A., D. Smithburg, and V. Thompson. *Public Administration*. New York: Knopf, 1950.

Simpson, George G. *The Major Features of Evolution*. New York: Columbia University Press, 1952.

Simpson, Richard L. "Social Control of Occupation and Work." In Ralph W. Turner, ed. *Annual Review of Sociology* 11(1985): 415–436.

Skinner, B. F. *Science and Human Behavior*. New York: Macmillan, 1953.

Skinner, G. William. *Chinese Society in Thailand*. Ithaca, NY: Cornell University Press, 1957.

———. "Marketing and Social Structure in Rural China." *Journal of Asian Studies* 24(1964–65): 3–43, 195–228, 363–399.

Skocpol, Theda. *States and Social Revolutions*. New York: Cambridge University Press, 1979.

———. "Cultural Idioms and political ideologies in the revolutionary reconstruction of state power: A rejoinder to Sewell." *Journal of Modern History* 57(1985): 86–96.

Skrynnikov, Roslan G. *Ivan the Terrible*. Translated by H. Graham. Academic International, 1981.

Skvoretz, John V., and R. H. Conviser. "Interests and Alliances." *Man* 9(1971): 53–67.

Skvoretz, John, and Thomas J. Fararo. "Languages and Grammars of Action and Interaction: A Contribution to the Formal Theory of Action." *Behavioral Science* 25(1980): 9–22.

Skvoretz, John, Thomas J. Fararo, and Nick Axten. "Role-Programme Models and the Analysis of Institutional Structure." *Sociology* 49–67, 1980.

Slater, J. C. *Quantum Theory of Matter*. New York: McGraw-Hill, 1960.

Sloan, Alfred P., ed., John McDonald. *My Years with General Motors*. New York: Doubleday, 1963.

Smith, Barbara Herrnstein. *Contingencies of Value: Alternative Perspectives for Critical Theory*. Cambridge, MA: Harvard University Press, 1988.

Smith, Charles W. *Auctions: The Social Construction of Value*. New York: Free Press-Macmillan, 1989.

Smith, David A., and Douglas R. White. "Structure and Dynamics of the Global Economy: Network Analysis of International Trade, 1965–1980." *Social Forces* 71: forthcoming.

Smith, Edward E., and Douglas Medin. *Categories and Concepts*. Cambridge, MA: Harvard University Press, 1981.

Smith, J. Maynard. *Evolution and the Theory of Games*. New York: Cambridge University Press, 1985.

Smith, Michael G. *Corporations and Society*. Chicago: Aldine, 1975.

Smith, Richard A. "Community Power and Decision Making." *American Sociological Review* 41(1976): 691–705.

Snyder, David, and Edward Kick. "Structural Position in a World System and Economic Growth, 1955–1970: A Multiple-Network Analysis of Transnational Interactions." *American Journal of Sociology* 85(1979): 1376–1395.

Socolefsky, H. E., and A. B. Spetter. *The Presidency of Benjamin Harrison*. Lawrence, KS: University Press of Kansas, 1987.

Sorenson, Aage. "The Structure of Inequality and the Process of Attainment." *American Sociological Review* 42(1977): 965–978.

Sorokin, Pitirim A. *Social and Cultural Mobility*. New York: Harper Bros., 1927.

———. *Social and Cultural Dynamics*. New York: American Books, 1937–41.

Spence, A. Michael. *Market Signalling*. Cambridge, MA: Harvard University Press, 1974.

Spence, A. Michael, and R. Zeckhauser. "Insurance, Information and Individual Action." *American Economic Review* 61(1971): 380–387.

Spencer and Gillen. *The Arunta*, 1903. Revised by Spencer for 1927 edition.

Sperling, L. H. *Introduction to Physical Polymer Science*. New York: Wiley, 1986.

Spilerman, Seymour. "Careers, Labor Market Structure and Socioeconomic Achievement." *American Journal of Sociology* 83(1977): 551–593.

Spilerman, S., and B. Singer. "The Representation of Social Processes by Markov Models." *American Journal of Sociology* 82(1976): 1–54.

Stark, Rodney, and W. S. Bainbridge. "Networks of Faith." *American Journal of Sociology* 85(1979): 1376–1395.

Stedry, A. C. *Budget Control and Cost Behavior*. New York: Prentice-Hall, 1960.

Steenstrup, Carl. "The Legal System of Japan." In *Law and the State in Traditional East Asia*, edited by Brian McKnight. 1987.

Steiber, Steven R. "The World System and World Trade: An Empirical Exploration of Conceptual Conflicts." *Sociological Quarterly* 20(1979): 23–36.

Steiner, Kurt. *Political Organization and Local Politics*. Princeton, NJ: Princeton University Press, 1981.

Stenton, Frank. *The First Century of English Feudalism*. Oxford: Oxford University Press, 1965.

Stevens, S. S. "On the Theory of Scales of Measurement." *Science* 103(1946): 677–689.

Stevenson, G. H. *Roman Provincial Administration*. Oxford: Blackwell, 1939.

Stevenson, Howard H., and Thomas V. Bonoma. "Goals, Measures and Judgement." Manuscript, Harvard Graduate School of Business Administration, Sept. 6, 1989.

Stewman, Shelby. "Markov Models of Occupational Mobility: Theoretical Development and Empirical Support; Part I, Careers." *Journal of Mathematical Sociology* 4(1976): 201–245.

———. "Organizational Demography." *Annual Review of Sociology* 14(1988): 173–202.

Stewman, Shelby, and S. L. Konda. "Careers and Organizational Labor Markets: Demographic Models of Organizational Behavior." *American Journal of Sociology* 88(1983): 637–685.

Stich, Stephen. *The Fragmentation of Reason: Preface to a Pragmatic Theory of Cognitive Evaluation*. Cambridge, MA: MIT Press, 1990.

Stinchcombe, Arthur L. "Social Structure and Organization." Pp. 142–193 in James G. March. *Handbook of Organizations*. Chicago: Rand McNally, 1965.

———. *Theoretical Methods in Social History*. New York: Academic Press, 1978.

———. "Contracts as hierarchical documents." In *Organization Theory and*

Project Management, edited by A. Stinchombe and C. Heimer. Bergen, Norway: Norwegian University Press, 1985.

———. "Comment" on Paul M. Hirsch, ed. "Rational Choice Models for Sociology: Pro and Con." Special issue of *Rationality and Society* 2(1990): 135–224.

Stokman, F. N., Rolf Ziegler, and J. Scott. *Networks of Corporate Power*. Oxford: Blackwell, 1985.

Stone, Lawrence. *The Crisis of the Aristocracy: 1558–1641*. Oxford: Oxford University Press, 1965.

Stouffer, Samuel A., et al. *The American Soldier*. Princeton, NJ: Princeton University Press, 1948

Straffin, P. D., and B. Grofman. "Parliamentary Coalitions: A Tour of Models." *Mathematics Magazine* 57(1984): 259–274.

Strathern, Andrew. *The Rope of Moka*. New York: Cambridge University Press, 1971.

Street, David, R. Vinter, and Charles Perrow. *Organizations for Treatment*. Glencoe, IL: Free Press, 1966.

Suleiman, Ezra N. *The Notaries and the State*. Princeton, NJ: Princeton University Press, 1987.

Suolahti, Jaakko. *The Junior Officers of the Roman Army*. Finnish Academy of Sciences, Monograph #97, 1955.

Svalastoga, Kaare. *Prestige, Class, and Mobility*. Copenhagen, Denmark: 1959.

Swanson, Guy E. *The Birth of the Gods*. Ann Arbor, MI: University of Michigan Press, 1960.

———. *Ego Defenses and the Legitimation of Behavior*. New York: Cambridge University Press, 1988.

Swart, Koenraad W. *Sale of Offices in the 17th Century*. The Hague: Nijhoff, 1949.

Swedberg, Richard. "Introduction" to translation of Myrdal 1930, University of Stockholm, Department of Sociology, July 21, 1989.

———. *Schumpeter—A Biography*. Princeton, NJ: Princeton University Press, 1991.

———, ed. *Economics and Sociology*. Princeton, NJ: Princeton University Press, 1990.

———, ed. *Explorations in Economic Sociology*. New York: Sage, 1992.

Swete, H. B., ed. *Essays of the Early History of the Church and the Ministry*. London: Macmillan, 1918.

Swidler, Ann. *Organization Without Authority: Dilemmas of Social Control in Free Schools*. Cambridge, MA: Harvard University Press, 1979.

———. "Culture in Action: Symbols and Strategies." *American Sociological Review* 51(1986): 273–286.

———. Unpublished paper, 1989.

Syme, Ronald. *The Roman Revolution*. Oxford: Oxford University Press, 1968 (pbk. ed.).

Tainter, Joseph A. *The Collapse of Complex Societies*. New York: Cambridge University Press, 1988.

Tarrow, Sidney. *Between Center and Periphery: Grassroots Politicians in Italy and France*. New Haven, CT: Yale University Press, 1977.

Taylor, Lily Ross. *Party Politics in the Age of Caesar*. Berkeley, CA: University of California Press, 1948.

Tellenbach, G. *Church, State and Civil Society*. Translated by R. F. Bennett. Toronto, Canada: University of Toronto Press, 1991.

Tex, Jan den. *Oldenbarnevelt*, 5 vols., abridgement in English, 1975.

Theil, H. *Statistical Decomposition Analysis*. Amsterdam: North-Holland, 1972.

Theissen, Gerd. *The Social Setting of Pauline Christianity*. Translated by John Schutz. Philadelphia, PA: Fortress Press, 1982.

Thomas, W. A. *The Finance of British Industry*. London: Methuen, 1978.

Thompson, Bard, ed. *Liturgies of the Western Church*. Cleveland, OH: World, 1961.

Thompson, E. P. *The Making of the English Working Class*. New York: Vintage Books, 1963.

Thompson, James D. *Organizations in Action: Social Science Bases of Administration*. New York: McGraw-Hill, 1963.

Thompson, V. A. *The Regulatory Process in OPA Rationing*. New York: King's Crown Press, 1950.

Thomson, Virgil. *The State of Music*. New York: Random House, 2d ed., 1962.

Thrupp, Sylvia L. *The Merchant Class of Medieval London*. Ann Arbor, MI: University of Michigan Press, 1948.

———. "The Gilds." Chap. 5 in *Cambridge Economic History*. vol. 3.

Tierney, Brian. *Foundations of the Conciliar Theory*. New York: Cambridge University Press, 1954.

Tillich, Paul. *Systematic Theology: Vol III*. Chicago: University of Chicago Press, 1963.

Tilly, Charles. *The Vendee*. New York: Wiley, 1964.

———. "Reflections on the History of European State-Making." In *The Formation of National States in Western Europe*, edited by Charles Tilly, 3–83. Princeton, NJ: Princeton University Press, 1975.

———. *From Mobilization to Revolution*. Reading, MA: Addison-Wesley, 1978.

———. "Flows of Capital and Forms of Industry in Europe: 1500–1900." *Theoretical Sociology* 13(1985): 123–142.

———. *Coercion, Capital and European States A.D. 990–1990*. Cambridge, MA: Blackwell, 1990.

Tilly, Richard. "Mergers, External Growth, and Finance in the Development of Large Scale Enterprise in Germany, 1880–1913." *Journal of Economic History*. 62(1982): 629–658.

Tooley, M. J., ed. *Six Books of the Commonwealth*, by Jean Bodin. Oxford: Oxford University Press, 1967.

Traugott, Mark. "Class and Organization in the Parisian Insurrection of June, 1849." *American Journal of Sociology* 86(1980): 32–48.

Trautmann, Thomas R. *Lewis Henry Morgan and the Invention of Kinship*. Berkeley, CA: University of California Press, 1987.

Travers, Jeffrey, and Stanley Milgram. "An Experimental Study of the Small World Problem." *Sociometry* 32(1969): 425–443.

Tuck, R. H. *An Essay on the Economic Theory of Rank.* Oxford: Blackwell, 1965.

Tufte, O. *The Visual Display of Quantitative Information.* Cheshire, CT: Graphics Press, 1983.

Tukey, John. *Exploratory Data Analysis.* Reading, MA: Addison-Wesley, 1977.

Tuma, Nancy. "Rewards, Resources and the Rate of Mobility: A Non-Stationary Multivariate Stochastic Model." *American Sociological Review* 41(1976): 338–360.

Tuma, Nancy, and Michael T. Hannan. *Social Dynamics: Methods and Models.* New York: Academic Press, 1984.

Turner, Victor. *The Ritual Process.* Chicago: Aldine, 1969.

———. *Dramas, Fields and Metaphors.* Ithaca, NY: Cornell University Press, 1974.

Udy, Stanley. *Organization of Work.* New Haven, CT: Human Relations Area Files, 1959.

———. *Work in Traditional and Modern Society.* Englewood Cliffs, NJ: Prentice-Hall, 1970.

———. "Structural Inconsistency and Management Strategy in Organizations." In Calhoun, Meyer, and Scott, 1990.

Uhlenbeck, G. E., and G. W. Ford. ""The Theory of Linear Graphs with Application to the Theory of the Virial Development of the Properties of Gases." Part B in deBoer and Uhlenbeck, eds., 1962.

Urban, Michael E. "Centralization and Elite Circulation in a Soviet Republic." *British Journal of Political Science* 19(1987): 1–23.

Useem, Michael. "Classwide Rationality in the Politics of Managers and Directors of Large Corporations in the United States and Great Britain." *Administrative Science Quarterly* 27(1982): 553–572.

Vancil, Richard F. *Decentralization: Managerial Ambiguity by Design.* Homewood, IL: Dow Jones-Irwin, 1979.

Vancil, Richard F., and Charles H. Green. "Top Management Committees." *Harvard Business Review.* 1984.

VanDeventer, George. Collected poems, Washington ME, 1988.

Van Schendelen, M.P.C.M., and R. J. Jackson, eds. *The Politicisation of Business in Western Europe.* London: Croom-Helm, 1987.

Van Vleck, J. H. *The Theory of Electric and Magnetic Susceptibilities.* New York: Oxford University Press, 1932.

Veblen, Thorstein. *The Engineer and the Price System.* New York: B. W. Huebsch, 1921.

Velez-Ibanez, Carlos G. *Bonds of Mutual Trust: The Cultural Systems of Rotating Credit Associations among Urban Mexicans and Chicanos.* New Brunswick, NJ: Rutgers University Press, 1983.

Viala, Alain. "Prismatic Effects." Translated by Paula Wissing. In Desan, Ferguson, and Griswold, 1989.

Vichniac, Judith E. "Union Organization in the French and British Iron and Steel Industries in the Late Nineteenth Century." In *Political Power and Social Theory* 6, edited by Maurice Zeitlin. 1985.

Vlachoutsicos, C., and Paul Lawrence. "What we don't know about Soviet Management." *Harvard Business Review*, 50–66, November–December 1990.

von Neumann, John, and O. Morgenstern. *The Theory of Games and Economic Behavior*. Princeton, NJ: Princeton University Press, 1944.

Wachter, K. W., et al., eds. *Statistical Studies of Historical Social Structure*. New York: Academic Press, 1978.

Waddington, C. H. *Behind Appearance*. Cambridge, MA: MIT Press, 1970.

Waldman, Don E. *Antitrust Action and Market Structure*. Lexington, MA: Lexington Books, 1978.

Waley, Daniel. *Medieval Orvieto*. Cambridge: Cambridge University Press, 1952.

———. *The Papal State in the 13th Century*. London: Macmillan, 1961.

———. *The Italian City Republics*. New York: McGraw-Hill, 1969.

Walker, Gordon. "Network Position and Cognition in a Computer Software Firm." *Administrative Science Quarterly* 30(1985): 103–130.

Walker, Gordon, and Laura Poppo. "Profit Centers, Single Source Suppliers and Transaction Costs." Wharton School, University of Pennsylvania, September 1989.

Waller, Willard. *The Sociology of Teaching*. New York: Wiley, 1932.

Wallerstein, I. *The Modern World-System*, vols. I and II. New York: Academic Press, 1974, 1980.

Walsh, E. *Democracy in the Shadows*. Westport, CT: Greenwood Press, 1988.

Wanderer, J. J. "In Defense of Popular taste: Film Rating among Professional and Lay Audiences." *American Journal of Sociology* 78(1970): 262–273.

Wang, Yuchung J., and George Y. Wong. "Stochastic Blockmodels for Directed Graphs." *Journal of the American Statistical Association* 82(1987): 8–19.

Warner, W. Lloyd. *A Black Civilization*. New York: Harper and Row, 1937.

Warriner, Charles K. "Levels in the Study of Social Structure." Chap. 6 in Blau and Merton, eds., 1981.

Washburn, Dorothy K., and Donald W. Crowe. *Symmetries of Culture: Theory and Practice of Plane Pattern Analysis*. Seattle, WA: University of Washington Press, 1988.

Wasserman, Stanley, and Carolyn Anderson. "Stochastic A Posteriori Blockmodels: Construction and Assessment." *Social Networks* 9(1987): 1–36.

Wasserman, Stanley, and K. Faust. *Social Network Analysis: Methods and Applications*. New York: Cambridge University Press, 1991.

Watkins, Susan C. "From Local to National Community: The Transformation of Demographic Regimes in Western Europe, 1870–1960." *Population and Development Review* 16(1990): 241–272.

Watson, James D. *Double Helix*. New York: New American Library, 1969.

Watson, William. *Tribal Cohesion in a Money Economy*. Manchester: Manchester University Press, 1958.

Watt, Ian. *The Rise of the Novel*. Berkeley, CA: University of California Press, 1957.

Weakliem, David L. "Relative Wages and the Radical Theory of Segmentation." *American Sociological Review* 55(1990): 573–590.

Webb, Diana. "Penitence and Peace Making in City and Contado: the Bianchi of 1399." *Studies in Church History* 16(1979): 243–256.

Weber, Max. *General Economic History*. Translated by Frank Knight. 1923.

———. *Economy and Society*. Edited by G. Roth and C. W. Mills. Berkeley, CA: University of California Press, 1978.

Weesie, Jeroen, and Henk Flap, eds. *Social Networks through Time*. Utrecht, NE: ISOR, 1990.

Weick, Karl E. "The Panglossian World of Self-Justification." Chap. 70 in Abelson et al., eds., 1968.

———. "Educational Organizations as Loosely Coupled Systems." *Administrative Science Quarterly* 21(1976): 1–19.

Weimann, Gabriel. "On the Importance of Marginality: One More Step in the Two-Step Flow of Communication." *American Sociological Review* 47(1983): 764–773.

Weissman, Ronald F. E. *Ritual Brotherhood in Renaissance Florence*. New York: Academic Press, 1982.

Wellman, Barry. "The Community Question." *American Journal of Sociology* 84(1981): 1201–1231.

Wellman, Barry, Peter J. Carrington, and Alan Hall. "Networks as Personal Communities." Chap. 6 in Wellman and Berkowitz, 1988.

Wellman, Barry, and S. D. Berkowitz, eds. *Social Structures: A Network Approach*. New York: Cambridge University Press, 1988.

Weyl, Hermann. *Philosophy of Mathematics and Natural Science*. Translated by O. Helmer. Princeton, NJ: Princeton University Press, 1949.

Whaley, Barton. *Codeword Barbarossa*. Cambridge, MA: MIT Press, 1973.

White, Douglas. "Notes on Compradzage." Irvine, CA: University of California Press, 1981.

———. "Cites and Fights: Material Entailment Analysis of the Eighteenth Century Chemical Revolution." In Wellman and Berkowitz, 1988.

———. "Rethinking Polygyny: Co-Wives, Codes and Cultural Systems." *Current Anthropology* 29(1988): 529–572.

White, Douglas, and Karl Reitz. "Graph and Semigroup Homomorphisms on Networks and Relations." *Social Networks* 5(1983): 193–234.

White, E. A., and J. A. Dykman. *Constitution and Canons for the Government of the Protestant Episcopal Church* (2 vols.). New York: Seabury Press, 1954.

White, Harrison C. "Management Conflict and Sociometric Structure." *American Journal of Sociology* 67(1961): 185–199.

———. "Chance Models of Systems of Casual Groups." *Sociometry* 25(1962): 153–172.

———. *An Anatomy of Kinship*. Englewood Cliffs, NJ: Prentice-Hall, 1963a.

———. "Cause and Effect in Social Mobility Tables: Combinatorial Models." *Behavioral Science* 8(1963b): 14–27.

———. "Uses of Mathematics in Sociology." In *Mathematics and the Social Sciences*, edited by J. C. Charlesworth, 77–94. Philadelphia: American Academy of Political and Social Science, 1963c.

———. "The Cumulation of Roles into Homogeneous Structures." Chap. 12 in *Perspectives in Organization Research*, edited by W. W. Cooper et al. New York: Wiley, 1964.

———. "Notes on the Constituents of Social Structure." Social Relations Department, Harvard University, Spring 1965a.

White, Harrison C. "Notes on Coupling and Decoupling." Social Relations Department, Harvard University, 1965b.

———. "Control and Evolution of Aggregate Personnel: Dual Flows of Men and Jobs." *Administrative Science Quarterly* 14(1969): 4–11.

———. "Search Parameters for the Small World Problem." *Social Forces* 49(1970a): 259–264.

———. *Chains of Opportunity: System Models of Mobility in Organizations.* Cambridge, MA: Harvard University Press, 1970b.

———. "Matching, Vacancies and Mobility." *Journal of Political Economy* 78(1970c): 97–105.

———. "Simon out of Homans by Coleman." *American Journal of Sociology* 75(1970d): 852–862.

———. "Stayers and Movers." *American Journal of Sociology* 76(1970e): 307–324.

———. "Multipliers, Vacancy Chains and Filtering in Housing." *Journal of the American Institute of Planners* 37(1971): 88–94.

———. "Everyday Life in Stochastic Networks." *Sociological Inquiry* 43(1973): 43–49.

———. "Models for Interrelated Roles from Multiple Networks in Small Populations." In *Proceedings of a Conference on Applications of Undergraduate Mathematics in the Engineering, Life, Managerial and Social Sciences,* edited by P. J. Knopp and G. H. Meyer, 52–101. School of Mathematics, Georgia Institute of Technology, Atlanta, GA, June 1973.

———. "Mobility from Vacancy Chains." In Ziegler, 1974, pp. 40–50.

———. "Probabilities of Homomorphic Mappings from Multiple Graphs." *Journal of Mathematical Psychology* 16(1977): 121–134.

———. "Fear and the Rhetoric of Confidence in Science." Pp. 199–209 in Markovitz and Deutsch, 1980.

———. "Production Markets as Induced Role Structures." Chap. 1 in Leinhardt, 1981a.

———. "Where do Markets Come From?" *American Journal of Sociology* 87(1981b): 517–547.

———. "Irvine Notes: Organizations in Comparative Historical Context." Manuscript, April–May 1981c.

———. *Research and Development as a Pattern in Industrial Management: A Case Study of Institutionalization and Uncertainty.* New York: Arno Press, 1981d.

———. "Notes on Where to go with a Theory of Markets as Role Structures." Department of Sociology, Harvard University, 1982a.

———. "Interfaces." *Connections* 5(1982b): 11–20.

———. "Going into Traffic." *Urban Affairs Quarterly* 18(1983): 473–484.

———. "Agency as Control." Chap. 8 in Pratt and Zeckhauser, 1985.

———. "Varieties of Markets." Chap. 9 in Wellman and Berkowitz, 1988a.

———. "Modelling Ideology as Configurations for Action." In Shafer, 1988b.

———. "Interview with Harrison White" in Swedberg, 1990.

———. "Values Come in Styles, Which Mate to Change." In Hechter and Nadel, 1992.

——. "Markets and Networks and Control." In Lindenberg and Schreuder eds., forthcoming, 1992.

——. "Markets in Production Networks." Chap. 7 in Swedberg, 1992.

——. "Cases are for Identity, for Explanation, or for Control." In Becker and Ragin, 1992.

White, Harrison C., and Vilhelm Aubert. "Sleep: A Sociological Interpretation." *Acta Sociologica 4*, fasc 3, 1–16, 1959.

White, Harrison C., Scott A. Boorman, and Ronald L. Breiger. "Social Structure from Multiple Networks: Part I. Blockmodels of Roles and Positions." *American Journal of Sociology* 81(1976): 730–780.

White, Harrison C., and Ronald L. Breiger. "Pattern Across Networks." *Society*. 12(July/August 1975): 68–73.

White, Harrison C., and Lee S. Christie. "Queuing with Preemptive Priorities or with Breakdown." *Operations Research* 6(1958): 79–95.

White, Harrison C., and Eric M. Leifer. "Markets as Pumps and as Arenas." Department of Sociology, University of North Carolina, September 1988.

White, Harrison C., and Cynthia A. White. *Canvases and Careers*. New York: Wiley, 1965; rev. ed., 1992. Chicago: University of Chicago Press.

White, Robert W. *The Abnormal Personality*, 4th ed. New York: Wiley, 1973.

——. *Lives in Progress*. New York: Holt-Rinehart-Winston, 1966.

Whitney, Joseph R. R. *China: Area, Administration and Nation Building*. University of Chicago, Department of Geography, Res. Paper #123, 1970.

Wholey, Douglas R. "Determinants of Firm Internal Labor Markets in large Law Firms." *Administrative Science Quarterly* 30(1985): 318–335.

Whyte, William F. *Street Corner Society*. Chicago: University of Chicago Press, 1943.

Wickelgren, Wayne. *Cognitive Psychology*. N.Y.: Prentice-Hall, 1979.

Wickner, William. "Assembly of Proteins into Membranes." *Science* 210(1980): 861–868.

Wiener, Norbert. *Time Series*. Cambridge, MA: MIT Press, 1949.

Wildavsky, Aaron. *Budgeting: A Comparative Theory of the Budgetary Processes*. Boston: Little, Brown, 1975.

Wilensky, Harold L. *Intellectuals in Labor Unions*. Glencoe, IL: Free Press, 1956.

Williams, George H. *The Mind of John Paul II*. New York: Seabury Press, 1981.

Williams, Gwyn A. *Medieval London from Commune to Capital*. London: Athlone, 1963.

Williams, Raymond. *Marxism and Literature*. New York: Oxford University Press, 1977.

Williamson, Oliver E. *Corporate Control and Business Behavior*. Englewood Cliffs, NJ: Prentice-Hall, 1970.

——. *Markets and Hierarchies: Analysis and Antitrust Implications*. New York: Macmillan, 1975.

Williamson, Samuel R., Jr. *The Politics of Grand Strategy: Britain and France Prepare for War, 1904–1914*. Cambridge, MA: Harvard University Press, 1969.

Willis, G. G. *Saint Augustine and the Donatist Controversy*. SPCK, 1950.

Willis, Paul. *Learning to Labour*. London: Gower, 1977.

———. *Common Culture*. Boulder, CO: Westview Press, 1990.

Wilson, E. O. *Insect Societies*. Cambridge, MA: Harvard University Press, 1970.

———. *Sociobiology: The New Synthesis*. Cambridge, MA: Harvard University Press, 1979.

Wilson, John. *The Boundaries of Conversation*. London: Pergamon, 1989.

Wilson, Kenneth. "Problems in Physics with Many Scales of Lengths." *Scientific American* 158–179, 1979.

Windmuller, John. *Labor Relations in the Netherlands*. Ithaca, NY: Cornell University Press, 1969.

Winn, D. N. "Industrial Market Share and Performance." Ann Arbor, MI: Division of Research, University of Michigan, 1975.

Winship, Christopher. "Thoughts about Roles and Relations." Department of Sociology, Harvard University, 1974.

———. "A Distance Model for Sociometric Structure." *Journal of Mathematical Sociology* 5(1977): 21–39.

———. "The Allocation of Time among Individuals." In *Sociological Methodology 1978*, edited by K. Schuessler. San Francisco: Jossey-Bass, 1978.

Winship, Christopher, and Michael J. Mandel. "Roles and Positions: A Critique and Extension of the Blockmodelling Approach." Chap. 10 in Leinhardt, 1984.

Wittkower, Rudolph. *Sculpture: Processes and Principles*. New Yord: Harper, 1978.

Wohlstatter, Roberta. *Pearl Harbor: Warning and Decision*. Stanford, CA: Stanford University Press, 1962.

Wolfe, Tom. *The Right Stuff*. New York: Bantam, 1980.

Wolin, Sheldon S. "Democracy and the Welfare State: The Political and Theoretical Connections between Staatsrason and Wohlfahrtsstaatrason." *Political Theory* 15(1987): 467–500.

Woo, J. Ph.D. thesis, Columbia University, Department of Political Science, 1988.

Wrapp, H. Edward. "Good managers don't make policy decisions." *Harvard Business Review* 45(1967): 91–100.

Wright, Gwendolyn. *Moralism and the Model Home: Domestic Architecture and Cultural Conflict*. Chicago: University of Chicago Press, 1980.

Wu, Lawrence L. "Local Blockmodel Algebras for Analyzing Social Networks." Chap. 9 in Leinhardt, 1984.

Wuthnow, Robert. *Meaning and Moral Order*. Berkeley, CA: University of California Press, 1987.

Wylie, Lawrence. *Village in the Vaucluse*. Cambridge, MA: Harvard University Press, 1964.

Wylie, Ruth C. *The Self Concept*, rev. ed., vols. I and II. Lincoln, NB: University of Nebraska, 1974.

Wynne-Edwards, V. C. *Evolution through Group Selection*. Oxford: Blackwell, 1985.

Yarbrough, Beth V., and Robert M. "Status and Contract: Identity as a Cooperation-Facilitating Mechanism." Department of Economics, Amherst College, 1989.

Yoshino, M. Y. *Japan's Managerial System*. Cambridge, MA: MIT Press, 1968.

Yoshino, M. Y., and Thomas Lifson. *The Invisible Link: Japan's Sogo Shosha in the Organization of Tradition*. Cambridge, MA: MIT Press, 1988.

Zadeh, Lofti, K. Fu, K. Taneka, and M. Shimura, eds. *Fuzzy Sets and their Applications to Cognitive and Decision Processes*. New York: Academic Press, 1975.

Zajac, Edward E. "Perceived Economic Justice: The Example of Public Utility Regulation." Chap. 7 in *Cost Allocation: Methods, Principles, Applications*, edited by H. Peyton Young. New York: Elsevier, 1985.

Zald, Mayer. *Organizational Change: The Political Economy of the YMCA*. Chicago: University of Chicago Press, 1970.

Zald, Mayer, ed. *Power in Organizations*. Nashville, TN: Vanderbilt University Press, 1970.

Zannetos, Z. S. *The Theory of Oil TankShip Rates*. Cambridge, MA: MIT Press, 1966.

Zeeman, Christopher, ed. *Catastrophe Theory*. Reading, MA: Addison-Wesley, 1977.

Zeigler, J. W. *Regional Theatre*. Minneapolis, MN: University of Minnesota Press, 1973.

Zelizer, Viviana A. "The Social Meaning of Money: 'Special Monies.'" *American Journal of Sociology* 95(1989): 342–377.

Ziegler, Rolf, ed. *Anwendung Mathematischer Verfahren Zur Analyse Sozialer Ungleicheit und Sozialer Mobilität*. Kiel, Germany: Christian Albrecht Universität, 1974.

Ziman, J. M. *Models of Disorder: The Theoretical Physics of Homogeneously Disordered Systems*. New York: Cambridge University Press, 1979.

Zipf, G. K. *Human Behavior and the Principle of Least Effort: An Introduction to Human Ecology*. Cambridge: Addison-Wesley, 1949.

Zuckerman, Harriet. *Scientific Elite*. New York: Macmillan Free Press, 1979.

Zukin, Sharon, and Paul DiMaggio, eds. *Structures of Capital: The Social Organization of the Economy*. Cambridge, UK: Cambridge University Press, 1990.

INDEX

Abbott, Andrew, 71, 223–25, 339
Abelson, Robert P., 329
academic research science, 122–26
accidents, 186
acquaintanceship scope, 76
agency, 95, 245–54, 315–16
Alford, Robert R., 224
Alonso, William, 130
altruism, 26n.5
ambage: versus ambiguity, 106–9; definition of, 17, 103, 106; and getting action, 271–73; in institutions, 170; and intimacy, 194
ambiguity: versus ambage, 106–9; in councils, 103–4; definition of, 17, 103; and getting action, 271–73; and strategy, 194; and styles, 170
Anderson, Perry, 20, 151
Annales school, 192
annealing, 230, 281–86
Ansell, Christopher K., 88, 96, 262, 291
Antal, F., 80–81, 143
anticareers, 221
arena markets, 51–52
arenas: ambiguity in, 104–5; definition of, 16, 30–32, 48–49, 331; as purifiers, 52–54; Shepard planes for, 49, 50
Arensberg, Conrad M., 195
Argyle, M., 29
Arrow, Kenneth J., 225
Ashford, Douglas E., 155, 270, 276n.24
associativity, 218n.31
Atkin, R. H., 337
atomic hypotheses, 132–33
attitudes, 171, 176, 204–5
auction markets, 169–70, 174
Augustine (saint), 132–33, 244
Austen, Jane, 87
authority trees, 178–79
autocracy, 58–60
Axelrod, R., 76n.18, 306
Axiom of Quality, 89n.29, 101–2

Badian, E., 150
Bailey, Robert W., 251, 253
balance theory, 337
Bales, Robert Freed, 29, 88, 337

Barth, Fredrik, 247, 249
Baruch, Bernard, 242, 252
Baxandall, Michael, 80–81, 129, 143, 285
Beame, Abraham, 253
Bearman, Peter, 270
Becker, Carl L., 301n.9
behavior, and stories, 83–84. *See also* behaviorism; cultural behavior
behaviorism, 26n.5, 306, 347
Bellman, Richard, 235–36n.6, 236
Berle, Adolf A., 182, 268, 297
Berman, Harold J., 215, 291
"big men," 194–95
biography, 314
biology, 14
Bjerstedt, Ake, 90
blocking actions, 147–50, 152–53, 172, 237, 245, 256, 273, 275, 295
blockmodel, 17, 93, 97, 107, 130, 220
Boorman, Scott A., 101, 336
Bosch, Johannes van den, 272
Bott, Elizabeth, 201
boundaries: cultural, 127–28; definition of, 92–93, 126–27; and envelopes, 186; in Indian castes, 118; and institutions, 126–36; and language, 133–35; and styles, 177; as theory, 127–29
Bourdieu, Pierre, 70
Bower, Joseph L., 10–11
Boyd, John P., 98, 254n.19, 332–33
Braudel, Fernand, 20, 192
Breiger, Ronald L., 35n.15, 101, 191, 332
Brzezinski, Z., 153, 223n.38
Buddha, 327
budget construction, 217–18, 277–81
bureaucracies, 171–72
Burns, Elisabeth, 67
Burns, Tom, 67
Burt, Ronald S., 71, 90–91, 185, 206–7, 280–81, 293, 337
Bush, R. R., 337
Bynum, Carolyn, 111, 198
Bythell, Duncan, 260

Calhoun, C. J., 202
careers: and anticareers, 220–21; and contingency chains, 219–20; creation